BASIC POST-TONAL
THEORY AND ANALYSIS

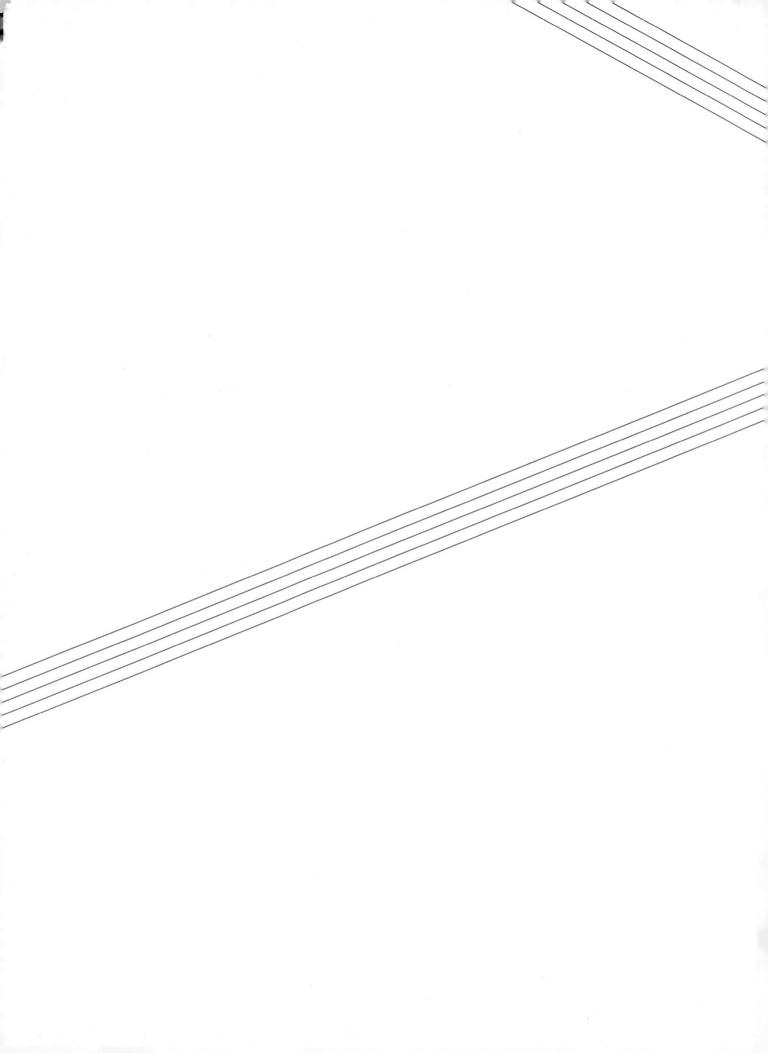

BASIC POST-TONAL
THEORY *AND* ANALYSIS

Philip Lambert

*Baruch College and the Graduate Center,
City University of New York*

New York   Oxford
OXFORD UNIVERSITY PRESS

Oxford University Press is a department of the University of Oxford. It furthers
the University's objective of excellence in research, scholarship, and education
by publishing worldwide. Oxford is a registered trade mark of Oxford University
Press in the UK and certain other countries.

Published in the United States of America by Oxford University Press
198 Madison Avenue, New York, NY 10016, United States of America.

© 2019 by Oxford University Press

Library of Congress Cataloging-in-Publication Data
Names: Lambert, Philip, 1958– author.
Title: Basic post-tonal theory and analysis / Philip Lambert.
Description: New York : Oxford University Press, [2018]
Identifiers: LCCN 2018010520 (print) | LCCN 2018011319 (ebook) | ISBN
   9780190864514 (ebook) | ISBN 9780190629649 (print text)
Subjects: LCSH: Music theory—Textbooks. | Atonality. | Musical analysis. |
   LCGFT: Textbooks.
Classification: LCC MT6.L1367 (ebook) | LCC MT6.L1367 B37 2018 (print) | DDC
   781.2/67—dc23
LC record available at https://lccn.loc.gov/2018010520

9 8 7 6 5 4 3 2 1
Printed by LSC Communications, United States of America

CONTENTS

PREFACE

This book addresses basic questions about concert music of the past hundred or so years. How have composers responded to the expansion of harmonic resources that reached its pinnacle around the turn of the twentieth century? If diatonic tonality was no longer a viable option, what resources and methods stood in its place? To what extent has diatonicism in some form or reconceptualization still had something to offer? What are the techniques composers have developed to give their music unity, or novelty, or artistry? What are the sonic environments of their works, and what is their architecture? How have things changed in the aftermath of the Second World War and in more recent times? More simply: How have post-tonal composers (re)conceived melody, harmony, rhythm, and form?

The process of answering such questions begins with tools, terminology, materials, and approaches. The book's first four chapters offer a step-by-step introduction to the methodology of post-tonal theory, also sometimes called "atonal theory" or "set theory." The remaining chapters build from this foundation, in studies of adaptations of the tonal system (Chapter 5); modeling techniques (6); formal designs (7); rhythmic organization (8); and twelve-tone music (9, 10). It is possible to skip around within the book after acquiring the background of Chapters 1–4, with two exceptions: the concepts in Chapter 5 are essential background for understanding the modeling techniques in Chapter 6, and the first twelve-tone chapter (9) is a necessary prequel to the second (10).

The book assumes no previous background in post-tonal repertoire, just an ability to add and subtract, and a solid understanding of the language and literature of the tonal era as exemplified by music of Bach, Mozart, Beethoven, and Wagner, and their contemporaries. Theoretical concepts are grounded in the close study of music by primary figures in twentieth-century music, including Arnold Schoenberg (1874–1951), Charles Ives (1874–1954), Béla Bartók (1881–1945), Igor Stravinsky (1882–1971), Anton Webern (1883–1945), Alban Berg (1885–1935), Olivier Messiaen (1908–1992), and many others.

The book is designed to maximize student engagement with the repertoire and the analytical machinery. In each chapter students will find:

- Frequent interplay of concepts and applications, with copious musical excerpts and graphic demonstrations;
- Recurring study of the same work or passage in shifting contexts and increasing depth;
- Division into brief sections, directing and organizing the learning process;
- A vocabulary list (words highlighted in **bold** within the main text and defined in the Glossary in Appendix 2);
- Study Questions for monitoring student comprehension at the end of each section, answered in full in Appendix 3;

- Exercises reinforcing theoretical concepts;
- Exercises in analytical applications, guided by specific questions and directives;
- Exercises in compositional applications;
- Lists of repertoire for further study (perhaps topics for term papers).

Students who have completed the book will have gained a basic understanding of many post-tonal works, and will be well equipped for more advanced study in topics such as transformational theory, similarity relations, contour theory, and twelve-tone theory. Curious researchers will find multiple valuable book-length studies of all of the principal composers, and pertinent articles in journals such as *Journal of Music Theory*, *Perspectives of New Music*, *Music Theory Spectrum*, *Music Analysis*, *Theory and Practice*, and *Intégral*.

The intellectual history of the theories presented here dates back to the pioneering work of Milton Babbitt and David Lewin in the 1950s and '60s, and draws direct inspiration from six foundational studies:

- George Perle, *Serial Composition and Atonality* (Berkeley: University of California Press, 1962; 6th ed., revised, 1991);
- Allen Forte, *The Structure of Atonal Music* (New Haven, CT: Yale University Press, 1973);
- Charles Wuorinen, *Simple Composition* (New York: Longman, 1979);
- John Rahn, *Basic Atonal Theory* (New York: Longman, 1980);
- Robert D. Morris, *Composition with Pitch-Classes: A Theory of Compositional Design* (New Haven, CT: Yale University Press, 1987);
- Joseph N. Straus, *Introduction to Post-Tonal Theory* (Englewood Cliffs, NJ: Prentice-Hall, 1990; 4th ed., Norton, 2016).

Students who have completed this book and who are motivated to explore these predecessors will find many areas of intersection, often involving contrasting approaches to and notations of the same basic ideas, but also offering ample opportunities for further inquiry and exploration.

Pitch designations throughout the book adopt the ASA (Acoustical Society of America) standard, where middle C = C_4. For the white keys of the piano, for example:

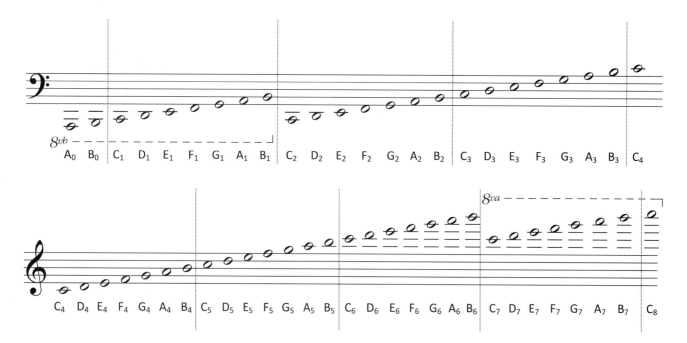

This book came to life under the watchful eye of Richard Carlin at Oxford University Press. I thank him for his guidance and support. I also thank his assistant, Jacqueline Levine, for help with myriad details. For their expertise during editing and production, I thank production editor Keith Faivre, copy editor Carrie Crompton, and Art Director Michele Laseau. I also acknowledge my personal support system: Diane, Alice, and Charlotte.

CHAPTER 1

MUSICAL UNITS

1.1 MUSICAL UNITS IN MOZART

A piece of music, like a building or a car or a novel, integrates a vast variety of individual components, brought together by some measure of skill and genius into a meaningful whole. To study what makes a piece of music interesting or beautiful or internally coherent is to consider the nature of these components, like exploring a feat of architecture or engineering or literature. In the process, we learn important details not only about the elements themselves but also about the methods by which they are created and combined, and, ultimately, about the person who did the creating.

That's what we do, for example, when we study a work from the tonal era, such as the Menuet from Mozart's String Quartet in E♭ Major (Ex. 1.1). The movement begins with two main musical ideas in the first five measures: (1) a motivic melody in running eighth notes in the first violin, starting each measure with a step down (in m. 5, a step up) followed by a leap up a third (in one case, a fourth) and then repeating the last note to the end of the bar (or in measure 3, jumping down to another chord tone); and (2) supporting chords in the second violin, viola, and cello, starting a harmonic movement toward the dominant key. The analytic shorthand beneath the score in Example 1.1 highlights these features.

EXAMPLE 1.1   Mozart, String Quartet in E♭ Major, K. 171, Menuet, mm. 1–5

This separation into two components—the melody and the supporting chords—is immediately apparent to the ear and eye. Right after that, however, orderly tranquility recedes. In measure 6, the dynamic level jumps from *piano* to *forte*, and the instruments pair off into contrasting duets, each presenting a three-note step-step motive, filling in a third: the violins unfold the motive slowly, rising in dotted half notes, while the viola and cello present it more rapidly and repeatedly and with changes in direction (bracketed in Example 1.2). Finally in measures 8 and 9, the instruments reach consonant agreement in a series of quarter-note chords, confirming tonal arrival in the dominant key. Since we have just heard the interplay of step-step motives in measures 6 and 7, even the ordinary cadential figure on scale degrees 2̂–1̂–7̂ in B♭ in measure 9 can be heard as part of the motivic fabric.

EXAMPLE 1.2   Mozart, String Quartet in E♭ Major, K. 171, Menuet, mm. 6–10

To make these observations, we've recognized a variety of musical groupings. The melody in the first five measures is grouped into repetitions of a one-measure motivic pattern. Supporting this is a harmonic grouping of notes into chords in the other three instruments. After that, the motivic and rhythmic groupings change to create the two duets and step-step motives in measures 6 and 7. And in the last three measures, the instruments come together into harmonic groupings of quarter-note chords expressing the cadential harmonies. These groupings constitute the basic **musical units** of Mozart's Menuet. The study of tonal music is traditionally focused on musical units of many varieties, including chords, motives, and phrases.

STUDY QUESTIONS 1.1[1]

1. **What are the two main musical ideas in the first five measures of Mozart's string quartet?**

2. **What is the primary motivic idea in the next five measures?**

---
[1]Answers to all Study Questions appear in Appendix 3.

1.2   MUSICAL UNITS IN WEBERN

The study of post-tonal music is also focused on musical units and their interrelationships. To find them, we can embark on this same sort of search for motivic, rhythmic, and harmonic groupings. Of course, our approach will necessarily be different from studying tonal music, in which some elements, such as triads or chord functions, can be anticipated even before we start the discovery process. Different tonal works by different composers can be presumed to share a vocabulary of harmonic resources. But post-tonal works carry no such inherent commonalities and depend on structural principles that are contextually defined. Grouping strategies and objects in post-tonal music may vary widely from one work to the next.

Listen to Anton Webern's Bagatelle for String Quartet, op. 9 no. 1, without looking at the score. Then listen again. It only lasts about thirty-five seconds; listen to it a few more times. Then try a few listenings while following the complete score of the work in Example 1.3. Because of the frequent clef changes and string harmonics, you may find it helpful to refer to the summary of the music on the bottom two staffs, which shows all the notes as they sound and in their approximate temporal locations.

EXAMPLE 1.3   Webern, *Six Bagatelles for String Quartet*, op. 9, no. 1

As you become familiar with Webern's Bagatelle, groupings emerge. In the first three measures, for example, notes are rhythmically grouped into twos and threes (Ex. 1.4). This starts right away with the initial cello/viola/first violin notes in measure 1, and then continues within individual instruments, starting with the second violin's C_4–$G\flat_4$–$A\flat_4$ in measure 2. The first violin has a five-note melody in measures 2 and 3, separated by slurs into a 3 + 2 grouping. The viola adds a rhythmically distinct oscillation in measure 2 between two notes, A_3 and B_3. And so forth. Throughout the remaining seven measures of the piece, these same sorts of two- and three-note groupings continue, defined by rhythm, articulation, and/or registral proximity.

EXAMPLE 1.4 Groupings in mm. 1–3 of Webern op. 9, no. 1

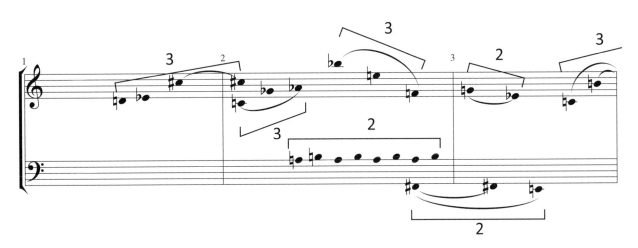

Look again through the entire score in Example 1.3. There are a few individual notes that don't relate as strongly with others to make two- or three-note groupings, but for the most part, the only obvious musical units of a size *other than* two or three are the four-note sonorities formed by concurrent double stops in the second violin and cello in measure 4, and in first violin and viola in measures 8 and 9. These chords are conspicuous because of their size and rhythmic uniformity, calling to mind the harmonies in uniform rhythms at the end of Mozart's Menuet (Ex. 1.2).

Groupings based on specific recurring intervals or rhythms are more of a rarity in Webern's Bagatelle. This music has nothing like the repeating motivic patterns in the first five measures of Mozart's Menuet. Webern writes tiny gestures that resemble each other, such as the viola's leap up followed by a step down in measure 4, recalled by the second violin in measure 9 (Ex. 1.5). But for the most part, the Bagatelle is distinguished by its *variety* of gesture, rhythm, and articulation, not by repeating rhythmic or motivic patterns.

EXAMPLE 1.5 Similar three-note gestures in Webern op. 9, no. 1

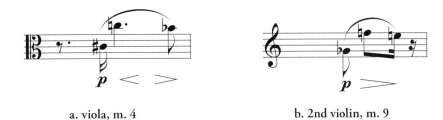

a. viola, m. 4   b. 2nd violin, m. 9

STUDY QUESTIONS 1.2

1. **How are some of Webern's musical groupings defined?**

2. **How is the motivic structure of Webern's Bagatelle different from the motivic structure of the Mozart excerpt studied earlier?**

3. **How does the importance of *context* affect the analytical process for post-tonal music in comparison to tonal analysis?**

1.3   HARMONIC GROUPINGS

The word "harmony" can have different meanings. For tonal music, it can refer to chords, such as the vertical formations in the second violin, viola, and cello in the first four measures of Mozart's string quartet studied earlier (Ex. 1.1). It can also apply to the relationships between chords in harmonic progressions. But the word can also be defined more broadly to apply to any element of consistency or structural salience within a work's pitch structure. In tonal music, that typically includes triads, but in post-tonal music, it can be pitch combinations of many different sizes and sounds.

So what constitutes a harmonic grouping in post-tonal music? Webern demonstrates one possibility in the first measure of his Bagatelle (Ex. 1.6a). The opening gesture combines notes from three different instruments: D$_4$ in the cello, E♭$_4$ in the viola, and C♯$_5$ in the first violin. Taken together as one musical unit, the three notes represent one way of presenting a **chromatic cluster**—a collection of consecutive notes from a chromatic scale (Ex. 1.6b).

EXAMPLE 1.6   Three-note chromatic cluster in m. 1 of Webern's op. 9, no. 1

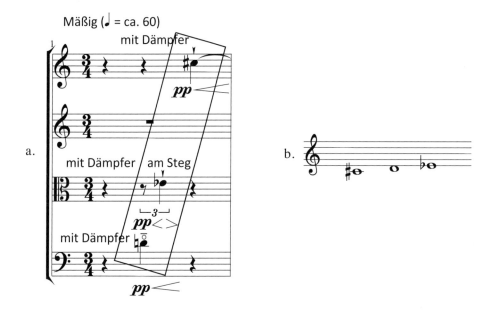

The chromatic cluster is an element of harmonic consistency in the Bagatelle. We see it again, for example, in the final measure (Ex. 1.7a), where the cello and viola present a chromatic clustering of B, C, and C♯ (Ex. 1.7b).

To say that these two musical units are both "chromatic clusters" doesn't mean they look and sound exactly like consecutive notes in a chromatic scale. In measure 1, the musical ordering is D–E♭–C♯, not C♯–D–E♭ as in the actual chromatic scale. In measure 10, the ordering is B–C♯–C, not B–C–C♯. And even if these notes were ordered as in a chromatic scale, they wouldn't all relate by actual steps. The D$_4$ and E♭$_4$ in measure 1 are literally a half step apart, but the C♯$_5$ is up in the next octave, many half steps away. All three notes clustered in measure 10 lie in different octaves—B$_2$, C♯$_4$, and C$_5$.

EXAMPLE 1.7   Three-note chromatic cluster in m. 10 of Webern's op. 9, no. 1

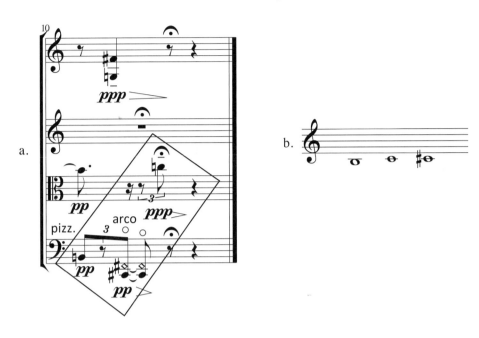

In describing the three-note groupings in measures 1 and 10 as chromatic clusters, we've given ourselves the freedom to reorder them and imagine them in the same register (Exx. 1.6b, 1.7b). We're asserting that the configurations in measures 1 and 10 are musical realizations of literal chromatic clusters, two of many possible realizations.

There are times when three-note collections such as these are better viewed in their actual states, preserving their original order and register. The three notes in measure 1 could be described as "a rising half step followed by a rising minor seventh (spelled here as an augmented sixth)"—rather than a cluster. The three notes in measure 10 could be described as "ascending major 9th, ascending major 7th (spelled here as a diminished octave)." For present purposes, however, we're going to stick with the more general view. We'll discover many useful reasons for adopting this strategy. One is that by reducing both gestures to the same general object—a three-note chromatic cluster—we're better able to make a connection between the beginning and the ending of the piece.

We're also able to tie together these gestures with events in other measures, thereby reaching some valuable conclusions about the Bagatelle's general harmonic language. To do this, we'll apply the designation "three-note chromatic cluster" to a realization of *any* three-note segment of a chromatic scale, not to any *particular* three-note segment. Thus, C♯–D–E♭, or B–C–C♯, or E–F–F♯, or A♭–A–B♭, or any other three-note chromatic segment all fall under this same rubric.

We make these same sorts of assumptions in studies of tonal music. When we describe the harmony of the first measure of Mozart's K. 171 Menuet (excluding the initial nonharmonic A♭) as an expression of the "E♭ major triad" (Ex. 1.8a), we similarly disregard details of the musical presentation. At no place in the measure do we literally find a simultaneously presented three-note chord with a major third between the bottom two notes and a minor third between the top two; rather, the triad tones are artfully distributed. But describing measure 1 as an expression of a major triad enables us, among other things, to recognize a connection between measure 1 and the beginning of measure 8 (Ex. 1.8b), where the instruments combine to realize a triad on a different root, B♭—again, without literally stacking a major third below a minor third in the actual instrumental combinations. Despite contrasting rhythmic profiles and note distributions, we can assert that both entities are members of the same family of chord type known as "major triad."

EXAMPLE 1.8   Triads in Mozart's K. 171 Menuet

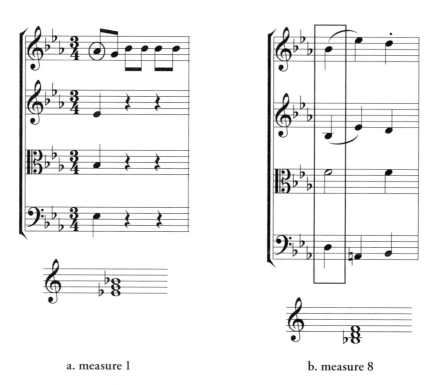

a. measure 1   b. measure 8

STUDY QUESTIONS 1.3

1. **How can the word "harmony" apply to post-tonal music?**

2. **How are Webern's expressions of chromatic clusters in measures 1 and 10 different from a literal three-note segment of a chromatic scale?**

3. **How are Mozart's expressions of triads in measures 1 and 8 of his string quartet different from a literal statement of a triad as root–third–fifth in close spacing?**

1.4   PRIMARY AND SECONDARY GROUPINGS

How pervasive are chromatic clusters in Webern's Bagatelle? Well, it's easy to find three-note groupings that *don't* represent segments of chromatic scales. The initial three-note grouping in the second violin is the nonchromatic segment C_4–$G\flat_4$–$A\flat_4$. Right after that, the first violin answers with $B\flat_5$–E_5–F_4. Clearly, the structure of the piece involves more than just recurrences of chromatic clusters, as we will later consider.

And yet chromatic clusters are still some of the most prominent musical units in the Bagatelle. Just before the last measure, for example, the second violin presents a three-note chromatic sequencing of $G\flat_4$–F_5–E_5. This is one of the three-note groupings we highlighted earlier (Ex. 1.5b) while noticing the prevalence of two- and three-note groupings throughout the score.

The presentations of chromatic clusters in measures 1, 9, and 10 involve notes that are closely associated by rhythm, articulation, instrumentation, and/or temporal proximity. These are **primary** groupings. Primary groupings arise from only the strongest grouping criteria.

Secondary groupings associate notes that can be reasonably extracted by collecting notes from different primary formations. Look, for example, at the sustained tones in the upper register in measures 8 and 9, just before the primary $G\flat_4$–F_5–E_5 in the second violin (Ex. 1.9). A secondary chromatic cluster begins with the viola's tremolo $C\sharp_7$ harmonic, followed by the cello's harmonic D_5, and concludes with the second violin's $E\flat_6$ in measure 9. In fact, this formation is another realization of the same three notes ($C\sharp$–D–$E\flat$) of the primary chromatic cluster in measure 1.

EXAMPLE 1.9   Chromatic cluster in Webern op. 9, no. 1, mm. 8–9

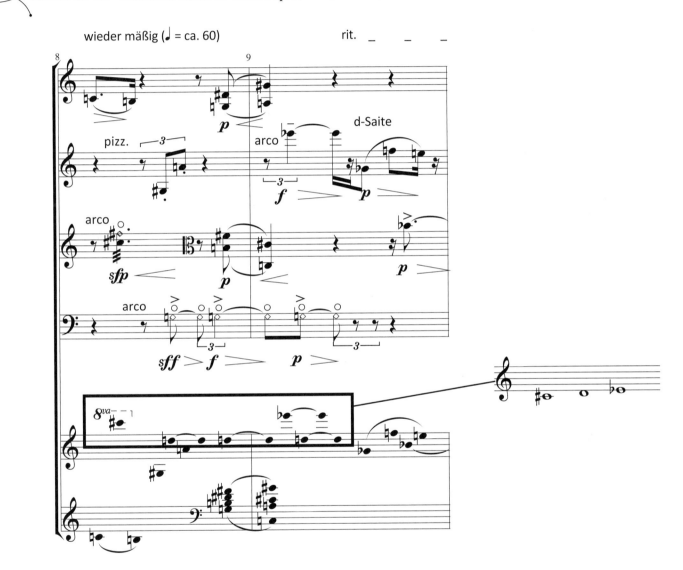

Secondary chromatic clusters often lurk in the Bagatelle, like a subtle subtext in a novel or play. Notice how often, for example, a two-note grouping can be joined with a third note from another grouping in close proximity to form a three-note chromatic cluster (Ex. 1.3). Here are a few such instances:

- As the viola moves back and forth between A_3 and B_3 in measure 2, the first violin completes the cluster with its $B\flat_5$.
- The next two first violin notes in measure 2—E_5 and F_4—similarly cluster with the cello's $F\sharp_2$.
- The beginning of the cello motive starting in measure 3, C_4–B_4, completes a chromatic cluster with the second violin's pizzicato $B\flat_3$ on the next downbeat.

- The viola's two-note gesture in measure 6, B_5–Bb_4, is followed by a cluster-completing A_6 at the beginning of the three-note motive in the first violin.
- Then the remaining two notes of the first-violin motive in measures 6 and 7, $F\#_6$ and G_5, are followed immediately by $G\#_4$ at the beginning of the two-note cello grouping at the beginning of measure 7.
- Likewise, the other note in the cello gesture in measure 7, E_5, creates a chromatic cluster with the subsequent viola F_5–Eb_5.
- The final cello pizzicato Bb_3–A_4 in measure 7 clusters with the nearly concurrent B_3 in the first violin.
- The first violin then goes on to express C_4–B_3 in measure 8, which cluster with the viola's tremolo $C\#_7$ harmonic.

Now listen to the Bagatelle a few more times, thinking about the structure and sound of the three-note chromatic cluster. At some point during the discovery process, the music starts to sound more familiar, more comprehensible, more engaging. You start noticing chromatic clusters of other sizes. (Consider, for example, the role of the next note after the cluster in measure 1.) You also start to notice recurring note groupings that aren't chromatically based.

You begin to make further and deeper connections between Webern and his predecessors in the string quartet tradition. You begin to realize that Webern and, for instance, his Austrian compatriot Mozart aren't actually as different as they might at first seem.

STUDY QUESTIONS 1.4

1. **What are some factors that help establish primary groupings?**

2. **How does Webern often form secondary three-note groupings in his Bagatelle?**

3. **What's an example of a secondary four-note chromatic cluster at the beginning of Webern's Bagatelle?**

4. **What's an example of a secondary four-note chromatic cluster at the end of Webern's Bagatelle?**

VOCABULARY

chromatic cluster   primary grouping   secondary grouping
musical unit

EXERCISES

A. RECOGNIZING CHROMATIC CLUSTERS

On the staff provided, organize the notes of each example as a chromatic cluster. The sizes of the clusters vary from **three** through **six**.

demo

1.

2.

3.

4.

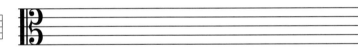

5.

6.

B. ANTON WEBERN (1883–1945), PIECE FOR VIOLIN AND PIANO, OP. 7, NO. 3 (1914)

1. Listen to the piece several times, first without the score, then while following along. Listen/look for primary groupings.

2. Directly on the score, circle four instances of three-note chromatic clusters (primary or secondary). Tag each one with a lowercase letter, "a" through "d."

3. Notate the three notes of each cluster as a segment of a chromatic scale on the staff below.

4. Indicate whether each cluster is a primary or secondary formation.

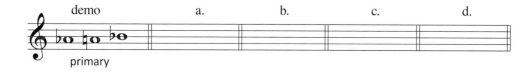

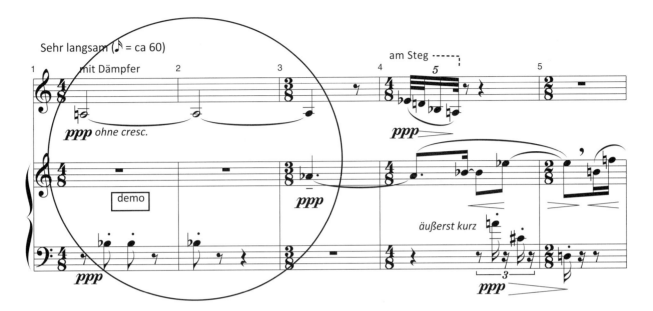

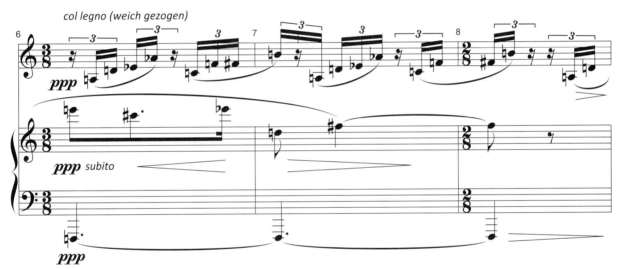

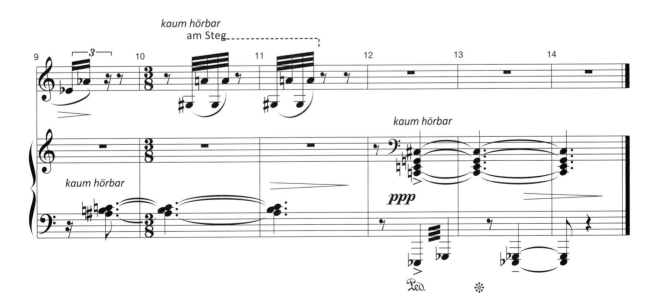

C. BÉLA BARTÓK (1881–1945), STRING QUARTET NO. 4 (1928), MVT. 1, MM. 1–13

1. Listen to the excerpt several times, first without the score, then while following along. Listen/look for primary groupings.

2. The primary motive (PM) of the excerpt is marked in measure 7. What is the four-note chromatic cluster presented by PM? Notate your answer in whole notes in tenor clef.

3. Find other places in the excerpt where instruments repeat the rhythm of PM, even if the actual notes are different from the PM in measure 7. How many other occurrences of the PM rhythm can you find, and what are their four-note chromatic clusters? Notate your answers on a staff in any clef.

4. Where in the excerpt do all four instruments combine to form vertical four-note chromatic clusters? Notate each of these clusters as whole notes on a staff in any clef.

5. Find all places in the excerpt where primary chromatic clusters are formed by two instruments working together. (Note: These must be *primary* groupings.) Draw a ring around these clusters, tag each one with a letter, and notate them separately as whole notes on a staff in any clef.

6. In whole notes on a staff in any clef, notate the chromatic cluster formed by all four instruments combined in the *sff* chord in measure 13.

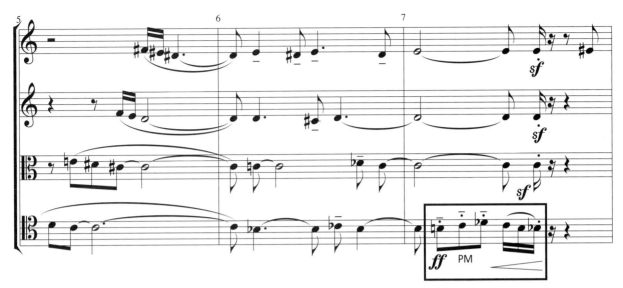

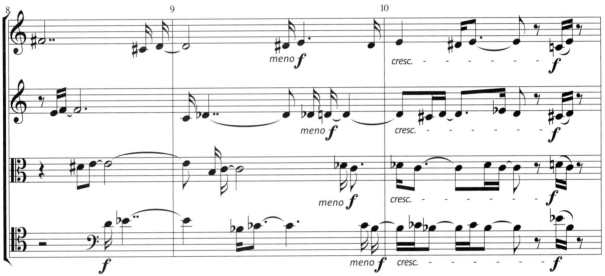

D. COMPOSITION EXERCISE

Use the given first two measures as the starting point for a short composition for string quartet inspired by Webern's Bagatelle, op. 9, no. 1. Employ chromatic clusters as primary and secondary musical units.

FOR FURTHER STUDY

BÉLA BARTÓK:

Mikrokosmos (1932–39): "Chromatics" (vol. 2, no. 54); "Chromatic Invention (1)" (vol. 3, no. 91); "Major Seconds Broken and Together" (vol. 5, no. 132); "Minor Seconds, Major Sevenths" (vol. 6, no. 144); "Chromatic Invention (3)," (vol. 6, no. 145)
String Quartet no. 5 (1934), mvt. 4

ERNST KRENEK:

String Quartet no. 1 (1921), mvt. 1

GYÖRGY LIGETI:

Étude 3 for Piano (1985): "Touches bloquées"

CHAPTER 2

MUSICAL SPACES

2.1 NOTE SPACE

Look again at the first measure of Webern's first opus 9 Bagatelle (Ex. 2.1a; Ex. 1.3 shows the complete work). In Chapter 1 we described the notes in this measure as a realization of the "chromatic cluster" C♯–D–E♭. To demonstrate, we rearranged them and wrote them in the same octave, as in Example 2.1b (repeating Ex. 1.6b). Let's explore this further: What else did we do, in making the reduction from the score (Ex. 2.1a) to the cluster (Ex. 2.1b)?

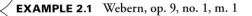

EXAMPLE 2.1 Webern, op. 9, no. 1, m. 1

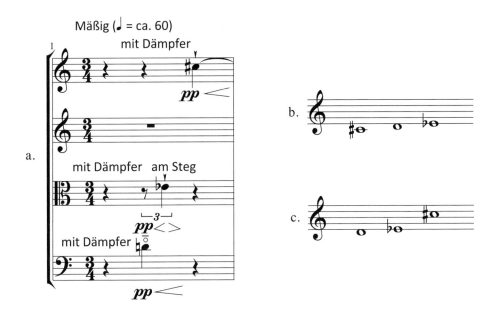

When we visually represented the cluster as a group of whole notes on a neutral staff, we also stripped the notes of their original durations, dynamic markings, and modes of articulation. We gave no special attention to the fact that all three instruments are muted (*mit Dämpfer*), nor to the bowing style, which is marked *am Steg* (at the bridge) for the viola. Further, we made no distinctions based on note spellings; the groupings wouldn't change, for example, if the viola's E♭ were respelled as D♯ or if the first violin's C♯ were respelled as D♭ (and so forth).

Even if we write out these notes in their original order and registers, as in Example 2.1c, we're still disregarding important aspects of their original musical presentation. When we make such leaps from the literal (Ex. 2.1a) to the abstract (Exx. 2.1b, 2.1c), we enter **note space**. In

19

note space, musical groupings are viewed in a neutralized state, without regard for their original rhythmic settings, durations, dynamic markings, modes of articulation, and spellings. Of course, any or all of these factors presumably influence our decision to make a musical grouping in the first place. But once we've made the grouping, they fall away, leaving us with just the notes themselves, in the analytic environment known as note space.

Any specifically defined perspective on a musical idea can be a **musical space**. The most literal musical space is the actual music (Ex. 2.1a). Note space is more abstract. Analyses of post-tonal music often move back and forth between spaces, as we did in Chapter 1 when comparing the literal presentation of the opening gesture in Webern's Bagatelle with the recurring primary and secondary chromatic clusters.

STUDY QUESTIONS 2.1

1. **What musical features are typically disregarded in note space?**

2. **Which is a more abstract description of the first measure of Webern's Bagatelle: "chromatic cluster" or "D_4–$E\flat_4$–$C\sharp_5$"?**

2.2   PITCH AND PITCH-CLASS SPACE

To make distinctions between notes in their original registers (Ex. 2.1c) and notes represented as a "chromatic cluster" within the same octave (Ex. 2.1b) is to differentiate between **pitch space (p space)** and **pitch-class space (pc space)**. Pitch space recognizes notes in their specific octaves. In pitch-class space, notes are identified without regard to register. When we describe Webern's opening measure using octave designations (D_4–$E\flat_4$–$C\sharp_5$, as in Ex. 2.1c), we're in p space. When we describe it as a chromatic cluster ($C\sharp$–D–$E\flat$, as in Ex. 2.1b), we're in pc space. Both spaces are subcategories of note space, where we disregard duration, dynamic markings, articulation, and spelling.

These are widely familiar concepts. If we refer, for example, to the first note of the cello melody at the beginning of Beethoven's "Eroica" Symphony as $E\flat_3$, we're in p space. But when we say that Beethoven's symphony is in the key of $E\flat$ major—when we use the phrase "Symphony no. 3 in $E\flat$ Major"—we're not referring to a specific $E\flat$, just to the overall tonality, which is expressed in numerous complex ways, including the soundings of $E\flat$'s in many different octaves; we're in pc space.

Pitch space is theoretically infinite, although we might limit it for practical purposes to the range of typical musical performance, roughly C_0 through C_9. Pitch-class space collapses all octave-equivalent and enharmonically equivalent notes into one collective known as the **pitch class (pc)**. While we'll continue to represent **pitches** using customary letters and octave designations, for labeling pitch classes we'll use the integers 0–11. In pc space, all C's and their octave and enharmonic equivalents constitute pc 0, all C$\sharp$'s and D$\flat$'s and their octave equivalents comprise pc 1, and so forth (Ex. 2.2). All F's (and enharmonic equivalents), regardless of register, are members of pc 5. All A$\sharp$'s or B$\flat$'s, regardless of register, are members of pc 10. And so forth. For convenience of labeling, pc 10 is represented as "T" and pc 11 as "E."

EXAMPLE 2.2   Pitch-class labels and note names on the piano keyboard

pc:	0	1	2	3	4	5	6	7	8	9	T	E
		C♯ D♭		D♯ E♭			F♯ G♭		G♯ A♭		A♯ B♭	
	B♯ C D♭♭	C𝄪 D E♭♭	D𝄪 E F♭	E♯ F G♭♭	F𝄪 G A♭♭	G𝄪 A B♭♭	A𝄪 B C♭					

So, the opening three notes of Webern's Bagatelle, pitches D₄, E♭₄, and C♯₅, are members of pitch classes 2, 3, and 1, which we earlier reordered as a segment of the chromatic scale, pc 1–2–3 (Ex. 2.3a). In Chapter 1 we noticed that the secondary chromatic cluster in the upper register of measures 8 and 9 recalls the same three notes from measure 1 (C♯, D, and E♭). The cluster in measures 8 and 9 comprises three different pitches—C♯₇, D₅, and E♭₆—but the same three pitch classes: 1, 2, and 3. The other two chromatic clusters we highlighted in Chapter 1 were pitches G♭₄, F₅, and E₅ (pc 6–5–4) in measure 9 (Ex. 2.3c), and pitches B₂, C♯₄, and C₅ (pc E–1–0) in measure 10 (Ex. 2.3d).

EXAMPLE 2.3   Four chromatic clusters from Webern's op. 9, no. 1 (see Ex. 1.3)

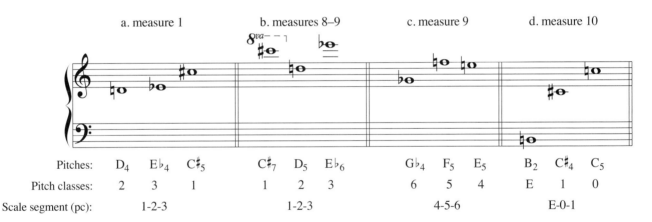

	a. measure 1			b. measures 8–9			c. measure 9			d. measure 10		
Pitches:	D₄	E♭₄	C♯₅	C♯₇	D₅	E♭₆	G♭₄	F₅	E₅	B₂	C♯₄	C₅
Pitch classes:	2	3	1	1	2	3	6	5	4	E	1	0
Scale segment (pc):		1-2-3			1-2-3			4-5-6			E-0-1	

STUDY QUESTIONS 2.2

1. **Which type of space(s) has/have the following features?**

   1.1. Disregard register and spelling.

   1.2. Notes in their specific octaves.

   1.3. Disregard duration, dynamic marking, articulation style, and spelling.

2. **Are the pitches listed below in order from low to high in pitch space? If not, rearrange them so that they are.**

   2.1. E₂–F♯₃–F₄

   2.2. E₄–F♯₃–F₄

   2.3. A₅–B₄–C₃

   2.4. G₆–C♯₃–G₄–G♭₄–F₅–B₂

3. **Rewrite each pitch series as a string of pitch–class integers (without changing the order):**

   3.1. E_2–$F\sharp_3$–F_4
   3.2. $A\flat_6$–$B\flat_2$–C_4
   3.3. G_6–$C\sharp_3$–G_4–$G\flat_4$–F_5–B_2
   3.4. $D\flat_4$–$C\times_4$–$D\sharp_4$–$F\flat_3$–$G\flat\flat_4$–$F\sharp_4$–G_5

2.3   INTERVAL SPACE

Pitch and pitch-class space are inhabited by objects. **Interval space** comprises distances between objects. The opening gesture in Webern's Bagatelle, for example, can be represented as pitches D_4–$E\flat_4$–$C\sharp_5$ or pitch classes 2–3–1 (or as a realization of chromatic scale segment 1–2–3), but also as a rising minor second from D_4 to $E\flat_4$ followed by a leap up an augmented sixth, from $E\flat_4$ up to $C\sharp_5$. To avoid the connotations of interval labels from tonal theory, we'll represent distances in interval space by counting half steps between notes: in measure 1 of the Bagatelle, D_4 rises to $E\flat_4$ by one half step, and $E\flat_4$ rises to $C\sharp_5$ by ten half steps.

Of course, interval identifications will change depending on whether you're in pitch- or pitch-class space. Let's first focus on the distance measurements within pitch space, known as **pitch intervals**. When one note follows another in pitch space, it moves a specific direction, up or down. Plus and minus signs specify these directions. (For intervals between notes that are presented simultaneously, omit the plus/minus signs altogether.) In Webern's four chromatic clusters, the pitch intervals are +1/+10, –23/+13, +11/–1, and +14/+11 (Ex. 2.4).

EXAMPLE 2.4   Pitch names and pitch intervals in op. 9, no. 1 chromatic clusters

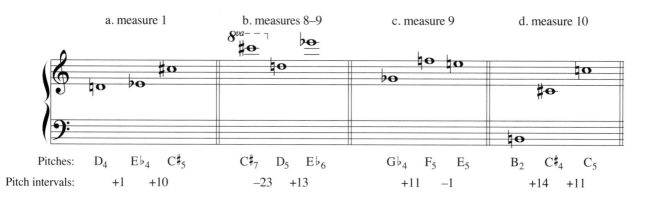

| | a. measure 1 | b. measures 8–9 | c. measure 9 | d. measure 10 |

When you first studied intervals in tonal theory, you may have learned half-step sizes for each quality/distance. The minor second spans one half step, the major second spans two, the major third is four, the perfect fifth is seven, and so forth (plus enharmonic respellings):

LABEL	DISTANCE IN HALF STEPS
P1 (d2)	0
m2 (A1)	1
M2 (d3)	2
m3 (A2)	3
M3 (d4)	4
P4 (A3)	5
A4/d5	6
P5 (d6)	7
m6 (A5)	8
M6 (d7)	9
m7 (A6)	10
M7 (d8)	11
P8 (A7)	12

We can use this information to calculate pitch intervals quickly. For pitch intervals larger than an octave, determine the half-step distance as if the two notes are in the same octave and then add 12 for each additional octave of separation. If the interval ascends, make all the values positive, and if the interval descends, make all the values negative. For the pitch interval from B_2 to $C\sharp_4$ in Example 2.4d, for example, imagine B to C$\sharp$ as a 2 (M2) and then add 12 for the one additional octave of separation: $2 + 12 = +14$. The pitch interval of the first two notes of Example 2.4b is a descending M7 (-11) plus an additional octave: $-11 + (-12) = -23$.

The distances between objects in pitch-class space are **pitch-class intervals (pc intervals)**. In pc space, objects don't move in particular directions; the musical motions "up" and "down" don't exist. A collection of all F$\sharp$'s in any octave and their enharmonic equivalents (pc 6) is not in any musical sense "higher" or "lower" than a collection of all D's (for example) including octave and enharmonic equivalents (pc 2).

Thus pitch-class intervals specify relationships that might be called "distances" between pitch classes, but we must keep in mind that these aren't the same as literal up or down distances in pitch space. For measuring distances between objects in pc space, we simply need to employ a method that's consistent for all circumstances. Here it is: Subtract the first pitch-class integer from the second. If the result is a negative number, add 12 ($10 = T$; $11 = E$). In the first measure of Webern's Bagatelle (Ex. 2.5a), the initial rise from D_4 to $E\flat_4$ is pitch interval $+1$, pc interval ($3 - 2 =$) 1:

Pitches:	D_4		$E\flat_4$	(*Ex. 2.5a*)
Pitch interval:		$+1$		(*$E\flat_4$ is one half step higher than D_4*)
Pitch classes:	2		3	(*D_4 is a member of pc 2; $E\flat_4$ is a member of pc 3*)
Pc interval		1		(*subtract the first pc from the second: $3 - 2 = 1$*)

The subsequent E♭$_4$ to C♯$_5$ in the Bagatelle is pitch interval +10, pc interval (1 − 3 + 12 =) T. After subtracting 1 − 3 = −2, change the negative result to positive by adding 12: −2 + 12 = 10:

Pitches:		E♭$_4$		C♯$_5$	(*Ex. 2.5a*)
Pitch interval:			+10		(*C♯$_5$ is ten half steps higher than E♭$_4$*)
Pitch classes:		3		1	(*E♭$_4$ is a member of pc 3; C♯$_5$ is a member of pc 1*)
Pc interval			T		(*subtract the first pc from the second: 1 − 3 = −2; because the result is negative, add 12: −2 + 12 = 10*)

Compare Webern's second and third chromatic motives (Exx. 2.5b, 2.5c). It's easy to think of both as segments of chromatic scales with octave displacements, and yet their pc-interval profiles look quite different: 1/1 versus E/E. But remember that pc interval E is not in any musical sense "larger" than pc interval 1. In fact, in the music itself, the actual distance traveled to create the second pc interval E in measure 9 is pitch interval −1, from F$_5$ to E$_5$. This is a substantially shorter distance than either of the realizations of pc interval 1 in measures 8–9 (−23 from C♯$_7$ to D$_5$; +13 from D$_5$ to E♭$_6$).

EXAMPLE 2.5   Pitch and pitch-class intervals in op. 9, no. 1 chromatic clusters

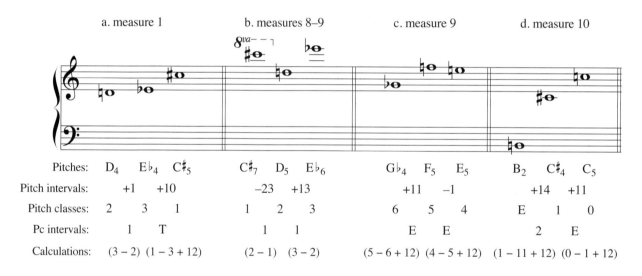

	a. measure 1	b. measures 8–9	c. measure 9	d. measure 10
Pitches:	D$_4$ E♭$_4$ C♯$_5$	C♯$_7$ D$_5$ E♭$_6$	G♭$_4$ F$_5$ E$_5$	B$_2$ C♯$_4$ C$_5$
Pitch intervals:	+1 +10	−23 +13	+11 −1	+14 +11
Pitch classes:	2 3 1	1 2 3	6 5 4	E 1 0
Pc intervals:	1 T	1 1	E E	2 E
Calculations:	(3 − 2) (1 − 3 + 12)	(2 − 1) (3 − 2)	(5 − 6 + 12) (4 − 5 + 12)	(1 − 11 + 12) (0 − 1 + 12)

Another term for the calculation process that produces a result between 0 and 11 is **mod-12 arithmetic**. For determining pc intervals, we would say that the result is "taken mod 12." As we've seen, to achieve a result mod 12, add 12 to a negative result. You can also backtrack and add 12 to the original starting number of the equation and then subtract; the result will be in the desired range. For the first pc interval in Example 2.5d:

$$1 − 11 = −10 + 12 = 2 \qquad or \qquad (1 + 12 =) \; 13 − 11 = 2$$

It may help to visualize these calculations around a circle of pitch-class integers (Ex. 2.6a). To determine the pc interval between two pitch classes, locate both on the circle and count the clockwise distance from the first pc to the second. For the first pc interval in Example 2.5d, locate the two pitch classes in the calculation, E and 1 (Ex. 2.6b). The distance clockwise from E to 1 is 2 (Ex. 2.6c). The pc interval from E to 1 is 2.

For the second pc interval in Example 2.5c, the pitch classes are 5 and 4 (Ex. 2.6d). The distance clockwise from 5 to 4 is 11 (Ex. 2.6e). The pc interval from 5 to 4 is E.

EXAMPLE 2.6   Circles of pitch classes

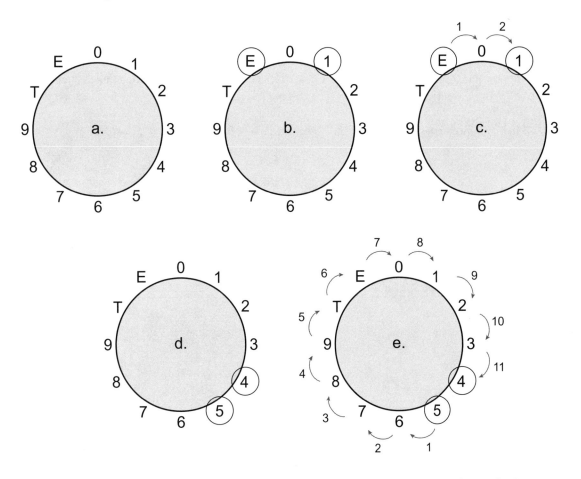

There is one final subcategory of interval space: **interval class (ic)**. Like pitch classes, interval classes collect together a theoretically infinite number of equivalent members, including all pitch intervals reducible to the same pc interval. But interval classes also include interval inverses, which are the familiar inverse intervals from tonal theory: perfect 4th inverts to perfect 5th, major 3rd inverts to minor 6th, diminished 5th inverts to augmented fourth, and so forth. These are also known as **mod-12 inverses** (or **mod-12 complements**) because they associate two inversional pc intervals that sum to 0, mod 12. So interval-class 2, for example, includes not only all whole steps, diminished thirds, major ninths, and any other spellings of pc interval 2 or larger intervals stretched by octaves, but also all instances of the inversion of the major second, the minor seventh, and its enharmonic equivalents and octave multiples. This collapses interval space into only six different classifications:

INTERVAL CLASS	INCLUDES PC INTERVALS:	
1	1, 11	(m2, M7, enharmonic equivalents, octave multiples)
2	2, 10	(M2, m7, enharmonic equivalents, octave multiples)
3	3, 9	(m3, M6, enharmonic equivalents, octave multiples)
4	4, 8	(M3, m6, enharmonic equivalents, octave multiples)
5	5, 7	(P4, P5, enharmonic equivalents, octave multiples)
6	6	(A4, d5, octave multiples)

To calculate interval-class values, simply convert any pc interval greater than 6 into its mod-12 inverse. Eleven converts to 1, 10 converts to 2, 9 converts to 3, 8 converts to 4, and

7 converts to 5. (Inverse pc intervals add to 12.) The initial gesture of Webern's Bagatelle, for example, which we can also describe as the succession of pitch intervals +1/+10 or pc intervals 1/T, presents members of interval classes 1 and 2 (Ex. 2.7a). The second and third chromatic clusters present literal half-step sequences that look different as pc intervals because one ascends (Ex. 2.7b, pc intervals 1/1) and the other descends (Ex. 2.7c, pc intervals E/E). In interval-class space, however, they are both 1/1. For the gesture in the Bagatelle's final bar (Ex. 2.7d), pc intervals 2 and E convert to interval classes 2 and 1.

EXAMPLE 2.7 Pitch and pitch-class intervals and interval classes in op. 9, no. 1 chromatic clusters

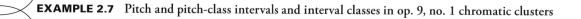

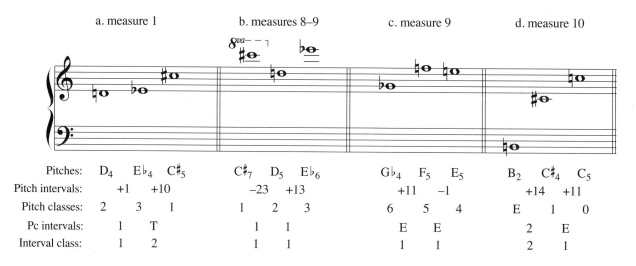

	a. measure 1			b. measures 8–9			c. measure 9			d. measure 10		
Pitches:	D_4	$E\flat_4$	$C\sharp_5$	$C\sharp_7$	D_5	$E\flat_6$	$G\flat_4$	F_5	E_5	B_2	$C\sharp_4$	C_5
Pitch intervals:		+1	+10		−23	+13		+11	−1		+14	+11
Pitch classes:	2	3	1	1	2	3	6	5	4	E	1	0
Pc intervals:		1	T		1	1		E	E		2	E
Interval class:		1	2		1	1		1	1		2	1

To use the pitch-class circle for calculating interval classes, find the shortest route between two points, clockwise or counter-clockwise. Let's say we want to determine the interval class between pitch classes 9 and 4. One way of getting from 9 to 4 on the circle is to move seven steps clockwise, as we do when we calculate the pc interval from 9 to 4 (Ex. 2.8a). But we can make the trip from 9 to 4 with fewer steps, five, if we move counter-clockwise (Ex. 2.8b). So the pc interval is 7, but the interval-class value is 5.

EXAMPLE 2.8 Using a pitch-class circle to calculate a member of interval-class 5

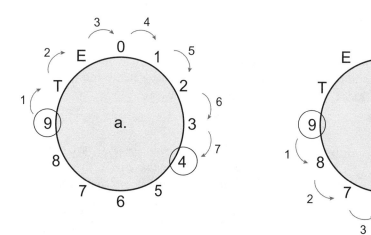

STUDY QUESTIONS 2.3

1. **Find the pitch interval between the pitches:**

   1.1. $D\flat_4/G\flat_4$ 1.2. $G\flat_4/D\flat_4$ 1.3. $G\flat_4/D\flat_5$ 1.4. $G\flat_3/D\flat_5$

   1.5. $C\sharp_6/F\sharp_4$ 1.6. $E\sharp_3/E_4$ 1.7. $E\sharp_3/E_3$

   1.8. $D_4/G\sharp_5$ 1.9. $G_4/E\flat_3$ 1.10. $D\sharp_3/A\flat\flat_5$

2. **Convert the pitches in question 1 to pitch classes and find the pc interval between them.**

3. **Express your answers to question 2 as interval classes.**

2.4   MUSICAL TRANSFORMATIONS IN PITCH SPACE

"Nacht," the eighth song in Arnold Schoenberg's twenty-one-song cycle *Pierrot Lunaire* for mezzo-soprano and chamber ensemble (1912), is subtitled "Passacaglia." The naming calls attention to a constant presence in the song of a three-note motive first clearly stated by the bass clarinet in measure 4 (Ex. 2.9). We'll refer to this motive as the "Nacht motive."

EXAMPLE 2.9   The "Nacht motive" in Schoenberg's "Nacht," bass clarinet, mm. 4–6.1 (sounds as notated)

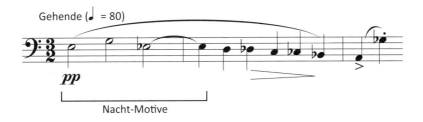

Unlike the chromatic clusters in Webern's op. 9, no. 1 Bagatelle, we'll define the Nacht motive as a specific sequence of pitch intervals in pitch space: +3/−4 (Ex. 2.10). The first clear presentation of the motive begins on E_3, a member of pc 4. Many other occurrences of the Nacht motive throughout the song also begin on an E in some octave—in other words, on some member of pitch-class 4.

EXAMPLE 2.10   Nacht motive

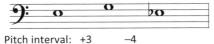

Pitch interval: +3   −4

But there are also a variety of other starting notes for statements of the motive throughout the song. In measure 8, for example, the bass clarinet expresses a rhythmically accelerated version of the motive starting on E_3, followed by identically rapid versions starting on G_3 and $E\flat_3$, designated X, Y, and Z in Example 2.11. Y is a transposition of X up three half-steps, and Z is a transposition of Y down four half steps. The pattern of transpositions outlines the +3/−4 structure of the motive itself.

EXAMPLE 2.11   "Nacht," bass clarinet, m. 8 (sounds as notated)

This exemplifies **ordered pitch-space transposition**, in which the pattern of pitch intervals is preserved while the starting note changes. To be specific about transpositional distances in pitch space, we'll use an uppercase "T" followed by the half-step amount as a subscript, with a plus or minus sign indicating direction. For this expression of the Nacht motive:

$$X \xrightarrow{\;T_{+3}\;} Y \xrightarrow{\;T_{-4}\;} Z$$

In algebraic notation, $Y = T_{+3}(X)$ ["Y is T_{+3} of X"], and $Z = T_{-4}(Y)$. Of course, $X = T_{0}(X)$.

Another word for this process is **mapping**. We can say that X maps to Y under T_{+3}, and Y maps to Z under T_{-4}.

Almost all of the singer's notes in *Pierrot Lunaire* are notated as *sprechstimme*, a combination of singing and speaking, indicated by a small "x" on the note stem. The next song in the cycle after "Nacht," "Gebet an Pierrot" (Prayer to Pierrot) features a *sprechstimme* D_4, $C\sharp_4$, and E_4 near the end in the vocal line ("J" in Ex. 2.12a). Although these pitches presumably aren't sung precisely, the first three notes Schoenberg wrote outline pitch intervals −1 and +3. Then, a few measures later, the song's final vocal gesture is a *sprechstimme* D_4, $E\flat_4$, and C_4, presenting those same pitch intervals with reversed directions, +1/−3 ("K" in Ex. 2.12b).

Identical distances in opposite directions constitute **ordered pitch-space inversion**. The "J" motive, which presents pitch intervals −1 and +3, is the ordered pitch-space inversion of "K," which expresses the same intervals in reverse directions, +1 followed by −3. We can say that J and K are inversionally equivalent.

EXAMPLE 2.12   "Gebet an Pierrot" motives

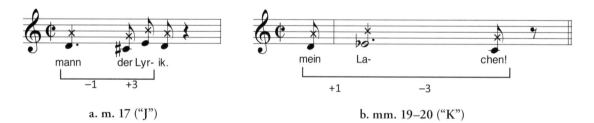

a. m. 17 ("J")   b. mm. 19–20 ("K")

Any pair of inversionally equivalent musical units shares a mathematical relation: corresponding notes, expressed as pitch-class integers, sum to the same number, mod 12. This consistent sum is known as the **index number**. For example, if we line up J and K, note-for-note (Ex. 2.13), the index number is 4, calculated by adding the pitch-class integers of the corresponding first notes (D + D = 2 + 2 = 4), second notes (C♯ + E♭ = 1 + 3 = 4), and third notes (E + C = 4 + 0 = 4).

EXAMPLE 2.13   "Gebet an Pierrot" inversional relations

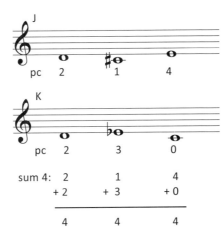

Symbolize inversion using an uppercase "I" followed by the index number as a subscript. J and K are equivalent via I_4. We can say that J maps to K by I_4. The reverse is also true: K maps to J by the same operation. A double-pointed arrow symbolizes this relationship:

$$J \xleftrightarrow{\quad I_4 \quad} K$$

The same is not true for all transpositional relations. Motive X from "Nacht" maps to Y by T_{+3}, but that same operation, T_{+3}, could not take us from Y back to X. The mapping from Y to X would be a literal reversal of T_{+3}, which is T_{-3}:

$$X \xrightarrow{\quad T_{+3} \quad} Y \qquad Y \xrightarrow{\quad T_{-3} \quad} X$$

A piece of music featuring these sorts of motivic recurrences is saturated with transpositional and inversional relations. Patterns can emerge not only from the multiple appearances of the motives themselves but also from specific transformational pathways that connect them. And when these relationships unfold in pitch space, they strike the ear with special clarity and resonance.

STUDY QUESTIONS 2.4

1. **What is the ordered pitch-space transposition from X to Z in Example 2.11?**

2. **What is the result of the indicated operations?**

   2.1. T_{+2} of $E_3\ G_3\ E\flat_3$ 2.2. T_{-2} of $E_3\ G_3\ E\flat_3$ 2.3. T_{+14} of $E_3\ G_3\ E\flat_3$
   2.4. T_{-5} of $G_4\ F_4\ D\flat_4\ E\flat_5$ 2.5. T_{-13} of $E_3\ F\sharp_4\ F_5\ E\flat_6$

3. **Find the pitch intervals in the given motive. Then reverse the directions in those pitch intervals to transform the motive by p-space inversion starting on the same note. Give the index number of the inversional transformation.**

   3.1. $G_3\ B\flat_3\ G\flat_3$ 3.2. $D\flat_4\ B\flat_3\ D_4$ 3.3. $F_5\ B\flat_5\ E_5\ D_5$
   3.4. $G_3\ D_4\ E\flat_4\ B_2$ 3.5. $B\flat_4\ B_4\ A_4\ C_5\ A\flat_4\ D\flat_5$

VOCABULARY

index number	musical space	pitch class (pc)
interval class (ic)	note space	pitch interval
interval space	ordered pitch-space inversion	pitch space (p space)
mapping	ordered pitch-space transposition	pitch-class interval (pc interval)
mod-12 arithmetic	pitch	pitch-class space (pc space)
mod-12 inverse		

EXERCISES

A. SYMBOLOGY FOR NOTES AND INTERVALS

On the staff provided, rewrite the notes of each melody as a series of whole notes in note space. Below that, in the blanks provided, translate the notes into pitch names and pitch-class integers; then indicate the pitch intervals, pitch-class intervals, and interval classes between consecutive notes.

Demo. Charles Ives (1874–1954), *The Unanswered Question* (1908, rev. 1930s)

Pitches:	B♭₄	C♯₄	E₄	E♭₅	C₅
Pitch classes:	T	1	4	3	0
Pitch intervals:		−9	+3	+11	−3
Pc intervals:		3	3	11	9
Interval classes:		3	3	1	3

1. Alban Berg (1885–1935), "Sahst du nach dem Gewitterregen," op. 4, no. 2, mm. 1–3 (1912)

Notes:

Pitches: ___ ___ ___ ___ ___ ___ ___ ___ ___ ___

Pitch classes: ___ ___ ___ ___ ___ ___ ___ ___ ___ ___

Pitch intervals: ___ ___ ___ ___ ___ ___ ___ ___ ___

Pc intervals: ___ ___ ___ ___ ___ ___ ___ ___ ___

Interval classes: ___ ___ ___ ___ ___ ___ ___ ___ ___

2. Anton Webern (1883–1945), *Drei kleine Stücke* for Cello and Piano, op. 11, no. 2, mm. 6–11 (1914)

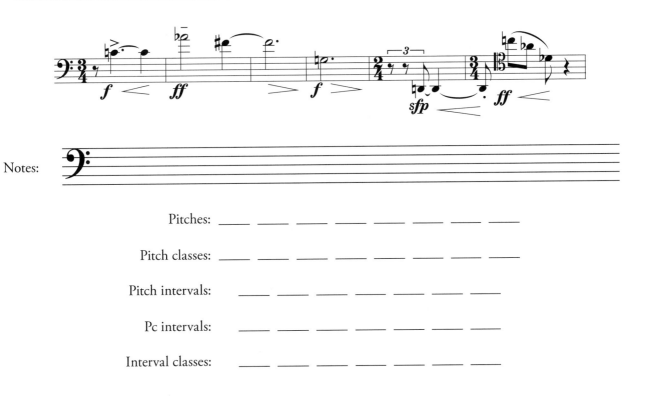

Notes:

Pitches: ___ ___ ___ ___ ___ ___ ___ ___

Pitch classes: ___ ___ ___ ___ ___ ___ ___ ___

Pitch intervals: ___ ___ ___ ___ ___ ___ ___

Pc intervals: ___ ___ ___ ___ ___ ___ ___

Interval classes: ___ ___ ___ ___ ___ ___ ___

3. Arnold Schoenberg (1874–1951), "Der kranke Mond" from *Pierrot Lunaire*, op. 21, mm. 8–10 (1912)

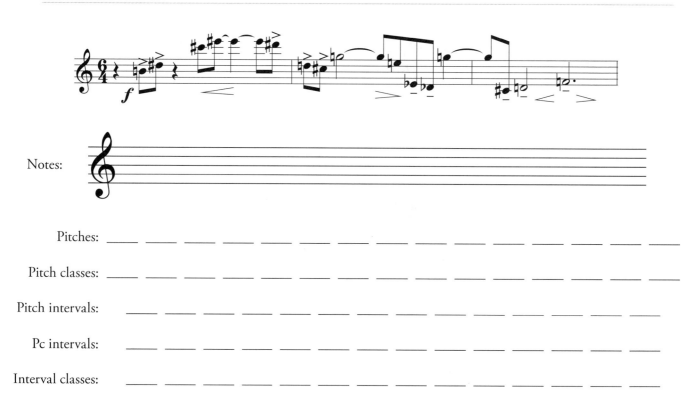

Notes:

Pitches: ____ ____ ____ ____ ____ ____ ____ ____ ____ ____ ____ ____ ____ ____ ____ ____

Pitch classes: ____ ____ ____ ____ ____ ____ ____ ____ ____ ____ ____ ____ ____ ____ ____ ____

Pitch intervals: ____ ____ ____ ____ ____ ____ ____ ____ ____ ____ ____ ____ ____ ____ ____

Pc intervals: ____ ____ ____ ____ ____ ____ ____ ____ ____ ____ ____ ____ ____ ____ ____

Interval classes: ____ ____ ____ ____ ____ ____ ____ ____ ____ ____ ____ ____ ____ ____ ____

B. NAVIGATING MUSICAL SPACES

Notate the specified notes on a staff.

Demo. Four different members of pc 5, labeled with pitch names.

1. **Five different members of pc 8, labeled with pitch names.**

2. **$D\sharp_2$ and four other members of the same pitch class as $D\sharp_2$ (labeled with pitch names).**

3. **C_3 followed by four other pitches displaying consecutive pitch intervals −3, +10, +17, −6 (labeled with pitch names).**

4. **$B\flat_4$ followed by four other pitches displaying consecutive pitch intervals +5, −23, −11, +7 (labeled with pitch names).**

5. **Eight pitches, all notated within the treble clef staff (i.e., without using ledger lines), starting with pc 7 and displaying consecutive pitch-class intervals 2, 5, 8, 1, 6, E, 3 (labeled as pitch classes).**

6. **Eight pitches, all notated within the bass clef staff (i.e., without using ledger lines), starting with pc 1 and displaying consecutive pitch-class intervals 7, T, 4, 6, 9, 5, E (labeled as pitch classes).**

7. **Four different pairs of pitches that all form different pitch intervals but are all members of interval-class 2, all with D$_4$ as the bottom note (labeled as pitch intervals).**

8. **Four different pairs of pitches that all form different pitch intervals but are all members of interval-class 5, all with G♭$_2$ as the bottom note (labeled as pitch intervals).**

C. ORDERED PITCH-SPACE TRANSPOSITION

Underneath the staff, indicate the pitch intervals of the given melodic segments. In the adjoining blank measures, notate the specified ordered pitch-space transpositions of those segments.

D. ORDERED PITCH-SPACE INVERSION

Indicate the pitch intervals of the given melodic segment. In the staff below, notate the p-space inversion of the given segment starting on the note provided. Then fill in the blanks to the side with the pitch-class integers of both the original segment and its inversion, and the index number (sum of corresponding pc's).

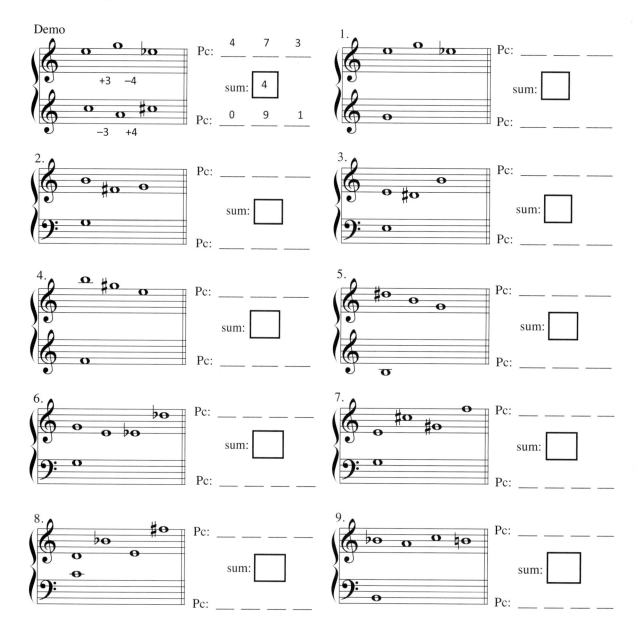

E. EQUIVALENCES VIA TRANSPOSITION OR INVERSION

Each melodic segment on the left is equivalent via ordered pitch-space transposition or ordered pitch-space inversion to a melodic segment on the right. Place a letter label in each box to identify the equivalent pairings. Label the arrows to indicate the equivalence operations (and remember to use +/− for transpositions to indicate directions).

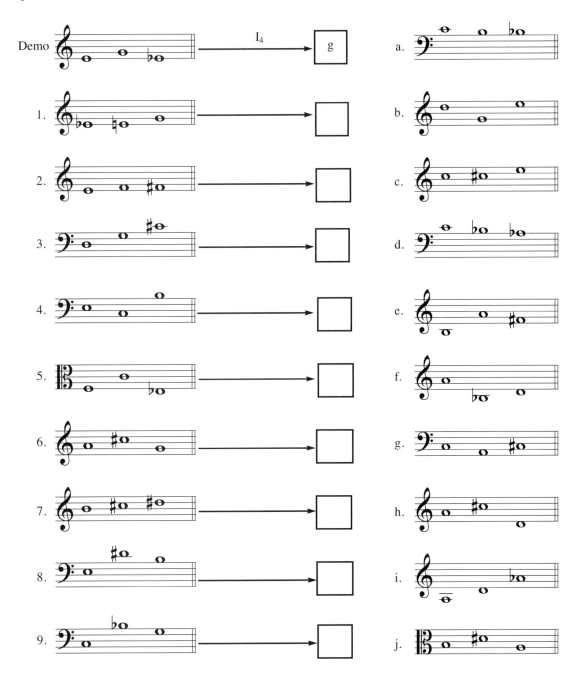

F. ARNOLD SCHOENBERG (1874–1951), "NACHT" FROM *PIERROT LUNAIRE* (1912), MM. 11–16

As we observed in Chapter 2.4, Schoenberg gives "Nacht" the subtitle "Passacaglia," highlighting the pervasive presence of a three-note motive we called the Nacht motive:

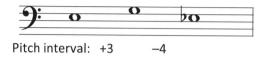

Pitch interval: +3   −4

Let's call it "NM" for short. The NM is an ordered pitch-space event, an ascent by three half steps followed by a descent by four half steps.

The middle section of the song excerpted below, which sets the second of three stanzas of the poem, begins with a clear restatement of NM starting on E_2 in the left hand of the piano (m. 11).

1. **In measure 11, the bass clarinet presents three transpositions of NM. Notate them on a staff as whole notes in pitch space. Draw arrows from the first to the second and from the second to the third, and label the arrows to specify the ordered pitch transpositions (don't forget +/− to indicate direction).**

2. **Now look for other ordered p-space transpositions of NM among consecutive pitches in the vocal part of the excerpt. Notate them as whole notes in pitch space and specify their locations.**

3. **Relate the versions of NM you found for Question 2 as p-space transpositions of NM itself, assuming that the primary version of NM is the one shown above (E_3 G_3 $E\flat_3$).**

4. **Next, look for ordered p-space transpositions of NM in the piano right hand in measures 11 and 12. On a blank staff, notate them as whole notes in pitch space and connect them with labeled arrows to specify their relationships with each other.**

5. **Do the same with the piano left hand in measure 12 . . .**

6. **. . . and with the piano left hand in measure 13.**

7. **Specifically describe the transpositional relationship between the piano left hand in measure 12 and the piano left hand in measure 13.**

8. **Look just at the first beat of the piano left hand in measure 14:**

   How many p-space transpositions of NM can you find just within this beat? Notate them on a staff as whole notes in pitch space. Connect them with labeled arrows to show ordered p-space transpositions.

9. **In the piano left hand in measure 14: Specifically explain the relationships between the notes on the first beat and the notes on the other two beats, and explain how these relationships tie in with a recurring organizational strategy in the composition.**

10. **Describe transposition patterns in the piano left hand of the entire excerpt. Explain how the recurrence of NM in the last measure (m. 16) is a logical conclusion of the longest of these patterns.**

11. **Finally, take a look at the chromatic lines in the cello (mm. 12–16), bass clarinet (mm. 13–15), and piano right hand (mm. 14–15). (Perhaps these help portray "sinister giant black butterflies.") What is the musical pattern shared by the chromatic lines in all three instruments, and how does this pattern relate to the Nacht motive?**

*These are the sounding pitches of the bass clarinet part.

Aus dem Qualm verlorener Tiefen	From dank forgotten depths of Lethe
Steigt ein Duft, Erinnrung mordend!	A scent floats up, to murder memory.
Finstre, schwarze Riesenfalter	Sinister giant black butterflies
Töteten der Sonne Glanz.	Eclipse the blazing disc of sun.

G. COMPOSITION EXERCISES

Compose motivic melodies using the given motives as starting points. Develop the motives within the melodies using techniques of ordered pitch-space transposition and ordered pitch-space inversion.

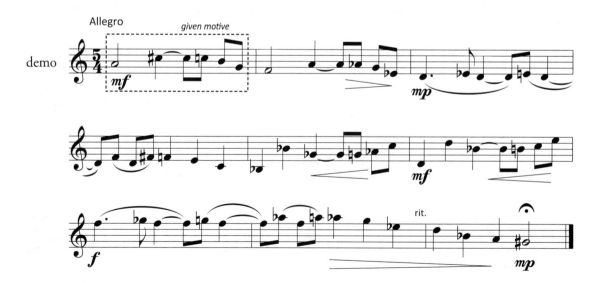

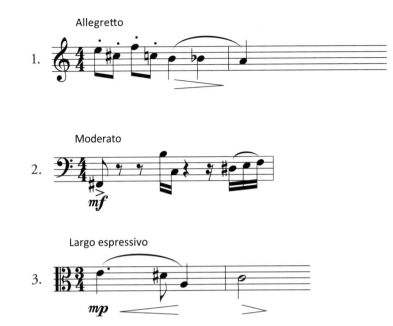

FOR FURTHER STUDY

IGOR STRAVINSKY:

Three Pieces for Clarinet Solo (1918), no. 1

EDGARD VARÈSE:

Density 21.5 (1936)

CHAPTER 3

TRICHORDS AND TRICHORD CLASSES

3.1 SETS AND SEGMENTS

In our exploration of Webern's first opus 9 Bagatelle for String Quartet in Chapter 1, we found musical groupings that could be somehow traced to three consecutive notes from a chromatic scale. We named these "chromatic clusters." Our definition of chromatic cluster didn't include a specific ordering or registral configuration, only the potential for notes to be moved into different octaves and reorganized until they look like a literal three-note sequence from a chromatic scale. The chromatic cluster is a type of **set**. A set is a musically meaningful collection of notes (pitches or pitch classes) that may appear in any possible ordering in a musical realization.

In Chapter 2, on the other hand, we defined the Nacht motive from Schoenberg's "Nacht" as a specific, ordered event in pitch space. It is, therefore, a **segment**. A segment is a meaningful musical grouping (in pitch- or pitch-class space) with a specific ordering.

To facilitate commentary and discussion, we'll notate sets using {curly braces}, segments in <angle brackets>.

Imagine borrowing the "A," "B," and "C" blocks from a kindergarten classroom. If we place them loosely in a bag, they have no particular order; they're a set. To describe the bag's contents, we could list the blocks in alphabetical order, {ABC}, but this wouldn't prioritize the alphabetical ordering over any other, just as the designation "chromatic cluster" doesn't prioritize a literal sequence of half steps over some other ordering of those same notes.

Now imagine removing the blocks from the bag, one by one, and lining them up on a table as they emerge. Each possible lineup is a specific ordering, a segment, one of six possibilities: <ABC>, <ACB>, <BAC>, <BCA>, <CAB>, or <CBA>.

Let's consider ordering issues further in Schoenberg's "Nacht." The main musical idea is the interval sequence $+3/-4$, first clearly presented as $<E_3-G_3-E\flat_3>$ in the bass clarinet in measure 4 (Ex. 3.1; see also Ex. 2.9).

EXAMPLE 3.1 Nacht motive from Schoenberg's *Pierrot Lunaire*

Pitch interval: +3   −4

In Chapter 2.4, and in the Chapter 2F exercises, we found many subsequent occurrences of the motive, some starting on E's in different octaves, some starting on other notes. The recurrences may have been presented in different rhythms and in different instruments, but they were all ordered pitch-space transpositions of each other.

Now let's make still more motivic connections in "Nacht." In the piano right hand of measures 17 and 18, for example, statements of <E–G–E♭> are stacked above <A–A♭–C> (Ex. 3.2a). This happens three times during the excerpt, first pairing <E_4–G_4–$E♭_4$> with <A_3–$A♭_3$–C_4>, then repeating that pairing up an octave, finally repeating it again up one more octave. We recognize the upper notes of the pairings as recurrences of the +3/−4 motive starting on different members of pc 4: <E_4–G_4–$E♭_4$>, <E_5–G_5–$E♭_5$>, <E_6–G_6–$E♭_6$>. The lower motive, however, is not +3/−4 but −1/+4 (Ex. 3.2b). And yet we can easily convert the lower motive to +3/−4 by reversing the second and third pitches (Ex. 3.2c). In other words, to recognize the close musical relationship between the upper and lower motives, we must disregard the original motivic ordering. We must treat the three-note grouping as a set, not a segment.

EXAMPLE 3.2   "Nacht," piano right hand, mm. 17–18.1

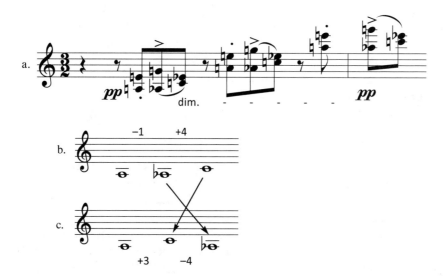

A two-step process gets us from the upper motive to the lower motive in each pairing: transpose down seven half steps, then reverse the order of the second and third notes. In the first pairing, for example:

$$E_4\text{–}G_4\text{–}E♭_4 \xrightarrow{\ T_{-7}\ } A_3\text{–}C_4 A♭_3 \xrightarrow{\ \text{reorder}\ } A_3\text{–}A♭_3\text{–}C_4$$

As we noticed in the scenario of the ABC blocks, a three-element set has six possible orderings. This transformation of the Nacht motive is just one of six possible orderings of the three elements in this set (Ex. 3.3). All six have the same pitch content but different orders and therefore different sequences of pitch intervals. In Example 3.3, the second possibility, −1/+4 (*), is the one used by Schoenberg as the lower motive in measure 17.

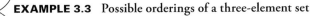

EXAMPLE 3.3 Possible orderings of a three-element set

+3 −4   −1 +4   −3 −1   −4 +1   +1 +3   +4 −3

STUDY QUESTIONS 3.1

1. **Set or segment?**

    1.1. {ABC}   1.2. <ABC>   1.3. {ACB}   1.4. <ACB>   1.5. <XYZ>

    1.6. chromatic cluster

    1.7. <D$_4$–E♭$_4$–C♯$_5$> in measure 1 of Webern's Bagatelle, op. 9, no. 1

    1.8. <E$_3$–G$_3$–E♭$_3$> in measure 4 of Schoenberg's "Nacht"

    1.9. The notes of the C-major scale as a source for all C-major melodies

    1.10. The notes C–D–E–F–G–A–B–C occurring consecutively within a melody by Mozart

    1.11. A chronological listing of the birth years of Schoenberg (1874), Webern (1883), and Berg (1885)

2. **Give the pitch-interval sequence for this segment: <F$_4$–A$_4$–E$_4$>. Then write out the other five possible orderings of these three pitches and give their pitch-interval sequences.**

3.2   THE NACHT TRICHORD

A close look at pitch groupings in "Nacht" will locate several other instances of three-note groupings that are equivalent to the Nacht motive through some transforming-plus-reordering process. Some are close relatives, as in Example 3.2; others involve more derivational steps. To understand their role in the pitch structure of the song, we need to refine our conception of the motive itself. Our analytical principles will need to allow for any possible ordering and registral configuration of this motive. In short, we need to redefine it as a **pitch-class set (pc set)**. A pitch-class set is a meaningful musical grouping, but because it's a set, its order is variable, and because its members are pitch classes, it has no fixed registral positioning.

Pitch-class sets come in different sizes. In the interest of thoroughness, a single pitch class can be viewed as a one-element set, or **monad**. What we called an interval class in Chapter 2 can also be described as a two-element pc set, or **dyad**. A pitch-class set of three elements, such as the Nacht motive, is a **trichord**. Size-specific names are also commonly used for pc sets of sizes four (**tetrachord**), five (**pentachord**), six (**hexachord**), seven (**septachord**), eight (**octachord**), and nine (**nonachord**).

For now, we're focusing on trichords. And we'll continue to use Schoenberg's Nacht motive as an example, although we need to give it a new name, because we originally defined it as an event in pitch space, a rising pitch interval 3 followed by a descending 4. To recognize its new status as a pitch-class set, let's call it the **Nacht trichord**.

Recurrences of the Nacht trichord in "Nacht" would of course include any of the many instances of the +3/−4 pitch-space motive, but would also include any other meaningful three-note grouping in the song that's equivalent to the Nacht motive through transposition or inversion in pc space and in any possible order variation. Let's summarize all the possibilities.

Start with the motive itself, <E–G–E♭>. We'll represent it as a pc set, {473}, keeping in mind that these pitch classes may occur in any order—not only {473} but also {437}, {743}, {734}, {347}, or {374}. In addition to the variable orderings, the set may also appear at any of its twelve transpositions. To derive these, take {473} and move it forward by half steps in pc space until you've identified all twelve possible transpositions:

{473}   {584}   {695}   {7T6}   {8E7}   {908}   {T19}   {E2T}   {03E}   {140}   {251}   {362}

It's easy to visualize this process on the staff or piano keyboard, or you can just make it a simple math problem, adding 1 to each integer, mod 12, as you move forward. For example, you could calculate the initial {473} to the subsequent {584} as follows:

$$
\begin{array}{ccccc}
\underline{\{473\}} & & & & \underline{\{584\}} \\
4 & + & 1 & = & 5 \\
7 & + & 1 & = & 8 \\
3 & + & 1 & = & 4 \\
\end{array}
$$

A complete list of possible forms of the Nacht trichord would also include all the inversional forms of the motive and their order variations. We can derive these through the same process. First, find a starting point by producing a trichord using the inverted pitch intervals: if the original trichord is +3/−4, the inversion is −3/+4. Arbitrarily choose a starting pitch class—let's say, pc 8—and create an inversional form of the trichord: pc 8 (−3 =), 5 (+ 4 =) 9. Then, start with {859} and move forward by half steps until you've listed all twelve transpositions of the inversion:

{859}   {96T}   {T7E}   {E80}   {091}   {1T2}   {2E3}   {304}   {415}   {526}   {637}   {748}

These twenty-four pc sets—twelve transpositions and twelve inversions—comprise the **equivalence class** for the Nacht trichord (Ex. 3.4). An equivalence class brings together elements whose structure and relations are specifically defined. In this case, the elements are defined as sets of three pitch classes, and their relations are equivalency by transposition or inversion. We might also describe this twenty-four-set group as a **set class**—an equivalence class in which the elements are pc sets.

EXAMPLE 3.4   Complete set-class of the Nacht trichord (sets in examples in bold)

	1	2	3	4	5	6	7	8	9	10	11	12
Transpositions:	**{473}**	{584}	{695}	{7T6}	{8E7}	**{908}**	**{T19}**	{E2T}	**{03E}**	{140}	**{251}**	{362}
Inversions:	{859}	{96T}	{T7E}	{E80}	{091}	**{1T2}**	**{2E3}**	{304}	{415}	{526}	{637}	{748}

So the equivalency demonstrated in Example 3.2bc is an order variation of the sixth set-class member on the transposition list, {908}. Let's look at some other recurrences in the song. The end of the vocal line in the middle section (Ex. 3.5a, and see Exercise 2F) includes the note succession E♭$_4$–E$_4$–G$_4$. This <347> is an order variation of the {437} at the beginning of the transposition list, and is followed immediately by E♭$_4$–D$_4$–B$_3$, <32E>, which is a reordering of the seventh set-class member on the inversion list, {2E3}. Then in the next measure (Ex. 3.5b), the cello presents four versions of the motive, each with the third note an octave higher than customary, and moving the motives upward by T$_{+10}$, stating set-class members <473>, <251>, <03E>, and <T19>. Just as that sequence is complete, the piano right hand responds with a temporary three-voice texture (Ex. 3.5c) presenting transpositions of the motive in the upper and lower voices (D$_6$–F$_6$–D♭$_6$ <251> and E♭$_5$–G♭$_5$–D$_5$ <362>). In addition, the combined notes of the voices themselves—the harmonies—comprise inversional set-class members in two instances, {2E3} and {1T2}.

EXAMPLE 3.5 Instances of the Nacht trichord in "Nacht"

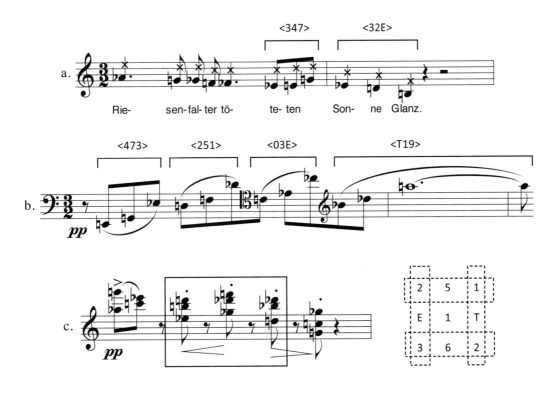

STUDY QUESTIONS 3.2

1. **What is the difference between the Nacht motive and the Nacht trichord?**

2. **Within the equivalence class of the Nacht trichord,**

   2.1. What operations produce equivalence?

   2.2. How many different members are included?

3. **Describe the differences between "segment," "set," and "set class."**

4. **List the entire contents of the set class that includes this pc set: {594}.**

   4.1. First, write the set and its eleven tranpositions.

   4.2. Then write the set in inversion (starting on any note) and write the eleven transpositions of this inversion.

3.3   MUSICAL TRANSFORMATIONS IN PITCH-CLASS SPACE

If you want to be specific about the transpositional relationship between two set-class members, use an uppercase "T" plus a pitch-class interval as a subscript. From {473} to {T19} in Example 3.5b, for example, pc interval 6 connects corresponding pitch classes; the operation is T_6. Thus, T_6 maps {473} to {T19}. You might prefer to line up the source and its transposition in tabular form and add the subscript value (mod 12) to get from the first set to the second:

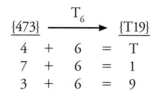

$$
\begin{array}{ccccc}
 & & T_6 & & \\
\{473\} & \longrightarrow & & \{T19\} \\
4 & + & 6 & = & T \\
7 & + & 6 & = & 1 \\
3 & + & 6 & = & 9 \\
\end{array}
$$

For inversions, the labeling is the same in pitch-space and in pitch-class space: use the uppercase "I" and the index number as a subscript. Between the reorderings of {473} and {2E3} in Example 3.5a, for example, line up corresponding notes and add their pitch-class integers to the same number, mod 12:

$$
\begin{array}{ccccc}
 & & I_6 & & \\
\{473\} & \longrightarrow & & \{2E3\} \\
4 & + & 2 & = & 6 \\
7 & + & E & = & 6 \\
3 & + & 3 & = & 6 \\
\end{array}
$$

I_6 maps {473} to {2E3}. It may help to visualize inversional mappings as reversals of direction in pitch space, whether or not they appear that way in a given musical context (Ex. 3.6).

EXAMPLE 3.6   Visualizing inversional relations

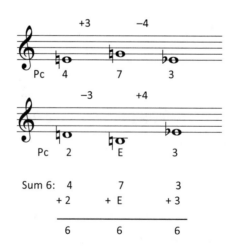

STUDY QUESTIONS 3.3

1. **Give the labels for these transpositions in pitch-space and in pc-space:**
   1.1.   The first to second trichord bracketed in Example 3.5b.
   1.2.   The first to third trichord bracketed in Example 3.5b.

1.3. The second to third trichord bracketed in Example 3.5b.

1.4. Within the box in Example 3.5c, the first chord (vertical sonority) to the third.

1.5. Within the box in Example 3.5c, the trichord formed by just the top notes of the chords to the trichord formed by just the bottom notes.

2. Give the labels for these inversions:

2.1. <473> to <96T>   2.2. <594> to <081>

2.3. <2T3> to <T29>   2.4. <482> to <739>

3.4 TRICHORDS IN NORMAL FORM

In Example 3.4 and surrounding discussion, we used the pitch-class ordering of the Nacht motive, <473>, as the point of reference for the set-class listing. This is a reasonable strategy for music such as "Nacht," in which a particular motivic ordering is so pervasive and influential. But in most cases, we will need to reference set-class members using an ordering standard that will apply in any piece or context. This universal standard is known as **normal form**.

To find the normal form of a trichord, follow this procedure:

1. List the pitch-class contents of the set in numerical order, from lowest to highest.
2. Move the pc positioned first in step 1 to the end and move the pc's in positions 2 and 3 in step 1 to positions 1 and 2. This is called a **rotation**.
3. Perform one more rotation on the step-2 ordering.
4. You now have three orderings, or rotations, of the set. The normal form is the rotation with the smallest pitch-class interval from beginning to end.
5. If more than one rotation has the same outer pc interval, look at the next pc intervals inward, from position 1 to 2.
6. If both outer and inner pc intervals are the same, the normal form is the rotation that starts on the smallest integer.
7. The normal form is notated using pitch-class integers without commas, enclosed in [square brackets].

To find the normal form of the Nacht motive, <473>, start with {347} (step 1). Rotate pc 3 to the end and move 4 and 7 back to positions 1 and 2: {473} (step 2). Perform the same rotation one more time: {734} (step 3). Calculate the outer pc interval of each rotation (step 4):

ROTATION	PITCH CLASSES	OUTER PC INTERVAL
1	**347**	**4**
2	473	E
3	734	9

The first rotation has the smallest outer pc interval (4). The normal form of the Nacht motive is [347].

Relatively compact sets such as this one (or the chromatic cluster) are usually easy to reduce quickly to normal form, because one rotation is so obviously smaller than the others. Here's one that might take a little longer, extracted from the end of Example 3.5c (after the box):

ROTATION	PITCH CLASSES	OUTER PC INTERVAL
1	067	7
2	**670**	**6**
3	706	E

The first two rotations differ by only one half step, but the second one has a smaller outer interval (6), so the normal form of the trichord is [670].

Here's a trichord with the same outer pc interval for two rotations:

ROTATION	PITCH CLASSES	OUTER PC INTERVAL
1	**279**	7
2	**792**	7
3	927	T

This activates the additional step 5 to break the tie:

ROTATION	PITCH CLASSES	OUTER PC INTERVAL	INNER PC INTERVAL
1	279	7	5
2	**792**	7	**2**
~~3~~	~~927~~	~~T~~	

Rotation 2 has the smaller pc interval (2) from its first to second pitch classes. The normal form is [792].

Only the augmented triad activates step 6 of the procedure:

ROTATION	PITCH CLASSES	OUTER PC INTERVAL	INNER PC INTERVAL
1	**159**	**8**	**4**
2	591	8	4
3	915	8	4

Because all rotations of this trichord have the same outer and inner pc intervals, the normal form is the rotation that begins on the smallest integer, [159].

STUDY QUESTIONS 3.4

Find the normal form of these pc sets:

1. All four bracketed trichords in Example 3.5b.
2. Both bracketed trichords in Example 3.5a.
3. The two highlighted horizontal trichords in Example 3.5c, then the two highlighted vertical trichords.
4. The middle chord (vertical sonority) in the box in Example 3.5c.
5. The trichord formed in the first measure of Webern's op. 9, no. 1 Bagatelle (Ex. 2.1).
6. $<B\flat_4–E_4–F_3>$
7. C$\sharp$° triad
8. B-minor triad
9. $<G\flat_3–C\flat_4–D\flat_5>$
10. $<B_2–F\times_4–E\flat_3>$

3.5   TRICHORDS IN PRIME FORM

We can now revise the set-class listing for the Nacht motive shown in Example 3.4 so that all members are given in normal form (Ex. 3.7).

EXAMPLE 3.7   Complete set class of the Nacht trichord showing normal forms

Transpositions: [347] [458] [569] [67T] [78E] [890] [9T1] [TE2] [E03] [014] [125] [236]
Inversions: [589] [69T] [7TE] [8E0] [901] [T12] [E23] [034] [145] [256] [367] [478]

We'll also rearrange that listing so that the normal forms starting on "0" are listed first (Ex. 3.8). This doesn't imply systematic or musical priority for the set-class members beginning on 0, but rather organizes the data in a neutral state that will facilitate comparisons with other set classes.

EXAMPLE 3.8   Complete set class of the Nacht trichord starting with [014]

Transpositions: [014] [125] [236] [347] [458] [569] [67T] [78E] [890] [9T1] [TE2] [E03]
Inversions: [034] [145] [256] [367] [478] [589] [69T] [7TE] [8E0] [901] [T12] [E23]

Also, we need to designate one member of the set-class as its identifier and representative. This is known as the **prime form**. The prime form is the one member that begins on 0 and has its smallest intervals on the left. In this set class, the two members that begin on 0 are [014] and [034]. Both span pc interval 4 from beginning to end, but [014] spans pc interval 1 from first note to second, while [034] has pc interval 3 from first note to second. So [014] is the identifier and representative of this set class. Notate the prime form using pc integers without commas and enclosed in parentheses: the prime form of this set class is **(014)**.

The twenty-four pitch-class sets listed in Example 3.8 are the complete contents of set-class (014). The Nacht motive, [347], is one very important member of this set class in the structure of Schoenberg's "Nacht," and we've also noticed several other members of (014) in the song, both transpositions and inversions. Very often, analysts of post-tonal music will say that a certain pc set, such as [347], "is (014)," or "is an instance of (014)." This is an informal way of saying that [347] "is a member of set class (014)."

STUDY QUESTIONS 3.5

Give the normal form and the prime form for each of these note groupings:

1. [034]
2. <B₄–B♭₃–G₃>
3. [594]
4. <A₄–D₅–C♯₅>
5. <B♭₄–E₄–F₃>
6. [E12]
7. [025]
8. B-minor triad
9. G-major triad
10. <G₄–A₃–E♭₄>

3.6 SET SYMMETRY

Let's explore the set class for the three-note "chromatic cluster" we studied in Chapter 1, also known as the **chromatic trichord**. Each of its members is both a transposition and an inversion of some other member. We can get from [012] to [345], for example, by T_3 or I_5:

$$
\begin{array}{ccccc}
& T_3 & & & \\
[012] & \longrightarrow & [345] & & \\
0 & + & 3 & = & 3 \\
1 & + & 3 & = & 4 \\
2 & + & 3 & = & 5 \\
\end{array}
\qquad
\begin{array}{ccccc}
& & I_5 & & \\
[012] & \longleftrightarrow & [345] & & \\
0 & + & 5 & = & 5 \\
1 & + & 4 & = & 5 \\
2 & + & 3 & = & 5 \\
\end{array}
$$

Any two members of the set class are equivalent both by some transpositional mapping and by some inversional mapping. Thus, [012] maps to [789] by both T_7 and I_9; [234] maps to [TE0] by both T_8 and I_2; and so forth.

As a result, the complete set-class has only twelve distinct members:

[012]   [123]   [234]   [345]   [456]   [567]   [678]   [789]   [89T]   [9TE]   [TE0]   [E01]

The prime form is easy to identify because only one set-class member, [012], begins with 0; the prime form is (012).

Sets with multiple equivalences, populating set classes with fewer than twenty-four members, are called **symmetrical sets**. In many cases, the symmetry is immediately apparent within the prime form itself. Just look at the pc intervals between adjacent notes:

$$
\begin{array}{ll}
\text{Prime form:} & (\ \mathbf{0}\ \ \mathbf{1}\ \ \mathbf{2}\ ) \\
\text{Pc intervals:} & \quad 1\ \ 1
\end{array}
$$

If the interval pattern in the prime form is the same reading left-to-right as it is right-to-left, the set is symmetrical.

Another method of detecting set symmetry is to find a way to add all of a set's pitch-class integers, with each other or with themselves, to equal the same index number. For the prime form of the chromatic trichord, add together 0 and 2, and add together 1 with itself, to equal index 2:

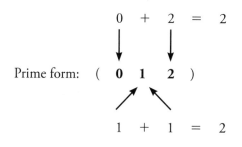

This indicates that the set can be mapped into itself at I_2:

$$
\begin{array}{ccccc}
 & & I_2 & & \\
[012] & \longleftrightarrow & [012] & & \\
0 & + & 2 & = & 2 \\
1 & + & 1 & = & 2 \\
2 & + & 0 & = & 2
\end{array}
$$

Symmetrical trichords (024) and (036) also have repeating interval patterns (pc intervals 2–2 and 3–3, respectively) and also have twelve-member set classes. Another symmetrical trichord, (027), however, doesn't have a repeating interval pattern in its prime form; the adjacent pc intervals are 2 and 5. To find its internal index number, add 0 and 2, and add 7 with itself (mod 12):

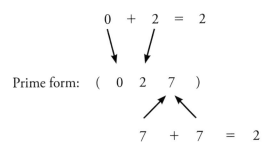

This indicates that the prime form of the set maps into itself at I_2:

$$
\begin{array}{ccccc}
 & & I_2 & & \\
[027] & \longleftrightarrow & [027] & & \\
0 & + & 2 & = & 2 \\
2 & + & 0 & = & 2 \\
7 & + & 7 & = & 2
\end{array}
$$

There's one more symmetrical trichord, the augmented triad (048), that also has a repeating pattern of pc intervals in its prime form (pc intervals 4–4). The set class of this trichord, however, contains only four distinct members. This is because the members of this set class transform into each other through multiple operations. Pitch-class set [159], for example, can be transformed into [26T] by three different transpositional mappings and three different inversional mappings (Ex. 3.9).

EXAMPLE 3.9   Multiple transformations between [159] and [26T]

$$[159] \xrightarrow{\ T_1\ } [26T] \qquad\qquad [159] \xleftrightarrow{\ I_E\ } [26T]$$

1	+	1	=	2		1	+	T	=	11
5	+	1	=	6		5	+	6	=	11
9	+	1	=	T		9	+	2	=	11

$$[159] \xrightarrow{\ T_5\ } [26T] \qquad\qquad [159] \xleftrightarrow{\ I_7\ } [26T]$$

1	+	5	=	6		1	+	6	=	7
5	+	5	=	T		5	+	2	=	7
9	+	5	=	2		9	+	T	=	7

$$[159] \xrightarrow{\ T_9\ } [26T] \qquad\qquad [159] \xleftrightarrow{\ I_3\ } [26T]$$

1	+	9	=	T		1	+	2	=	3
5	+	9	=	2		5	+	T	=	3
9	+	9	=	6		9	+	6	=	3

You can see this capability just by inspecting the prime form itself, noticing six different ways of mapping the set into itself (including T_0). (048) retains the same pitch-class content after transformation by T_0, T_4, T_8, I_0, I_4, and I_8.

STUDY QUESTIONS 3.6

1. **What are the prime forms of the symmetrical trichords?**

2. **Which symmetrical trichord has fewer than twelve members in its set class?**

3. **Give the index number that maps these pc sets to themselves:**

   3.1. [345]   3.2. [258]   3.3. [T02]   3.4. [681]

3.7   TRICHORD CLASSES

In all, there are twelve distinct set classes for three-element sets, also known as **trichord classes**. Any combination of three different pitch classes is reducible to a normal form that's a member of one of these twelve set classes. Five of them are symmetrical and contain twelve members or fewer, while the other seven each contain the full complement of twenty-four pitch-class sets.

Besides transpositional and inversional equivalences, we can also characterize a trichord class by its interval-class content. To accomplish this, make a record of all possible dyads among its three notes. This is called the **total interval-class content (TIC)**.

To find the TIC of (012), for example, break the set down into the three possible dyadic pairings: [01], [12], and [02]. That's two members of ic 1, [01] and [12], and one member of ic 2, [02]. The TIC organizes these in a number array showing the amount for each interval class within this set (Ex. 3.10).

EXAMPLE 3.10   Total interval-class content of (012)

Interval class:	<u>1</u>	<u>2</u>	<u>3</u>	<u>4</u>	<u>5</u>	<u>6</u>
Amount:	2	1	0	0	0	0

The TIC for (012) shows two instances of ic 1, one instance of ic 2, and no instances of ic's 3, 4, 5, and 6.

Example 3.11 gives the prime forms and TICs for all twelve trichord classes. Take special notice of these aspects of this table:

- The list is ordered numerically, if you think of each prime form as a two-digit number (disregarding the 0's). Or if you view each TIC as a number (starting with 210,000), those numbers become increasingly smaller (ending on 300).
- The **bold** type highlights prime forms of symmetrical sets. These set classes have fewer than twenty-four members, as specified in the second column. All entries in regular type are nonsymmetrical and represent set classes with twenty-four members.
- Look at the values in the first column of the TIC for all of the trichords. Only the first five trichord types contain at least one ic 1. This is also evident in the prime forms, the first five of which start with "01." Because post-tonal music often features members of ic 1, as we've seen in Webern's Bagatelle and Schoenberg's "Nacht," these first five trichord classes are some of the most common pitch resources in music of the post-tonal era.
- The next four, with prime forms beginning "02," feature milder dissonance than the first five and are often associated with music derived from diatonic or whole-tone scales.
- The trichords better known as "triads" appear at the end of the listing. The diminished triad (036) and augmented triad (048) are symmetrical and so have fewer than twenty-four members in their set classes. The major and minor triads, which aren't symmetrical, are both contained in set-class (037); they're inversions of each other.

EXAMPLE 3.11   Trichord classes

PRIME FORM	NO. OF SETS IN SET CLASS	TIC <u>1</u> <u>2</u> <u>3</u> <u>4</u> <u>5</u> <u>6</u>
(012)	12	2 1 0 0 0 0
(013)	24	1 1 1 0 0 0
(014)	24	1 0 1 1 0 0
(015)	24	1 0 0 1 1 0
(016)	24	1 0 0 0 1 1
(024)	12	0 2 0 1 0 0
(025)	24	0 1 1 0 1 0
(026)	24	0 1 0 1 0 1
(027)	12	0 1 0 0 2 0
(036)	12	0 0 2 0 0 1
(037)	24	0 0 1 1 1 0
(048)	4	0 0 0 3 0 0

STUDY QUESTIONS 3.7

1. **Break down these prime forms into their three constituent dyads, notated in normal form:**

    1.1. (014)   1.2. (024)   1.3. (026)   1.4. (037)   1.5. (048)

2. **Which trichord classes . . .**

    2.1. Include members of three different interval classes?

    2.2. Include an ic 6?

    2.3. Exclude *both* ic 2 and ic 4?

    2.4. Are known by other names in tonal theory?

VOCABULARY

chromatic trichord	octachord	set class
dyad	pentachord	symmetrical set
equivalence class	pitch-class set (pc set)	tetrachord
hexachord	prime form	total interval-class content (TIC)
monad	segment	trichord
nonachord	septachord	trichord class
normal form	set	

EXERCISES

A. SPECIFYING PITCH-CLASS TRANSPOSITION (NONSYMMETRICAL TRICHORDS)

Place a transposition label in each box to specify the pitch-class transposition from the first trichord to the second.

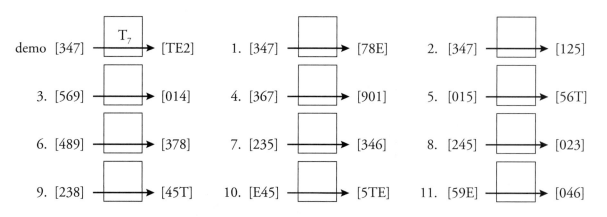

B. SPECIFYING PITCH-CLASS INVERSION (NONSYMMETRICAL TRICHORDS)

Place an inversion label in each box to specify the pitch-class inversion from the first trichord to the second.

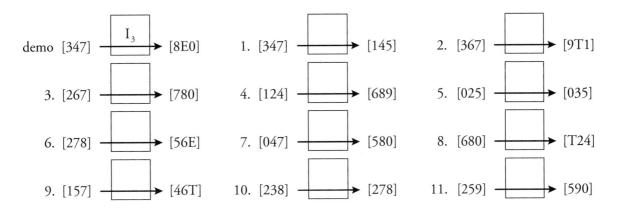

C. SPECIFYING PITCH-CLASS TRANSPOSITION OR INVERSION (NONSYMMETRICAL TRICHORDS)

Place a label (T_n or I_n) in each box to specify the pitch-class transformation from the first trichord to the second.

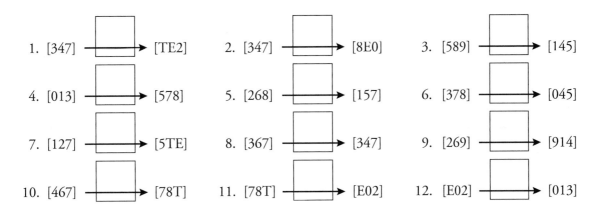

D. CALCULATING PITCH-CLASS TRANSPOSITION (NONSYMMETRICAL TRICHORDS)

Complete the transposition operations. Your answer must be in normal form.

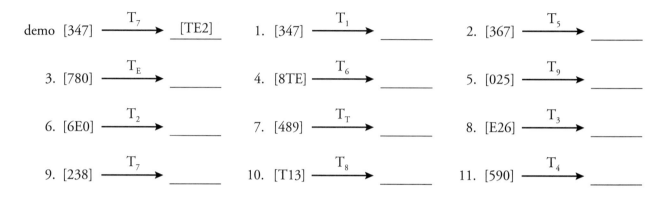

demo [347] $\xrightarrow{T_7}$ [TE2]   1. [347] $\xrightarrow{T_1}$ _____   2. [367] $\xrightarrow{T_5}$ _____

3. [780] $\xrightarrow{T_E}$ _____   4. [8TE] $\xrightarrow{T_6}$ _____   5. [025] $\xrightarrow{T_9}$ _____

6. [6E0] $\xrightarrow{T_2}$ _____   7. [489] $\xrightarrow{T_T}$ _____   8. [E26] $\xrightarrow{T_3}$ _____

9. [238] $\xrightarrow{T_7}$ _____   10. [T13] $\xrightarrow{T_8}$ _____   11. [590] $\xrightarrow{T_4}$ _____

E. CALCULATING PITCH-CLASS INVERSION (NON-SYMMETRICAL TRICHORDS)

Complete the inversion operations. Your answer must be in normal form.

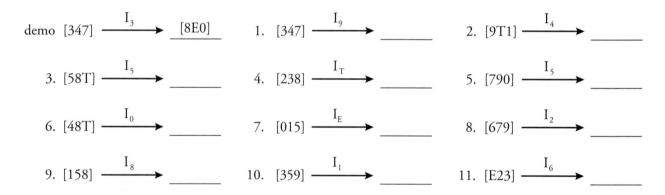

demo [347] $\xrightarrow{I_3}$ [8E0]   1. [347] $\xrightarrow{I_9}$ _____   2. [9T1] $\xrightarrow{I_4}$ _____

3. [58T] $\xrightarrow{I_5}$ _____   4. [238] $\xrightarrow{I_T}$ _____   5. [790] $\xrightarrow{I_5}$ _____

6. [48T] $\xrightarrow{I_0}$ _____   7. [015] $\xrightarrow{I_E}$ _____   8. [679] $\xrightarrow{I_2}$ _____

9. [158] $\xrightarrow{I_8}$ _____   10. [359] $\xrightarrow{I_1}$ _____   11. [E23] $\xrightarrow{I_6}$ _____

F. RELATING SYMMETRICAL TRICHORDS

Indicate both a transpositional and an inversional operation that could relate the given trichords.

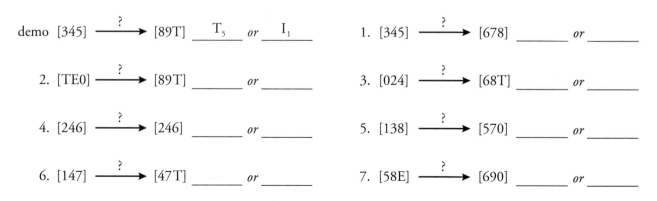

demo [345] $\xrightarrow{?}$ [89T] T_5 or I_1 1. [345] $\xrightarrow{?}$ [678] _____ or _____

2. [TE0] $\xrightarrow{?}$ [89T] _____ or _____   3. [024] $\xrightarrow{?}$ [68T] _____ or _____

4. [246] $\xrightarrow{?}$ [246] _____ or _____   5. [138] $\xrightarrow{?}$ [570] _____ or _____

6. [147] $\xrightarrow{?}$ [47T] _____ or _____   7. [58E] $\xrightarrow{?}$ [690] _____ or _____

G. NORMAL FORM, PRIME FORM

Give the [normal form] and (prime form) for the pc set comprising all the notes in each excerpt.

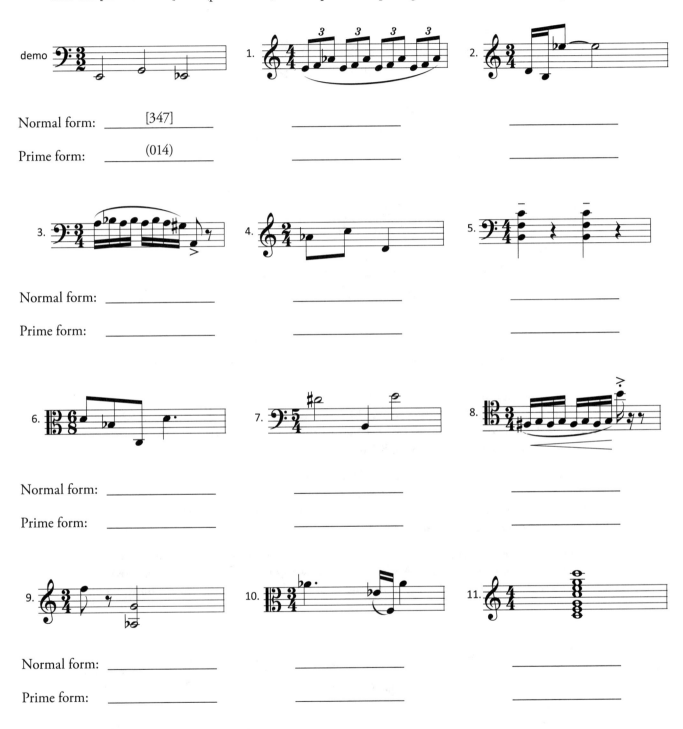

Normal form: _____[347]_____

Prime form: _____(014)_____

H. ARNOLD SCHOENBERG (1874–1951), "NACHT" FROM *PIERROT LUNAIRE* (1912), MM. 1–3, 19–20.

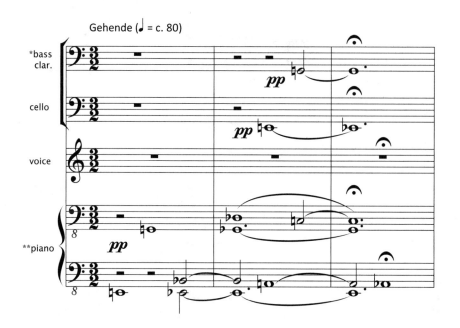

*Sounds as notated.

**Both hands of the piano part in these three measures are played one octave lower than notated.

1. The Passacaglia theme, or Nacht motive, begins right away in the piano in the first measure: E_1–G_1–$E\flat_1$. Then the texture thickens from interlocking recurrences of the motive. How many different transpositions of the motive are formed in these three measures, and how are they related? List them in normal form.

2. Combine the second and third notes of the first statement of the motive, G_1 and $E\flat_1$, with the $G\flat_1$ on the downbeat of measure 2. What's the normal form of this trichord? How is it related to the actual motive? How is this trichord integrated within the motivic network described in question 1?

3. Now look at the piano part in measures 19 and 20. In what sense are the motivic relations in these measures a recollection and development of ideas first presented in the introduction? Use technical terms and analytical methodology from Chapter 3 whenever possible.

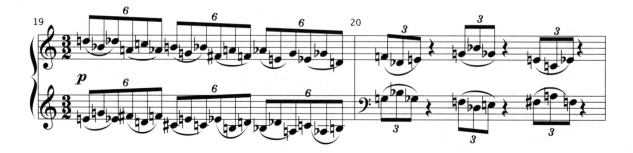

I. ANTON WEBERN (1883–1945), FIVE MOVEMENTS FOR STRING QUARTET, OP. 5, NO. 3 (1909)

1. Listen to the movement several times without looking at the score. Reach some preliminary conclusions about its overall form. Then listen several times while following the score. How would you describe the overall form of the movement? What are the recurring themes? What other factors contribute to the formal structure?

2. Look at the pitch structure carefully and thoroughly. Find primary three-note groupings and translate them into normal form and prime form. Also look for instances of these same trichord types formed by secondary groupings. Identify the *three* most prevalent trichord types in the movement, and rank them in order of importance within the overall pitch structure. Describe the most prominent occurrences of these trichords in the movement.

3. In what sense are trichords expressed as pitch-space "motives," and in what sense should they be considered unordered pitch-class sets?

4. How do the last two measures summarize the pitch structure of the entire movement?

J. COMPOSITION EXERCISE

Below is a sketch for the beginning of a piano piece inspired by some of the trichord-oriented music of Schoenberg ("Nacht") and Webern (String Quartet Movement, op. 5 no. 3). Using the provided measures as a starting point—and Schoenberg and Webern as models—compose your own brief trichord-oriented piano piece.

FOR FURTHER STUDY

BÉLA BARTÓK:

"Jack-in-the-Box," *Mikrokosmos* (1932–39), vol. 5, no. 139

GEORGE CRUMB:

"No piansan en la lluvia" from *Madrigals* I (1965)
"Gargoyles" from *Makrokosmos* II (1973)

CHAPTER 4

THE SET-CLASS UNIVERSE

4.1 NORMAL FORM FOR ALL SETS

Alongside the three-note chromatic clusters in Webern's first opus 9 Bagatelle for String Quartet that we studied in Chapter 1 are prominent trichords of other types. (The complete score of the Bagatelle is Ex. 1.3.) Just after the cluster of the opening measure, for example, the second violin, which is the only instrument not involved in measure 1, answers with $<C_4-G\flat_4-A\flat_4>$, a member of the very different trichord class (026) (Ex. 4.1a). The first violin responds with $<B\flat_5-E_5-F_4>$, still another trichord type, (016), heard again in the work's final measure (Ex. 4.1b).

EXAMPLE 4.1 Webern, *Six Bagatelles* for string quartet op. 9, no. 1, mm. 1–3, 10

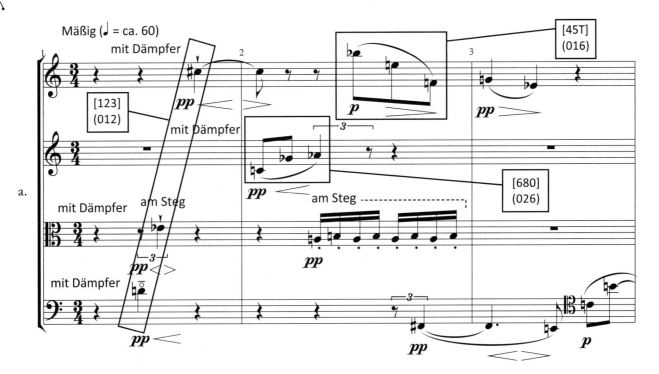

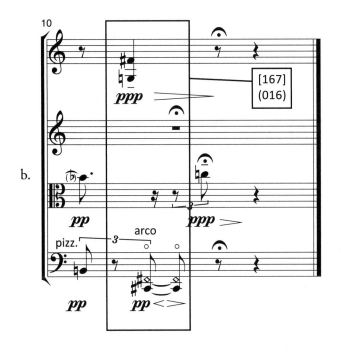

A recurring theme in the middle portion of the piece is set class (sc) (013) as a melodic gesture, in the cello, viola, and first violin (Ex. 4.2). A complete study of Webern's Bagatelle would recognize these and other trichords and their interactions with the chromatic clusters, which are members of sc (012).

EXAMPLE 4.2   Members of (013) as melodic gestures in Webern's op. 9, no. 1

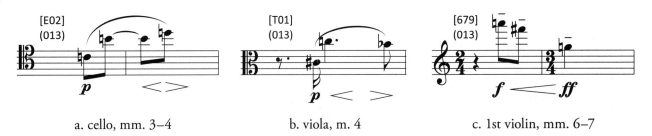

a. cello, mm. 3–4   b. viola, m. 4   c. 1st violin, mm. 6–7

But of course, trichords aren't the only story. Note groupings of other sizes occur with comparable resonance. The complete opening melodic gesture in the first violin is a pentachord (Ex. 4.1a, mm. 2–3). Trichords often combine to form hexachords. Three tetrachords especially attract attention because they are the only places in the movement where instruments come together to form harmonies, brief though they may be. This first happens between second violin and cello in measure 4 (Ex. 4.3a). The other two instruments take their harmonic turn with two vertical tetrachords surrounding the measure 9 barline (Ex. 4.3b).

EXAMPLE 4.3   Tetrachordal harmonies in Webern's op. 9, no. 1

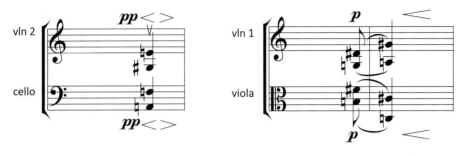

a. 2nd violin, cello, m. 4   b. 1st violin, viola, mm. 8–9

Finding normal form for tetrachords and larger sets is slightly different from the trichord procedure, but only because more notes in a set translates to more rotations and potentially more tie-breaking maneuvers. Here again is the normal-form routine, updated to apply to sets of any size:

1. List the pitch-class contents of the set in numerical order, from lowest to highest.
2. Write out all rotations of the set. The number of rotations to be made will be the same as the number of pitch classes in the set.
3. The normal form is the rotation with the smallest pitch-class interval from beginning to end.
4. If rotations have the same outer pc interval, look at the next pc intervals inward (from first pc to next-to-last), and continue to work inward until you find a smallest interval.
5. If all outer and inner pc intervals are the same in two or more rotations, the normal form is the rotation that starts on the smallest integer.

The tetrachord {9584} in measure 4 (Ex. 4.3a) has the first rotation {4589} (step 1). The other three rotations are {5894}, {8945}, and {9458} (step 2). Calculate the outer pc interval of each rotation (step 3):

ROTATION	PITCH CLASSES	OUTER PC INTERVAL
1	**4589**	**5**
2	5894	E
3	8945	9
4	9458	E

The first rotation has the smallest outer pc interval. Steps 4 and 5 of the procedure aren't necessary. The **normal form** is [4589].

Now jump ahead to the tetrachord in measure 9, which reads, in registral order, {0918} (Ex. 4.3b). Again, one rotation is clearly preferable. The **normal form** is [8901]:

ROTATION	PITCH CLASSES	OUTER PC INTERVAL
1	0189	9
2	1890	E
3	**8901**	**5**
4	9018	E

Look further at these two tetrachords, [4589] and [8901]. Both normal forms start with pc-interval 1, then have a gap of three half steps, and end with another pc interval 1. The intervallic structure of the normal forms is 1–3–1. This tells us two things. One is that they are equivalent; normal forms with identical intervallic structures are members of the same set class. This may not be immediately noticeable as they appear in the score, with different pitch intervals between adjacent notes, but it is evident after close inspection of the normal forms.

The other revelation is that the set is symmetrical. We can see this because the 1–3–1 intervallic pattern reads the same forward and backward. Indeed, the first occurrence ([4589] in m. 4) is p-space symmetrical in Webern's scoring, displaying pitch intervals 8–3–8 (see Ex. 4.3a). (Plus and minus signs for pitch intervals are omitted when notes are presented simultaneously.) And as we know from Chapter 3.6, symmetrical sets are equivalent by both transposition and inversion. In this case, both T_4 and I_5 map [4589] to [8901]:

$$
\begin{array}{ccccccc}
 & T_4 & & & & I_5 & \\
[4589] & \longrightarrow & [8901] & \qquad & [4589] & \longleftrightarrow & [8901] \\
4 + 4 & = & 8 & \qquad & 4 + 1 & = & 5 \\
5 + 4 & = & 9 & \qquad & 5 + 0 & = & 5 \\
8 + 4 & = & 0 & \qquad & 8 + 9 & = & 5 \\
9 + 4 & = & 1 & \qquad & 9 + 8 & = & 5 \\
\end{array}
$$

Let's look at another tetrachord, the {7E36} in measure 8 (Ex. 4.3b). It has the first ordering {367E} (step 1) and other rotations {67E3}, {7E36}, and {E367} (step 2). Calculating the outer pc intervals of each rotation (step 3) reveals two that are the same:

ROTATION	PITCH CLASSES	OUTER PC INTERVAL
1	**367E**	**8**
2	67E3	9
3	7E36	E
4	**E367**	**8**

So to find the normal form we can rule out rotations 2 and 3 and look at the next interval inward in rotations 1 and 4 (step 4). Rotation 1 wins the tie-breaker because the pc interval 4 from pc 3 to pc 7 in rotation 1 is smaller than the pc interval 7 from pc E to pc 6 in rotation 4:

The normal form is [367E].

You can also determine normal form by placing the notes of a set around a pitch-class circle and counting distances clockwise, looking for the intervallic pattern that's most compact, with the smallest intervals at the beginning. For the measure 4 tetrachord (Ex. 4.3a), the notes congregate in the circle's lower region and are clearly most compact when starting on pc 4 (Ex. 4.4a). The tetrachord in measure 8 (Ex. 4.3b) is more spread out around the circle, but the preference for {367E} over {E367} is still easily visualized (Ex. 4.4b).

EXAMPLE 4.4   Tetrachords in pitch-class circles

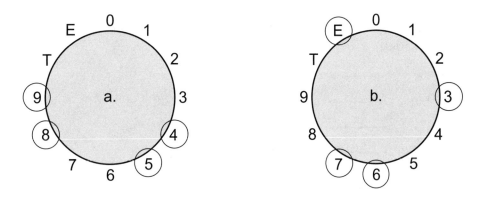

STUDY QUESTIONS 4.1

Find the normal form of these pc sets:

1. The first four pitch classes in Webern's op. 9, no. 1 (Ex. 4.1a).

2. The cello's tetrachord in measures 2 and 3 of Webern's op. 9, no. 1 (Ex. 4.1a).

3. The first violin's pentachord starting with the B♭$_5$ in measure 2 (Ex. 4.1a).

4. The last four pitch classes in Webern's op. 9, no. 1 (Ex. 4.1b).

5. $<F_2–A_2–D_3–F\sharp_3>$

6. $<D\flat_4–G_4–F_4–B_3>$

7. F dominant seventh chord.

8. All the black keys within one octave on the piano.

9. G fully diminished seventh chord.

10. $<A\flat_4–G_3–F\sharp_4–D_3–D\sharp_3–A_4>$

4.2   PRIME FORM FOR ALL SETS

As we learned in Chapter 3, the prime form of a trichord begins on 0 and has the smallest intervals on the left. The same is true for sets of other sizes, although the process of finding them may take longer. Some larger sets are tricky, and may make you want to throw up your hands and seek comfort in an online set class calculator. This is understandable, but you'll benefit by working through the process, by getting to know your sets inside and out. The better you understand the sets you're working with, the more you'll be able to do with them, as analyst and composer.

Prime forms are generally easiest to determine when sets are symmetrical. As we noticed in Chapter 3.6 and 3.7, the set class of a symmetrical set has fewer than twenty-four members, and only one of them begins with 0; that's the prime form. Here, for example, is the set class that includes the **two equivalent tetrachords** in Example 4.3:

[0145] [1256] [2367] [3478] **[4589]** [569T] [67TE] [78E0] **[8901]** [9T12] [TE23] [E034]

Only one member of this set class begins with 0. The prime form is (0145).

So for symmetrical sets, simply transpose the normal form to begin on 0 and you'll have the prime form. Here are some examples:

SYMMETRICAL SET IN NORMAL FORM		TRANSPOSED TO BEGIN ON 0	PRIME FORM
[2345]	$\xrightarrow{T_T}$	[0123]	(0123)
[9TE01]	$\xrightarrow{T_3}$	[01234]	(01234)
[35679]	$\xrightarrow{T_9}$	[02346]	(02346)
[567TE0]	$\xrightarrow{T_7}$	[012567]	(012567)

For sets that aren't symmetrical, use this procedure to find prime form:

1. Write the set in normal form, and transpose so that the normal form begins on 0.
2. Transform the result of step 1 by I_0 and write it in normal form.
3. Transpose the result of step 2 so that the normal form begins on 0.
4. The prime form is either the result of step 1 or the result of step 3, whichever has the smallest intervals on the left.
5. Notate the prime form using pc integers without commas and enclosed in parentheses.

Let's use the procedure to find the prime form of the first violin's pentachord in measures 2 and 3 of Webern's Bagatelle (see Ex. 4.1a, starting on the $B\flat_5$):

1. *Write the set in normal form, and transpose so that the normal form begins on 0.* $\qquad$ [3457T] $\xrightarrow{T_9}$ [01247]

2. *Transform the result of step 1 by I_0 and write it in normal form.* $\qquad$ [01247] $\xrightarrow{I_0}$ [58TE0]

3. *Transpose the result of step 2 so that the normal form begins on 0.* $\qquad$ [58TE0] $\xrightarrow{T_7}$ [03567]

4. *The **prime form** is either the result of step 1 or the result of step 3, whichever has the smallest intervals on the left.* $\qquad$ step 1 result = **[01247]** $\qquad$ step 3 result = [03567]

5. *Write the prime form using pc integers without commas and enclosed in parentheses.* $\qquad$ (01247)

Make the choice in step 4 using the same process we use for breaking ties in normal form. Look at the pc intervals from beginning to end, then beginning to next-to-last, and so forth:

Step 1 result: 0   1   2   4   7 $\qquad$ Step 3 result: 0   3   5   6   7

(with bracket annotations: Step 1 result has outer interval 7, inner interval 4; Step 3 result has outer interval 7, inner interval 6)

Both candidates have the same outer pc interval (7), but the step 1 result is the prime form, because its next interval inward—**4**—is smaller than the next interval inward—6—in the step 3 result.

Here's an application of the prime form procedure to the first tetrachord in Example 4.3b, {7E36}:

1. *Write the set in normal form, and transpose so that the normal form begins on 0.*

    $[367E] \xrightarrow{\text{T}_9} [0348]$

2. *Transform the result of step 1 by I_0 and write it in normal form.*

    $[0348] \xrightarrow{\text{I}_0} [8904]$

3. *Transpose the result of step 2 so that the normal form begins on 0.*

    $[8904] \xrightarrow{\text{T}_4} [0148]$

4. *The **prime form** is either the result of step 1 or the result of step 3, whichever has the smallest intervals on the left.*

    step 1 result = [0348]
    step 3 result = **[0148]**
    (0148)

5. *Write the prime form using pc integers without commas and enclosed in parentheses.*

The tricky aspect of this tetrachord is getting the result of I_0 in step 2 into normal form. The initial inversional mappings in step 2 look like this:

$$[0348] \xrightarrow{\text{I}_0} [?]$$

$$
\begin{array}{ccccc}
0 & + & 0 & = & 0 \\
3 & + & 9 & = & 0 \\
4 & + & 8 & = & 0 \\
8 & + & 4 & = & 0 \\
\end{array}
$$

For many sets, the result of the I_0 mappings in step 2 will be the normal form in reverse. For this tetrachord, however, {4890} is not the normal form. To complete step 2, we'll need to look at all four rotations:

ROTATION	PITCH CLASSES	OUTER PC INTERVAL	NEXT INNER PC INTERVAL
~~1~~	~~0489~~	~~9~~	
2	4890	8	5
3	**8904**	**8**	**4**
~~4~~	~~9048~~	~~E~~	

The second and third rotations both span pc interval 8 from beginning to end, but the next pc interval inward is smaller in rotation 3. The normal form is [8904].

Here's one more example, using the hexachord formed by all the notes in the last measure of Webern's op. 9, no. 1 (see Ex. 4.1b):

1. *Write the set in normal form, and transpose so that the normal form begins on 0.*

    $[67TE01] \xrightarrow{\text{T}_6} [014567]$

2. *Transform the result of step 1 by I_0 and write it in normal form.*

    $[014567] \xrightarrow{\text{I}_0} [5678E0]$

3. *Transpose the result of step 2 so that the normal form begins on 0.*

    $[5678E0] \xrightarrow{\text{T}_7} [012367]$

4. *The **prime form** is either the result of step 1 or the result of step 3, whichever has the smallest intervals on the left.*

    step 1 result = [014567]
    step 3 result = **[012367]**
    (012367)

5. *Write the prime form using pc integers without commas and enclosed in parentheses.*

[012367] wins out over [014567] because it has the smallest intervals on the left, in this case a chromatic tetrachord [0123]. In [014567], the chromatic tetrachord [4567] is pushed to the right.

STUDY QUESTIONS 4.2

Find the prime forms of the sets you wrote in normal form for Study Questions 4.1.

4.3   Z-RELATIONS

Let's now look at two unique tetrachords formed as secondary sets in Webern's Bagatelle. The first consists of all the notes sounding together at the end of measure 2. This tetrachord is [569E], a member of set class (0146) (Ex. 4.5a). The other is the outburst in cello and first violin in the upper register of measure 6, ending on the downbeat of measure 7. This tetrachord is [6791], a member of sc (0137) (Ex. 4.5b).

EXAMPLE 4.5   All-interval tetrachords as secondary sets

[6791]
(0137)

Look at the interval-class contents of these two sets:

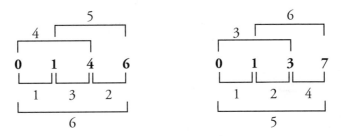

They aren't transpositionally or inversionally equivalent—aren't members of the same set class—and yet they have the same TIC:

Interval class:	1	2	3	4	5	6
Amount:	1	1	1	1	1	1

Further, the TIC itself is unique: every interval class is represented once. Set classes (0146) and (0137) are known as the **all-interval tetrachords**.

Nonequivalent sets with identical TICs are known as **Z-relations**.[1] We say that (0146) and (0137) are "Z-related" or are "Z-correspondents" or "Z-partners." No trichords have this

---

[1] So named by Allen Forte, *The Structure of Atonal Music* (New Haven, CT: Yale University Press, 1973), 21. The letter "Z" has no special significance.

feature, and only these two tetrachords do. The set class universe also includes three pairs of Z-related pentachords and fifteen pairs of Z-related hexachords.

The Z-relation represents a special connection between two nonequivalent sets. Although the two instances in Webern's Bagatelle have no direct musical relationship, composers do sometimes associate Z-partners in musically meaningful ways. It's certainly possible to imagine a variety of contexts that might draw attention to this special relation, such as Example 4.6, which contrasts the symmetrical tetrachord (0127) as rising arpeggios with different all-interval Z-related tetrachords as descending arpeggios.

EXAMPLE 4.6   Musical context showing equivalences and Z-relations among tetrachords

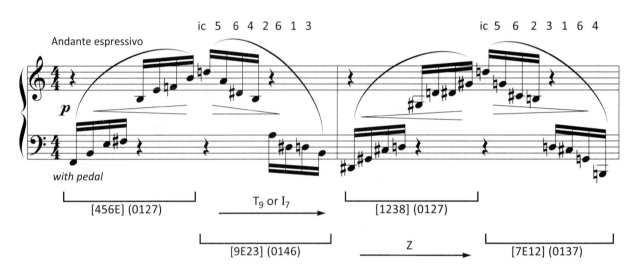

The descending arpeggios are structured to highlight their intervallic connections. The first presents melodic interval classes 5–6–4–2–6–1–3, then the second answers with the same adjacencies in a slightly different order, 5–6–2–3–1–6–4. This helps emphasize the close relationship between the two nonequivalent sets.

STUDY QUESTIONS 4.3

1. **How is the relationship between Z-partners the same as the relationship between two members of the same set class?**

2. **Why aren't Z-related sets members of the same set class?**

3. **Among the tetrachordal set classes, only one pair is Z-related. What else is unique about these two tetrachords?**

4.4   SET COMPLEMENTATION

Here's how Webern described his compositional process for his six opus 9 string quartet Bagatelles:

> *I had the feeling, "When all twelve tones had gone by, the piece is over." Much later I realized that all this was part of the necessary development. In my sketch-book I wrote out the chromatic scale and crossed off the individual notes. . . . In short, a rule of law emerged; until all twelve notes have occurred, none of them may occur again. The most*

important thing is that each "run" of twelve notes marked a division within the piece, idea, or theme.[2]

We can see evidence of this approach right from the beginning of the first Bagatelle (Ex. 4.7). Except for the F♯$_2$ in the cello in measure 2, which duplicates the pitch class of the G♭$_4$ in the second violin earlier in the bar, every pitch class through the G$_4$ in measure 3 is new. The first two measures plus that G$_4$ amass a complete statement of one member of each of the twelve pitch classes.

EXAMPLE 4.7   Webern, op. 9, no. 1, mm. 1–3

One result of this comprehensive presentation is the close association of set groupings that combine to exhaust the pitch classes, or **complete the aggregate**. This is called **set complementation**. The complement of any set is the set containing all the remaining pitch classes. The combination of any set with its complement produces a complete aggregate.

For example, one way to parse the opening of the Bagatelle would be to isolate the opening trichord, [123], from its complement, the remaining nonachord, [456789TE0]. Another way would be to combine the opening trichord with the second violin trichord, forming the [012368] hexachord that complements the remaining [4579TE] hexachord through the downbeat of measure 3. The sizes of complementary sets add to twelve: 2 and 10, 3 and 9, 4 and 8, 5 and 7, 6 and 6.

The 3 + 9 complementation at the beginning of the Bagatelle associates [123], a member of sc (012), with [456789TE0], a member of the set class of the nine-tone chromatic cluster, (012345678). These two sets literally combine to complete the aggregate. That's called **literal complementation** (Ex. 4.8).

---

[2]Anton Webern, *The Path to the New Music*, ed. Willi Reich, trans. Leo Black (Bryn Mawr, PA: Presser, 1963), 51.

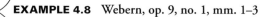

EXAMPLE 4.8   Webern, op. 9, no. 1, mm. 1–3

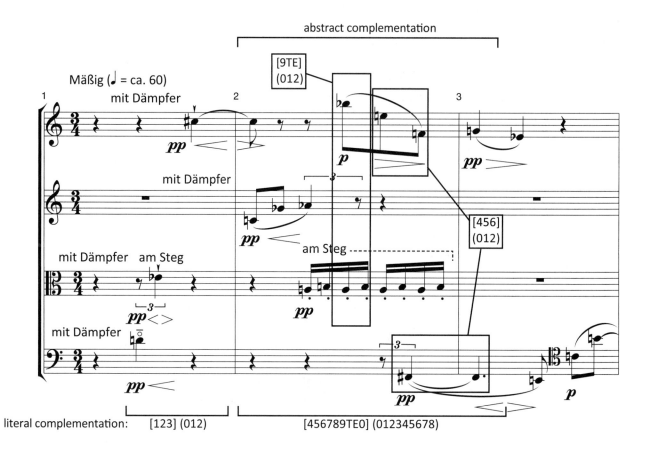

If other members of these two set classes associate but include pitch-class overlaps—in other words, don't literally combine to present all twelve pitch classes—that's called **abstract complementation**. Within the nine-tone chromatic cluster in measures 2–3 of the Bagatelle, for example, are two members of (012), [9TE] and [456], formed as secondary sets (Ex. 4.8). Of course, these two sets cannot combine with the nine-tone set (of which they're subsets) to complete the aggregate. A set formed within its abstract complement is known as an **embedded complement**. By definition, an embedded complement always involves abstract complementation.

The TICs of complementary non-hexachords differ by a fixed amount, equal to the difference in size of the two sets, except for ic 6, which differs by half of the size difference. Compare, for example, the TIC of (012) with the TIC of its complement, (012345678):

Interval class:	<u>1</u>	<u>2</u>	<u>3</u>	<u>4</u>	<u>5</u>	<u>6</u>
(012) TIC:	2	1	0	0	0	0
(012345678) TIC:	8	7	6	6	6	3

The entries for interval-classes 1–5 differ by 6, which is equal to the difference in size between a trichord and a nonachord. The entries for interval-class 6 differ by 3, which is half the difference in size between a trichord and a nonachord.

Now look at the complementation of hexachords in the Bagatelle's opening (Ex. 4.9). Set [012368], a member of (012368), is followed by set [4579TE], a member of (012467). These two hexachords are not transpositionally or inversionally equivalent, but they have the same TIC; they're Z-related (Ex. 4.10).

EXAMPLE 4.9   Webern op. 9, no. 1, mm. 1–3

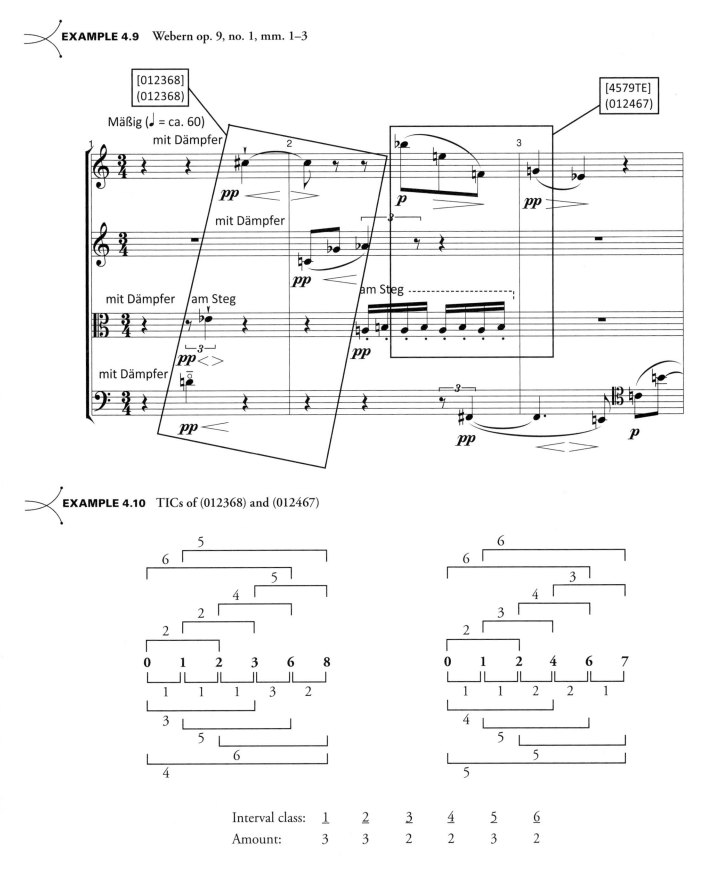

EXAMPLE 4.10   TICs of (012368) and (012467)

Interval class:	1	2	3	4	5	6
Amount:	3	3	2	2	3	2

Within the set class universe are fifty different hexachords, but thirty of these are paired off into Z-partnerships. In other words, fifteen pairs of hexachords have identical interval-class contents but cannot be transposed or inverted into each other; they are members of different set classes. The remaining twenty hexachord types *can* be transposed or inverted into their complements—and because they're hexachords, their complements are simply transformations of themselves. That's called **self-complementation**. Within the set class of the six-note chromatic cluster (012345), for example, [345678] complements [9TE012].

So, for non-hexachords, complements are always members of different set classes. But for hexachords, complementation occurs either *between* or *within* set classes: between when they are Z-related, within when they are self-complementary. Whether or not two complementary hexachords are transpositionally or inversionally equivalent, they have identical TICs.

STUDY QUESTIONS 4.4

1. **What is the literal complement of [23678]? (Give your answer in normal form.)**

2. **Which type of set complementation does *not* result in the formation of an aggregate?**

3. **Describe the numerical difference between the TICs of a tetrachord and its complement.**

4. **Describe the numerical difference between the TICs of a pentachord and its complement.**

5. **Which type of hexachord cannot map to its complement?**

4.5   THE SET-CLASS CATALOG

The set-class universe encompasses 208 set classes of sizes three through nine. This includes the twelve trichords and an equal number of complements (nonachords); the twenty-nine tetrachords and an equal number of complements; the thirty-eight pentachords and an equal number of complements; and the fifty hexachords, consisting of thirty members of Z-pairs and twenty that are self-complementary:

$$
\begin{array}{rl}
24 & \text{(12 trichords + 12 nonachords)} \\
58 & \text{(29 tetrachords + 29 octachords)} \\
76 & \text{(38 pentachords + 38 septachords)} \\
+\ 50 & \text{(hexachords)} \\
\hline
208 &
\end{array}
$$

Appendix 1 lists them all, in ascending numerical order as if the prime form were an integer. Symmetrical sets are shown in **bold**, and the number of members in each set class is provided in the second column. The third column shows the TIC.

The fourth column in the catalog affixes the labels for each set class in Allen Forte's pioneering study, *The Structure of Atonal Music*.[3] These are known as the **Forte names**. (Don't pronounce the "e" in Forte: think "Fort Knox," not "*mezzo-forte*.") A Forte name consists of a number specifying the set size followed by a hyphen and then a number indicating its placement on Forte's list (which isn't in numerical order by prime form). Set class "3-1" is the first trichord on his list. Set class 4-2 is the second tetrachord. Set class 5-4 is the fourth

---

[3]Forte, *Structure of Atonal Music*, 179–81.

pentachord. In Forte's nomenclature, the number after the hyphen is the same for a set and its complement: the set class of the complement of 3-1 (012) is 9-1 (012345678). Set class 4-5 (0126) is the complement of 8-5 (01234678). Forte names for sets with Z-partners include the "Z" in the label ("4-Z29," "5-Z17"). In the fifth column of Appendix 1, each Z set is cross-referenced to the Forte name of its Z-correspondent. Many post-tonal commentaries use Forte's labels when referring to pentachords and larger sets but identify trichords and tetrachords by their prime forms.

Our observations about the twelve trichord classes in Chapter 3.5, 3.6, and 3.7 also apply to the comprehensive catalog, with necessary adjustments for set types of larger sizes. Nonsymmetrical trichords barely outnumber symmetrical ones (7 to 5), and symmetrical tetrachords actually appear more often than nonsymmetrical ones (15 to 14), but symmetries are much less common in pentachords (10 of 38) and hexachords (20 of 50). Also, all of the set classes of the symmetrical pentachords contain twelve members, whereas the symmetrical tetrachords include set classes of six or three members, and the set class sizes of the symmetrical hexachords are also more diverse. The most redundant symmetrical set is the whole-tone scale (hexachord (02468T)), whose set class has only two distinct members, either the collection of "even" or "odd" pitch classes. This set transforms into itself under six different transpositional mappings and six different inversional mappings.

Identifying symmetry within a larger set follows the same process as for trichords (see Chapter 3.6): try to find a way to transform a set into itself. For a set such as the (0145) of Webern's two harmonic tetrachords (Ex. 4.3), it's easy to see the symmetry within the prime form itelf, in the symmetrical 1–3–1 pattern of pc intervals. So to transform the prime form into itself, pair up the 0 and 5 and then the 1 and 4. Because both pairs sum to 5, the index number is 5; the prime form maps into itself under I_5. But a larger symmetrical set whose prime form doesn't have a symmetrical interval pattern may take a little longer to figure out.

Look at the hexachord (014679), for example. The set class catalog tells us that it's symmetrical, and that its set class contains twelve members, but the interval succession of its prime form doesn't display a symmetrical pattern of pc intervals:

$$\text{Prime form:} \quad (\ \mathbf{0} \quad \mathbf{1} \quad \mathbf{4} \quad \mathbf{6} \quad \mathbf{7} \quad \mathbf{9} \ )$$
$$\text{Pc intervals:} \qquad 1 \quad 3 \quad 2 \quad 1 \quad 2$$

Even so, the pc-interval sequence "2–1–2" between pc's <4679> within the prime form reveals a moment of symmetry that we can use to find the index number. Add together 6 + 7 and 4 + 9 within the 2–1–2 segment, and the other two pc's 0 and 1, to total the index number, 1:

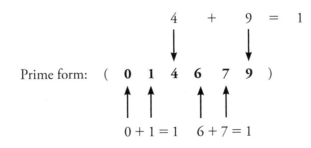

(014679) inverts into itself at I_1. From this we can infer that the set is symmetrical, and that every member of the set class is equivalent to every other member under both transposition and inversion.

STUDY QUESTIONS 4.5

1. **What are the prime forms and Forte names of the all-interval tetrachords?**

2. **What is the prime form and Forte name of the third pentachord on Forte's list?**

3. **How can you use Appendix 1 to find the prime form of the complement of a set?**

4. **In set types of which size do symmetrical sets occur in greater numbers than non-symmetrical sets?**

4.6   MAXIMAL SUBSETS

Let's return one last time to the three vertical tetrachords in Webern's Bagatelle (Ex. 4.3). At first glance, the second one, a member of sc (0148), appears distinct from the other two, which are both members of (0145). The (0148) is more triadic, the (0145)s more dissonant. Indeed, the contrast provided by the second one is an important aspect of its role within the pitch language of the Bagatelle.

On the other hand, we might also want to consider ways in which the second tetrachord somehow relates to its surroundings. To accomplish this, we can examine the **maximal subsets** of these tetrachords. A subset is an extraction of notes from a larger set. A maximal subset is a subset that is one element smaller than that larger set. Trichords are maximal subsets of tetrachords, pentachords are maximal subsets of hexachords, and so forth. We've already studied maximal subsets of trichords, which are also known as interval classes.

So let's compare all the maximal subsets of (0145) and (0148). Extract every possible three-note grouping within the prime form and place these trichords in normal and prime form:

	(0145)			(0148)	
SUBSET	**NORMAL FORM**	**PRIME FORM**	**SUBSET**	**NORMAL FORM**	**PRIME FORM**
{014}	[014]	**(014)**	{014}	[014]	**(014)**
{015}	[015]	**(015)**	{018}	[810]	**(015)**
{045}	[045]	**(015)**	{048}	[048]	(048)
{145}	[145]	**(014)**	{148}	[148]	(037)

From this we can see that the four trichordal subsets of (0145) are all members of two set classes, (014) and (015), and that these two set classes are also represented in the subsets of (0148). Of course, (0148) also has two triadic subsets—(048) and (037)—and these set it apart from (0145) and many other tetrachords. Still, it's useful to know that (0145) and (0148) have some sort of structural similarity. It's a connection that (0148) doesn't have with some other tetrachords, (0127) for example:

(0127)

SUBSET	NORMAL FORM	PRIME FORM
{012}	[012]	(012)
{017}	[701]	(016)
{027}	[027]	(027)
{127}	[127]	(016)

The harmony in measure 8 of Webern's Bagatelle connects to its surroundings in other ways, as well. When the (0148) tetrachord sounds in the first violin and viola at the end of the bar, it forms a secondary pentachord with the cello's simultaneous D$_5$ harmonic (see Ex. 1.3). This pentachord is [E2367] (01458), whose maximal (tetrachordal) subsets include (0145):

(01458)

SUBSET	NORMAL FORM	PRIME FORM
{0145}	[0145]	**(0145)**
{0148}	[0148]	(0148)
{0158}	[0158]	(0158)
{0458}	[4580]	(0148)
{1458}	[1458]	(0347)

In a sense, then, all three of the vertical tetrachords in the Bagatelle participate in forming members of (0145). The first and third ones do so with primary formations, while the second embeds that tetrachord within a secondary pentachord.

The amount of maximal subsets within a given set will always be equal to the size of the set itself. As we've seen, trichords have three maximal subsets (interval classes), tetrachords have four trichordal subsets, and pentachords have five tetrachordal subsets. Hexachords have six pentachordal subsets, septachords have seven hexachordal subsets, and so forth.

STUDY QUESTIONS 4.6

1. **Calculate the normal forms and prime forms of the maximal subsets of (0135).**

2. **Calculate the normal forms and prime forms of the maximal subsets of (0235).**

3. **Compare the maximal subsets of (0135) and (0235).**

VOCABULARY

abstract complementation	Forte name	self-complementation
aggregate completion	literal complementation	set complementation
all-interval tetrachords	maximal subset	Z-relations
embedded complement		

EXERCISES

A. NORMAL FORM AND PRIME FORM FOR SYMMETRICAL SETS

A symmetrical set is given. Demonstrate the two-step procedure for finding its prime form:

1. *Rotate*: **List all the rotations of the set and their outer pc intervals. Draw a ring around the rotation that represents normal form.**

2. *Transpose*: **Transpose the normal form to start on 0. Write the prime form without commas and enclosed in parentheses.**

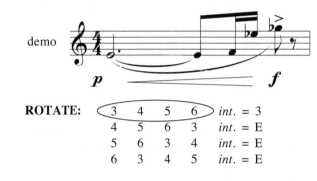

ROTATE:

	3	4	5	6	*int.* = 3
	4	5	6	3	*int.* = E
	5	6	3	4	*int.* = E
	6	3	4	5	*int.* = E

TRANSPOSE: (0123)

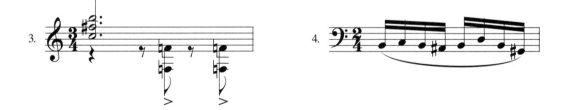

B. NORMAL FORM AND PRIME FORM FOR NONSYMMETRICAL SETS

A nonsymmetrical set is given. Demonstrate the six-step procedure for finding its prime form:

1. *Rotate*: **List all the rotations of the set and their outer pc intervals. Draw a ring around the rotation that represents normal form.**

2. *Transpose*: **Transpose the circled set to start on 0.**

3. *Invert*: **Invert the normal form at I_0.**

4. *Rotate*: **List all the rotations of I_0 and their outer pc intervals. Draw a ring around the rotation that represents normal form.**

5. *Transpose*: **Transpose the circled set in step 4 to start on 0.**

6. *Prime Form*: **Choose the prime form from the results of step 2 or 5 and write it without commas and enclosed in parentheses.**

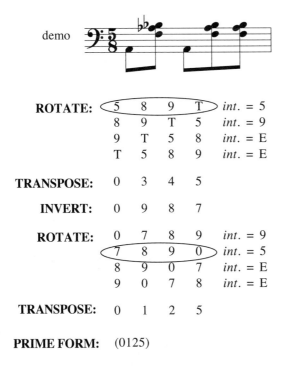

C. SETS IN POST-TONAL MELODIES

Give the [normal form] and (prime form) for the bracketed sets in each melody.

Demo. Arnold Schoenberg (1874–1951), *Das Buch des hängenden Gärten*, op. 15, no. 11, mm. 8–10 (1909)

1. [8TE03] (02347)   2. [89TE03] (012347)   3. [E025] (0136)   4. [03478] (01458)

1. Arnold Schoenberg (1874–1951), *Das Buch des hängenden Gärten*, op. 15, no. 1, mm. 1–5 (1909)

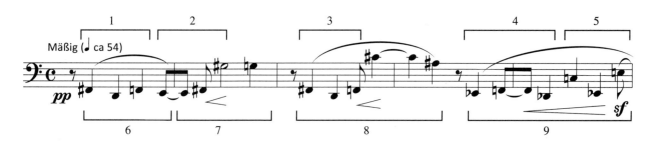

2. Anton Webern (1883–1945), "Gleich und Gleich," op. 12, no. 4, mm. 4–9 (1917)

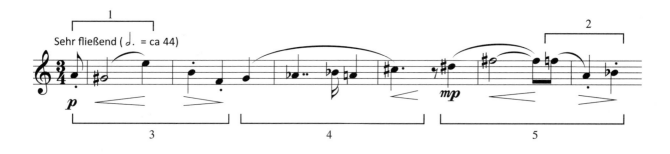

3. Alban Berg (1885–1935), "Nichts ist gekommen," op. 4, no. 4, mm. 2–7 (1912)

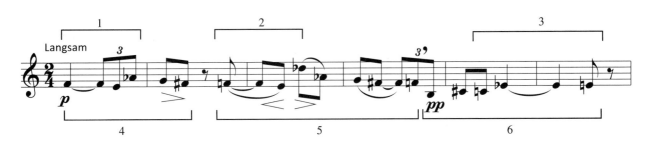

4. Charles Ives (1874–1954), "Luck and Work," mm. 1–4 (1916)

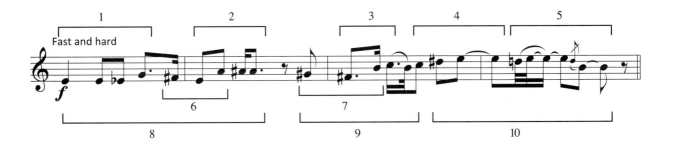

5. John Harbison (b. 1938), "Where Did You Go?" from _Mirabai Songs_, mm. 3–12 (1982)

D. IDENTIFYING TRANSFORMATIONAL MAPPINGS IN PITCH-CLASS SPACE

If the two given sets are equivalent, label the arrow to specify the equivalence operation in pitch-class space. The possible arrow labels to indicate equivalence are: T_n (transposition); I_n (inversion); both T_n and I_n (for symmetrical sets). If the two given sets aren't equivalent, label the arrow with an "X."

Demo [458T] $\xrightarrow{I_1}$ [3589]   1. [3589] $\longrightarrow$ [2478]   2. [E1345] $\longrightarrow$ [579TE]

3. [1256] $\longrightarrow$ [4589]   4. [456890] $\longrightarrow$ [012458]   5. [346T] $\longrightarrow$ [E356]

6. [569T] $\longrightarrow$ [1267]   7. [467E0] $\longrightarrow$ [2378T]   8. [8E04] $\longrightarrow$ [236T]

9. [02345] $\longrightarrow$ [5689T]   10. [12589] $\longrightarrow$ [347TE]   11. [258E] $\longrightarrow$ [1479]

12. [5678T0] $\longrightarrow$ [E01246]   13. [E01246] $\longrightarrow$ [E13456]   14. [1368] $\longrightarrow$ [2479]

15. [579E1] $\longrightarrow$ [2468T]   16. [57TE] $\longrightarrow$ [0146]   17. [569TE0] $\longrightarrow$ [78E012]

18. [13579E] $\longrightarrow$ [02468]   19. [3489T] $\longrightarrow$ [TE045]   20. [E03568] $\longrightarrow$ [23689E]

E. THE SET-CLASS CATALOG

Answer the questions by consulting the Set Class Catalog in Appendix 1.

1. **What is the TIC of (0246)?**

2. **What is the prime form of the set class with the TIC 060603?**

3. **What is the Forte name for (01347)?**

4. **What is the prime form of the set class with Forte name 6-1?**

5. **What is the prime form of the complement of (02479)?**

6. **What is the Forte name of the complement of set class 4-9?**

7. **What are the Forte names of the all-interval tetrachords?**

8. **Give the Forte names of the Z-partners of these set classes: 5-Z18 5-Z37 6-Z3 6-Z45**

9. **How many pentachords are symmetrical?**

10. **Which symmetrical pentachord has the same TIC as a nonsymmetrical pentachord? (Give prime forms and Forte names for both.)**

11. **What are the prime forms and Forte names of the tetrachordal set classes containing only six distinct pitch-class sets?**

12. **How many hexachords are self-complementary?**

13. **What are the prime forms and Forte names of the hexachords that are both self-complementary and symmetrical?**

F. FINDING MAXIMAL SUBSETS

Extract all possible maximal subsets of the given sets. Notate the subsets in normal form and prime form, and give their Forte names.

Demo. (0127)

Subsets:	{012}	{017}	{027}	{127}
Normal form:	[012]	[701]	[027]	[127]
Prime form:	(012)	(016)	(027)	(016)
Forte name:	3-1	3-5	3-9	3-5

1. (0125)   2. (0236)   3. (0167)   4. (01256)   5. (02346)   6. (012357)   7. (013467)

G. ANTON WEBERN (1883–1945), FIVE MOVEMENTS FOR STRING QUARTET, OP. 5, NO. 4 (1909)

1. **Listen to the movement several times without looking at the score. Reach some preliminary conclusions about its overall form. Then listen several times while following the score. How would you describe the overall form of the movement? What are the distinguishing features of each section? What are the recurring musical ideas that contribute to the articulation of form? How does Webern create contrast within the form (be specific)?**

2. **The opening of the movement features two different tetrachords played by the violins, muted, tremolo, and *am Steg* (at the bridge). What are the normal forms, prime forms, and Forte names of these two tetrachords? How are they structurally similar, and how are they similarly presented? What impact do they have on the music up through the beginning of measure 5?**

3. **What is the hexachord formed by all the notes in both violin tetrachords in measures 1 and 2 plus the concurrent E♭ in the cello (normal form, prime form, Forte name)? What is the hexachord formed by the cello line from the F♯$_3$ in measure 4 through the C♯$_2$ in measure 6 (normal form, prime form, Forte name)? Specifically how are these two hexachords related?**

4. **What are the normal form, prime form, and Forte name of the septachord in the second violin in measure 6? What is the significance of this septachord in the remainder of the movement?**

5. **What are the normal form, prime form, and Forte name of the pizzicato chord in measure 12? It's a symmetrical set, and therefore can be viewed as both a transposition and an inversion of other set-class members. In this case, however, which type of transformation better interprets the chord's structuring?**

6. **What are the normal form, prime form, and Forte name for the octachord that combines the pizzicato chord in measure 12 with the subsequent final gesture in the second violin? How does this octachord relate to previous tetrachords?**

H. ARNOLD SCHOENBERG (1874–1951), *DAS BUCH DES HÄNGENDEN GÄRTEN*, OP. 15, NO. 14 (1909)

1. **Listen to the song several times. The setting suggests four distinct phrases. Where are the phrase divisions, and how do the phrases interact with the structure and meaning of the poem?**

1.	*Sprich nicht immer*	*Don't always talk*
2.	*Von dem Laub,*	*About the leaves,*
3.	*Windes raub,*	*Stolen by the wind,*
4.	*Vom Zerschellen*	*About the fall*
5.	*Reifer Quitten,*	*Of ripe quinces,*
6.	*Von den Tritten*	*About the traces*
7.	*Der Vernichter*	*Of the destroyer [harvester]*
8.	*Spät im Jahr.*	*Late in the year.*
9.	*Von dem Zittern*	*About the trembling*
10.	*Der Libellen*	*Of dragonflies*
11.	*In Gewittern,*	*In thunderstorms.*
12.	*Und der Lichter,*	*And the fires [candles],*
13.	*Deren Flimmer*	*Twinkling*
14.	*Wandelbar.*	*Variably.*

2. **The song opens and closes with two similar gestures in the piano. Give the normal forms, prime forms, and Forte names for the pentachords formed by the first five piano notes in measures 1 and 11. How are the two gestures similar, both in their internal structure and in their manner of presentation?**

3. **Where else in the song do these same pentachord types occur?**

4. **What are the maximal subsets of these two pentachords, and which of these are subsets of both pentachords? Where are some prominent occurrences of some of these maximal subsets (of either or both pentachords) in the song?**

5. **Study the vocal line alone from measure 2 through the downbeat of measure 4. What are the most prominent trichords formed among adjacent notes in this phrase? How do they relate to the piano part in phrase 1?**

6. **The piano part in measure 6 has two arpeggios, one in the right hand, the other in the left hand starting on the B$_2$. What are the normal form, prime form, and Forte names of these two set-class types? How do these relate to music happening elsewhere in the song?**

7. **Describe Schoenberg's use of sequential patterns in the middle portion of the song. Include in your observations an identification of the set-class type for the first five notes in the piano in measure 7. Relate the sequential patterns to other parts of the song whenever possible.**

I. COMPOSITION EXERCISE: "VOCALISE"

Imagine the repeating piano chords below as the beginning of, and possibly the repeating accompaniment for, a wordless song for voice and piano, inspired by Charles Ives's song "Serenity." Create a vocal line that interacts with the repeating chords. Decide if the chords should continue to repeat as shown or if they should undergo some sort of transformation in the course of the song. Determine the set classes of the two chords and identify some structural properties that you might also use in the vocal line. Craft your vocal line so that it not only interacts inventively with the piano but also displays internal cohesion and unifying set relationships within and among phrases.

FOR FURTHER STUDY

BÉLA BARTÓK:

"Bulgarian Rhythm (2)," *Mikrokosmos* (1932–39) vol. 4, no. 115

ALBAN BERG:

Pieces for Clarinet and Piano, op. 5, nos. 1, 4 (1913)

ARNOLD SCHOENBERG:

Three Pieces for Piano, op. 11, no. 1 (1909)
Das Buch des hängenden Gärten, op. 15, nos. 1, 6, 11, 13 (1908–9)
Six Little Piano Pieces, op. 19, nos. 1, 3 (1911)
Pierrot Lunaire, op. 21, nos. 7, 9 (1912)

ANTON WEBERN:

Five Movements for String Quartet, op. 5, no. 2 (1909)
Six Bagatelles for String Quartet, op. 9, nos. 2, 3 (1911, 1913)
Five Pieces for Orchestra, op. 10, no. 2 (1911–13)
Three Short Pieces for Cello and Piano, op. 11 (1914)

CHAPTER 5

TONALITY IN TRANSITION

5.1 SOURCE SETS AND CENTRICITY

Listen to the beginning of Mozart's C-major piano sonata (Ex. 5.1), then to a climactic phrase from Debussy's "The Sunken Cathedral" (Ex. 5.2). These two works, composed about 122 years apart, reflect radically different artistic sensibilities, one epitomizing late-eighteenth-century Viennese classicism, the other turn-of-the-century French culture on the cusp of modernism. Yet they share one very important musical feature: their melodies and harmonies are formed entirely from notes of the C-major scale. As we know, this doesn't mean that the actual C-major scale, moving step-by-step upwards from C, <C–D–E–F–G–A–B>, is present in the music. But it does mean that the notes of this scale provide the composers with the pitch classes they used in the music they wrote.

In other words, for both Mozart and Debussy, the notes of the C-major scale are treated as a "set," as defined in Chapter 3.1. The notes may appear in any order, register, and combination. In the traditional scalar ordering, they would be listed in curly braces: {C–D–E–F–G–A–B}. In normal form and translated to pitch-class integers, this septachord is [E024579]. It's a member of set class (013568T).

EXAMPLE 5.1 Mozart, Sonata in C Major, K. 545, mvt. 1, mm. 1–4

EXAMPLE 5.2 Debussy, *Préludes* I, "La cathédrale engloutie" (The Sunken Cathedral), mm. 28–32

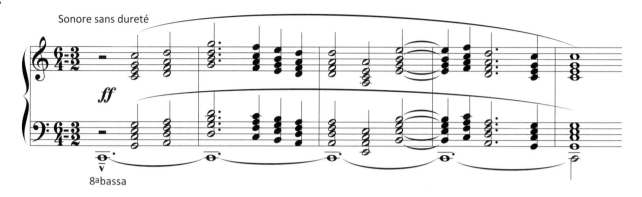

To simplify discussion, let's refer to this set by its Forte name, 7-35. We'll say that 7-35 provides the **source set** for both Mozart and Debussy. This means that a particular member of set class 7-35, [E024579], is a collection of the primary pitch-class content of the music. The source set doesn't define a specific order or register for its notes, and it doesn't restrict how different note combinations may be pulled out and combined to form "triads" and "seventh chords" and the like. It just represents the complete listing of all the pitch classes the composer has used.

Think about the implications of the source-set designation for these excerpts. A set class label, such as (013568T) or 7-35, doesn't give priority to any one pitch class over another—and yet one note, which we call "C" or "pitch-class 0," clearly is more important in both cases. For Mozart, we say that C is the "tonic" and the "key" of the music; in fact, the title of the work is "Sonata in C Major." For Debussy, we hear C as the primary anchor of the passage, sounding as a **pedal point** in the bass and represented by the C major triads that start and end the phrase.

When a certain note takes on a leading role within a source set, that's called **centricity**. Both Mozart's Sonata and Debussy's "Cathédrale" employ C centricity: they use a total of seven pitch classes, but C is more important than the other six. The excerpts demonstrate the 7-35 source set with C centricity. It's possible to employ a source set without defining a centricity, but usually one note takes precedence over the others. It's also possible for the centricity to change, even while the source set remains the same.

But how is C centricity different in the two passages? Mozart's C is established within a hierarchical system in which not just C but the C-major triad is primary. The C-major triad holds the tonic function, and other triads within the system hold lesser functions, such as dominant and predominant, with the shared goal of establishing the primacy of C. Debussy's C is also an arrival point, but not within a hierarchical system: it's simply the first and last triad of the phrase. The other triads within the phrase don't have functional connections to C, as they do in Mozart.

Consider, for example, the role of G-major triads in the two excerpts. When the left hand forms a G-major triad in the fourth measure of the Mozart phrase, it serves a dominant function, preparing and anticipating the subsequent return of tonic (Ex. 5.3a). The addition of the chord 7th (F) in the melody helps intensify the forward momentum of the progression. But Debussy's G-major triad at the beginning of his second measure cannot be considered a "dominant" in the same way (Ex. 5.3b). It's the high point of the phrase, but it carries no expectation of resolution to tonic. It's one of several identically structured chords helping to convey the composer's expressive message.

EXAMPLE 5.3   G-major triads in Mozart and Debussy

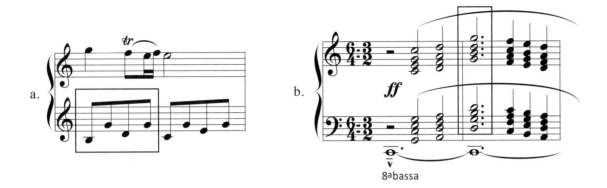

Notice the parallel movement of Debussy's triads: C major, D minor, G major, F major, E minor, D minor, and so forth. Given the prohibitions on parallel voice leading in tonal harmony, it's hard to imagine a more radical, more subversive implementation of triads. Debussy values the triads purely for their sonic effects. Their functional roles in tonal harmony are meaningless. He's painting a musical picture, and these are his colors.

STUDY QUESTIONS 5.1

1. **What other triad, besides C major and G major, is formed in both the Mozart phrase (Ex. 5.1) and the Debussy phrase (Ex. 5.2)?**

2. **How is the function of the triad identified for question 1 different in the two excerpts?**

3. **What musical techniques help to establish C centricity in the Debussy excerpt?**

5.2   THE DIATONIC SOURCE SET

Many composers of the early twentieth century explored ways to redefine traditional concepts such as "harmony" and "progression." Some, such as Schoenberg and Webern, tried dispensing with the source set idea altogether. Others shared Debussy's interest in exploring new possibilities for source sets that had been in constant use for centuries.

Let's think about what happens when a composer employs the **diatonic** (major or minor) scale as a **source set**. As long as the music faithfully draws from this single seven-note source, all musical groupings—melodies or chords of various sizes—will come from a finite group of possibilities. If we make a list of these possibilities, we'll have a reasonable summary of the pitch language of that music.

What does the list of possible subsets for a septachord look like? When you extract sets of smaller sizes from a septachord, you come up with seven hexachords (maximal subsets), twenty-one pentachords, thirty-five tetrachords, and thirty-five trichords. That's a total of ninety-eight different note combinations of sizes three through six. But these are ninety-eight different pitch-class sets, not ninety-eight different set classes. Many of the subsets are equivalent to others. In the diatonic source set, for example, six of the trichordal subsets are members of set class (037), better known as three major and three minor triads. The number of different set-class *types* formable within the diatonic source set is much smaller: thirty-five. Example 5.4 lists them all.

EXAMPLE 5.4 Subsets of the diatonic source set

(013568T) 7-35

Hexachords	Pentachords	Tetrachords	Trichords
(013568) 6-Z25	(01356) 5-Z12	(0135) 4-11	(013) 3-2
(013578) 6-Z26	(01357) 5-24	(0136) 4-13	(015) 3-4
(023579) 6-33	(01358) 5-27	(0137) 4-Z29	(016) 3-5
(024579) 6-32	(01368) 5-29	(0156) 4-8	(024) 3-6
	(01568) 5-20	(0157) 4-16	(025) 3-7
	(02357) 5-23	(0158) 4-20	(026) 3-8
	(02358) 5-25	(0235) 4-10	(027) 3-9
	(02469) 5-34	(0237) 4-14	(036) 3-10
	(02479) 5-35	(0246) 4-21	(037) 3-11
		(0247) 4-22	
		(0257) 4-23	
		(0258) 4-27	
		(0358) 4-26	

Of course, not all of these subsets will be equally effective indicators of the source set. Trichords (036) or (037)—the "triads"—will certainly carry implications of diatonicism, but others, such as (015) and (016), are more characteristic of strictly atonal idioms, as we've seen in previous chapters. Similarly, the tetrachordal subsets include "seventh chords" (0258) and (0358), or the diatonic scale segments (0135) and (0235), but also the starkly dissonant (0156). A composer working within the diatonic source set has options for highlighting or obscuring the music's allegiances to tonal traditions.

STUDY QUESTIONS 5.2

1. **How many pitch-class sets of sizes three through six can be extracted from a septachord?**

2. **How many different set classes (sizes 3–6) are represented in the subsets of the diatonic source set (7-35)?**

3. **How many different members of set class (037) are formable within a diatonic source set?**

4. **How many different members of set class (036) are formable within a diatonic source set?**

5. **What are the familiar names for the seventh chords in set class (0258)?**

6. **How many different members of set class (0258) are formable within a diatonic source set?**

5.3   THE DIATONIC MODES

Now let's turn our attention to the next phrase after the C-major passage in Debussy's piano piece (Ex. 5.5). The parallel triads continue, the pedal point keeps the centricity on C, but now all the B's are flatted. Debussy has shifted the source set into the diatonic collection with one flat in its key signature. But we can't say that the music is in F major (or D minor), however, because the pedal point keeps the centricity on C.

EXAMPLE 5.5   Debussy, *Préludes* I, "La cathédrale engloutie" (The Sunken Cathedral), mm. 32–38

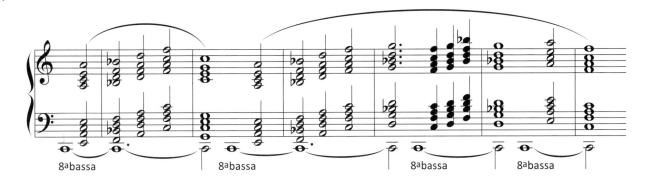

In other words, it's now the "one-flat key with C centricity." The best way to conceptualize the source set for this passage is to take the F-major scale and rotate it to start on C. Traditional tonal theory already has names for scales rotated to start on different notes: the **diatonic modes**. Minor, also known as **Aeolian**, can be defined as the major scale rotated to begin on its sixth scale degree. Debussy's phrase uses F major rotated to begin on degree $\hat{5}$, also known as **Mixolydian**. Each of the seven possible starting notes has its own name:

F Ionian:	F	G	A	B♭	C	D	E	
G Dorian:		G	A	B♭	C	D	E	F
A Phrygian:			A	B♭	C	D	E	F	G
B♭ Lydian:				B♭	C	D	E	F	G	A
C Mixolydian:					C	D	E	F	G	A	B♭
D Aeolian:						D	E	F	G	A	B♭	C
E Locrian:							E	F	G	A	B♭	C	D

So when Debussy starts flatting his B's, he has shifted from C major (Ionian) into C Mixolydian. That's another way of describing the [4579T02] source set with C centricity.

Six of the diatonic modes can be grouped into families of similar structures (Ex. 5.6). The "major" family includes **Ionian**, which is more commonly known as major, and the two modes that differ from major by only one note: **Lydian** (major with #$\hat{4}$) and **Mixolydian** (major with ♭$\hat{7}$). (The "#" before the scale degree indicates a chromatic alteration upward, not necessarily the addition of a sharp sign, and the "♭" indicates a chromatic alteration downward, not necessarily the addition of a flat sign.) In the "minor" family are **Aeolian**, more commonly known as minor, and the two modes that differ from minor by one note: **Dorian** (minor with #$\hat{6}$) and **Phrygian** (minor with ♭$\hat{2}$). Only **Locrian** is excluded from the family groupings. It differs from minor at two places (♭$\hat{2}$ and ♭$\hat{5}$) and is rarely found in the literature.

EXAMPLE 5.6   Modal families and examples

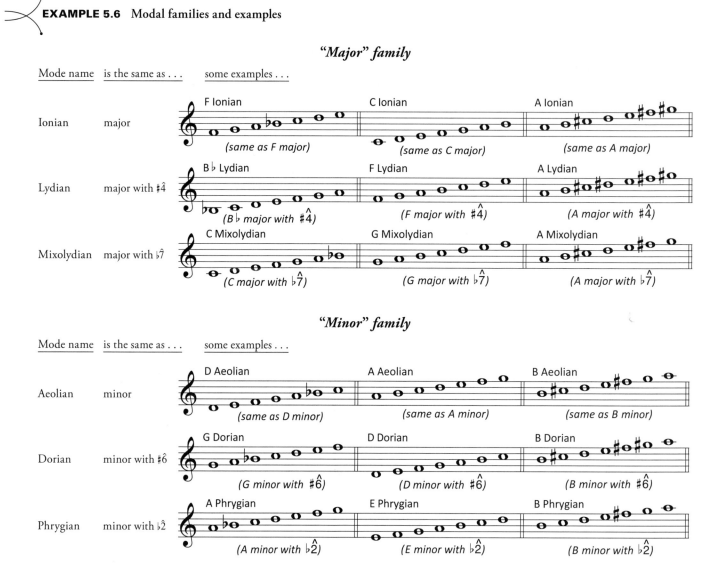

To determine the mode of a melody, then, look for chromatic inflections. If it's mostly minor but has sixth scale degrees that are a half step higher than they would be in minor, it's Dorian (Ex. 5.7). If it's mostly major but has fourth scale degrees that are a half step higher than they would be in major, it's Lydian (Ex. 5.8). And so forth.

EXAMPLE 5.7   Casella, *11 pezzi infantili*, no. 6, melody

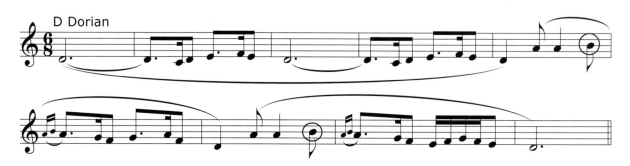

EXAMPLE 5.8 Bartók, *For Children*, no. 20, melody

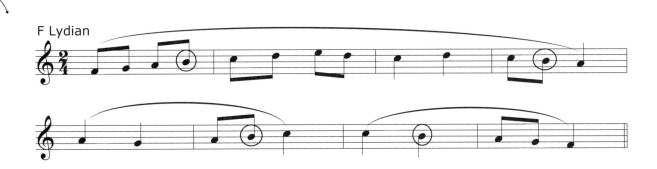

F Lydian

Likewise, modal harmony often resembles family members except for certain chords. Harmonies formed from chromatic inflections will have different qualities than they would in major or minor. In Dorian, for example, the i, III, v, and VII don't include the inflected scale degree $\hat{6}$ and sound just like they do in minor, while the chords built on scale degrees $\hat{2}$, $\hat{4}$, and $\hat{6}$ do include the inflected tone and thus have different qualities. The most common result is a major quality for the triad built on scale degree $\hat{4}$. The harmony of the Dorian setting in Example 5.9 alternates between the minor tonic and the major subdominant, which includes the inflected $\hat{6}$ (B♮) as its third.

EXAMPLE 5.9 Casella, *11 pezzi infantili*, no. 6, mm. 1–9

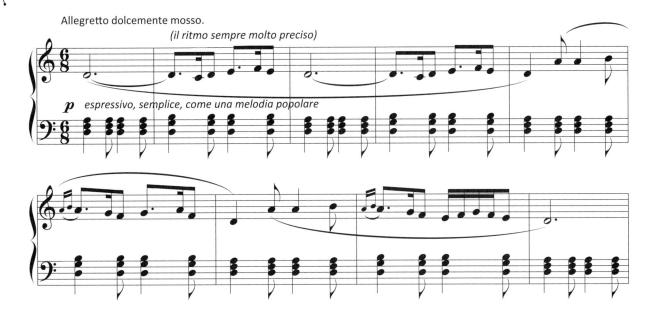

Allegretto dolcemente mosso.
(il ritmo sempre molto preciso)

p *espressivo, semplice, come una melodia popolare*

STUDY QUESTIONS 5.3

1. **Which of the two diatonic modes are most commonly used, and what are their more familiar names?**

2. **How would you make these conversions?**

    2.1. Ionian to Lydian.

    2.2. Aeolian to Phrygian.

2.3. Mixolydian to Ionian.

2.4. Dorian to Aeolian.

3. What are the qualities of these chords?

3.1. Dorian subdominant.

3.2. Lydian supertonic.

3.3. Mixolydian dominant.

3.4. Phrygian subtonic (rooted on $\hat{7}$).

5.4   THE OCTATONIC SOURCE SET

The concept of the source set is extendable in many different directions, with vastly different results. In theory, any large set can be established as a source set, subject to fragmentation and reordering. Simply designate a large set, let's say a septachord, as your source, then write music employing subsets of that source as melodies and chords. But not every large set is equally attractive for such purposes. Composers have preferred sets like the diatonic septachord because of its limited subset content. This gives the music composed within that source set a unique and distinctive sound.

Let's determine the source set for the excerpt from a piano prelude by Olivier Messiaen provided in Example 5.10. Centricity isn't strongly established, but A is the most important note in the stems-up right-hand melody, so let's use that note as the starting point. The source set consists of eight different notes: A–B♭–C–C♯–D♯–E–F♯–G. Every musical unit in the excerpt is extracted from this eight-pitch-class source. To put it another way, of the twelve pitch classes, eight are present, and the remaining four—pc's [258E]—are nowhere to be found.

EXAMPLE 5.10 Messiaen, *Préludes pour piano*, "Les sons impalpables du rêve" (The ethereal sounds of a dream), m. 7

When the notes of this source set are ordered as a scale, the adjacent intervals alternate ascending half and whole steps, pc intervals 1 and 2 (Ex. 5.11). A scale with this type of intervallic alternation is known as **octatonic**. Octatonic source sets appear in music of many composers in the early twentieth century and later, including Olivier Messiaen, Igor Stravinsky, and Béla Bartók.

EXAMPLE 5.11   Source set for the music shown in Example 5.10

Pc interval: 1   2   1   2   1   2   1

Consider the appeal of the octatonic scale as a source set. Its simple alternating interval pattern approaches an extreme of redundancy. Because of this structural property, the set can transform into itself via several operations. Transposing at T_3, for example, produces no change in pitch-class content. Imagine this operation in pitch space: moving every note up a minor third (T_{+3}) is the same as rotating the first two notes to the end, transposed up an octave (Ex. 5.12). The pitch-class content of this collection is likewise preserved under T_6 and T_9.

EXAMPLE 5.12   Redundancy of octatonic scale after transposition

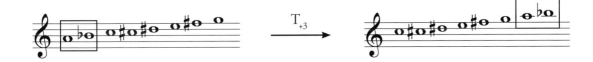

To put it another way, four different rotations of the octatonic scale notated in Example 5.11—starting on A, C, D♯, or F♯—have identical sequences of pitch-class intervals: 1–2–1–2–1–2–1. The other four rotations of this scale—starting on B♭, C♯, E, or G—also have identical interval patterns: 2–1–2–1–2–1–2 (Ex. 5.13). But we don't need to make a strict distinction between the rotations starting with pc interval 1 and the rotations starting with pc interval 2. Because they're reducible to the same normal form, in this case [0134679T], they're fundamentally the same source set.

EXAMPLE 5.13   Rotation of octatonic scale to begin with pc interval 2

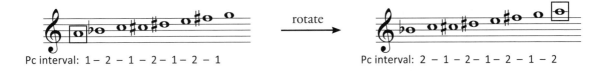

Pc interval: 1 – 2 – 1 – 2 – 1 – 2 – 1   Pc interval: 2 – 1 – 2 – 1 – 2 – 1 – 2

Now think about the inherent symmetry of the octatonic scale. Its repetitive interval pattern reveals, among other things, that the scale transforms into itself under inversion. You can discover this by finding ways to add scale tones together to total the same index number. In the A octatonic that we extracted from Messiaen's score, start with the two notes in the center of the scale and work your way outward to find note pairs that sum to index 4 (Ex. 5.14a). This scale inverts into itself at I_4. In the T_3 transposition of this scale (Ex. 5.14b), the nested pairs sum to index 10, indicating that it inverts into itself at I_T. This octatonic scale also inverts into itself at I_1 and I_7.

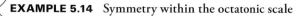

EXAMPLE 5.14   Symmetry within the octatonic scale

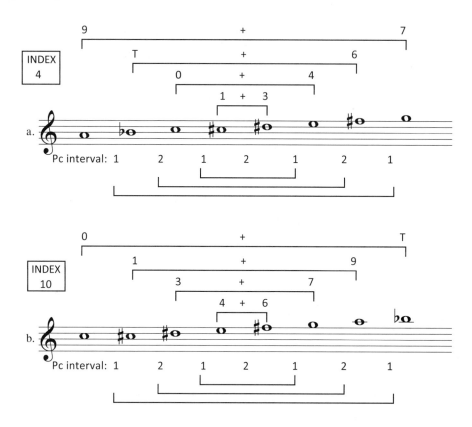

Amid such redundancy, the total subset content of the octatonic source set is extremely limited. The total number of pitch-class sets of sizes 3–7 formable within any octachord is 218: 8 septachords, 28 hexachords, 56 pentachords, 70 tetrachords, and 56 trichords. But the actual number of different set-class *types* within the octatonic source set is only 34. Example 5.15 lists them all.

EXAMPLE 5.15   Subsets of the octatonic source set

(0134679T) 8-28

Septachords	Hexachords	Pentachords	Tetrachords	Trichords
(0134679) 7-31	(013467) 6-Z13	(01346) 5-10	(0134) 4-3	(013) 3-2
	(013469) 6-27	(01347) 5-16	(0136) 4-13	(014) 3-3
	(013479) 6-Z49	(01367) 5-19	(0137) 4-Z29	(016) 3-5
	(013679) 6-30	(01369) 5-31	(0146) 4-Z15	(025) 3-7
	(014679) 6-Z50	(01469) 5-32	(0147) 4-18	(026) 3-8
	(023568) 6-Z23	(02358) 5-25	(0167) 4-9	(036) 3-10
		(02368) 5-28	(0235) 4-10	(037) 3-11
			(0236) 4-12	
			(0258) 4-27	
			(0268) 4-25	
			(0347) 4-17	
			(0358) 4-26	
			(0369) 4-28	

Just for practice, let's see how many members of (014) we can extract from this octatonic scale (Ex. 5.16). Start with the (014) member formed by the first, second, and fourth notes, A–B♭–C♯ (normal form [9T1]), and then assume, because of the source set's redundancy, that you can extract transpositions of this same trichord type starting with the third note [014], fifth note [347], and seventh note [67T]. Then go back and start with the (014) member formed by the first, third, and fourth notes, A–C–C♯ (normal form [901]), and again extract transpositions starting with the third note [034], fifth note [367], and seventh notes [69T]. Eight different members of set class (014) can be extracted from this (or any) octatonic scale.

EXAMPLE 5.16   (014) subsets within the octatonic scale

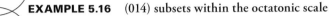
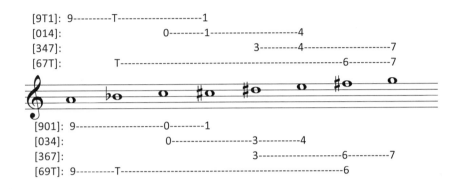

In fact, you can perform similar surgeries and extract eight different members of any of the trichord classes listed in Example 5.15. That includes (037): the octatonic collection includes four major and minor triads with roots related by minor third (Ex. 5.17). Perhaps you noticed three of these—C minor, E♭ major, and C major—in the left hand of Messiaen's piano piece (Ex. 5.10), despite some unusual spellings.

EXAMPLE 5.17   (037) subsets within the octatonic scale

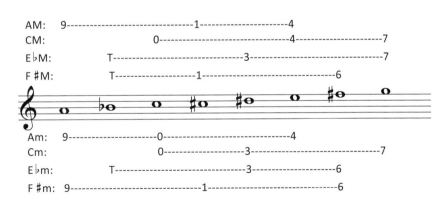

The tetrachordal subsets of the octatonic source set include eight members of (0258), the set class that includes both half-diminished and dominant seventh chords, and four members of (0358), the set class of the minor seventh chord. (In other words, it's possible to add a minor seventh from within the source set to any of the triads highlighted in Ex. 5.17.) But the most revelatory tetrachordal subsets may be the fully diminished seventh chords (0369), because they offer a clue to the source set's structure. One way to think of the formation of an octatonic scale, for example, is to interlock two different fully diminished seventh chords (Ex. 5.18).

EXAMPLE 5.18   Interlocking (0369)s within an octatonic scale

We can use this information to explore the octatonic source set more generally. As we know from tonal theory, in terms of pitch-class content, it's possible to form only three different fully diminished seventh chords, rooted on C, C♯, and D (Ex. 5.19a). Any other fully diminished seventh chord is a different transposition/spelling of one of these three. So if we make three different pairings of any two of these tetrachords, we'll have the three different octatonic pitch-class sets—that is, the three different members of set class (0134679T) 8-28 (Ex. 5.19b).

EXAMPLE 5.19   Three octatonic collections from three diminished seventh chords

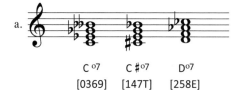

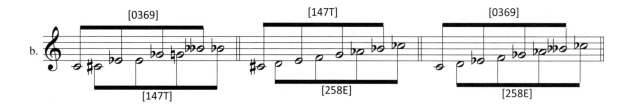

These are the only three members of set class (0134679T) 8-28. Start on any pitch class and enact the interval sequence 1–2–1–2–1–2–1 or 2–1–2–1–2–1–2, and you'll end up with some rotation of one of these three collections. We'll label the three octatonic collections with the symbol "OCT" and a subscript giving the first two pc's of the normal form:

$$\text{OCT}_{01}: \quad [0134679T]$$
$$\text{OCT}_{12}: \quad [124578TE]$$
$$\text{OCT}_{23}: \quad [235689E0]$$

The subscript gives the beginning of the normal form, not necessarily the first two notes of any given source set. To illustrate the source set for the excerpt from Messiaen's piano piece in Example 5.10, for example, we used the octatonic scale starting on A–B♭ (Ex. 5.11). But the collection being implemented is OCT_{01}. In other words, the source set Messiaen uses is a reordering of the OCT_{01} collection to begin on pc 9.

Charles Ives's song "Evening," excerpted in Example 5.20, employs OCT_{12} in the first three-and-a-half measures plus the voice's C♯ in measure 4. In many cases, when you're looking for an octatonic source set, you may find it easier to keep account of the notes that are *missing* from the octatonic environment—these missing notes are also a fully diminished seventh chord, the complement of the source set. In the Messiaen excerpt (Ex. 5.10), for example, the absent fully diminished seventh chord is the one rooted on D, or [258E]. In the Ives, it's the one rooted on C, or [0369].

EXAMPLE 5.20 Ives, "Evening," *114 Songs*, mm. 1–6

STUDY QUESTIONS 5.4

1. **How many pitch-class sets of sizes 3–7 can be extracted from an octachord?**

2. **How many different set classes (sizes 3–7) are represented in the subsets of the ocatonic source set (Forte name 8-28)?**

3. **How many different members of set class (014) are formable within an octatonic source set?**

4. **How many different members of set class (016) are formable within an octatonic source set?**

5. **How many different major triads can be formed within a single octatonic collection? What is the relationship between the roots of these triads?**

6. **How many different fully diminished 7th chords can be formed within a single octatonic collection?**

7. **Give the normal forms and labels for all of the members of set class 8-28.**

5.5   THE WHOLE-TONE SOURCE SET

Notice what happens in Ives's "Evening" when the vocal C♯ in measure 4 arrives (Ex. 5.20). This is the note that completes the octatonic source set (OCT_{12}) of the first three-and-a-half measures, and yet the piano's accompanying harmony underneath the C♯ suddenly shifts away from octatonicism. The new source set in the second half of measure 4 is the **whole-tone** collection, a scale consisting of only whole steps between adjacent notes. In the second half of measure 4, Ives essentially demonstrates one way of conceptualizing the whole-tone scale—as a pair of interlocking augmented triads (Ex. 5.21).

EXAMPLE 5.21   Interlocking augmented triads forming the whole-tone source set in measure 4 of Ives's "Evening" (see Ex. 5.20)

piano bass clef and upper treble

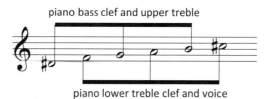

piano lower treble clef and voice

The whole-tone source set is the most redundant of all. Any hexachord encompasses 41 different trichordal, tetrachordal, and pentachordal subsets, but the whole-tone hexachord includes only 7 different set-class *types* among its subsets: 1 pentachord, 3 tetrachords, and 3 trichords (Ex. 5.22). Because of this exclusivity, any of these sets has a strong association with its whole-tone parentage.

EXAMPLE 5.22   Subsets of the whole-tone source set

(02468T) 6-35

Pentachords	Tetrachords	Trichords
(02468) 5-33	(0246) 4-21	(024) 3-6
	(0248) 4-24	(026) 3-8
	(0268) 4-25	(048) 3-12

In the next two measures of "Evening," for example, Ives continues to employ whole-tone materials, even while including other note formations suggestive of other source sets (Ex. 5.23). First, the left hand in measure 5 echoes the end of the previous bar with the penta-chordal whole-tone cluster [579E1], a member of sc (02468). Then in measure 6, the vocal line unfolds consecutive whole steps as if starting an actual whole-tone scale but stopping after four notes, stating a member of (0246), while the piano essentially harmonizes these notes with a whole-tone tetrachord [68T2], a member of (0248), in beat two, and the complete hexachord after that.

EXAMPLE 5.23 Whole-tone elements in mm. 4–6 of "Evening"

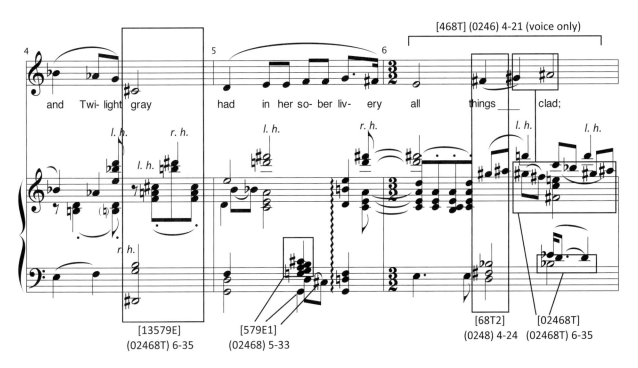

This excerpt also helps demonstrate the full pitch-class availability for the whole-tone source set. Because of its excessive redundancy, the whole-tone hexachord transposes and inverts into itself in multiple ways. The set class of this hexachord consists of only two members: the even-numbered pitch classes [02468T], and the odd-numbered pitch classes [13579E]. Ives's whole-tone environment in this part of "Evening" begins with the odd collection (mm. 4–5) and shifts to even (m. 6).

Similar to the octatonic labels, we'll specify whole-tone collections using the first number of the normal form as a subscript:

$$WT_0: \quad [02468T]$$
$$WT_1: \quad [13579E]$$

You could also describe them as "even" (WT_0) and "odd" (WT_1); Ives shifts from odd to even. In Bartók's piano piece "Whole-Tone Scales," the pianist's hands sometimes cooperate to present members of the same whole-tone collection (Ex. 5.24a), and other times present odd and even collections in opposition between the hands (Ex. 5.24b).

EXAMPLE 5.24 Bartók, "Whole-Tone Scales," *Mikrokosmos* 136 (vol. 5), mm. 20–23 (a), 35–37 (b)

STUDY QUESTIONS 5.5

1. **How many pitch-class sets of sizes 3–5 can be extracted from a hexachord?**

2. **How many different set classes (sizes 3–5) are represented in the subsets of the whole-tone source set (6-35)?**

3. **What type of triad can be interlocked to form a whole-tone scale?**

4. **Give the normal forms and labels for all of the members of set class 6-35.**

5. **Find the normal form and prime form of each set and indicate the whole-tone collection from which it's extracted:**

    5.1. $<A_3–G_2–E\flat_3>$

    5.2. $<F\sharp_4–D_4–E_4–A\sharp_4>$

    5.3. B♭ augmented triad

    5.4. Degrees $\hat{1}–\hat{2}–\hat{3}–\hat{4}$ of the G Lydian scale

5.6   THE HEXATONIC SOURCE SET

Like the octatonic source set, the **hexatonic** source set, when ordered as a scale, alternates pitch-class intervals: 1–3–1–3–1 or 3–1–3–1–3. Like the whole-tone source set, the hexatonic can be conceptualized as a pair of interlocking augmented triads (Ex. 5.25). Its prime form is (014589), its Forte name 6-20.

EXAMPLE 5.25 Hexatonic source set

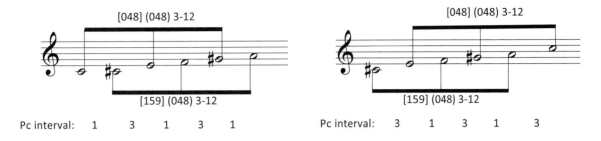

The hexatonic hexachord is almost as internally redundant as the whole-tone hexachord: among its 41 different pitch-class subsets are just 9 different set types—1 pentachord, 4 tetrachords, and 4 trichords (Ex. 5.26).

EXAMPLE 5.26 Subsets of the hexatonic source set

(014589) 6-20

<u>Pentachords</u>	<u>Tetrachords</u>	<u>Trichords</u>
(01458) 5-21	(0145) 4-7	(014) 3-3
	(0148) 4-19	(015) 3-4
	(0158) 4-20	(037) 3-11
	(0347) 4-17	(048) 3-12

The hexatonic set class has four members, labeled with "HEX" and the subscripted first two integers of the normal forms:

$$HEX_{01}: \quad [014589]$$
$$HEX_{12}: \quad [12569T]$$
$$HEX_{23}: \quad [2367TE]$$
$$HEX_{34}: \quad [3478E0]$$

When implementations of the hexatonic source set emphasize the triadic subsets (major, minor, and augmented), the music can leave a mostly consonant, somewhat traditional impression. Webern's hexatonicism, however, often highlights subsets such as (014) and (015) that avoid tonal implications. The last four bars of his last Opus 9 Bagatelle, for example, begin with a formation of HEX_{12} and then move directly to an accumulation of HEX_{34} (Ex. 5.27). Of course, HEX_{12} and HEX_{34} are literal complements, completing the aggregate just as the Bagatelle is coming to an end. As if in response, the final beats saturate a certain range of pitch space (G_4–$E\flat_5$) with a concluding chromatic cluster, recalling how the entire opus began (see Chapter 1).

EXAMPLE 5.27   Webern, Bagatelle for String Quartet, op. 9, no. 6, mm. 6–9

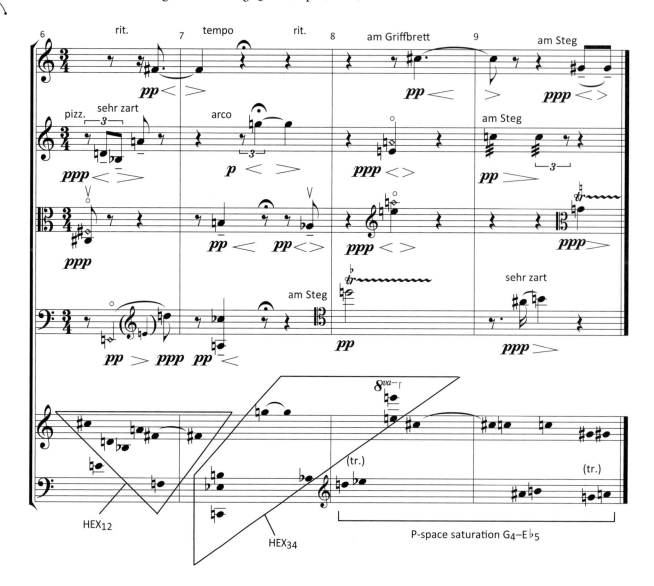

STUDY QUESTIONS 5.6

1. Which sets interlock to form both the whole-tone and the hexatonic source sets? How is this interlocking differently positioned in the two instances?

2. How many pitch-class sets of sizes 3–5 can be extracted from a hexachord?

3. How many different set classes (sizes 3–5) are represented in the subsets of the hexatonic source set (6-20)?

4. Give the normal forms of all members of set class (0347) that are subsets of [12569T].

5. Give the normal forms and labels for all of the members of set class 6-20.

6. **Find the normal form and prime form of each set and indicate the hexatonic collection from which it's extracted:**

   6.1. $<G_3–B_2–F\sharp_3>$
   6.2. $<C\sharp_5–A\sharp_4–D_4–A_4>$
   6.3. F-major triad
   6.4. Degrees $\hat{5}–\hat{6}–\hat{7}–\hat{8}$ of the C harmonic minor scale

5.7 INTERVAL CYCLES AND COMBINATION CYCLES

The commonly used source sets are specific types within broader categories of repeating intervallic patterns. A repetition of a single interval over and over, as in the whole-tone source set, is a type of **interval cycle**. Interval cycles are designated with the number of the repeating pitch-class interval: the chromatic scale is the 1-cycle, the whole-tone scale is the 2-cycle, and so forth. Repeating two different intervals in alternation, as in the octatonic or hexatonic source sets, generates a **combination cycle**. For combination cycles, the two alternating pitch-class interval numbers are separated by a dash and enclosed in angle brackets: the octatonic is the <1-2> cycle; the hexatonic is the <1-3> cycle. Let's explore some other possibilities within these general categories.

Most of the interval cycles are too short to have practical value as source sets. The 3-cycle (or its inverse, the 9-cycle) yields only a fully diminished seventh chord, and the 4-cycle (or 8-cycle) generates but an augmented triad. The 6-cycle consists of just the two notes in a tritone.

What about the 1-cycle (or its inverse, the 11-cycle) and the 5-cycle (or its inverse, the 7-cycle)? These have the opposite problem: they aren't limiting enough. When repeated to their completion, they generate complete aggregates. Literally speaking, if you consider one of these cycles to be your source set, then any music can somehow be considered its derivative. The subset content of one of these source sets would be Appendix 1, a listing of every set class.

Even if these aggregate-completing cycles can't be actual source sets, however, they can be broken up into segments to provide material for melodies and harmonies. The "chromatic clusters" in Webern's string quartet Bagatelle that we studied in Chapter 1 were essentially segments of incomplete 1-cycles. And let's not forget that the diatonic scale itself is a reordering of a seven-note segment of a 5- or 7-cycle:

B major (E Lydian, G♯ Aeolian, etc.)

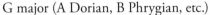

7-cycle: 0   7   2   9   4   E   6   1   8   3   T   5

G major (A Dorian, B Phrygian, etc.)

A **pentatonic** scale is a reordering of a five-note segment of a 5- or 7-cycle. The classic ordering is demonstrated by the piano black keys starting on pc 6, with adjacent pc intervals 2–2–3–2 (Ex. 5.28a). You can also think of it as the major scale minus degrees $\hat{4}$ and $\hat{7}$. (Insert C♭ and F at appropriate places in Example 5.28a and you'll have a G♭-major scale.) If you rotate the pentatonic scale to begin on its last note (pc 3 in this case), you'll derive the **minor pentatonic**, which has adjacent pc intervals 3–2–2–3 (Ex. 5.28b). This is like a minor scale missing degrees $\hat{2}$ and $\hat{6}$. (Insert F and C♭ at appropriate places in Ex. 5.28b and you'll have an E♭-minor scale.)

EXAMPLE 5.28 Pentatonic scales

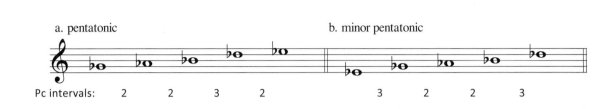

a. pentatonic

b. minor pentatonic

Pc intervals: 2   2   3   2   3   2   2   3

The melody in Darius Milhaud's pentatonic piano piece for children "Touches noires" (Black Keys) is solidly anchored on G♭, although the harmonic dyads in the left hand do their best to bring the music in the direction of other centricities (Ex. 5.29a). Maurice Ravel's passacaglia theme from the third movement of his Piano Trio (Ex. 5.29b) likewise hints at different tone centers but most strongly reinforces a C♯ centricity, and a pentatonic minor source set C♯–E–F♯–G♯–B.

But these are fairly conventional musical results. The pentatonic environment lacks interval class 1's and can never be harshly dissonant. It has a long history of association with simple harmonies and traditional melodies ("Amazing Grace," for example).

A more progressive approach creates a melody or harmony from the cyclic segment with its generating intervals intact. Chords formed of literal segments of incomplete 5-cycles in pitch space, without reordering, are often described as **quartal harmonies**. Chords formed of intact p-space segments of 7-cycles are often described as **quintal harmonies**.

Charles Ives's quartal chords (plus a concluding chord formed of a variety of intervals) in the introduction to his song "The Cage" (Ex. 5.30a) establish a chord pattern that persists after the voice enters and throughout the remainder of the song.[1] Because each of the quartal sonorities consists of a five-note segment of a 5-cycle, the pitch-class content is the same as the pentatonic scale (sc (024579) 5-35). Debussy's quintal chords at the beginning of "The Sunken Cathedral" piano prelude (Ex. 5.30b) exploit the haunting hollowness of open fifths.

---

[1]See Philip Lambert, *The Music of Charles Ives* (New Haven, CT: Yale University Press, 1997), 150–59.

EXAMPLE 5.29   Pentatonic source sets in (a) Milhaud, "Touches noires"; (b) Ravel, Piano Trio III

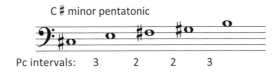

EXAMPLE 5.30   Quartal and quintal harmonies in (a) Ives's song "The Cage," m. 1; and (b) Debussy's *Préludes* I, "La cathédrale engloutie" (The Sunken Cathedral), mm. 1–2

a.

All notes not marked with sharp or flat are natural.

Profondément calme (Dans une brume doucement sonore)

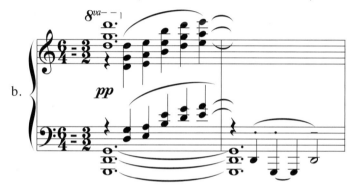

b.

As we've seen, combination cycles, such as the octatonic or hexatonic scales, can be viewed as interlockings of single-interval cycles. So if a <1-2> combination cycle—that is, an octatonic scale—interlocks two 3-cycles (fully diminished seventh chords; Ex. 5.18), then a <6-5> combination cycle alternates two 11-cycles (Ex. 5.31). The mod-12 sum of the two intervals being alternated equals the size of the intervals in the interlocked single-interval cycles (in this case, 6 + 5 = 11).

EXAMPLE 5.31   <6–5> combination cycle

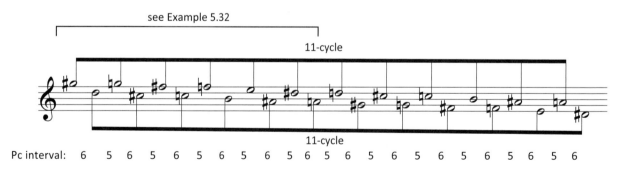

Olivier Messiaen's vibraphone melody heard throughout the sixth movement of his *Turangalîla-Symphonie* (Ex. 5.32) is freely based on the first half of the <6-5> combination cycle. The melody begins with the combination cycle's first six notes in order (see Ex. 5.31), then jumps ahead to pc E, repeats pc's 6, 0, and E, omits pc's 4 and T, and finally finishes with pc's 5, 3, and 9.

EXAMPLE 5.32   Messiaen, *Turangalîla-Symphonie*, mvt. 6, mm. 4–7, vibraphone

Messiaen's concluding pc 9 represents the place in the combination cycle where the aggregate has been completed, after which pitch-class repetitions begin. The next note in the combination cycle after the pc 9 is pc 2 in the upper 11-cycle, which is the same pc as the first note in the lower 11-cycle (see Ex. 5.31). Of course, pitch-class repetitions are inevitable when you're interlocking two complete 11-cycles. But in this particular combination, each of the twelve pitch classes occurs exactly once before a pitch class recurs.

The concept of the combination cycle vastly expands a composer's options for composing with cycles. Any of the aggregate-completing single-interval cycles can be interlocked to create combination cycles with maximal pitch-class variety before the first pitch-class repetition. We should observe, however, that the preservation of adjacent intervals in a cyclic source, as in Examples 5.30 and 5.32, is a tangent in our study of the "source set." Creating a melody or chord from the adjacent notes in a certain intervallic repetition isn't the same as treating that cycle as an unordered source set for chords and pitch relationships. An intact subsegment values the generating intervals themselves as distinctive elements of structure.

STUDY QUESTIONS 5.7

1. **Give the more familiar names for these note patterns:**

    1.1. 1-cycle   1.2. 2-cycle   1.3. 3-cycle   1.4. 4-cycle

    1.5. <1-2> combination cycle   1.6. <1-3> combination cycle

    1.7. five consecutive notes extracted from a 5-cycle and rearranged

    1.8. seven consecutive notes extracted from a 7-cycle and rearranged

    1.9. 6-cycle

2. **What is the term for chords formed by intact p-space segments of 7-cycles?**

3. **What is the term for chords formed by intact p-space segments of 5-cycles?**

4. **What single-interval cycles interlock in the <6-5> combination cycle?**

5. **How does the label for a combination cycle reveal the size of the intervals in its interlocking single-interval cycle?**

6. **For each combination cycle:**

    (a)   notate the entire cycle as a <pc string>;

    (b)   specify which type of single-interval cycle is being interlocked;

    (c)   give the number of different pitch classes in the string prior to a pc repetition;

    (d)   give the more familiar name for the resulting source set, if any.

    6.1. <2-1> starting on pc 8

    6.2. <7-6> starting on pc 4

    6.3. <3-5> starting on pc 1

    6.4. <8-3> starting on pc 3

    6.5. <5-9> starting on pc 0

    6.6. <2-3> starting on pc E

VOCABULARY

Aeolian	interval cycle	pedal point
centricity	Ionian	pentatonic
combination cycle	Locrian	Phrygian
diatonic mode	Lydian	quartal harmony
diatonic source set	minor pentatonic	quintal harmony
Dorian	Mixolydian	source set
hexatonic source set	octatonic source set	whole-tone source set

EXERCISES

A. SOURCE SET NOTATION

Notate each specified source set as an ascending scale starting on the given note. Don't repeat the first note at the end.

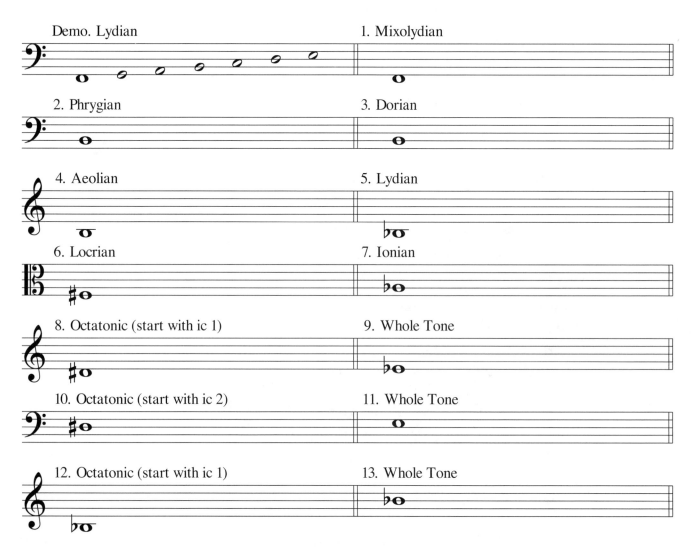

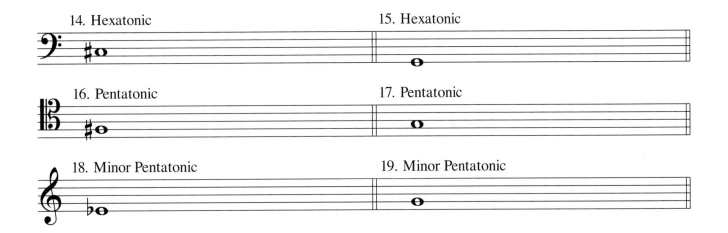

14. Hexatonic   15. Hexatonic

16. Pentatonic   17. Pentatonic

18. Minor Pentatonic   19. Minor Pentatonic

B. SOURCE SET IDENTIFICATION

Find the tonal center of the given excerpt. On a staff in treble clef, arrange the notes of the excerpt as an ascending scale starting on the tonal center. (For music without a clear tonal center, a starting note is provided.) If notes are missing from the complete source set, place them in parentheses. Circle any notes in the excerpt that aren't part of the source set ("nonharmonic tones").

Specify the name of the source set for each excerpt. Options: Ionian, Dorian, Phrygian, Lydian, Mixolydian, Aeolian, Locrian, OCT_{01}, OCT_{12}, OCT_{23}, WT_0, WT_1, HEX_{01}, HEX_{12}, HEX_{23}, HEX_{34}, pentatonic, minor pentatonic. Or if the source set is a combination cycle (but not octatonic or hexatonic), give the identifier for that cycle (e.g., <6-5>).

Demo. Igor Stravinsky (1882–1971), Octet for Wind Instruments (1923), mvt. 2, flute, mm. 1–8

Source set: OCT_{01}

1. Claude Debussy (1862–1918), *L'isle joyeuse* (1904), mm. 68–71

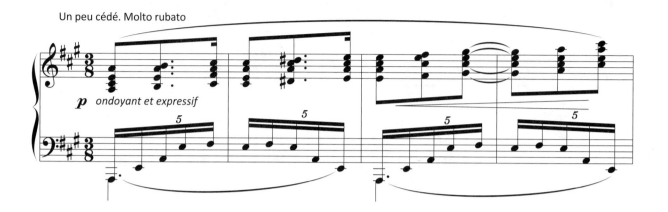

2. Sergei Prokofiev (1891–1953), *Alexander Nevsky* (1938), III, mm. 43–46

3. Paul Dukas (1865–1935), *Ariane et Barbe-bleue* (1907), I, page 45

START SOURCE SET ON A♭

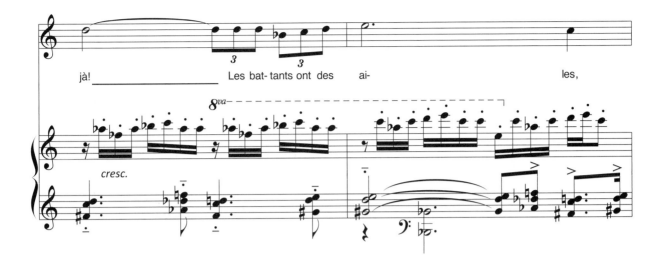

jà! _____ Les bat- tants ont des ai-   les,

4. Ernest Bloch (1880–1959), "Simchas Torah," *Baal Shem* for violin and piano (1923), rehearsal 26

Tempo I (♩ = 120–126)

5. Olivier Messiaen (1908–1992), *Quartet for the End of Time* (1941), mvt. 7, mm. 1–3

START SOURCE SET ON A

Rêveur, presque lent (♪ = 50 env.)

VC

p espress.

pno

p

6. Béla Bartók (1881–1945), "Free Variations," *Mikrokosmos* 140 (vol. 6), mm. 52–55

7. Alfredo Casella (1883–1947), "Minuetto," *11 Pezzi Infantili* (1920), no. 8, mm. 37–41

8. Alberto Ginastera (1916–1983), Piano Sonata no. 1 (1952), mvt. 1, mm. 41–43

RIGHT HAND ONLY

9. Wallingford Riegger (1885–1961), *Who Can Revoke* (1948), mm. 24–25

10. Charles T. Griffes (1884–1920), "So-fei Gathering Flowers" (1917), mm. 1–4

11. Erik Satie (1866–1925), *Socrate* (1918), "Mort de Socrate," mm. 97–101

12. Béla Bartók (1881–1945), "Five-Tone Scale," *Mikrokosmos* 78 (vol. 3), mm. 1–8

13. Joan Tower (b. 1938), *Silver Ladders* (1986), clarinet (sounds as notated), mm. 127–36

14. Giacomo Puccini (1858–1924), *Madama Butterfly* (1904), act 3, after rehearsal 32 (sounds as notated)

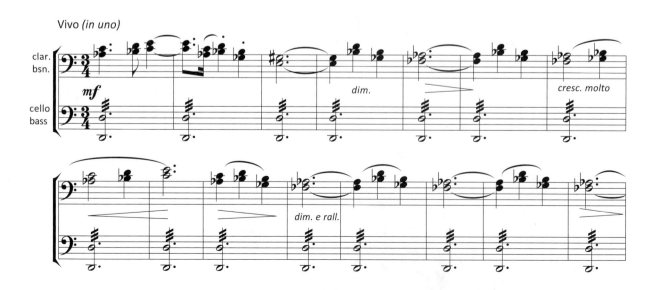

15. Igor Stravinsky (1882–1971), "Ritual of the Abduction," *Le sacre du printemps*
(The Rite of Spring) (1913), rehearsal 42, representative instruments (sounds as
notated)

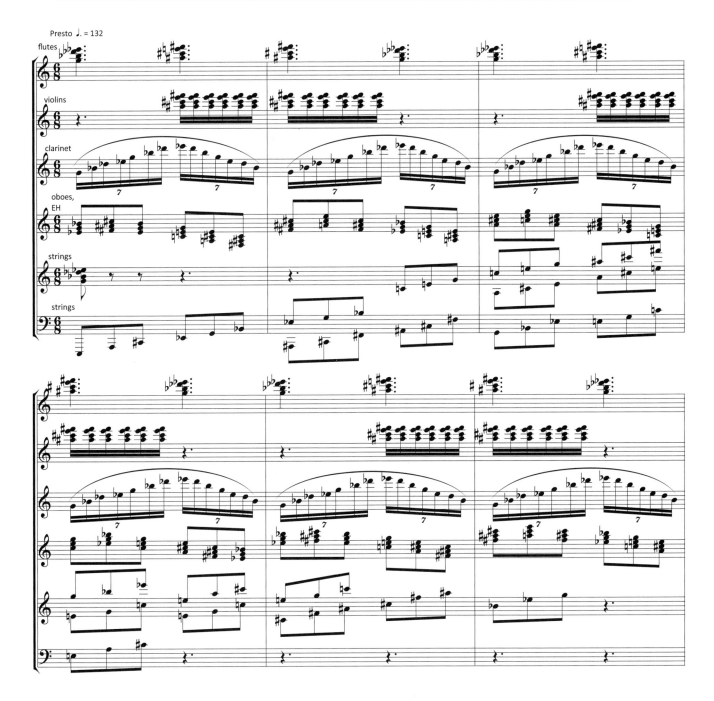

C. SUBSET CONTENTS

Identify the collection of the given source set. Notate the specified subsets of that source set on the blank staff and in normal form.

Demo    collection =   OCT₂₃

Extract eight different members of set-class (014):

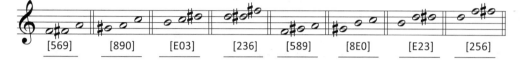

[569]   [890]   [E03]   [236]   [589]   [8E0]   [E23]   [256]

1.    collection =

Extract eight different members of set-class (013):

2.    collection =

Extract six different members of set class (024):

3.    collection =

Extract two different members of set class (0369):

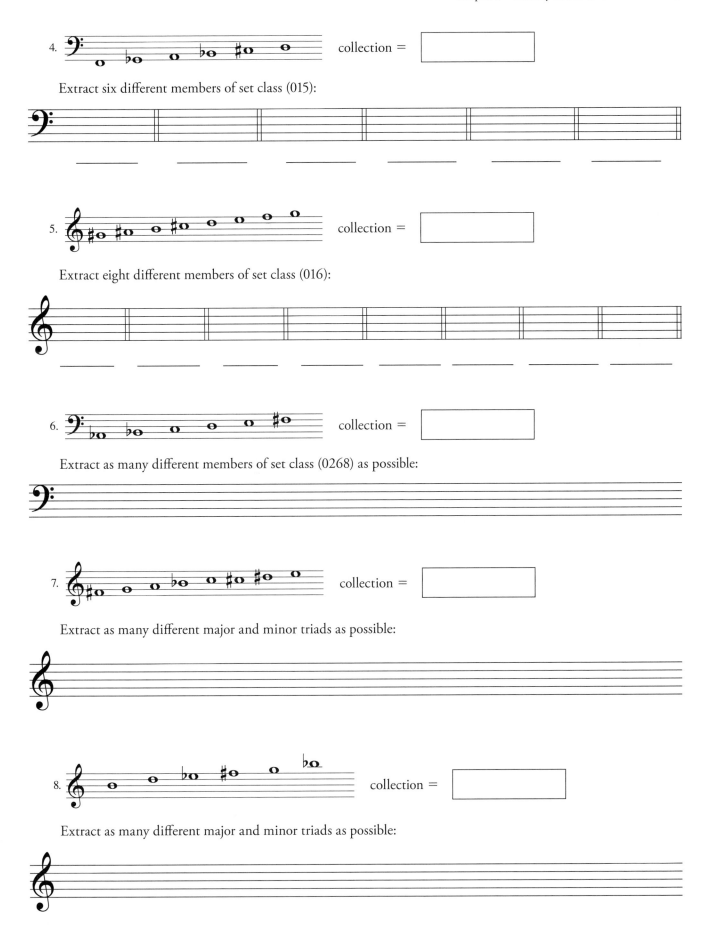

4. collection = _____

Extract six different members of set class (015):

5. collection = _____

Extract eight different members of set class (016):

6. collection = _____

Extract as many different members of set class (0268) as possible:

7. collection = _____

Extract as many different major and minor triads as possible:

8. collection = _____

Extract as many different major and minor triads as possible:

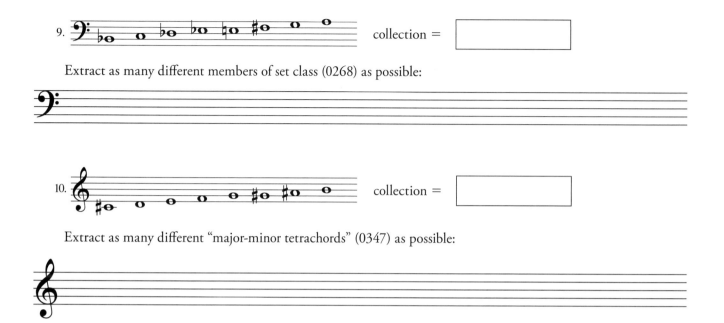

9. collection =

Extract as many different members of set class (0268) as possible:

10. collection =

Extract as many different "major-minor tetrachords" (0347) as possible:

D. CLAUDE DEBUSSY (1862–1918), PRÉLUDE TO ACT 1, *PELLÉAS ET MÉLISANDE* (1902)

Here at the beginning of the opera, Debussy is presenting some of its principal themes. Notice how frequently the music shifts from one theme or atmosphere to another. During the five acts of the opera to come, Debussy will use these and other themes to tell the tragic story of two young lovers, Pelléas and Mélisande.

In this Prelude to act 1, we hear three main musical ideas. The first four measures present the **Allemonde** theme, which is associated with the mythical, dark forest where the action of the opera takes place. Just after that, in measures 5–7, we're introduced to the **Golaud** theme, which Debussy uses to dramatize the character Golaud, who is the brother of Pelléas. Then a short while later, in measures 14–18, we hear the theme that becomes associated with the character of **Mélisande**.

The different thematic introductions and recurrences give the Prelude a seven-part form:

Measures:	1–4	5–7	8–11	12–13	14–17	18–20	21–23
Theme:	Allemonde	Golaud	Allemonde	Golaud	Mélisande	Golaud	transition to scene 1

1. **Look closely at the harmonies in the first Allemonde section (mm. 1–4). How would you describe the chord structures, centricity, and source set?**

2. **What's different about the chords, centricity, and source set when the Allemonde theme returns in measures 8–11?**

3. **Describe in detail the source set of the first occurrence of the Golaud theme in measures 5–7.**

4. **What's different about the return of the Golaud theme in measures 12–13? Organize all the notes in these measures as a scale: although it's not a source set specifically discussed in this chapter, can you describe it using similar terminology?**

5. **In the first two measures of the first Mélisande theme (mm. 14–15), what is the normal form and prime form of the set in the accompaniment (everything but the stems-up treble clef melody)? This set is a subset of which two collections studied in this chapter?**

6. **Now look at the melody of the first Mélisande theme (mm. 14–15, stems up in the treble clef). What are the normal form and prime form of the melody alone, and how might you relate it to the set of the accompaniment?**

7. **In the third appearance of the Golaud theme (mm. 18–20), where and how does the source set change?**

8. **Discuss the harmony of the transition to scene 1 (mm. 21–23) in relation to the music that precedes it.**

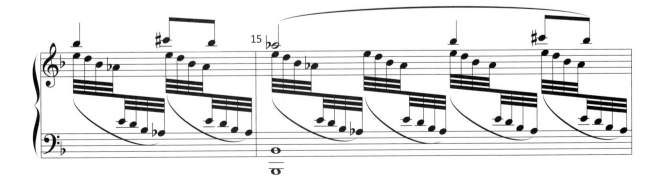

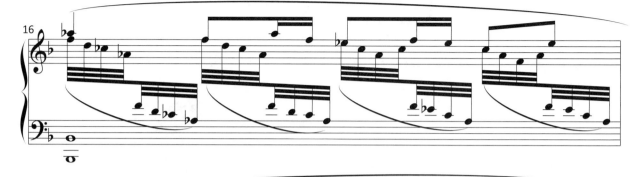

En augmentant un peu

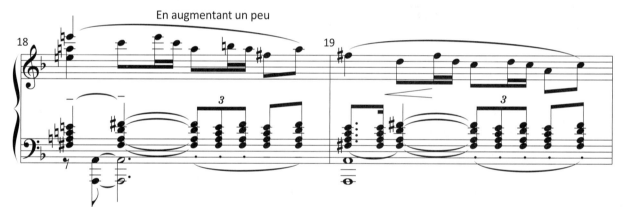

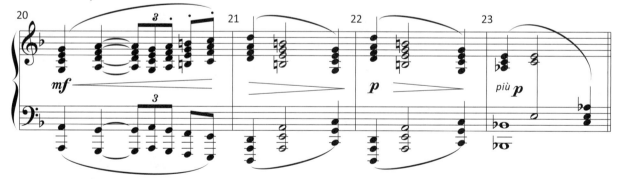

E. OLIVIER MESSIAEN (1908–1992), PREMIÈRE COMMUNION DE LA VIERGE (FIRST COMMUNION OF THE VIRGIN), *VINGT REGARDS SUR L'ENFANT-JÉSUS* (TWENTY CONTEMPLATIONS ON THE INFANT JESUS) FOR PIANO (1944), NO. 11.

Messiaen's monumental work is a soulful meditation on the early life of Jesus Christ. The eleventh movement contemplates the Virgin Mary's first communion with her unborn child.

The form of the movement is anchored on a recurring theme, described by the composer as the "Thème de Dieu," or "Theme of God." This same theme is prominent in other movements, as well. In the eleventh movement, we first hear the God theme in the opening bars, then again in a large central section, repeated with variation, and finally in a recapitulatory coda. These sections are the beginning, middle, and end of a five-part form:

Section	A	B	A¹	C	A
Measures:	1–16	17–20	21–42	43–72	73–80

Because the sections involve repetition of material, we can get a good sense of the complete movement just by looking at some representative excerpts.

1. **First examine only the left-hand part (lower staff) at the beginning of the A section (Ex. 5.33). What is the source set for this material? (Be specific.) What aspects of the source set are highlighted in this setting?**

2. **Now look at the right-hand part in the same excerpt (treble staff of Ex. 5.33). How does the right-hand material relate to the source set in the left hand? When you find correspondences between right hand and left hand, explain similarities and differences in the presentation of the source set. When you find contrasting pitch material in the two hands, describe specifically the right-hand set(s) and their presentation (normal form, prime form).**

3. **Next look at the B section (Ex. 5.34). Messiaen's inscription below the lower staff, "Rappel de 'la Vierge et l'Enfant,'" indicates that he is borrowing from a movement from one of his other works, a nine-movement contemplation for organ on the birth of Christ (*La nativité du Seigneur*, 1935). Again, look at the material in the two hands separately: Do they cooperate within the same source set or present notes from different source sets? Be specific about both the source sets and their manner of presentation.**

4. **Finally, look at the chords in measure 43, which are typical of the material in section C (Ex. 5.35). What are the set types of the hands separately and together? Assuming that other pitch structures in this part of the piece are similar, describe the contrast between section C and section A.**

EXAMPLE 5.33   Messiaen, *Vingt regards*, no. 11, mm. 1–4

EXAMPLE 5.34   Messiaen, *Vingt regards*, no. 11, mm. 17–20

EXAMPLE 5.35   Messiaen, *Vingt regards*, no. 11, m. 43

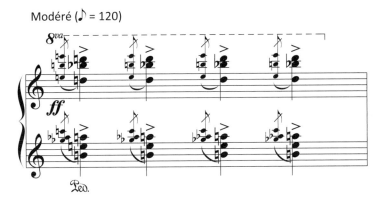

F. COMPOSING MODAL MELODIES

Determine the modality of the given melodic fragment, then compose a melody that starts with the given fragment and retains the same mode and tonal center.

G. CHORALE HARMONIZATIONS

Let's use this chorale phrase as a starting point:

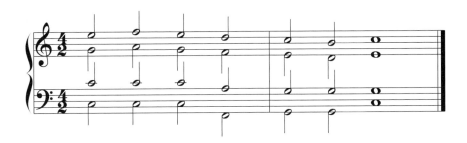

If we wanted to reharmonize this phrase in the Aeolian mode, we could simply add accidentals to shift to the parallel minor:

A reharmonization in the Dorian mode also works pretty well, just by leaving the notes where they are but changing accidentals to stay within C Dorian:

But if we use that same strategy for Lydian, the result isn't nearly as interesting:

For a Lydian reharmonization of the melody, it sounds better to rethink all the chord structures, in addition to using the notes of the C-Lydian mode:

Take that same melody and try a few reharmonizations of your own. Do more than change a few accidentals in the original chorale, however. Experiment with different chord structures and surprising dissonances. Savor the opportunity to relax (ignore) traditional part-writing rules. Don't change the notes of the melody, except to add an accidental that's consistent with the changes you're making in the underlying harmonies.

1. Mixolydian

2. Phrygian

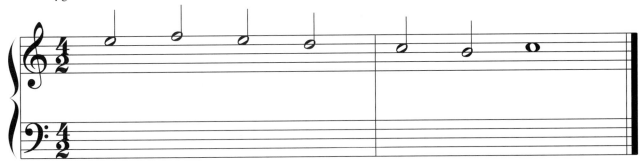

3. Whole Tone

4. Octatonic

5. Quartal/Quintal

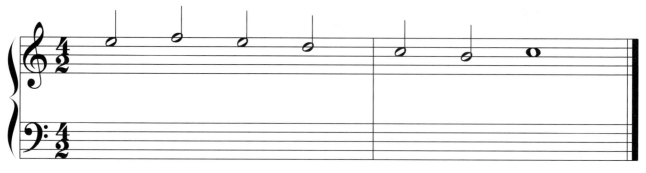

H. COMPOSITION PROJECT 1

Compose an "Octatonic Invention" using the given measures as a springboard. Restrict yourself to a single octatonic source set throughout, but create variety by highlighting subsets of different sizes and types.

I. COMPOSITION PROJECT 2

Compose a "Hexatonic Dance" using the given measures as a springboard. For example, you might repeat the given measures as an accompaniment pattern underneath a lyrical melody from the same hexatonic source set (perhaps with an occasional nonharmonic tone). Or you might use the given measures as the first utterance in a dialogue between the hands. However you proceed, consider shifts between different hexatonic collections as a means of adding variety and articulating form.

FOR FURTHER STUDY

BÉLA BARTÓK:

Eight Improvisations on Hungarian Peasant Songs (1920), op. 20, no. 6
For Children (1908–10): "I Lost My Young Couple" (part 1, no. 3); "Frisky" (part 2, no. 20)
Mikrokosmos (1932–39): "In Dorian Mode" (vol. 1, no. 32); "In Phrygian Mode" (vol. 1, no. 34); "In Lydian Mode" (vol. 2, no. 37); "In Mixolydian Mode" (vol. 2, no. 48); "Triplets in Lydian Mode" (vol. 2, no. 55); "Hands Crossing" (vol. 4, no. 99); "Game (with two five-tone scales)" (vol. 4, no. 105); "Whole-Tone Scales" (vol. 5, no. 136)
"Harvest Song," Violin Duos (1931), no. 33
Three Rondos on Slovak Folk Tunes (1927)

ERNEST BLOCH:

Macbeth (1904–09)
Sonata no. 1 for Violin and Piano (1920)
Suite Modale for Flute and Strings (1956)

ALFREDO CASELLA:

Eleven Children's Piano Pieces (1920): "Preludio" (no. 1); "Canone" (no. 3); "Siciliano" (no. 6); "Carillon" (no. 9)

CARLOS CHAVEZ:

Ten Preludes for Piano (1937), no. 1

AARON COPLAND:

"An Immortality" (1925)

CLAUDE DEBUSSY:

Piano Preludes (1910–13): "Feuilles mortes" (book 1, no. 2); "Les collines d'Anacapri" book 1, no. 5; "Voiles" (book 2, no. 2); "La fille aux cheveux de lin" (book 2, no. 8)

PAUL DUKAS:

Ariane et Barbe-bleu (1899–1907)

CHARLES IVES:

114 Songs, "The Cage," (1906), p. 144; "Mists," p. 131

OLIVIER MESSIAEN:

Quartet for the End of Time (1940–41)
Vingt regards sur l'Enfant-Jésus (1944)

DARIUS MILHAUD:

Protée, op. 17 (1913–19), "Prelude and Fugue," mm. 98–113

FRANCIS POULENC:

Album des six (1919), Valse

IGOR STRAVINSKY:

Petrushka (1910–11)
Le sacre du printemps (1911–13)
Les noces (1923)

CHAPTER 6

STRUCTURAL MODELS

6.1 INTERVAL PATTERNS

Composers of tonal music work with well-established musical resources and frameworks. Post-tonal composers must conceive resources and frameworks anew, either for a group of works, consistently within an established style and compositional practice, or from one piece to another. The first five chapters of this book concentrate on some of the resources post-tonal composers have developed and implemented. Now we turn our attention to the frameworks. A **structural model** is the organizing principle of a musical passage, possibly involving a musical analogy to a geometric shape or some sort of patterned repetition of intervals or harmonies or durations.

Example 6.1 is a transcription-translation of a structural model created by Alban Berg and sent to his mentor, Arnold Schoenberg, in 1920. On the bottom staff Berg wrote an ascending chromatic scale, or 1-cycle, starting on C_2, and then on the staff above that he notated an ascending whole-tone scale, or 2-cycle, starting on that same pitch. Because the 2-cycle has half as many notes as the 1-cycle, Berg repeated the 2-cycle on the second staff through a second octave, so that the repeating 2-cycle fills the space of two octaves with the same number of notes used by the 1-cycle to fill one octave. Berg then continued the cyclic layering with three consecutive 3-cycles on the third staff up, spanning three octaves, and four consecutive 4-cycles on the fourth staff from the bottom, spanning four octaves—all starting on the same note, C_2. As he moved upward in the chart, he continued using C_2 as the starting note for cycles of increasingly larger intervals spanning increasingly more octaves. He evidently discovered, however, that these octave expansions cannot be contained within the customary range of pitch space, so he stopped notating the cycles on the top five lines when he reached the top note on the piano (C_8), adding "etc." to indicate their conceptual continuation. The actual final note of the 12-cycle on the top line of the chart would be twelve octaves higher than C_2—that is, C_{14}, six octaves higher than the highest note on the piano!

In his annotations below and to the side of the chart, Berg points out that the patterns of repeating intervals occur in two dimensions: not only as ascending cycles on each staff, but also as chords of increasingly wider intervals from one column to the next. The unison C's in the first column, and the octave C's in the last column, correspond to the series of octaves on the top staff. The half-step chord in column two mimics the 1-cycle on the bottom staff. The whole-step chord in column 3 has its counterpart in the 2-cycle on the next-to-bottom staff, and so forth. After the tritone chord in the center column, the chords begin to recall their inverse intervals earlier in the pattern but in reverse order, as Berg's arrows indicate: the quintal chord in column 8 matches up with the quartal chord in column 6, the interval-8 chord in column 9 recalls the stacked augmented triads (interval-4 chord) in column 5, and so on.

EXAMPLE 6.1   Berg's chart of interval cycles

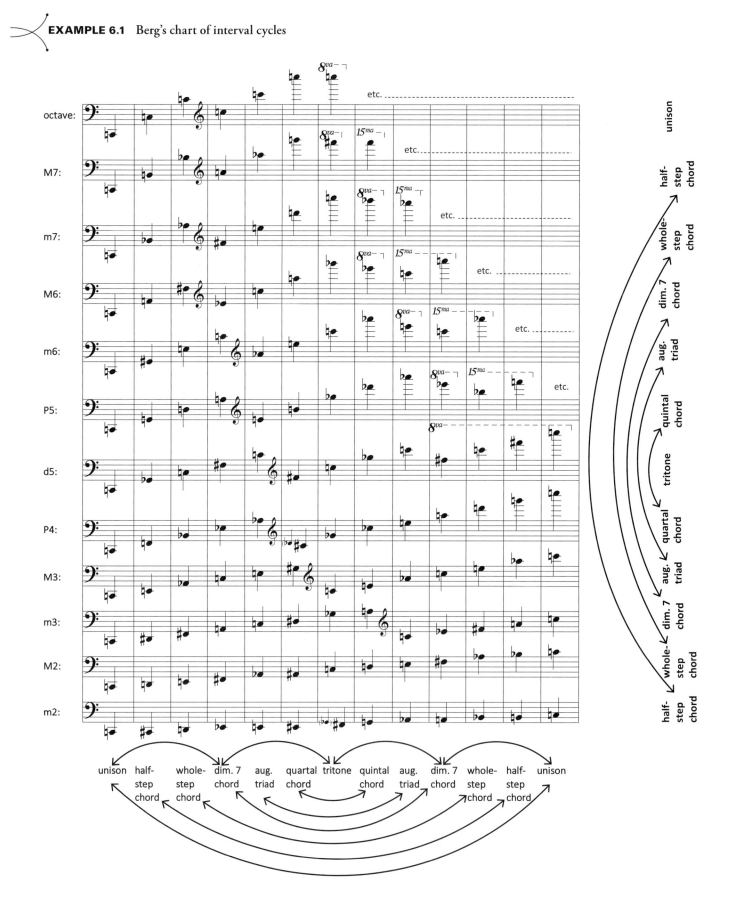

Berg humbly described the chart as a "theoretical trifle,"[1] but it was clearly a source of fascination, and he found ways to incorporate some of the chart's pitch combinations within his compositions. In other words, he used the chart as a structural model. That doesn't mean that he literally orchestrated the entire chart as a piece of music—not a possibility anyway, given its extreme upper range—but that he occasionally drew inspiration from the chart's organizing principles and combined lines of repeating intervals so that they create chords of increasing size.

In act 2 of his opera *Wozzeck*, for example, in a rapid instrumental flourish, Berg aligns portions of 1-, 2-, 3-, and 4-cycles underneath a noncyclic solo violin line (Ex. 6.2). For this realization of the structural model, he has extracted the first eight notes of the bottom four staffs of Example 6.1, transposed them up two octaves, and assigned them to the solo cello, oboe, solo viola, and clarinet, respectively. The structural model provides an underlying logic for the passage, an orderliness of intervallic relations.

EXAMPLE 6.2   Berg, *Wozzeck*, act 2, m. 380 (all parts sound as notated)

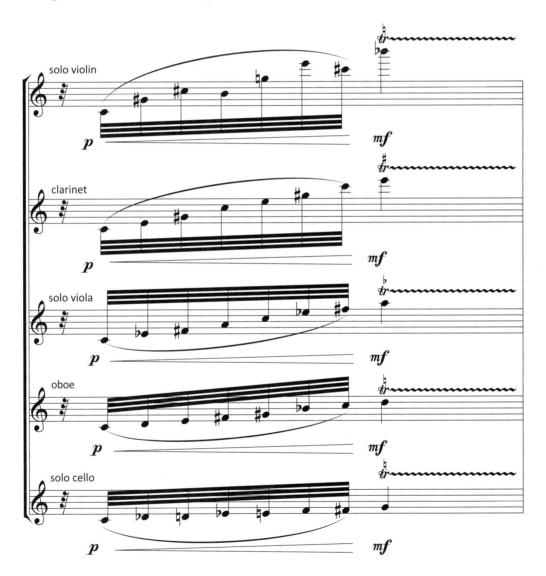

---

[1]George Perle, "Berg's Master Array of Interval Cycles," *The Musical Quarterly* 63, no. 1 (1977): 1–30. His exact words were "theoretische Spielerei."

Imagine what other compositional contexts this structural model might inspire. We could, for example, present chords taken from columns of the chart in a chorale setting, perhaps occasionally connecting chords from nonadjacent columns. The structural model would be the basis of our chord progression. Or we might pair off cycles from different lines of the model, adjacent or not, and create musical interactions between the pairs as if in dialogue. The nature of the governing structural model might be as evident as it is in the *Wozzeck* excerpt (Ex. 6.2), or it might be considerably varied, perhaps with subtle reorderings or pitch-space manipulations.

Even a brief set of intervallic combinations like those at the beginning of Berg's String Quartet op. 3 (Ex. 6.3) is traceable back to the multi-cycle structural model. In response to the second violin's opening gesture, the viola answers with three notes of an 11-cycle (A♭–G–F♯), aligned with three notes in the cello from a 7-cycle (F–C–G), forming harmonic intervals 3, 7, and E. It's much more subtle than the densely layered model, but it nevertheless has its roots in the model's orderly configuration of interval patterns.

EXAMPLE 6.3   Berg, String Quartet op. 3, opening to mvt. 1

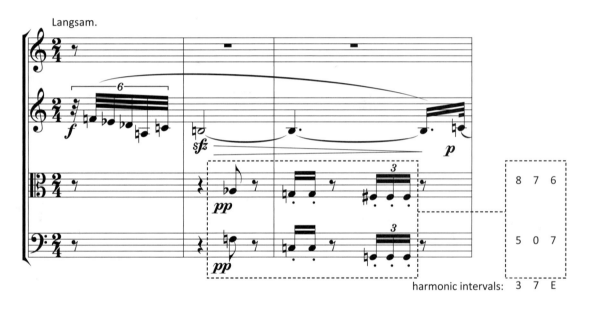

Charles Ives's conception of a cyclically based structural model focused less on the correspondence between vertical and horizontal dimensions and more on the relationships of the generating intervals. In the introduction to his song "On the Antipodes," for example, two pianists create huge chords of gradually changing interval size (Ex. 6.4). The first chord consists of ten of the twelve notes in a 7-cycle, from D_2 to F_7. For the next chord, Ives wanted to progress to a chord with slightly smaller intervals, but he apparently didn't want to build a chord only from a 6-cycle, which has only two pitch classes in it, so his second chord is a <7-6> combination cycle, spanning G_1 to G_7. This combination cycle interlocks two 1-cycles, completing the aggregate at the midway point, after one pitch-class repetition (Ex. 6.5). Ives uses only the first twelve notes of this combination cycle for his second chord, and thus duplicates pitch-class 7 at the bottom and top.

EXAMPLE 6.4   Ives, "On the Antipodes," mm. 1–4

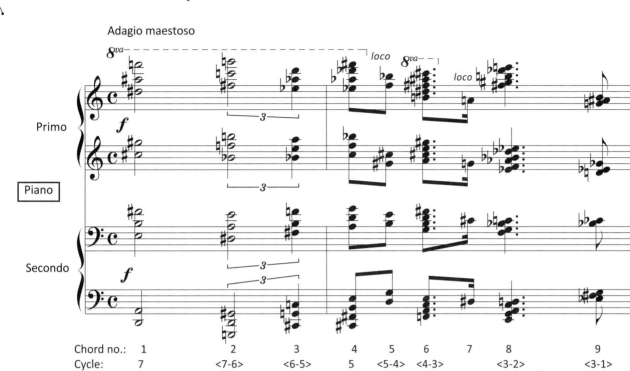

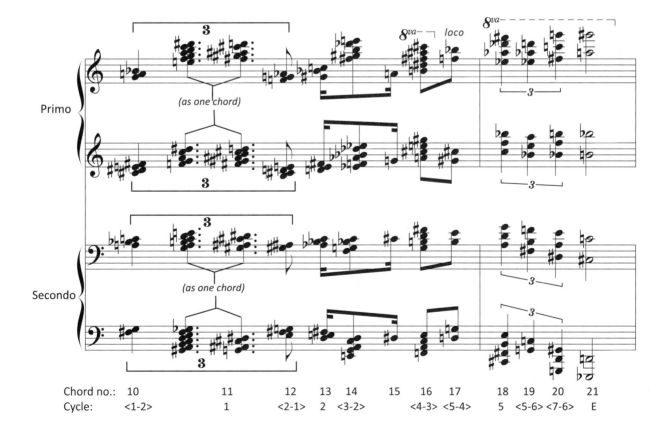

EXAMPLE 6.5 The <7-6> combination cycle

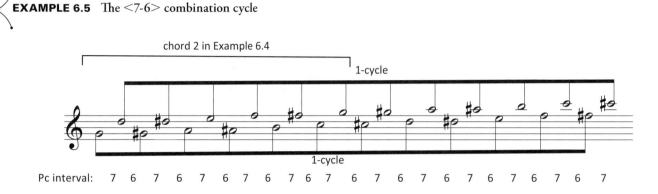

Pc interval: 7 6 7 6 7 6 7 6 7 6 7 6 7 6 7 6 7 6 7 6 7 6 7

Ives's chord 3 is a <6-5> combination cycle that interlocks 11-cycles to complete the aggregate without pc duplication, from C#$_2$ to B$_7$ (Ex. 6.6). This is the same combination cycle we observed in Messiaen's *Turangalîla-Symphonie* in Chapter 5 (Exx. 5.31, 5.32).

EXAMPLE 6.6 The <6-5> combination cycle

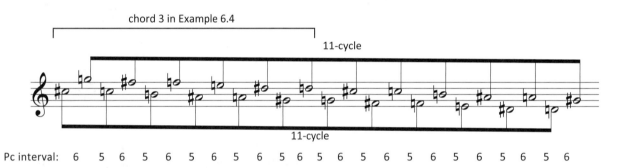

Pc interval: 6 5 6 5 6 5 6 5 6 5 6 5 6 5 6 5 6 5 6 5 6 5 6

So the <7-6> and <6-5> combination cycles enable Ives to make a suitably gradual progression of intervallic reductions in his structural model, connecting the quintal harmony at the beginning with the quartal sonority (5-cycle) in chord 4. After that are a series of chords built from combination cycles of gradually diminishing interval sizes up to the chromatic cluster at chord 11, followed by chords with gradually increasing interval sizes, almost restating the previous chord series in reverse (Ex. 6.5).[2] (Chords 14–18 repeat chords 4–8 in reverse; other chords recall previous ones without restating them exactly.) The progression ends with a stacking of interval 11's (chord 21) that has no previous counterpart.

Ives apparently didn't write out his structural model on a separate page as Berg did, but it's easy to imagine what such a model would look like. It would look like Example 6.5 in neutral rhythms, perhaps showing more complete cyclic repetitions from which selections were made for the musical setting. (Chord 1, for example, might be notated as a complete 7-cycle in the model, from which Ives selected ten of the twelve pitch classes to form his chord.) It might also include chords that could also contribute to the pattern but that weren't used for one reason or another. In the model, for example, the 2-cycle in chord 13 might have a symmetrical counterpart earlier in the progression that was skipped over in the musical realization.

---

[2]Chord 12 actually begins, from bottom to top, with intervals <2-1-1> before continuing upward with a <2-1> alternation. The sharp sign before the F$_3$ may be a notational error. If the F$_3$ is natural, chord 12 would be a representation of a <1-2> combination cycle, more precisely matching chord 10.

Indeed, Ives repeats the progression later in the song and uses more complete versions of some cycles or combination cycles. When chord 1 reappears in measure 28, for example, it's a complete 7-cycle, without missing pitch classes.

Further, the model not only supplies the logic of the mostly symmetrical chord sequence. It also unfolds much more slowly as the harmonic setting for the vocal line. Right after the first presentation of the model (Ex. 6.5), for example, the 7-cycle, <7-6> combination cycle, and <6-5> combination cycle are arpeggiated, with reorderings and embellishments, underneath the first vocal phrase (Ex. 6.7). Varied arpeggiations of chords continue up until the midway point of the pattern, where another statement of the chord sequence itself is inserted, and then the second half of the model similarly provides harmonic support for additional vocal phrases, leading up to one final, more complete, presentation of the chord sequence as the song's conclusion. The structural model essentially becomes the backbone for the entire song.

EXAMPLE 6.7   Ives, "On the Antipodes," mm. 5–6

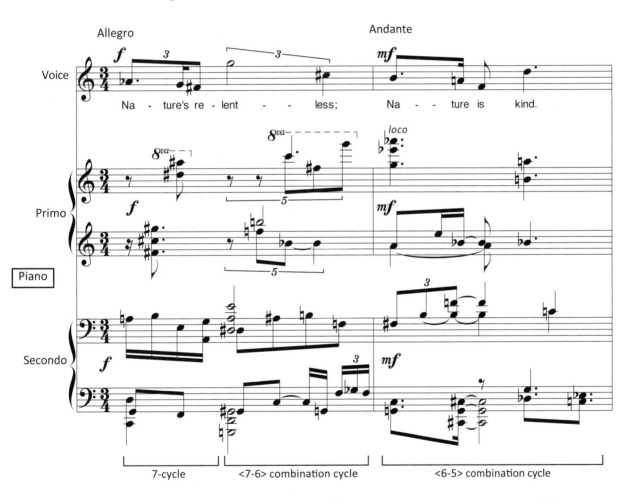

Berg's chart and Ives's chord series are part of the answer to an important question: What is a "progression" in post-tonal music? While tonal composers are able to draw from centuries of practice and well-established chord relations, post-tonal composers must define progressions using their own contextual criteria. Berg's and Ives's cyclically generated structural models provide frameworks for how particular musical moments are formed, and how they might generate progressive musical action.

STUDY QUESTIONS 6.1

1. **What is the appeal of a structural model to a post-tonal composer?**

2. **What are some basic similarities between Berg's structural model in Example 6.1 and Ives's structural model as realized in Example 6.5?**

3. **How are vertical and horizontal dimensions related in Berg's structural model in Example 6.1?**

4. **In what sense is the introduction to Ives's song in Example 6.5 a model for the entire work?**

6.2 THE WEDGE MODEL

In another song, "Like a Sick Eagle," Ives aligns a 1-cycle and a 2-cycle as if extracting a portion of Berg's chart of interval cycles (Ex. 6.1). There's no evidence that Ives actually notated any kind of separate structural model for the music, but let's imagine that he did. It might have looked something like Example 6.8, which combines two consecutive 2-cycles (stems up) with one complete 1-cycle (stems down), just like the bottom two staffs of Berg's chart but starting on B♭₃. In the song itself, Ives moves back and forth in the model to symbolize the uncertain aerial movements of a sick eagle, and at one point steps through slightly more than half of the model in order, a complete 2-cycle from F♯₄ to F♯₅ aligned with seven notes of a 1-cycle (Ex. 6.9).

EXAMPLE 6.8 Structural model for Ives, "Like a Sick Eagle," *114 Songs*

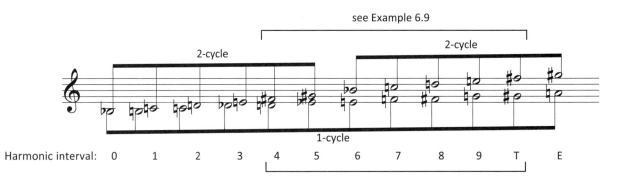

Like Berg in his annotations (Ex. 6.1), Ives is interested here in the gradually changing distances between musical lines. His harmonic intervals progress incrementally from pitch interval 4 up to T (Ex. 6.9), selecting from a more complete structural model (Ex. 6.8) that ranges from interval 0 to E. The eagle can soar up to F♯₅, forming the next-to-largest harmonic interval in the model, but is too infirm to fly any higher and starts to float back down.

With respect to the pattern of changing distances between lines, Ives's "Sick Eagle" model is not that different from **wedge voice leading**, in which identical or similar lines move simultaneously in opposite directions to unfold an incremental progression of harmonic intervals. It's a familiar pattern from tonal music, as in the converging wedge of scale figures at the end of the first movement of Beethoven's "Waldstein" sonata (Ex. 6.10a), or the diverging wedge of rich chords near the end of Gershwin's *Rhapsody in Blue* (Ex. 6.10b). The "Sick Eagle" version skews the model by unfolding gradually changing harmonic intervals between voices moving in the *same direction*.

EXAMPLE 6.9   Ives, "Like a Sick Eagle," initial vocal phrases

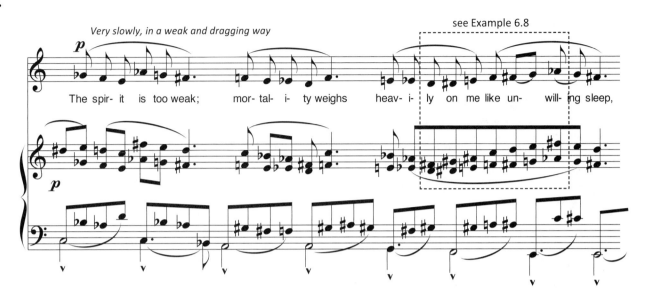

EXAMPLE 6.10   Wedges in tonal music

a. Beethoven, Piano Sonata, op. 53, mvt. 1, mm. 298–302

b. Gershwin, *Rhapsody in Blue*, last section

Let's look at a more orthodox post-tonal wedge in the first theme of Bartók's Bagatelle for Piano, op. 6, no. 2 (Ex. 6.11). First the right hand establishes a repeating $A\flat_4/B\flat_4$ dyad (labeled "a" in Ex. 6.11), and then the left hand responds with two notes just above and below the dyad, B_4 and G_4 (b), followed by other dyads that continue to wedge outward: $C_5/G\flat_4$ (c), $D\flat_5/F_4$ (d), and $D_5/F\flat_4$ (e). The progress of the expanding wedge leads us to expect that the final $E\flat_5$ of measure 4 will be paired with an $E\flat_4$, but instead we hear a heavily accented $E\flat_4$ at the beginning of measure 5, repeated for emphasis in measure 6.

EXAMPLE 6.11   Bartók, *14 Bagatelles* for piano, op. 6, no. 2, mm. 1–6

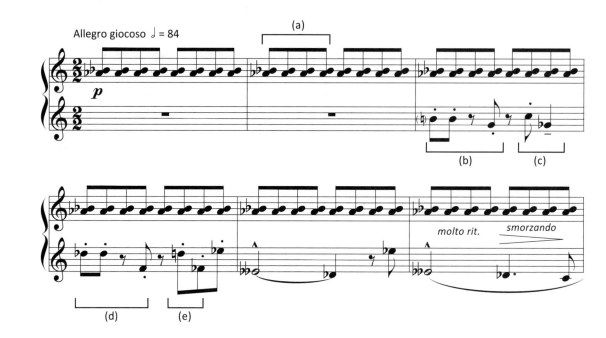

So the structural model for this melody would be a wedge of chromatic lines expanding outward from A_4 (Ex. 6.12). Bartók's music features each of the five dyads of the model (labeled a–e in the examples) plus the final $E\flat_5$ but playfully avoids the single note on which the model begins. You might say that the A_4 is conspicuous by its absence.

EXAMPLE 6.12   Structural model for Example 6.11

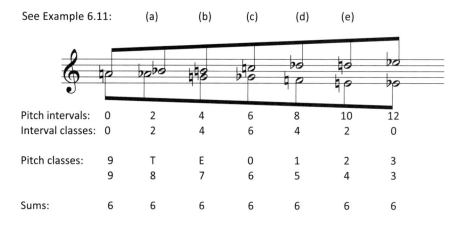

See Example 6.11:		(a)	(b)	(c)	(d)	(e)	
Pitch intervals:	0	2	4	6	8	10	12
Interval classes:	0	2	4	6	4	2	0
Pitch classes:	9	T	E	0	1	2	3
	9	8	7	6	5	4	3
Sums:	6	6	6	6	6	6	6

Let's explore this wedge model further. Its harmonic intervals increase by two in pitch space, from pitch intervals 0 through 12; the progression of interval classes is symmetrical, 0–2–4–6–4–2–0. The starting note is called the **axis of inversion**, or **inversional axis**, or **axis of symmetry**. This A_4 axis is the pitch-space midpoint between the notes of each of the dyads (a–e in Ex. 6.12) and between the two notes of the final Eb_4/Eb_5 octave. We can say that this model exhibits pitch-space symmetry "about" A_4.

Because the initial A_4 belongs to both wedge voices, it's paired with itself at the beginning, just as the Eb is paired with its octave at the end. Notes that pair with themselves within a wedge are known as **singletons**. The distance between the two singletons in this type of wedge is always a tritone, ic 6. As pitch classes, the mod-12 sums of the singletons with themselves, and of the notes in the dyads with each other, will always be the same, following the principle of the index number between inversionally equivalent sets that we studied in previous chapters. In this case, the constant sum is 6: $9 + 9$ and $3 + 3$ for the singletons, $T + 8$ (a), $E + 7$ (b), $0 + 6$ (c), $1 + 5$ (d), and $2 + 4$ (e) for the dyads. For that reason, we'll refer to this wedge model as the **6-wedge**.

Either singleton can be an axis of inversion for the same wedge type. In other words, if we know that a 6-wedge fans out from pc 9 (Ex. 6.12), we also know that a different 6-wedge can start a tritone away from that, at pc 3 (Ex. 6.13). Regardless of axis, both versions of the 6-wedge feature exactly the same sum-6 pitch-class pairs but in reverse order: compare the sum-6 pc pairs in Example 6.12 from left to right with the sum-6 pc pairs in Example 6.13 from right to left. Or think of it this way: transposing the model by T_6 preserves the pc pairs and index number (Ex. 6.13 is T_6 of Ex. 6.12 and vice versa).

EXAMPLE 6.13   A different 6-wedge

Pitch intervals:	0	2	4	6	8	10	12
Interval classes:	0	2	4	6	4	2	0
Pitch classes:	3	4	5	6	7	8	9
	3	2	1	0	E	T	9
Sums:	6	6	6	6	6	6	6

Any wedge with an even index number (including 0) works the same way. The 0-wedge, 2-wedge, 4-wedge, 6-wedge, 8-wedge, or 10-wedge each includes two singletons that sum with themselves to equal the index number and five dyads whose elements sum together to equal the index number (Ex. 6.14). Any of these wedges can be reconfigured to make the other singleton the axis of symmetry, without changing the index number.

EXAMPLE 6.14   Wedge models with even index numbers, including 0

0-WEDGE

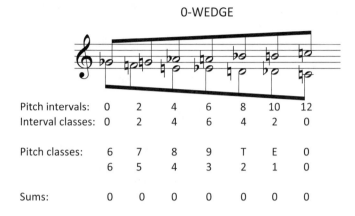

Pitch intervals:	0	2	4	6	8	10	12
Interval classes:	0	2	4	6	4	2	0
Pitch classes:	6	7	8	9	T	E	0
	6	5	4	3	2	1	0
Sums:	0	0	0	0	0	0	0

2-WEDGE

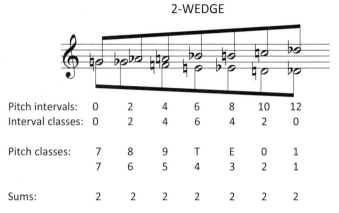

Pitch intervals:	0	2	4	6	8	10	12
Interval classes:	0	2	4	6	4	2	0
Pitch classes:	7	8	9	T	E	0	1
	7	6	5	4	3	2	1
Sums:	2	2	2	2	2	2	2

4-WEDGE

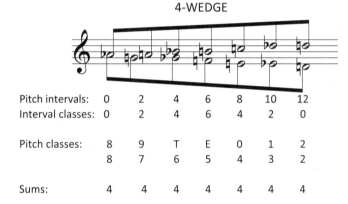

Pitch intervals:	0	2	4	6	8	10	12
Interval classes:	0	2	4	6	4	2	0
Pitch classes:	8	9	T	E	0	1	2
	8	7	6	5	4	3	2
Sums:	4	4	4	4	4	4	4

6-WEDGE

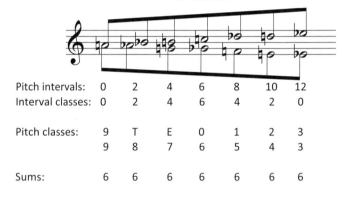

Pitch intervals:	0	2	4	6	8	10	12
Interval classes:	0	2	4	6	4	2	0
Pitch classes:	9	T	E	0	1	2	3
	9	8	7	6	5	4	3
Sums:	6	6	6	6	6	6	6

8-WEDGE

Pitch intervals:	0	2	4	6	8	10	12
Interval classes:	0	2	4	6	4	2	0
Pitch classes:	T	E	0	1	2	3	4
	T	9	8	7	6	5	4
Sums:	8	8	8	8	8	8	8

10-WEDGE

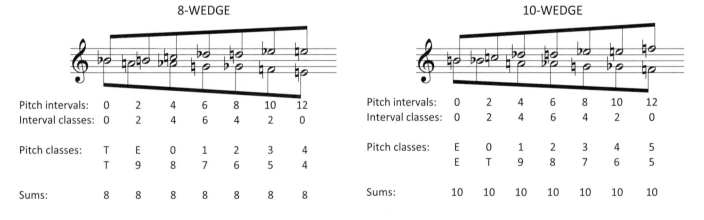

Pitch intervals:	0	2	4	6	8	10	12
Interval classes:	0	2	4	6	4	2	0
Pitch classes:	E	0	1	2	3	4	5
	E	T	9	8	7	6	5
Sums:	10	10	10	10	10	10	10

The wedges with odd-numbered index numbers emanate from an ic-1 dyad rather than from a single note, forming identical arrays of odd-numbered harmonic intervals (Ex. 6.15). You might prefer to imagine that the axis of inversion for these wedges falls in the cracks between the two notes of a half step. Corresponding notes in the model form six different dyads, not singletons.

EXAMPLE 6.15   Wedge models with odd index numbers

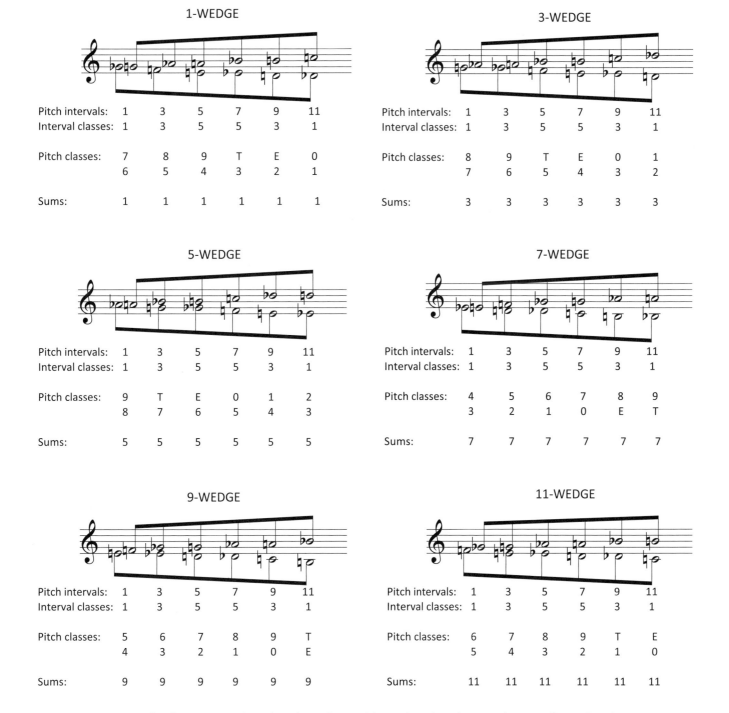

Like the even-numbered wedges, these odd-numbered wedges can be reconfigured without changing the index number, by renotating the final ic 1 as a half step and using that dyad as the initiating axis. Transposing the model by T_6 has the same effect.

Realizations of wedge models in post-tonal literature rarely preserve every detail of order and voice leading. As in Bartók's Bagatelle melody (Ex. 6.11), something about the model is usually embellished or implied. The second movement of Berg's String Quartet op. 3 begins with a portion of a contracting 8-wedge, played pizzicato in the second violin and cello, that is submerged among bowed non-wedging lines in the other two instruments (Ex. 6.16).

Although relatively inconspicuous when it first occurs, the wedge model gains resonance as the movement progresses, in further bursts and snippets of assorted wedging actions.

EXAMPLE 6.16   Berg, String Quartet op. 3, mvt. 2, mm. 1–2

The seventh song from Schoenberg's *Book of the Hanging Gardens*, op. 15 (a collection also known as the *George-Lieder*) ends with a series of trichords in the piano in which two of the three notes almost always participate in a contracting 0-wedge (Ex. 6.17). In the first three chords, the wedge occurs overtly in the outer voices (C$_5$–B$_4$–B♭$_4$ against C$_4$–C♯$_4$–D$_4$), completing a phrase, but then as the piece's final phrase begins, the lower wedge note moves to the inner voice. The wedge continues in this fashion up to the axis note G♭$_4$, missing only F$_4$ from a complete realization of the model.

EXAMPLE 6.17   Schoenberg, op. 15, no. 7, mm. 14–19

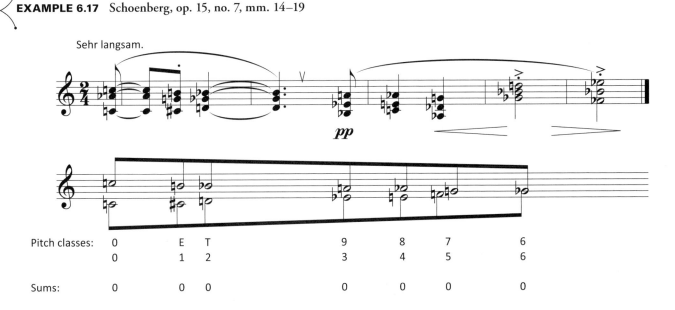

As few as two different chords can be enough to invoke, or at least hint at, a wedge model. In the first of his opus 5 String Quartet pieces, Webern uses wedging motions to connect eighth-note chords, played with double stops in each instrument (Ex. 6.18). Individually, the first violin, viola, and cello, create mini-wedges of their own. (For example, the first violin plays two dyads from a 10-wedge: $D_4/G\#_4$ wedging out to $C\#_4/A_4$.) Because the instruments registrally overlap, however, it makes more sense to collect notes together from different instruments to make separate multi-voice wedges. In the upper register, two rising voices ($G\#$–A_4 in the first violin, F_4–$F\#_4$ in second violin) oppose one falling voice (D_4–$C\#_4$ in first violin), and in the lower register, three rising voices (Bb_3–B_3 in viola, A_3–Bb_3 in second violin, G_3–$G\#_3$ in cello) complement two falling voices (E_3–Eb_3 in viola, $C\#_3$–C_3 in cello).

EXAMPLE 6.18   Webern, *Five Movements* for string quartet, op. 5, mvt. 1, mm. 4–6

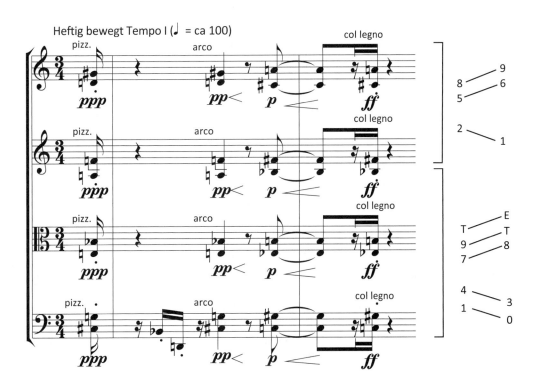

A primary theme in Berg's *Altenberg Lieder* illustrates other typical variants on the wedge model (Ex. 6.19). The melody begins with the axis pitch, C_4, and quickly states two upper and two lower surrounding pitches as if starting to unfold a melodic wedge similar to that in Bartók's Bagatelle (Ex. 6.11). After two more notes of the model (A_3 and $E\flat_4$), however, the melody suddenly leaps upward to a different register. The next five notes—$A\flat_4$, G_5, $F\sharp_5$, F_5, and E_5—are essentially a continuation of the lower arm of the wedge but in the upper register and extending beyond the normal terminal note for this wedge. It's as if Berg has stolen notes from the upper arm of the standard model and packed them in the lower arm, drawing attention to the theft with an expressive shift to a new area of pitch space.

EXAMPLE 6.19   Berg, *Altenberg Lieder*, op. 4, no. 1, viola, mm. 10–15

STUDY QUESTIONS 6.2

1. **Which types of wedges always have singletons?**

2. **In wedges with singletons, what are the two possible axis notes?**

3. **How are inversional axes typically defined in non-singleton wedges?**

4. **What are the wedge models (as shown in Examples 6.14 and 6.15) for the given pitch strings?**

   4.1. $<G_4–A\flat_4–G_4–F\sharp_4–G_4–A_4–G_4–F_4–G_4–B\flat_4–E_4–G_4–B_4>$
   4.2. $<B_3–C_4–B_3–C_4–B\flat_3–C\sharp_4–B\flat_3–C\sharp_4–A_3–D_4–A\flat_3–D\sharp_4–G_3>$
   4.3. $<F\sharp_4–G_4–E_4–A_4–C\sharp_4–C_5–F_3–G\sharp_5>$
   4.4. $<C\sharp_4–C_4–D\sharp_4–B\flat_3–D_4–B_3–E_4–A_3–F_4–G\sharp_3–F\sharp_4–G_3>$
   4.5. $<D_3–D_4–D\sharp_3–D\flat_4–E_3–C_4–F\sharp_3–B\flat_3–G_3–A_3–G\sharp_3>$

6.3   GENERAL INVERSIONAL SYMMETRY

The most distinctive, and compositionally inviting, aspect of a wedge is its pitch-space symmetry. As voices move by equivalent distances in opposite directions, they articulate equivalent pitch intervals above and below an axis. We can't say that the axis represents any sort of "tonic" in the conventional sense, but we can regard the axis as a very important note, possibly a point of centricity, that can help give focus and coherence to a post-tonal soundscape.

Pitch-space symmetries may also occur without literal chromatic wedges. Any motive, theme, or chord, regardless of its structuring intervals, may be combined or otherwise associated with a mirror of itself. The result may or may not involve a wedge-like voice-leading pattern. Nevertheless, a wedge can still lurk in the background as a structural model for basic inversional symmetry.

Bartók's piano piece "Minor Seconds, Major Sevenths," for example, begins with a tetrachordal cluster moving quickly to half steps above and below, establishing symmetry about the $G\sharp_4/A_4$ axis (Ex. 6.20). This chromatic mass is then repeated twice before continuing an outward movement to D_5 and $E\flat_4$ in measure 2, subsequently stretched farther to $E\flat_5/D_6$ in the right hand and $E\flat_3/D_4$ in the left hand.

Let's relate this music to the 5-wedge about $G\sharp_4/A_4$. The opening tetrachordal cluster combines the first two dyads of the model, labeled (a) and (b) in Example 6.20, and the subsequent outward movement states the (c) dyad. But the (d) and (e) dyads aren't sounded at all in the music, as the second measure dwells on different presentations of the model's (f) dyad.

EXAMPLE 6.20   Bartók, "Minor Seconds, Major Sevenths," *Mikrokosmos* 144 (vol. 6), mm. 1–2

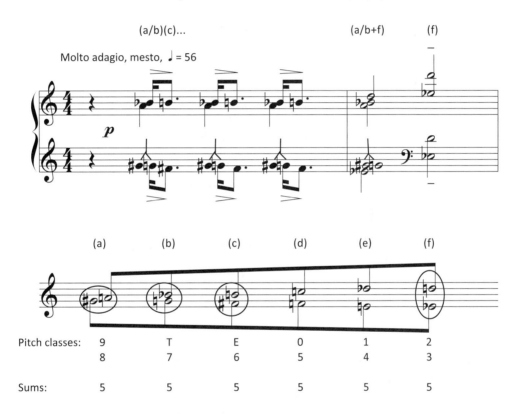

So, despite the overall wedge-like expansion, it's not completely accurate to say that these measures are a "realization" of the 5-wedge. Only four of the model's six dyads occur, and we don't get a pervasive sense of uniform chromatic movement among diverging lines. Rather than providing a literal voice-leading model, the 5-wedge simply shows the range of possibilities within this particular inversional environment. When we encounter music such as this, it's useful to know all the possible inversional pairings about a given axis, even if they don't all appear in the score.

Let's say, for example, that we want to investigate the inversional symmetry in measure 7 of the third of Webern's *Five Movements* for String Quartet op. 5 (Ex. 6.21). We can see at first glance, and/or hear at first listening, that the cello is answering the first violin in inversion, one eighth note later. So there is a wedging motion, but it's not a strict unfolding of the wedge model. Rather, the violin alternates pitch intervals −4 and −1 (that's a segment of the <8-E> combination cycle), while the cello mirrors this, alternating +4 and +1 (<4-1> combination cycle). In set-class terms, any three consecutive notes in either instrument forms a member of (015). So, what, specifically, is the inversional relationship between the lines, and what is the inversional axis?

EXAMPLE 6.21   Webern, *Five Movements* for string quartet, op. 5, mvt. 3, m. 7

	(a)	(b)	(c)	(d)	(e)	(f)
Pitch classes:	1	2	3	4	5	6
	0	E	T	9	8	7
Sums:	1	1	1	1	1	1

First, line up corresponding notes. The violin's initial $C\sharp_6$ is answered by the cello's C_2. So the index number is the mod-12 sum of these two pitch classes: $1 + 0 = 1$. Any other pair of corresponding notes (for example, the second notes of both lines, A_5 and E_2, or the last notes of both lines, $B\flat_4$ and $E\flat_3$) will also add to 1.

Now for the axis. Since we're working with an odd index number, we know that the inversional axis will be a dyad, not a singleton. We also know that there are two ways to add pitch classes together to equal that index number, each T_6 of the other. So the two possible axis dyads for index 1 are the two ic 1 dyads whose pitch classes can be added together to total 1: (0 + 1) and (6 + 7). Choose any two corresponding notes in the inversional lines and find the 0/1 or 6/7 dyad that lies precisely halfway between them. Any pair of corresponding notes will do; let's choose the last notes of the two lines, $B\flat_4$ and $E\flat_3$. The pitch-space midpoint between $B\flat_4$ and $E\flat_3$ is $C_4/C\sharp_4$. This 0/1 dyad is the axis of inversion for the entire inversional mirroring.

So to display the underlying inversional relations, we'll use $C_4/C\sharp_4$ as the starting point for a 1-wedge (Ex. 6.21). Again, we're not consulting this wedge as a voice-leading model, expecting to find these specific notes in pitch space. We're using the model to help keep track of all the inversional dyads between two musical objects in the index-1 environment. By consulting the wedge model, for example, we can easily determine that Webern's inversional lines involve five of the six possible dyads: the first notes of the lines comprise the first dyad in the model (a), a pairing of the second notes in the lines (A_5/E_2) realizes the fourth dyad in the model (d), and so forth.

An inversional pairing at the beginning of Bartók's piano piece "From the Island of Bali" occurs in consecutive measures, like an inversional canon, although the music doesn't continue canonically (Ex. 6.22). The left hand begins with pitch intervals −1/−5/−1/+1/+5, and the right hand responds with the same pitch intervals in reverse directions, +1/+5/+1/−1/−5. So we know that the notes in both hands can be displayed on a wedge model, even though the music exhibits no chromatic lines in contrary motion.

EXAMPLE 6.22 Bartók, "From the Island of Bali," *Mikrokosmos* 109 (vol. 4), mm. 1–2

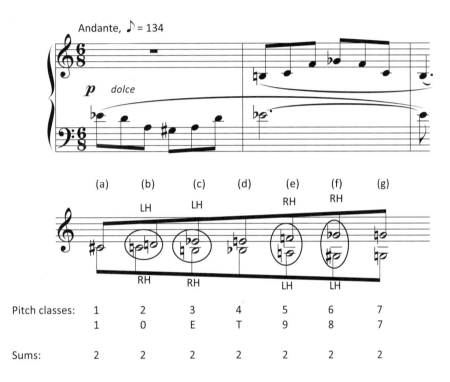

As before, start by looking at two corresponding notes. Let's take the first notes in both hands, $E\flat_4$ and B_3, because they are obvious correspondents and are very close together (making it easy to locate the axis pitch). Their mod-12 sum is $3 + 11 = 2$, and the pitch-space midpoint between them is $C\sharp_4$. The underlying model is a 2-wedge starting on $C\sharp_4$ (Ex. 6.22).

Because the hands overlap—the highest left-hand notes are higher than the lowest right-hand notes—both the upper and lower strands of the model include notes from both hands. The (b) and (c) dyads (Ex. 6.22) have left-hand notes above right-hand notes, and the (e) and (f) dyads have right-hand notes above left-hand notes. The (d) dyad isn't represented at all, nor is the axis pitch (a) or the other singleton (g). The four dyads that are used combine to complete the octatonic collection OCT_{23}.

One common way of compactly realizing a collection of inversional relations is to place them in a large inversionally symmetrical chord, as Berg does at the end of his Piece for Clarinet and Piano, op. 5, no. 4 (Ex. 6.23). The ending begins with the clarinet's falling pitch interval 10, $G\flat_5$–$A\flat_4$, which is echoed first in the next measure, three half steps lower, by the clarinet's $E\flat_5$–F_4, and then again an octave lower at the end of the bar. The clarinet's two middle notes in this measure, F_4 and $G\flat_4$, articulate the pitch-space midpoint of the piano's symmetrical chord, and thus can be interpreted as the axis for an 11-wedge to model the symmetrical relations. So the (a) dyad appears in the clarinet, while the (b) and (f) dyads comprise the piano chord. Further, the clarinet's highest and lowest notes in this measure

(E♭₅ and A♭₃) also surround the F₄/G♭₄ axis at equal distances, reversing the notes of the (c) dyad and placing them at the upper and lower extremes of the entire symmetrical display.

EXAMPLE 6.23 Berg, *Piece for Clarinet and Piano*, op. 5, no. 4, mm. 18–20 (sounds as notated)

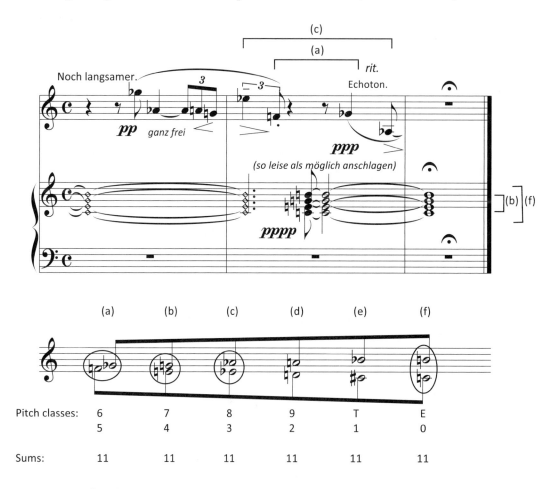

Pitch classes:	(a)	(b)	(c)	(d)	(e)	(f)
	6	7	8	9	T	E
	5	4	3	2	1	0
Sums:	11	11	11	11	11	11

Some of Webern's symmetrical configurations are a little less orderly, a little more rhythmically dispersed. At the beginning of the third of his Six Bagatelles for string quartet, op. 9, for example, he creates index-10 symmetry in three configurations, illustrated using boxes in Example 6.24:

Box 1:   First, the piece begins on an axis tone, F₄ in the viola (that's the (a) singleton in Ex. 6.24), and then the viola's E₄, A♭₄, and D₄ (excluding the viola's highest note, which associates with the violins) plus the cello's F♯₄ surround the axis with dyads (b) and (d) of the 10-wedge model. (The cello's harmonic sounds two octaves higher.)

Box 2:   At the same time in the upper register, the viola's E♭₅ along with the second violin's C♯₅/A₅ and the G₅ of the first violin establish index-10 symmetry surrounding a different (implied) axis, F₅, representing dyads (c) and (e) of the model.

Box 3:   That leaves out the upper first-violin note, which is subsequently associated with the next note in that instrument, B♭₃, in a symmetrical pairing surrounding the second violin's B₄, which is the other singleton in the index-10 model, the tritone relation to the previous axes. The F₅ occurring in alternation with the B₄ in the second violin is, of course, the implied axis tone in Box 2.

EXAMPLE 6.24 Webern, *Six Bagatelles* for string quartet, op. 9, no. 3, mm. 1–2

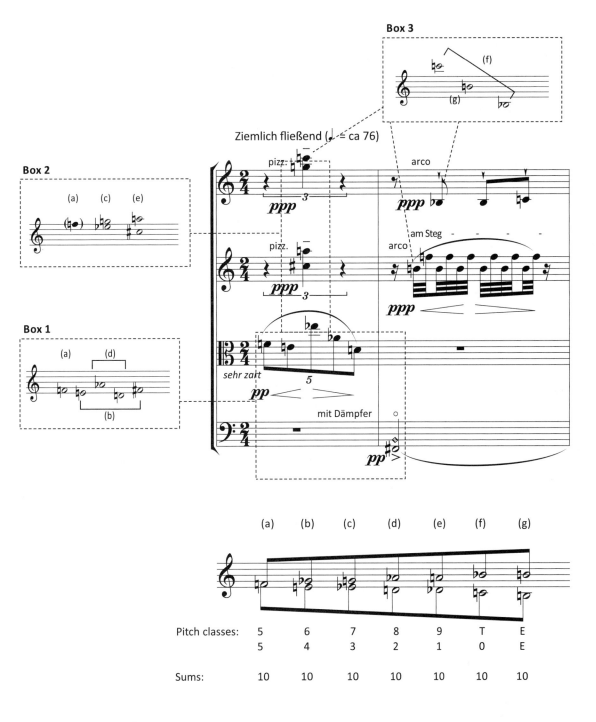

STUDY QUESTIONS 6.3

1. How can any set, of any size or type, be used to create a symmetrical chord?

2. If the tetrachord $<A_4–B_4–D_5–F\sharp_5>$ appears at the top of a symmetrical chord about an A_4 axis, what are the chord's other notes? What is the wedge model that summarizes the chord's symmetrical relations?

3. If the tetrachord $<\flat D_2–\flat A_2–C_3–F_3>$ appears at the bottom of a symmetrical chord about an implied $G_3/G\sharp_3$ axis, what are the chord's other notes? What is the wedge model that summarizes the chord's symmetrical relations?

4. In our study of the excerpt from Webern's string quartet movement shown in Example 6.21, we observed that the first pair of corresponding notes, $C\sharp_6/C_2$, realizes the "a" dyad in the model, and that the second pair of corresponding notes, A_5/E_2, realizes the "d" dyad. What are the remaining five pairs of corresponding notes in the excerpt, and which dyads from the model do they realize?

VOCABULARY

axis of inversion (inversional axis, axis of symmetry)   structural model

n-wedge (n = 0–11)   wedge voice leading

singleton

EXERCISES

A. CYCLIC JUXTAPOSITIONS

Add an interval cycle above the given cycle to form the specified pitch intervals between corresponding notes. Write your notes as half notes with stems pointing upward and beamed together. Above and below the staff, identify both cycle types.

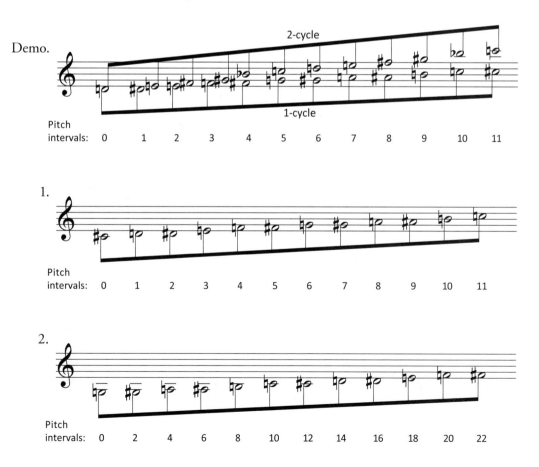

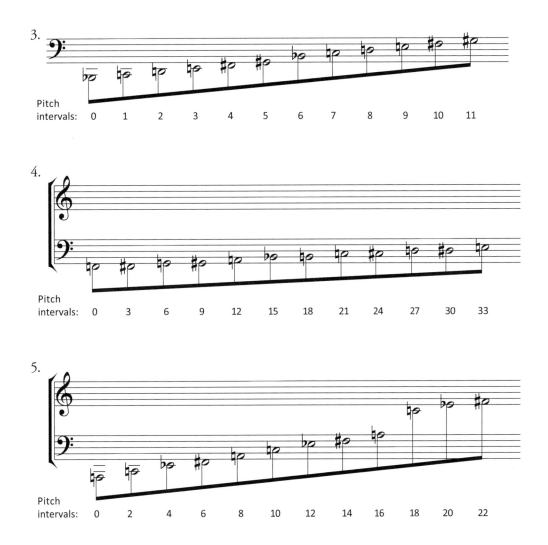

B. INTERVAL PATTERNS

Write a pitch-class integer in each blank to create a potential structural model with two different patterns of repeating pitch-class intervals, one in all the rows, the other in all the columns. Patterns could be single-interval cycles or combination cycles.

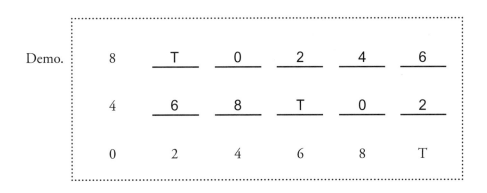

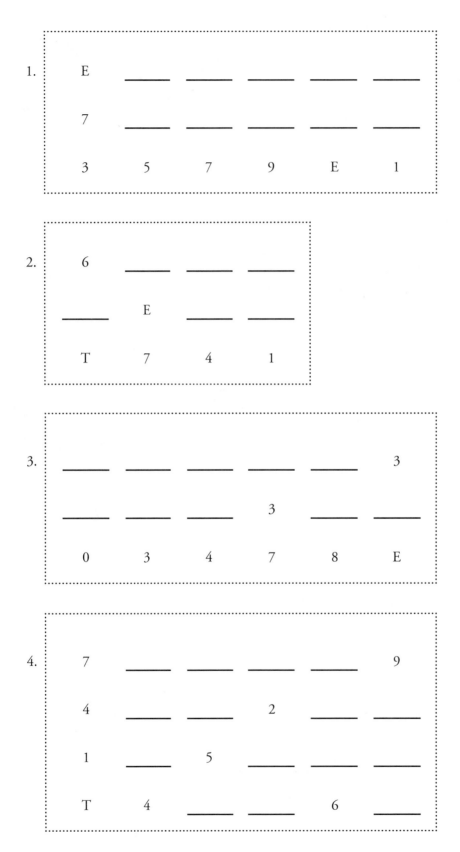

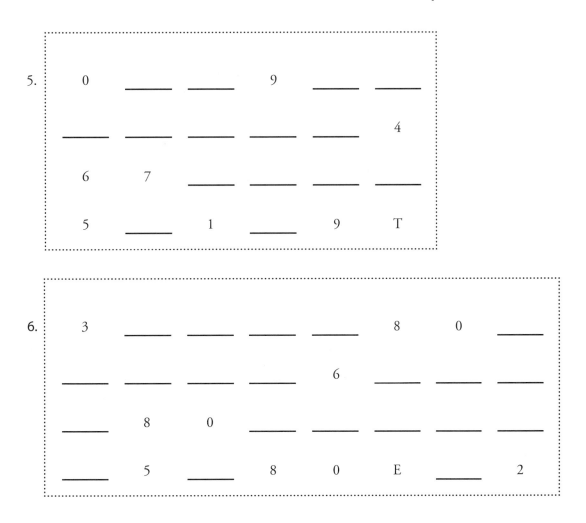

C. WEDGE REALIZATIONS

Notate and identify the wedge model underlying each excerpt and respond to any questions or instructions.

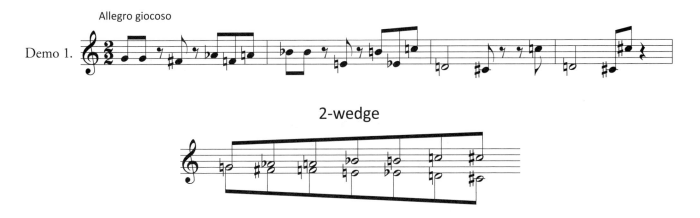

Demo 2.

5-wedge

1. Leonard Bernstein (1918–1990), "Quiet," *Candide* (1956)

2. Sofia Gubaidulina (b. 1931), String Quartet no. 1 (1971), I, R6, mm. 4–7

The first violin, second violin, and cello are primarily responsible for the wedge realization.
What happens in the viola part?

3. György Ligeti (1923–2006), Invention for Piano (1948), mm. 1–3

Notate and identify the *two* wedge models realized in the first two measures.
How are these two wedge models related?
What wedges are implied in measure 3?

4. Charles Ives (1874–1954), "Soliloquy" (c. 1917), excerpt from vocal line

Hint: See Example 6.19

5. Béla Bartók (1881–1945), String Quartet no. 5 (1934), mvt. 5, mm. 189–95

D. ANALYSIS OF STRUCTURAL MODELS

1. Alban Berg (1885–1935), "Der Glühende," voice and piano, op. 2, no. 2 (1910), mm. 1–4

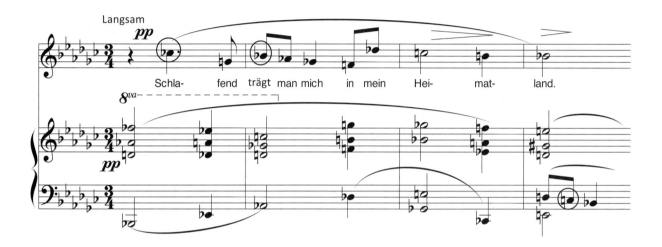

1.1 View the passage as a series of seven chords, expressed by voice and piano together. The circled notes are nonharmonic tones, not included in those chords. What are the chords (normal form, prime form)? What are the possibilities for relating them as pitch-class sets?

1.2 Make a rectangular structural model for the passage using pitch-class integers. Start with the normal form of the first chord from bottom to top on the left side of the rectangle. Then write the subsequent chords, also notated vertically, to fill out the rectangle. Structure the chords in your model so that they demonstrate minimal voice-leading movement from one chord to the next. (They won't all be in normal form from bottom to top.) The lines of your model will not necessarily be the same as the musical lines in the song.

1.3 Where and how does Berg's music highlight aspects of the model, and where and how does the music draw attention to aspects of the model that may not be immediately apparent or prominent?

2. Charles Ives (1874–1954), *Tone Roads*, no. 3 (c. 1914), mm. 24–26

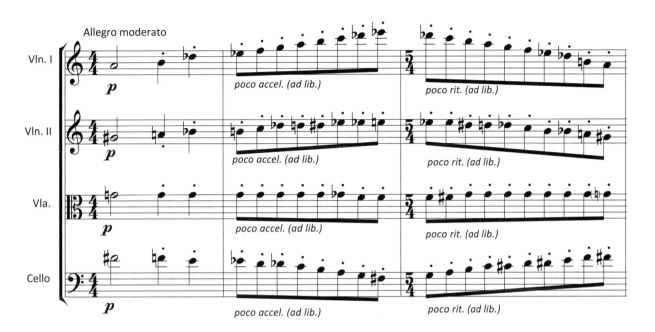

Describe the structural model. Compare it to Berg's structural model partially realized in *Wozzeck* (Ex. 6.1) and Ives's structural model for "On the Antipodes" (Ex. 6.4).

E. CREATING INVERSIONAL SYMMETRY

Demo. Construct a chord that's symmetrical about F_4 and exhibits the following intervallic structure: 5–2–3–6–5–5–6–3–2–5. Highlight the axis tone by notating it differently than the others. Notate and identify the wedge model for the inversional symmetry.

1. **Construct a chord that's symmetrical about $A_3/B\flat_3$ and exhibits the following intervallic structure: 6–7–4–2–3–1–3–2–4–7–6. Highlight the axis tones by notating them differently than the others. Notate and identify the wedge model for the inversional symmetry.**

2. **Construct an eleven-pitch-class chord that's symmetrical about D$_4$ and includes the following:**

   - Notes surrounding the axis by whole steps above and below
   - E♭$_3$
   - B♭$_4$
   - Intervals 8–8 between the bottom three notes

   Highlight the axis tone by notating it differently than the others. Beneath the chord, specify its intervallic structure. Notate and identify the wedge model for the inversional symmetry.

3. **Imagine that this is the beginning of a leading voice in an inversional canon:**

   (a) Notate a two-measure answer to this voice in inversion (exhibiting the same melodic intervals in opposite directions) that begins one measure after the leading voice begins and pairs with the leading voice to create symmetry about D$_4$. Notate and identify the wedge model for the inversional symmetry.

   (b) Notate a two-measure answer to this voice in inversion (exhibiting the same melodic intervals in opposite directions) that begins on A$_3$ one measure after the leading voice begins. Notate and identify the wedge model for the inversional symmetry, starting with the inversional axis between the two voices.

F. RECOGNIZING INVERSIONAL SYMMETRY

Demo. Locate the axis of symmetry of the given symmetrical chord. Notate the inversional relations as a wedge model beginning on the axis. Identify the model ("X-wedge," where X = index number), and circle the dyads in the model that are part of the chord. Beneath the chord, specify its intervallic structure.

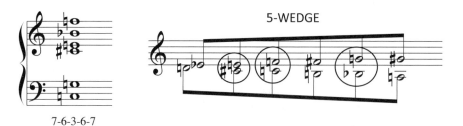

5-WEDGE

7-6-3-6-7

1. Symmetrical Chords

Locate the axis of symmetry of the given symmetrical chord. Notate the inversional relations as a wedge model beginning on the axis. Identify the model ("X-wedge," where X = index number), and circle the dyads in the model that are part of the chord. Beneath the chord, specify its intervallic structure.

2. Béla Bartók (1881–1945), "From the Island of Bali," *Mikrokosmos* 109 (vol. 4), mm. 40–43

Locate the axis of symmetry of the passage. Notate the inversional relations as a wedge model beginning on the axis. Identify the model ("X-wedge," where X = index number), and circle the dyads in the model that are employed in the music.

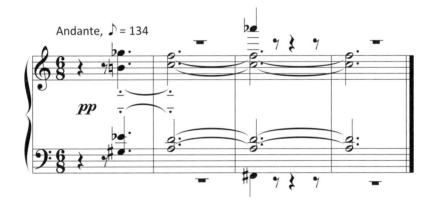

3. Vincent Persichetti (1915–1987), *Mirror Etude* no. 3 (1980), mm. 1–2

Locate the axis of symmetry of the passage. Notate the inversional relations as a wedge model beginning on the axis. Identify the model ("X-wedge," where X = index number). Above the model, label its components with lower-case letters. (Because the index number is even, you'll use letters "a" through "g"—a and g will be singletons, b–f will be dyads.) Annotate the score with lowercase letters, showing the musical occurrences of components of the model.

4. Charles Ives (1874–1954), "Harvest Home," *Three Harvest Home Chorales*, no. 1, (c. 1902), mm. 6–10

Locate the axis of symmetry between corresponding notes in the two canonic voices. Notate the inversional relations as a wedge model beginning on the axis. Identify the model ("X-wedge," where X = index number).

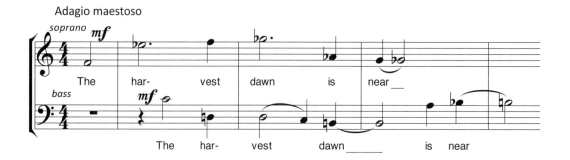

5. Arnold Schoenberg (1874–1951), "Parodie," *Pierrot Lunaire* (1912), initial phrases

The clarinet (which sounds as notated) answers the viola in inversion, with the minor exception of the written-out embellishments. Locate the symmetrical axis between corresponding notes in the two lines. Notate the inversional relations as a wedge model beginning on the axis. Identify the model ("X-wedge," where X = index number).

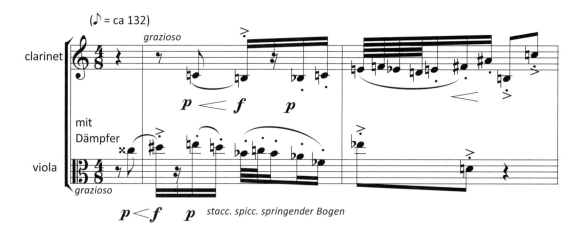

6. Dmitri Shostakovich (1906–1975), Sonata for Violin and Piano (1968), mvt. 1, mm. 1–8

Locate the axis of symmetry between corresponding notes in inversionally equivalent musical units. Notate the inversional relations as a wedge model beginning on the axis. Identify the model ("X-wedge," where X = index number).

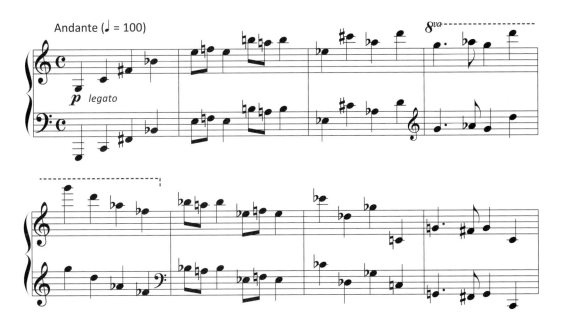

G. BÉLA BARTÓK (1881–1945), "DRAGONS' DANCE," *MIKROKOSMOS* 72 (VOL. 3)

Molto pesante, ♩ = 104

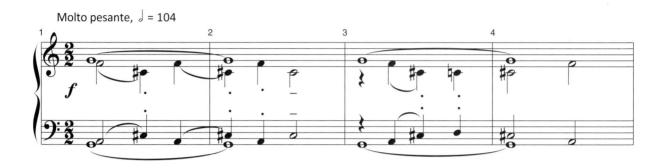

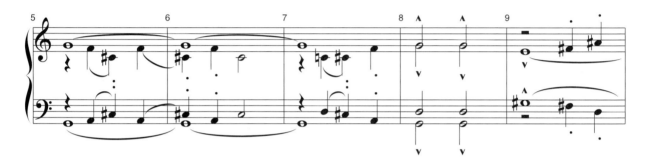

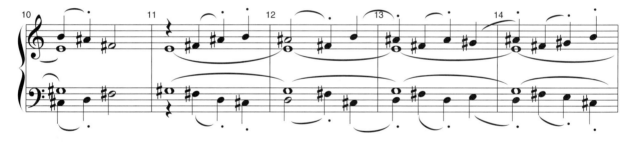

1. Listen to the piece several times without the score, noticing places where musical changes occur. Then listen several times while following the score. What are the primary sectional divisions?

2. Look closely at the first subphrase, measures 1 and 2. Notice Bartók's division of the music into four voices. How are these voices grouped into two pairs in measures 1 and 2? Describe the music in each pair.

3. Notate and identify ("X-wedge," where X = index number) the wedge model for the inversional symmetry in measures 1 and 2, beginning with the axis. Circle the components of the model that are employed in measures 1 and 2.

4. What is the pitch-class set (normal form, prime form) of all the notes in measures 1 and 2 combined? What source set does this set bring to mind?

5. Now look at the next subphrase, measures 3 and 4. Two new notes are added to the pitch-class collection of measures 1 and 2. Find the pitch-class set of all the notes in measures 3 and 4 combined. What is the impact of the two new notes on: (1) the inversional symmetry; and (2) the source-set affiliation?

6. In what sense could the two new notes be understood as "nonharmonic tones?"

7. Locate the place where the axis of inversion changes and notate and identify the new wedge model, starting with the new axis. Circle the dyads in the model that are employed in this section of the piece.

8. Besides the new axis of inversion, what else is similar and different about the second section in comparison to the music that preceded it? Consider all the factors explored earlier.

9. Where does the axis change again? What's similar and different about the music in this section in comparison to earlier music? Illustrate with wedge models where appropriate.

10. How does the inversional symmetry in measure 23 relate to previous sections?

11. On a grand staff, summarize the structure of the entire piece by showing each axis of inversion and the measure numbers where they appear.

12. What are the moments in the piece that *aren't* inversionally symmetrical? Discuss the role of these moments in the articulation of the form.

H. ANTON WEBERN (1883–1945), SIX BAGATELLES FOR STRING QUARTET, OP. 9, NO. 5 (1913)

1. Listen to the Bagatelle several times, first without the score, then while following along. It's possible to identify sectional divisions, based on moments of silence, but we'll think of the entire thirteen-measure piece as essentially one musical gesture.

2. Focus on the first two measures. On a blank staff, notate and identify ("X-wedge," where X = index number) the wedge model for the inversional symmetry in measures 1 and 2, starting with the axis. Above the model, label its components (dyads or singletons) with lowercase letters. (If the model has an even index number, you'll use letters "a" through "g": a and g will be singletons, b–f will be dyads. If the model has an odd index number, you'll use letters "a" through "f" for the six dyads.)

3. The first seven measures are an embellished unfolding of this wedge model. Explain how this happens. Describe the appearances of each of the model's components (singletons/dyads or just dyads). Discuss the roles of the notes in the score that don't participate in this unfolding.

4. Now transpose the axis of this model up by a tritone and notate a new wedge model starting on this axis.

5. From measure 6 (overlapping with the end of the earlier unfolding) through measure 12, this new model underlies important pitch relations. Describe them.

6. Now transpose your axis from question 4 down an octave and notate a new wedge model starting on this axis.

7. Find prominent dyads from this new model starting in measure 7 and especially emerging in the piece's conclusion.

8. How might you associate the viola's final D_5 with the cello's earlier D_3 (m. 9) as an appropriate ending for the piece? In what sense do the final measures encapsulate the entire structure?

I. COMPOSITION PROJECTS

1. Imagine other realizations of the structural models we studied at the beginning of this chapter. For example, a pattern of changing intervals might be realized as a repeating series of arpeggiated chords, perhaps an accompaniment for a song or instrumental solo:

Compose a short piece based on a repeating intervallic pattern. Use pattern changes to articulate form. To change the pattern, for example, you could transpose it to a different pitch level, or rhythmically vary its presentation, or extend or truncate it, or shift to a new pattern (or to nonpatterned music) altogether.

2. Compose a melody based on a wedge model and inspired by Berg's melody shown in Example 6.19. Start your melody with an obvious wedging action, but break out

of strict wedge voice leading (as Berg does) by shifting notes to other octaves and by presenting more notes in one arm of the wedge than in the other.

3. Use the measures below as a starting point for a piano etude featuring inversional symmetry. Articulate form by changing to different inversional axes.

FOR FURTHER STUDY

BÉLA BARTÓK:

Mikrokosmos (1932–39): "Reflection" (vol. 1, no. 12); "Contrary Motion (1)" (vol. 1, no. 17); "Imitation Reflected" (vol. 1, no. 29); "Line against Point" (vol. 2, no. 64a/b); "Diminished Fifth" (vol. 4, no. 101); "Subject and Reflection" (vol. 6, no. 141)
Concerto for Orchestra (1945), first movement, mm. 242ff
String Quartet no. 5 (1934)

ALBAN BERG:

String Quartet, op. 3 (1910)
Three Pieces for Orchestra, op. 6 (1914–15)

CHARLES IVES:

The Celestial Country, interlude before no. 4 (1912–13)
Study no. 20 for piano (1917–19), mm. 21–24
Psalm 90 for chorus (1923–24), mm. 60–65
Hallowe'en (1914), mm. 1–8
"Processional: Let There Be Light" (1902–3; 1912–13; late 1930s)
Varied Air and Variations (1920–22), variation 2

GYÖRGY LIGETI:

Musica Ricercata (1951–53), no. 11
Requiem, "Kyrie" (1963–65)

VINCENT PERSICHETTI:

Mirror Etudes for piano (1979)

DMITRI SHOSTAKOVICH:

Fugue for Piano, op. 87, no. 15 (1950–51)

IGOR STRAVINSKY:

Octet for Wind Instruments (1923), mvt. 2, variation D

STEFAN WOLPE:

Passacaglia for Orchestra (1937)

CHAPTER 7

INSTRUMENTAL FORMS

7.1   FORMAL FUNCTIONS AND RELATIONS

As a piece of music unfolds before your ears, momentous changes—perhaps in key, melody, rhythm, and texture—help to define units of structure and design. These units can be small, such as a motive, phrase, or sentence, or large, as in sections or movements. **Form** is the collection and collaboration of these units within a coherent plan. It is the framework for a composer's expressive agenda, like the stanzas in a poem or chapters in a novel. Form guides and manages the musical experience by giving listeners a sense of orientation and perspective.

Just as there is no coherent, definable system of post-tonal harmony, there is no such thing as a "post-tonal form." Post-tonal music has form, of course, just as it has melody and harmony, but the principles of formal organization in this repertoire vary as widely as do aesthetic values and artistic philosophies. In the early years of the post-tonal era, progressive composers were consistently willing to fall back on tonal forms and traditional concepts of musical structure. Only decades later, amid the seismic cultural shifts of the aftermath of the Second World War, do we find radical reconceptions of what constitutes "form" in music—indeed, questions about the very essence of "music" itself.

A section of a piece of music generally fulfills one of three **formal functions**:

- **Thematic**. A section with a thematic function presents an important melody. The music sounds stable and settled, with fully formed phrases and well-defined cadential gestures.
- **Connective**. Connective material is transitory and often unstable, serving to link, lead to, or lead away from sections with other functions. Typical connective sections are **introductions**, **transitions**, and **closings**.
- **Developmental**. A section with a developmental function features previous musical ideas that are fragmented and combined in ways that distort and transform their original structure and character.

The classical sonata form, for example, contains two **thematic** areas within its exposition and recapitulation, possibly bolstered by connective introductory, transitory, and closing material, and a section preceding the recapitulation that fulfills a developmental function.

While fulfilling one of the three formal functions, a section may utilize one of three **constructive techniques**:

- **Repetition**. Music heard previously occurs again, either exactly as first presented, or with very minor alterations (such as a change in dynamic level).

- **Variation**. Music heard previously is presented with significant alterations, while keeping important elements intact (such as an embellished melody that preserves original harmony and phrasing).
- **Contrast**. A new musical idea occurs, in a contrasting style and/or character.

For example, a section with a thematic function—with stable phrasing and cadences—might repeat a section previously heard, or present a variation on earlier material, or introduce a contrasting, entirely new melody. A section fulfilling a connective function could also employ any of the three constructive techniques: a transitional passage, for example, could feature repetitions or variations of musical ideas previously heard, or could present contrasting material, as in a "transition theme." The fragmentation within a developmental section is likewise apt to call upon all three constructive techniques, especially variation.

Let's keep these factors in mind as we explore Bartók's piano piece "From the Island of Bali" (Exx. 7.1, 7.2). The music begins thematically, without an introduction. After an initial four-bar phrase (measures 1–4), an answering phrase begins with a variation on the first phrase (measures 5–8), which is extended into connective (closing) material in measures 9–11.

After two-and-a-half beats of silence, the thematic material starting in measure 12 presents vivid contrasts:

- The tempo speeds up, from *Andante* to *Risoluto*;
- The meter changes, from $\frac{6}{8}$ to $\frac{4}{4}$;
- The texture becomes monophonic, with octave doublings;
- The dynamic level jumps from *piano* to *forte*;
- And, of course, the melody is different (although motivically related).

These contrasts help define measure 12 as the beginning of a new section, not a continuation of the previous one. If measure 1 begins section A, then measure 12 would be labeled the beginning of section B.

What else happens in section B? After an initial thematic phrase (measures 12.3–16.2), motives from the new theme are developed, through imitation and fragmentation, in measures 16.3–22. Then the phrase starting in measure 23 at first sounds thematic but ultimately dissipates into connective (closing) material in measures 27–30.

After that, the A material returns (measures 31–39), not in repetition but in variation. The last four measures (40–43) fulfill the connective function; they are a closing tag, or coda. The overall form of the piece is best described as ABA′ (Ex. 7.1).

EXAMPLE 7.1   Formal overview of Bartók, "From the Island of Bali"

	A			B				A′	
Measure:	1	5	9	12	16	23	27	31	40
Function:	thematic	thematic	connective	thematic	developmental	thematic	connective	thematic	connective
Technique:		variation	variation	contrast	variation	variation	variation	variation	

EXAMPLE 7.2   Bartók, "From the Island of Bali," *Mikrokosmos* 109 (vol. 4)

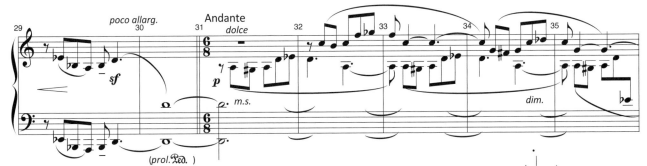

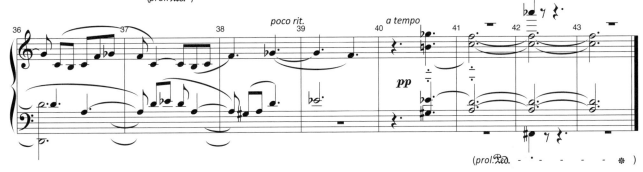

STUDY QUESTIONS 7.1

1. **What constructive techniques might be used in a section that has a developmental function?**

2. **Variation techniques could be employed in sections that fulfill what formal functions?**

3. **What is the source set for the music in the A section of "From the Island of Bali?" (Be specific.)**

4. **What is the role of inversional symmetry in the A section?**

5. **How does the pitch material in the B section relate to the source set of the A section?**

6. **How does your answer to question 5 relate to the formal function and techniques in section B?**

7. **Address these same issues in the A′ section of "From the Island of Bali."**

7.2   SIMPLE SECTIONAL FORMS

It's fair to say that composers in the early years of the post-tonal era often aspired to challenge listeners with melodies and harmonies that were radically different from anything they had heard before. At the same time, many of their formal structures were just the opposite: clear and conventional. Perhaps one reason for this was a fear of sensory overload, a suspicion that listeners could easily reach their limits of tolerance. Formal innovations would have to wait.

So, simple two-part or three-part forms, as in "From the Island of Bali," are relatively easy to find within the post-tonal repertoire of the first half of the twentieth century. In many cases, post-tonal works adopt traditional formal procedures in places where you'd expect to find these same forms in tonal music. Many of the inner movements of Bartók's String Quartets, for example, are ABA forms, following the tradition of the Minuet–Trio or Scherzo–Trio in inner movements of eighteenth- and nineteenth-century string quartets (or symphonies).

It's likewise no surprise to find ABA forms in the instrumental miniatures of Bartók's Austrian contemporaries. We saw one such example in the Chapter 3 exercises, in Webern's Movement for String Quartet, op. 5, no. 3. Other Webern works aren't long enough to include sufficient formal contrast and are essentially elaborated phrases or sentences. On the other hand, Berg's nine-measure-long piece for clarinet and piano, op. 5, no. 2, outlines a convincing ABA in miniature. Schoenberg's piano piece op. 11, no. 2 is a bit more expansive (sixty-six measures) but uses a distinctive ostinato to set apart the outer A sections from the contrasting B material in the center.

A **rondo** form essentially extends the ABA concept into additional sections of contrast followed by additional thematic returns. The form of Bartók's third "Rondo on a Slovak Folk Tune," for example, is ABABACABA. The rondo in the fourth movement of his *Concerto for Orchestra* is more elaborate, although with fewer main sections, ABACBA. The third movement of Stravinsky's Concerto in D for String Orchestra follows a similar pattern.

Berg conceived a more challenging rondo in the second act of his opera *Wozzeck*. We know he thought of it this way because he left behind an elaborate explanation of the instrumental forms underlying each scene.[1] Although he described act 1, scene 5 as a "quasi-rondo"—which is probably difficult for most listeners to follow—the "Rondo con introduzione" in the last scene of act 2 is detectable after a few intense listenings. Perception of the formal units

---

[1] See Douglas Jarman, *Alban Berg: Wozzeck* (Cambridge: Cambridge University Press, 1989), 42.

can be challenging, because Berg's interpretation of a "thematic return" may include substantial variation, or may involve only a recurring set-class progression in contrasting rhythms.

STUDY QUESTIONS 7.2

1. **How is a rondo form different from simple ternary?**

2. **What are typical forms for inner movements of string quartets by Haydn, Mozart, and Bartók?**

7.3 SONATA FORMS

In the Classical and Romantic periods, first movements of works with titles such as "Sonata," "Symphony," and "String Quartet," and sometimes finales and other movements, often displayed the same basic formal scheme.

In its earliest and simplest manifestation, the form was essentially **binary**, featuring a move away from tonic in the first section, often involving two contrasting themes, followed by a second section that begins with an elaborate return to tonic, typically featuring harmonic instability and some sort of fragmentation and variation of previous themes or motives, and then concludes with a restatement of the earlier thematic material minus the harmonic mobility (i.e., without a key change). Later commentators gave the names **exposition** to the first section, **development** to the beginning of the second section, and **recapitulation** to the thematic return in the latter part of the second section (Ex. 7.3). The overall structure was known as **sonata form** (or "sonata-allegro form").

EXAMPLE 7.3 Overview of the 18th-century (binary) sonata form

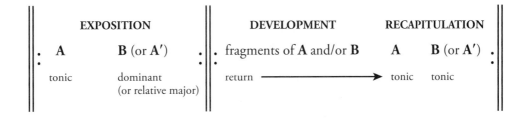

Composers in the Romantic period generally expanded and elaborated the dimensions of the form, yielding an inflated development section and a **ternary** design (Ex. 7.4). Nineteenth-century sonata forms are also likely to include additional themes, and key relations other than tonic–dominant (or minor tonic and relative major). It was also common in this era to expand introductions and codas, creating a four- or five-part overall form.

EXAMPLE 7.4 Overview of the 19th-century (ternary) sonata form

EXPOSITION		DEVELOPMENT	RECAPITULATION	
1st theme group	2nd theme group	theme fragments or new theme(s)	1st theme group	2nd theme group
tonic	dominant (or other non-tonic key)	distant keys and/or harmonic instability	[return to tonic at some point]	

Although composers after 1900 generally sought to break with tradition, the sonata paradigm retained its allure. The results fall into three categories. Some modern composers followed standard practices quite closely, even while avoiding traditional principles of melodic construction and harmonic progression. The first movement of Sergei Prokofiev's Fifth Symphony, for example, presents two contrasting theme groups with tonal centers related by ascending fifth (alluding to tonic and dominant); a development of this material; and then a recapitulation of the earlier themes, now mostly within the tonic key. Some early works of Shostakovich, such as the first movement of his Second String Quartet, also follow the sonata-form tradition with minimal variation.

In a second category are works that preserve some essential features of the traditional sonata form while radically reconceptualizing others. The first movement of Bartók's Piano Sonata, for example, presents an exposition with two clear theme groups, a development of that material, and a recapitulation of the earlier themes followed by a substantial coda. Instead of an interplay of "tonic" and "dominant," however, Bartók unfolds a T_5 transposition pattern for the first theme group in the exposition, counterbalanced by a T_7 transposition pattern in the second theme group. When these ideas return in the recapitulation and coda, we hear no sense of resolution of an earlier disparity, but instead a more extensive continuation of the previous transposition patterns. So the movement essentially upholds the thematic structure of the traditional sonata form while advancing a new approach to its tonal structure.

The most radical reconceptions, constituting a third category, challenge the definition of the form itself, raising questions about what elements are necessary in order for a sonata form to be recognized. For example, Berg explained that he conceived scene 1 of act 2 of *Wozzeck* as a sonata form, including contrasting themes and developments. Because these elements are some of many aspects of a complex dramatic scene, however, the sense of a "sonata form" survives mainly as an intriguing aspect of the composer's creative process, not as a perceptual reality for most listeners. The same is true of the first movement of Pierre Boulez's Second Piano Sonata, which exhibits only hints of a sonata structure, and which was described by the composer himself as an effort to "destroy the first-movement sonata form."[2]

Let's take a close look at music that falls in the second category, the first movement of Stravinsky's Sonata for Piano (1924). Stravinsky wrote the three-movement work in the early years of his "neoclassical" period, when he shifted away from the earlier modernism of *The Firebird* (1910) and *The Rite of Spring* (1913) and toward a style rooted in the idioms and gestures of the past.

When the first movement begins, however, we realize that the categorization "neoclassical" doesn't necessarily connote the Classical style period and music of Haydn and Mozart. The composer most strongly referenced in the opening twelve bars of Stravinsky's movement (Ex. 7.5) is J. S. Bach. The constant motor rhythms and irregular phrasing call to mind one of Bach's keyboard preludes or instrumental concertos—more "neo-Baroque" than "neo-Classical."

Further, Stravinsky explicitly stated that when he wrote the work, and gave it its Classical-sounding name, he did not "give it the Classical form that we find in Clementi, Haydn, and Mozart, and which (as is generally known) is conditioned by the use of the so-called Sonata Allegro."[3] Indeed, the opening music of the first movement (Ex. 7.5), which returns in the middle of the movement and at the end, functions not like the first theme in a sonata form but more like a refrain, or "ritornello," in a Baroque concerto.

---

[2]Pierre Boulez, *Conversations with Célestin Deliège*, foreword by Robert Wangermée (London: Eulenburg, 1976), 41–42.

[3]Eric Walter White, *Stravinsky: The Composer and His Works*, 2nd ed. (Berkeley: University of California Press, 1984), 320.

EXAMPLE 7.5   Stravinsky, Piano Sonata (1924), mvt. 1, mm. 1–6

But there is a lesson to be learned here about a composer's account of his own creations. Despite assertions to the contrary, the first movement of Stravinsky's Sonata does recall fundamental aspects of Classical sonata form. It's not a faithful replica, of course, but that's what makes it interesting. The style is known as *neo*classical because it distorts and reimagines elements of earlier music. Stravinsky creates a hybrid form and style in this movement that are at the same time Baroque, Classical, and Modern.

Let's explore elements of Classical sonata form in the movement. After the introductory music (Ex. 7.5), we hear a primary theme with C centricity (Ex. 7.6a) and its repetition at T_{+2}, where it exhibits D centricity (Ex. 7.6b). The melody features a three-note motive that we'll call "M." M is defined for this music as any three-note stepwise ascent, not a specific pitch-class series. (Exx. 7.6a and 7.6b make no distinction between statements of M starting on different notes; they're all just "M.") And the designation "stepwise" can refer to either half or whole steps.

EXAMPLE 7.6   Stravinsky, Piano Sonata (1924), mvt. 1, exposition section beginnings

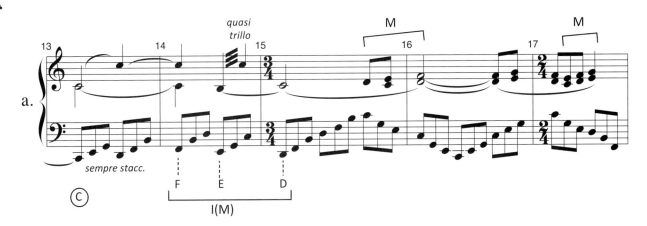

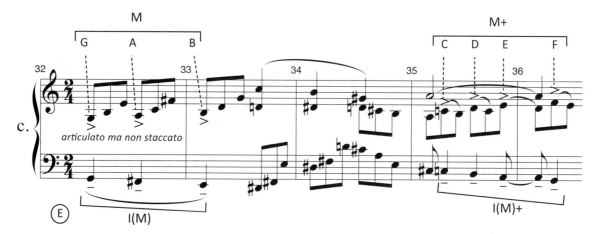

Notice that an inverted form of M appears a few beats earlier within the eighth notes in the left hand (Exx. 7.6a, 7.6b). We'll call this "M-inverse," or "I(M)," defined as a three-note stepwise descent, again without specifying pitch-class content or differentiating between half and whole steps. I(M) is secondary when it first appears here—because it's buried within a stream of eighth notes, and not emphasized like the three-note motive in the right hand is—but when the second theme area begins, I(M) becomes the central musical idea (Ex. 7.6c). It's still in the left hand, but now presented in quarter notes as the primary melodic element, while the right hand has the decorated version of the motive (not inverted). The normal and inverted versions of M now appear together, at first establishing E centricity. Subsequently, the M motive is extended by one note and again mirrored between the hands (I(M)+ and M+ in Ex. 7.6c).

Let's consider how Stravinsky's exposition relates to sonata traditions. Despite sharing a motive, the first and second theme areas are contrasting in customary ways. The second theme is more aggressive than the lyrical first theme, and it is inverted, shifted to the left hand, mirrored against itself, and more prominently featured. The second theme also suggests minor tonality, unlike the pure major of theme one.

Further, the exposition is harmonically organized not by tonic–dominant polarity but through an organic connection to the primary motive. The three main centricities in the exposition project a three-stage stepwise ascent, just like motive M itself: C in the introduction and beginning of the first theme group (Exx. 7.5, 7.6a), D when the first theme recurs at T_{+2} (Ex. 7.6b), and E at the beginning of the second theme group (Ex. 7.6c). The completion of the projection of the motive becomes the completion of the exposition itself.

Before looking at the development, let's investigate the return of these ideas in the recapitulation. The first theme recurs with tiny variants (in measures 126–36), resuming C centricity and ending as it did earlier, with a preparation for a move to D. After that, the music does move to D as in the parallel place in the exposition, but instead of a repetition of theme 1 at T_{+2} (as in Ex. 7.6b), we now hear the music of the second theme group, featuring the inverted form of the motive, with D centricity (first three measures of Ex. 7.7). This is Stravinsky's adaptation of the sonata-form principle whereby the second theme group in the recapitulation occurs in the tonic key. Here it's not in the tonic but a whole step lower than it was earlier (compare the first three measures of Exx. 7.6c and 7.7). The implication is that a motivic projection through the C–D–E tonicities has begun again (as in the exposition), but has reached an opposing force in the desirability of the second theme group to descend in the direction of tonic (Ex. 7.8). You might say that the expression of this material with D centricity is a sort of compromise.

EXAMPLE 7.7   Stravinsky, Piano Sonata (1924), mvt. 1, second theme group in recapitulation

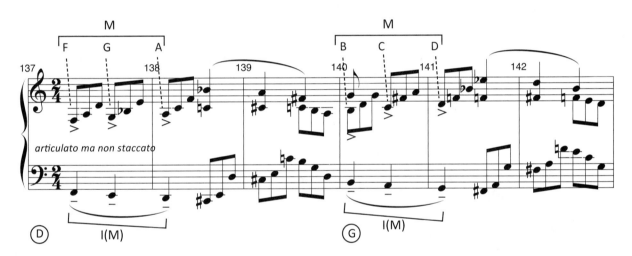

EXAMPLE 7.8   Exposition vs. recapitulation in Stravinsky's movement

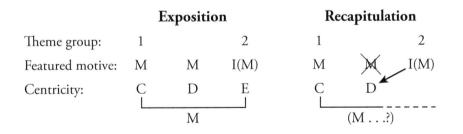

But this lasts for only three measures. Subsequently, starting in measure 140, we hear the second theme group material again, now with G centricity (compare the beginning of Ex. 7.6c with the last three measures of Ex. 7.7). And the music thereafter provides exactly the kind of tonal resolution that a recapitulation typically requires: it transposes the end of the exposition into C centricity. For the remainder of the movement, the C home base is further confirmed by a repetition of the introductory material (Ex. 7.5), curiously renotated in triple meter but otherwise the same as earlier, followed by a brief ending and a final C-major chord (Ex. 7.9).

EXAMPLE 7.9 Stravinsky, Piano Sonata (1924), mvt. 1, ending

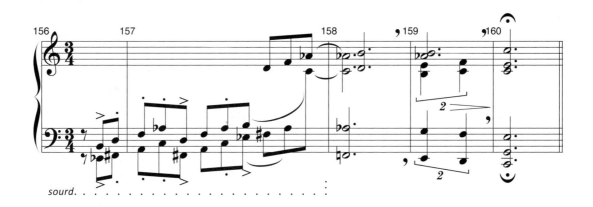

The development section begins with another projection of the M motive, starting with a reworking of the introductory triplets and diminished seventh chords with A centricity (Ex. 7.10a), and continuing to a reminiscence of the first theme group with B centricity (Ex. 7.10b), followed by a recurrence of the motive itself in C♯ (starting in m. 56 of Ex. 7.10b). These ideas and centricities continue to swirl for a while, leading up to a cadence at the end of measure 80 that splits the development into two parts.

EXAMPLE 7.10 Stravinsky, Piano Sonata (1924), mvt. 1, development excerpts

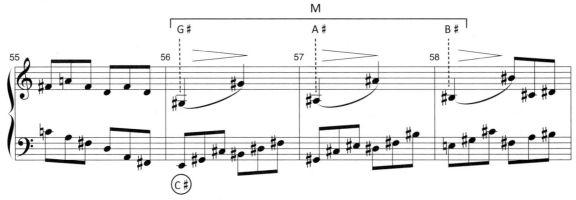

The second part of the development begins with a T_{+11} version of the introduction (compare Exx. 7.5 and 7.11), briefly resuming B centricity. This is followed by a syncopated, more lyrical treatment of the M motive with E♭ centricity (Ex. 7.12), highlighting the inversional form in the right-hand melody while the regular form appears in the left hand—reminiscent of the second theme group in the exposition but now with the I(M) form in the right hand.

EXAMPLE 7.11 Stravinsky, Piano Sonata (1924), mvt. 1, development excerpt

EXAMPLE 7.12 Stravinsky, Piano Sonata (1924), mvt. 1, development excerpt

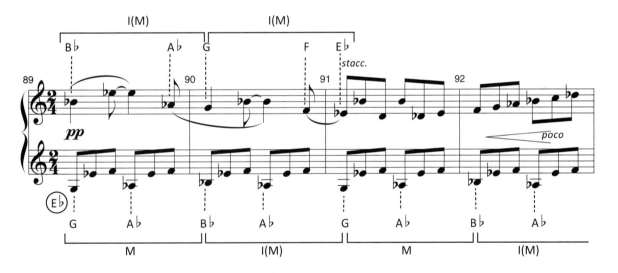

After that, the music continues to develop the primary themes, moving centricity away from E♭ to a splash of F♯ (mm. 96–97), followed by hints of more E♭ (mm. 99–103), then again to hints of A sounding like a dominant of D but never resolving as such (mm. 104–8), followed by more suggestions of E♭ (mm. 109–14). The final retransition (mm. 115–25) also veers to C♯ but reverts to E♭ centricity one last time (mm. 122–24).

Stravinsky's development section falls in line with inherited traditions. It fragments, distorts, and recontextualizes the main thematic material while destabilizing the tonal structure. At the same time, it also relates very directly to the unfolding formal plan (Ex. 7.13). At first, the material being developed simply echoes the rising stepwise motions of the movement's primary motive (mm. 41–56). Then in the second part of the development, the predominance of one centricity—on E♭—suggests a deeper engagement with the movement's overall form. To reflect the interplay of motive M and its inversion heard so often on the musical surface, the prevalent E♭ can be interpreted as the beginning of a long-range inverted form of M that continues with the D-centered recurrence of the second theme (m. 137) and concludes with the final return to C centricity (mm. 149–end). Because this projection begins on E♭, it presents the minor form of the motive, answering the exposition's major version of M in the same way that the second theme's I(M) in minor answers the first theme's M in major.

EXAMPLE 7.13 Stravinsky, Piano Sonata (1924), mvt. 1 overview

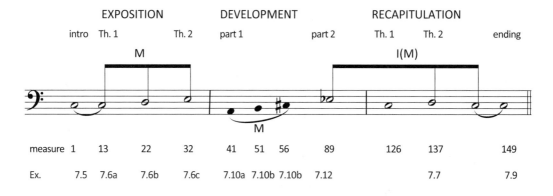

Stravinsky's take on sonata form is both typical and unique. It's typical of adaptations of this form by other composers in the post-tonal era in that it preserves essential features of the basic design while reimagining others. But it's also unique because we can't necessarily expect to find the same sorts of organizing methods in other works of this period, by Stravinsky or by others. We might find them, but we can't expect to. It's not like the classic sonata harmonic structure, in which countless works of the late eighteenth century set up a tonic–dominant polarity in the exposition that was resolved into tonic continuity in the recapitulation. The means of achieving organizational clarity in music since 1900 may vary from composer to composer, and from work to work.

Which elements or techniques in post-tonal sonata forms are most likely to recur in music of different composers? Recapitulations are likely to be substantially different from expositions, as we saw in Stravinsky's Piano Sonata. In some works, the drama of the thematic return after the development is radically revised by a reversal of the two main theme groups: the second group returns first in the recapitulation, and is followed by the return of the first theme. These modifications join a tradition of sonata variants already well developed in the nineteenth century in the music of Franz Liszt and Anton Bruckner, among others. Examples of "reversed recapitulations" from the twentieth-century repertoire include the first movements of Hindemith's Third Piano Sonata, Stravinsky's Octet and Symphony in Three Movements, and Bartók's *Concerto for Orchestra*.

You might think of these structures as formal "arches," with similar material arranged symmetrically around the central development section. Bartók in particular explored the arch form and symmetrical placement of material, conceiving entire multi-movement works according to symmetrical plans. His Fifth String Quartet, for example, consists of five movements, with close relationships between the first and fifth movements and between the second and fourth, surrounding the Scherzo–Trio–Scherzo in the third. And the first movement is itself symmetrical, with themes from the exposition returning in reverse order and in inversion in the recapitulation.

STUDY QUESTIONS 7.3

1. **In which time period did sonata forms follow a binary model?**

2. **What part of the sonata form was expanded to create the ternary model?**

3. **What aspects of the first movement of Stravinsky's Piano Sonata sound more "neo-Baroque" than "neo-Classical?"**

4. **How does Stravinsky use the motive (M) to organize the movement?**

7.4 FUGUE

The sonata-form development section in the fifth movement of Bartók's Fifth String Quartet demonstrates another favorite carryover from common-practice music to the post-tonal era: the **fugato**. As a development of the first theme of the quartet's first movement, the viola presents a ten-measure theme (Ex. 7.14) that's subsequently echoed with tiny variations at T_6 in the second violin (mm. 380–90), then at T_0 (literally, T_{+12}) in the first violin (mm. 390–99), and finally at T_6 again in the cello (mm. 400–408). It is, in other words, just like the beginning of the classic fugal **exposition**, in which the main theme, or **subject**, is stated in each of the fugue's parts, or **voices**. This instance is termed **fugato** because it consists mainly of the exposition of the four voices followed by some related motivic interplay. It is, after all, only one small section within a long movement and a complex form.

EXAMPLE 7.14   Bartók, String Quartet no. 5, mvt. 5, viola, mm. 370–79

A full-fledged **fugue** would normally involve more extensive development of the subject and its motives. In a typical fugue, the exposition is followed by passages of motivic fragmentation and combination, known as **episodes**, alternating with restatements of the subject in various closely related keys. There is no standard fugal format, just a presumption that the alternation of episodes and subject entries will ultimately negotiate a return to the main key, perhaps ending with a final statement of the subject in the tonic.

Here are some additional devices commonly found in fugues:

- **Countersubject**. A secondary contrapuntal line paired with the subject in the exposition and usually accompanying the subject as it recurs throughout the remainder of the fugue.
- **Stretto**. Overlapping subject entries.
- **Augmentation**. A presentation of the subject in longer note values.
- **Diminution**. A presentation of the subject in shorter note values.

Further, the expositions of Baroque or Classical fugues typically alternate between subject entries in tonic and dominant keys. J. S. Bach's G-Minor Fugue from Book 2 of *The Well-Tempered Clavier*, for example, begins with a subject in the tenor voice in G minor, answered by the subject in the alto in D minor. The soprano soon follows with an entry back in G minor, and the exposition concludes with the subject in the bass in D minor.

So Bartók mimics this structure in his string quartet fugato, substituting T_6 for transpositions to the dominant. In fact, he employs the same sequence of voices as in Bach's fugue: T_0 in the tenor (viola), T_6 in the alto (second violin), T_0 in the soprano (first violin), T_6 in the bass (cello). Of course, Bartók wasn't bound by principles of dissonance treatment and tonal harmonic progression as Bach was, but he had his own standards of harmonic consistency to follow.

Bartók's approach is typical of many fugues in the post-tonal era. The transposition levels of their subject entries call to mind principles of earlier fugues, even if their pitch combinations and harmonic practices don't. Charles Ives, for example, wrote a "Fugue in Four Keys" that begins with subject entries by rising fifths, in C, G, D, and A, like a traditional fugue that forgot to return to tonic. Paul Hindemith did something similar in a three-voice fugue in the fourth movement of his Third Piano Sonata, with subject entries at T_0, T_7, and T_2 ($= T_7$ of T_7).

Actually, Hindemith's movement is a **double fugue**, with two subjects and two separate expositions, both of which feature subject entries transposed by rising fifths. Stravinsky's four-voice double fugue in the second movement of his *Symphony of Psalms* presents subject entries at T_0, T_7, T_0, and T_7 in two different expositions, but then gives the subjects a completely choral setting with voices related by *descending* fifth—a mirror of Ives's transpositional plan in "Fugue in Four Keys."

The extreme instance of extending traditional fugal subject relations is the first movement of Bartók's *Music for Strings, Percussion, and Celesta*. It begins with a chromatic subject played by violas in four phrases (Ex. 7.15). The high points of the phrases rise gradually from $C\sharp_4$ (phrase 1) to $E\flat_4$ (phrase 2) and $E\natural_4$ (phrase 3) before falling back to $E\flat_4$ (phrase 4). Each phrase saturates a certain area of pitch space with the notes of a chromatic pentachord or hexachord.

EXAMPLE 7.15   Bartók, *Music for Strings, Percussion, and Celesta*, mvt. 1, fugue subject (violas)

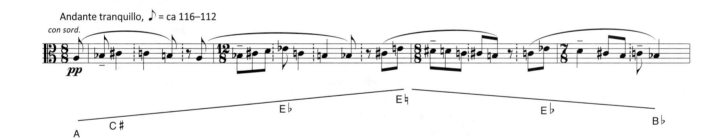

Next, as the violas continue their chromatic weaving, we hear a p-space transposition of the subject up a perfect fifth played by violins ("$T_{+7}(S)$" in Ex. 7.16). After the violins have completed their statement, the cellos enter with a p-space transposition down by that same distance ("$T_{-7}(S)$" in Ex. 7.16). In other words, Bartók takes the traditional pitch relations in a fugal exposition and extends them both upward and downward, in pitch space. He continues to do so in the next two subject entries, again transposing upward and downward by p-space perfect fifths.

EXAMPLE 7.16 Bartók, *Music for Strings, Percussion, and Celesta*, mvt. 1, mm. 1–12

Because the full subject is absent for the next few measures, the first five subject entries constitute the fugue's exposition. After that episode, however, the transposition pattern continues with more subject entries, moving upward and downward by p-space perfect fifths from the previous ones. Example 7.17 summarizes this portion of the movement, representing each subject entry by its first note (compare Ex. 7.16). The last two entries, starting on $F\sharp_5$ in the first violins and on C_2 in the basses, are the first to appear simultaneously, helping to draw attention to their relationship by a very important interval in the movement, the tritone.

EXAMPLE 7.17 Bartók, *Music for Strings, Percussion, and Celesta*, mvt. 1, overview of mm. 1–31

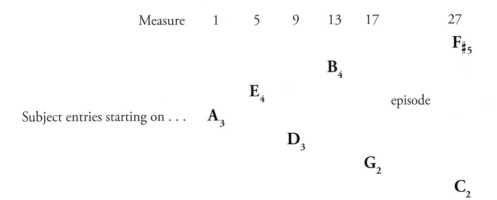

Indeed, just like the fugue subject itself (Ex. 7.15), the subject entries are on their way to a big climax on E♭, a tritone away from where they began. The pathway to this E♭ involves more pitch relations by rising and falling fifths, although now the subject is fragmented and varied, and pitch regions may be present more as moments of centricity than as starting points of subject transpositions. After the climax we hear mostly the subject in inversion, or fragments thereof, as the transposition pattern reverses itself and returns to its starting tone, A. The coda presents the subject and its inversion together, both starting on A, and in the final bars the violins play an expanding-contracting wedge based on subject motives to summarize the structure of the entire movement (Ex. 7.18).

EXAMPLE 7.18   Bartók, *Music for Strings, Percussion, and Celesta*, mvt. 1, mm. 86–88

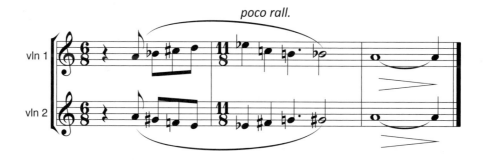

Bartók's fugue reflects radically and persuasively on fugal traditions. It joins the legacy of the great fugues of Bach and Beethoven, while mastering the methods and sensibilities of its own era. Many of Bartók's contemporaries and their artistic descendants likewise found ways to reimagine the fugue. For the second scene of act 2 of his opera *Wozzeck*, for example, Berg wrote a triple fugue, each of its three subjects representing a different character in the drama. After the subjects are presented separately in their own expositions, they are variously combined as a reflection of dynamic interactions and interrelationships of the three characters.

The first tableau of Darius Milhaud's ballet *The Creation of the World* (1923) features a fugue in a new musical style that was attracting attention on both sides of the Atlantic in the early 1920s: jazz. The fugue's subject, with jazzy rhythms and blue notes, is introduced in the exposition by instruments that feel right at home in jazz style: double bass, trombone, alto saxophone, and trumpet. Each new subject entry represents a new stage in an African creation myth, a new world emerging from a chaotic mass.

Even more unique is Ernst Toch's *Geographical Fugue* (1930) for four-part speaking chorus, which employs standard fugal techniques among contrapuntal lines that consist of rhythmically spoken place names, including Nagasaki, Mississippi, Titicaca, and Popocatépetl. The work has no overt sociopolitical agenda but simply explores the sonic variety within geographical names as a celebration of cultural diversity.

Later applications of fugal techniques fall in line with shifting compositional trends of the postwar period. The Kyrie movement from György Ligeti's *Requiem* (1963–65) is an adaptation of a double fugue, with one subject presenting the "Kyrie" text, the other the "Christe" text. The two themes are initially presented together, each in four-part canon, gradually creating massive blocks of sound that shift, undulate, and shimmer. The fugue in Witold Lutosławski's Preludes and Fugues for Thirteen Solo Strings (1972) has six different subjects but actually begins with an episode, and can take on a number of different forms in performance, depending on choices made by the performers.

STUDY QUESTIONS 7.4

1. **What moment in a fugue marks the end of the exposition section?**

2. **What techniques of fugal construction involve restating the subject with altered rhythms?**

3. **In the first movement of *Music for Strings, Percussion, and Celesta*, how does Bartók mimic tonal aspects of the conventional fugue?**

4. **What structural model summarizes the structure of Bartók's movement?**

7.5   THEME AND VARIATIONS

The traditional theme and variations is very different from the other form types because it's so uniformly sectionalized. Once a theme has been stated at the beginning of this type of piece in the hands of a Classical composer, you can usually be pretty sure that its structure—the number and length of phrases—will be replicated in most or all of the subsequent variations. So a traditional set of variations based on, let's say, a twenty-four-bar theme, is likely to have a fairly conspicuous sectional division every twenty-four bars.

This kind of formal transparency and regularity has often been an attractive option for post-tonal composers who are otherwise focused on breaking new ground in their melodies and harmonies. One popular formal model has been the **passacaglia**. In this type of variation form, a repeating bass melody, also known as a **ground bass**, doesn't change at all from section to section but serves as the backbone for continuous variation in the music that surrounds it. (If the bass line also supports a repeating chord progression, the result can also be called a **chaconne**.) Passacaglias in the finale of Hindemith's Fifth String Quartet and in the fourth movement of Shostakovich's Eighth Symphony follow these conventions quite closely. Ligeti's *Passacaglia ungherese* for harpsichord likewise keeps its primary melody mostly intact while substantial changes occur around it, although the melody itself begins in the upper register and works its way downward as the piece progresses.

Compare these examples with Schoenberg's treatment of his three-note theme in "Nacht," the song from *Pierrot Lunaire* that we studied in Chapters 2 and 3. Although the movement is subtitled "Passacaglia," we can't expect to find a sectionalized repetition of an unchanging theme. Rather, the three-note motive (E–G–E♭) recurs in varying durations and in transpositions and inversions (see Chapter 2.4, Exercise 2F; Chapter 3, Exercise 3H). In some parts it's broken down into its constituent intervals, like fragmenting a theme in the development section of a sonata form. That, in fact, may be a better way to characterize Schoenberg's treatment of the "Nacht" theme: in traditional terms, as much "development" as "variation."

We can make the same comparison between post-tonal variation forms in general (passacaglias aside). The second movement of Prokofiev's Third Piano Concerto (1917–21) and the march section of the first movement of Shostakovich's Seventh Symphony (1941) present well-defined themes followed by series of separately articulated variations whose connections to the original themes are never in doubt. Frederic Rzewski's thirty-six variations on "The People United Will Never Be Defeated" (1975) call to mind monumental variation sets of the past, such as J. S. Bach's *Goldberg Variations* (theme and thirty variations) or Beethoven's *Diabelli Variations* (theme and thirty-three variations).

Composed during the same time period, however, are variation sets in which themes are deconstructed and reinterpreted in countless ways. We can't even assume that the theme itself—the subject of variation—will be identifiable and distinctive. In Luciano Berio's *Cinque variazioni* for piano, we don't hear the actual theme until the end, *after* the variations. Although the word "variation" may be in the title of some post-tonal works, the music isn't necessarily "about" the theme but may be more about the process of development, about traveling diverse and unpredictable transformational pathways.

Let's see how this happens in one of Berg's variation forms, the first scene of the third act of his opera *Wozzeck*. In the composer's own description, act 3 is a series of "inventions," and scene 1 is "Invention on a Theme." [4] According to Berg's annotations on the score, the scene begins with a seven-measure theme, which is followed by seven variations and then concludes with a fugato based on material from the theme. The scene features Marie, who is Wozzeck's lover and the mother of his child, regretting a romantic tryst with one of Wozzeck's rivals, the Drum Major. Overcome with guilt, she reads Bible passages about an adulterous woman and about Mary Magdalene, and tells her child a dark fairy tale.

The theme has two parts (Ex. 7.19). First, a quiet imitated motive in solo muted strings, clarinet, horn, and flute underlies the beginning of Marie's Bible reading, delivered in *Sprechstimme* (mm. 1–5.1, "And no guile is found in his mouth"). Then, suddenly, she explodes with grief, in sung high notes accompanied by motivic outbursts in the strings, trumpets, and clarinets (mm. 5.2–7, "Lord God, Lord God! Don't look upon me!"). Her last four notes ("Sieh mich nich An!") recall one of the opera's primary motives, first heard in act 1, scene 1, when Wozzeck utters a central thematic idea: "Wir arme leut!," which roughly translates as "We poor people" or "How the poor live." When we hear Marie sing those notes in this scene at the beginning of act 3, we know that Wozzeck is on her mind as she expresses her anguish over betraying her lover.

EXAMPLE 7.19 Berg, *Wozzeck*, act 3, scene 1, mm. 1–7, condensed score (sounds as notated)

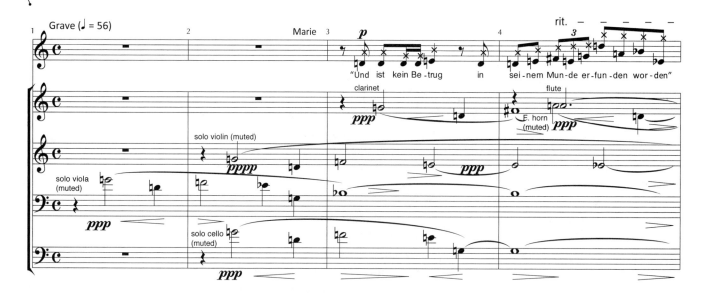

---

[4] See Douglas Jarman, *Alban Berg:* Wozzeck (Cambridge: Cambridge University Press, 1989), 42.

In the variations that follow, Berg focuses on three musical ideas from this theme. One is the four-note motive that dominates the theme's first half, beginning in the viola and then imitated with alterations in the cello, violin, and clarinet. Let's call it "M" (Ex. 7.20a). The other two important ideas are the main elements of the second half of the theme, "P" in the first violins (Ex. 7.20b), and "Q" in the low strings and bassoons (Ex. 7.20c). P winds downward, as if selecting notes from a descending chromatic scale (Ex. 7.21a), while Q subtly rearranges all the notes of an ascending chromatic scale (Ex. 7.21b). Because P and Q unfold roughly in tandem, they hint at one of Berg's favorite structural models, the chromatic wedge (see Chapter 6.2).

EXAMPLE 7.20   M, P, and Q in *Wozzeck* act 3, scene 1 theme

EXAMPLE 7.21   P and Q as variants of chromatic scales

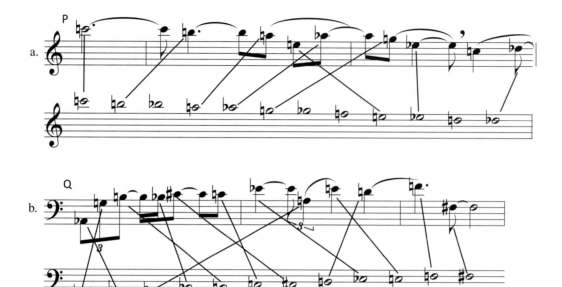

The moment where each variation begins is indicated by Berg in the published score. Calculated in amounts of beats, each variation on the theme is a multiple of seven: variation 1 is notated in seven four-beat bars like the theme (= twenty-eight beats); variation 2 consists of just two bars totaling seven beats; variation 3 is notated in seven three-beat bars (= twenty-one beats); and so forth:

SECTION	NO. OF BEATS
Theme	28
Variation 1	28
Variation 2	7
Variation 3	21
Variation 4	21
Variation 5	28
Variation 6	14
Variation 7	7

The structures of the variations also strongly relate, each variation beginning with a presentation of some form of motive M. In variations 1, 5, and 6, the recurrences of M echo both the rhythm and the contour of the original, while others strip the rhythm away and just recall the motive's pitch contours. Variation 2 begins with triplets in the oboe that repeat M and its two varied imitations as first heard in the theme (see the viola, violin/cello and clarinet lines in Ex. 7.19, mm. 1–4). These imitations are designated M1, M2, and M3 in Example 7.22a. Variation 3 begins with T_{11} transpositions of M1 and M2 in the solo violins and solo viola, respectively, followed by a variant of M3 in the oboe that starts like another T_{11} transposition but then stretches its second interval (Ex. 7.22b).

In the final variation, however, M is not represented by pitch classes, rhythms, or contours. Instead, the variation begins with two trichords in the bass clarinet and bassoons that replicate only the set-class types of the initial trichords of, first, M3, and then of M1/M2 (Ex. 7.22c). To recognize these two trichords as variants of M, we must recall that M1, M2, and M3 all begin with an ic 5 from G to D followed by a third note that's either F or F♯ and hear an analogy in variation 7 when the ic 5 E–B is followed by first C, then C♯.

EXAMPLE 7.22   Recollections of M in (a) variation 2; (b) variation 3; (c) variation 7

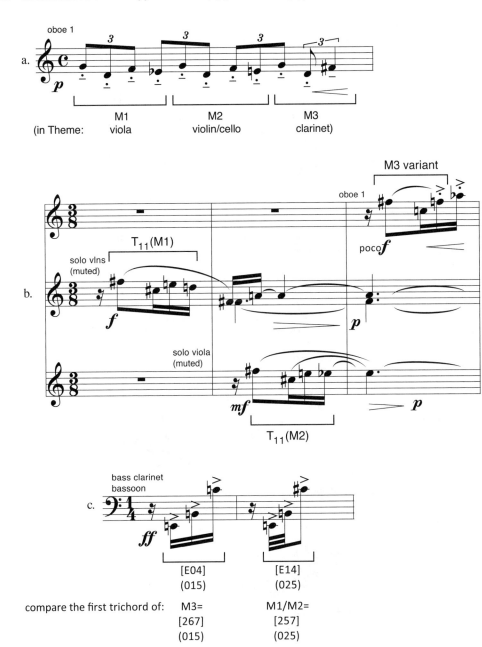

P and Q undergo reworkings of a different sort in the course of the scene. In the first variation, for example, while a not-that-different variant of P occurs in the bass trombone, a derivation from Q in the French horns strips away the original rhythms almost entirely and combines adjacent notes from the theme into simultaneous dyads (Ex. 7.23). Despite this, the sense of a wedge variant remains in variation 1, with P generally descending while Q generally ascends. It's a diverging (opening) wedge model now, however, because P is below Q—by contrast with the converging (closing) wedge suggested by the positioning of P above Q in the theme (Exx. 7.19, 7.20bc).

EXAMPLE 7.23   Derivations from P and Q in variation 1 (sounds as notated)

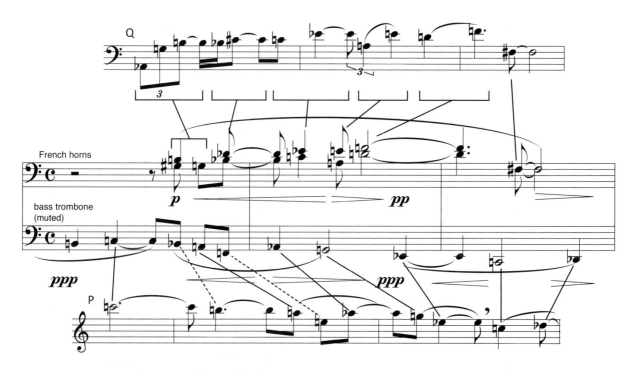

The other variations also feature unpredictable recollections of P and Q. Each of variations 3 and 4 features only one of the themes while hinting at the other, thereby abandoning the illusion of a wedge-like pairing. Further, the variant of P in the flute in variation 4 also revises its rhythm and contour, obscuring the original melody's chromatic downward thrust (Ex. 7.24).

EXAMPLE 7.24   Variant of P in variation 4 (flutes)

In addition, the latter variations add one more alteration into the mix. While the original rhythms and contours of P and Q may or may not be preserved or suggested, the pitch classes themselves reappear in transposition. We first hear the pitch classes of $T_{11}Q$ in variation 3, later T_{10} of both P and Q in variations 5 and 6. T_9 transpositions dominate the final variation, first T_9P <98615409T> in the clarinets, answered by T_9Q <5487T9061E23> in the bassoons (Ex. 7.25). (In the latter, the order of the first two notes is reversed.) Although the rhythms of these variants bear little resemblance to those in the original melodies, their shapes hold true to their original downward (P) and upward (Q) directions, as if the two arms of a converging wedge have fallen out of sync.

EXAMPLE 7.25   Variants of $T_9(P)$ and $T_9(Q)$ in variation 7 (sounds as notated)

The scene ends with a double fugato whose subjects are based on M and P. It is, essentially, the eighth variation, but expanded to serve as the finale, in the tradition of the fugal finales for Beethoven's *Diabelli Variations* and Brahms's *Variations and Fugue on a Theme by Handel*. Around the same time as *Wozzeck*, Stravinsky closed the variation set in the second movement of his Octet in the same fashion, as did Berg's mentor Schoenberg about twenty years later, in Variations on a Recitative for Organ, op. 40. For Berg, the fugal finale in *Wozzeck* was one more step along a developmental pathway, one more opportunity to work within his materials while moving forward with the drama, on the stage and in the pit.

STUDY QUESTIONS 7.5

1. **What elements of a theme are typically preserved in a classical-era theme and variations?**

2. **What elements of the theme are developed in act 3 scene 1 of Berg's *Wozzeck*?**

3. **In what sense is Berg's conception of theme and variations more radical than Stravinsky's version of sonata form, or than Bartók's approach to fugue?**

7.6   NEW CONCEPTS OF ORGANIZATION

Later in the twentieth century, George Rochberg likewise ended a large variation set, his twelve-movement *Partita-Variations* for Piano (1976), with a fugue. But Rochberg's fugue also exemplifies another important trend because of its full adoption of tonality. In fact, Rochberg's fugue is more than just a general recollection of earlier variation sets with fugal finales: it specifically recalls motives and idioms from Brahms's finale to his *Variations and Fugue on a Theme by Handel*. Elsewhere in the *Partita-Variations* we hear tonal echoes of other musical ancestors, including Bach (in mvt. 9, Menuetto) and Chopin (in mvt. 11, Nocturne). And yet other movements embrace atonality with equal conviction (mvt. 4, Cortege; mvt. 5, Impromptu). Among other things, Rochberg's work challenges traditional assumptions of stylistic heterogeneity and continuity.

We might make an analogy between the *Partita-Variations* and a work of visual art that combines diverse images and materials: the **collage**. Listening to Rochberg's musical collage is the aural equivalent of scanning your eyes across a diverse canvas that juxtaposes simply drawn images, abstract shapes, and mixed media. As a musical experience, it has few precedents before 1900 and is essentially a modern (eventually postmodern) phenomenon. Around the turn of the twentieth century, we hear hints of the collage aesthetic in many works of Mahler—for example, the funeral march in the third movement of his First Symphony—and in Charles Ives's juxtapositions of American folk tunes, marches, and hymns (e.g., Fourth Symphony, *The Fourth of July*). More recently, the concept has been fully embraced by, among others, Luciano Berio (*Sinfonia*), Alfred Schnittke (First Symphony, Second Violin Sonata), Sofia Gubaidulina (Piano Sonata), Arvo Pärt (*Collage on the Theme BACH*), and Bernd Alois Zimmermann (*Musique pour les soupers du roi Ubu*).

The form of a musical collage may not be abstract and may in fact rely on traditional principles of variation, contrast, and return. More common, however, are collages that actively subvert such values, that revel in their inscrutability. The third movement of Berio's *Sinfonia*, for example, moves rapidly between recurring snippets of the Scherzo from Mahler's Second Symphony; quotations from music of Beethoven, Debussy, Ravel, Schoenberg, and Berg; spoken excerpts from Beckett and Joyce; and so forth. We don't hear a strong sense of shape or architecture in the movement; rather, the listening experience feels subversively, delightfully random. By conventional standards, the music is formless.

The notion that music may deny the experience of continuity or progression eventually became one of modernism's primary tenets. It's one facet of what Karlheinz Stockhausen described as **moment form**.[5] In a moment form, sections of music are static and self-contained; they belong together in the same composition but otherwise do not relate to each other as stages in a progressive narrative. We hear precedents for this approach in the early twentieth century, in the contrasting blocks of music variously juxtaposed by Stravinsky in *Petrushka*. A few decades later, Olivier Messiaen adopted similar approaches to juxtaposition and recombination (e.g., *L'ascension* [1935], *Turangalîla-Symphonie* [1948]). Stockhausen's moment forms, in works such as *Kontakte* (1960), *Mixtur* (1964), and *Momente* (1972), realize the concept to its fullest, stringing together musical events that are individually coherent but collectively unconnected within any sort of continuity or conventional musical progression.

If a moment form may seem randomly created, then its overall impact may be not that different from music whose conception is essentially arbitrary from the start. From the avant-garde movement of the 1950s and 1960s came **aleatory music**—music created by chance operations, minimizing the role of the composer in the creative process, and raising questions about the art of "music" as traditionally defined. In works such as *Music of Changes* (1951) and *Atlas Eclipticalis* (1962), John Cage used random processes of selection (coin flips, for example) to determine pitches, durations, textures, and so forth. Similarly, music of **indeterminacy** uses nontraditional notation to provide performers outlines for improvisation (e.g., Lukas Foss, *Echoi*). In such works, the performer becomes an integral part of the creative act; the form of a musical event can differ substantially from one performance to the next. We might group all such radical reconceptions of musical structure under the general rubric of **open form**.

But that's where the study of form ends, because, essentially, anything goes.

---

[5]Karlheinz Stockhausen, "Momentform," in *Texte zur elektronischen und instrumentalen Musik*, vol. 1 (Cologne: DuMont, 1963), pp. 189–210.

STUDY QUESTIONS 7.6

1. In what sense can a musical collage be considered formless?

2. What are similarities and differences between aleatoricism and indeterminacy?

VOCABULARY

aleatory music	double fugue	passacaglia
augmentation	episode	recapitulation
binary form	exposition (fugue)	repetition
chaconne	exposition (sonata form)	rondo form
closing	form	sonata form
collage	formal function	stretto
connective formal function	fugato	subject
constructive technique	fugue	ternary form
contrast	ground bass	thematic formal function
countersubject	indeterminacy	transition
development	introduction	variation
developmental formal function	moment form	voice (contrapuntal)
diminution	open form	

EXERCISES

A. VARIATION TECHNIQUES IN FREDERIC RZEWSKI (B. 1938), *THE PEOPLE UNITED WILL NEVER BE DEFEATED!*

1. Study the first sixteen measures of the theme. (The entire theme encompasses thirty-six measures.) Describe the passage, then explain how measures 5–16 could be considered the first variation, even though the officially designated first variation starts in measure 37.

2. Describe the first twelve measures (mm. 37–48) of variation 1 with respect to the first sixteen measures of the theme. (Variation 1 in its entirety encompasses twenty-four measures.) Exactly what portion of the theme provides the source for each measure in the variation? What aspects of the theme are retained, and what aspects are altered?

3. Within variation 1 alone, describe the relationship between the music in the first two measures (mm. 37–38) and the next two (39–40). Similarly describe musical relationships between the next four measures (mm. 41–44) and the next four (mm. 45–48). How does Rzewski give musical shape and continuity to the passage in its entirety (mm. 37–48)?

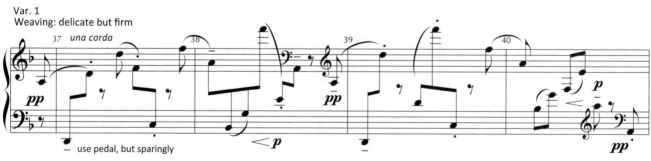

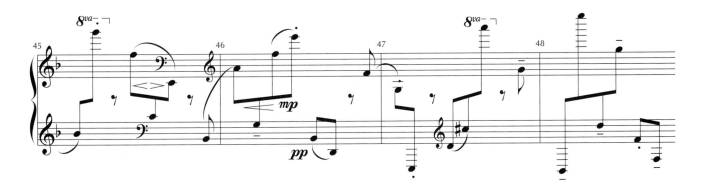

B. VARIATION TECHNIQUES IN AARON COPLAND (1900–1990), *PIANO VARIATIONS*

1. What are the phrases of the theme and how are they created? In your explanation, incorporate discussion of the main motive stated by the first four notes. Identify the motive by normal form and prime form and explain its subsequent reappearances and development throughout the theme.

2. Exactly how is the four-note motive from the theme developed and varied in variation 17? How does the structure of the entire variation relate to the structure of the entire theme?

3. Specifically how does the music in the first measure of variation 18 relate to the four-note motive? Also discuss how these ideas are extended and developed when this material returns later in the variation (mm. 3–4, 7–9, 17, 20–21).

4. What are some other ways in which the four-note motive is developed in variation 18?

5. What structural correspondences do you notice between the complete theme, and variation 18 in its entirety?

C. VARIATION TECHNIQUES IN ARNOLD SCHOENBERG (1874–1951), SERENADE, OP. 24, MVT. 3

1. The clarinet alone plays the theme at the beginning of the movement (mm. 1–11). First, break down the theme into interlocking trichords: trichord 1 is formed by the first three notes, trichord 2 is formed by notes 2, 3, and 4 (A_3–$D\flat_4$–C_4), and so forth. List the normal forms of all instances of the trichord type occurring most often among these interlocking trichords.

2. How does the structure of the second half of the theme relate to the structure of the first half? In what way(s) are these relationships highlighted, and in what way(s) are they obscured?

3. Look first at the second part of variation 1, starting in measure 17. Describe the manipulation of the theme in these measures. Which aspects of the theme are preserved, and which are changed (and how)?

4. Now look at the clarinet line in the first part of variation 1 (mm. 12–16). How is it related to the theme? (Be specific; apply methodology from previous chapters.) What is the logic behind stopping where it does, at the beginning of measure 16?

5. What is the structure of the cello line in the first part of variation 1 (mm. 12–16)? How does it relate to the concurrent clarinet line and to the theme?

all parts sound as notated

D. TERNARY FORM: BÉLA BARTÓK (1881–1945), 14 BAGATELLES FOR PIANO, OP. 6, NO. 11

1. **What are the distinguishing features of the music at the beginning of the piece? The trichords in the right hand all look very similar, but they're not all transpositionally equivalent: how many different trichord types are there? What's going on in the left hand at the same time, and how does it relate to the right hand?**

2. **The third section of the ternary form, the return of the A material, begins in measure 61, an octave higher than originally presented. What else is different about the returning material, in comparison to the music at the beginning of the piece?**

3. **What is the source of the closing material starting in measure 77?**

4. Now focus on the middle section. The trichordal gestures in the right hand end after measure 18. What is the function of the next section, measures 19–39? Is it thematic, connective, or developmental? Support your answer with evidence from the music.

5. List at least five ways in which the music in measures 40–60 contrasts with the A material.

6. How does the end of the B section, measures 55–60, create an effective retransition by bringing together aspects of both A and B?

E. SONATA FORM: PAUL HINDEMITH (1895–1963), STRING QUARTET NO. 4, OP. 22, MVT. 2

1. **Add measure numbers to complete the chart:**

Exposition

	Theme 1	Transition 1	Transition 2	Theme 2	Theme 2 again	Theme 2 again	Closing material
Measure:	1	☐	☐	☐	☐	☐	☐

Recapitulation   **Coda**

	Theme 1	Transition 1		Theme 2	Theme 2 again		
Measure:	☐	☐		☐	☐		☐

2. The first theme initally alternates between repeating-note unison downbows (e.g., measure 1) and agitato sixteenth notes (e.g., mm. 3 and 4). How is the agitato material structured? How do the downbow gestures evolve over the first eleven measures?

3. Besides these two elements, what other important musical ideas are introduced within the first theme area?

4. Which aspects of the transition 1 section are new, and which are developed from the previous section?

5. List at least four ways in which the theme 2 section contrasts with theme 1.

6. Describe differences between the transitional material in the exposition and recapitulation.

7. In a traditional sonata form, the second theme is transposed to the tonic key in the recapitulation, as a resolution of the tonal disparity created when the two main themes appeared in different keys in the exposition. How does Hindemith's treatment of the second theme in his recapitulation reflect an analogous approach to formal resolution?

8. What are the musical sources for Hindemith's brief development section? How is the beginning of the development different from any other part of the movement?

F. FUGUE: DMITRI SHOSTAKOVICH (1906–1975), STRING QUARTET NO. 8, MVT. 5

This is the final movement of one of Shostakovich's most popular—and most personal—string quartets. He wrote the music in 1960, during a short stay in East Germany. Its dedication reads: "In remembrance of the victims of facism and war."

Throughout the first four movements of the quartet, Shostakovich includes musical quotations from his own works, and from a song well-known to his Russian compatriots, "Exhausted by the Hardships of Prison." Most conspicuously, he frequently features a four-note motive derived from letters of his name, his personal musical signature:

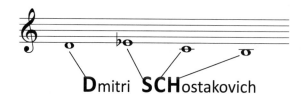

Dmitri **SCH**ostakovich

To create the motto, Shostakovich used a Germanic spelling of his name.

"S" is used to represent E♭ because the German pronunciation of that note name ("Es") sounds like the letter.

"H" is the German name for B♮ ("B" = B♭.)

1. In this four-voice fugue, the exposition section ends after the fourth entry of the subject. What is the last measure of the exposition section in this fugue? What are the transpositional relationships between the subject entries in the exposition?

2. A countersubject appears along with the subject, in a different part. Describe the countersubject in this fugue.

3. Locate every other entry of the subject and countersubject in the fugue. Organize this information in the form of a chart, using measure numbers to show the location of each event. In your chart, indicate exact transposition levels of subject entries, and use the terms "link" or "episode" to describe any passage in which the complete subject isn't present. Also highlight instances of varied subject entries.

4. Comment on the form. How does the composer use fugal conventions to give his movement shape and coherence? Consider also that the music of the stretto section (mm. 54–69) is a precise recollection of the beginning of the entire work (mm. 1–15 of the first movement), and that the rising half-step motive heard in the fugue's final measures has been a recurring idea throughout all of the previous movements.

G. COMPOSITION PROJECT: THEME AND VARIATIONS

Study this theme:

Compose variations on the theme using the given measures as starting points.

If you feel inspired, compose more variations by expanding the basic conception. Instead of restricting yourself to a single staff, for example, write variations for piano or instrumental duo or string quartet or some other instrumental combination.

H. OTHER COMPOSITION PROJECTS

1. Compose a movement for piano in ternary form modeled after Bartók's "From the Island of Bali" (Chapter 7.1) and Bagatelle, op. 6, no. 11 (Exercise 7D). Explore different ways of producing contrast in the central section while tying the entire structure together with a recurring musical idea.

2. Compose a fugue in four voices for instrumental ensemble. Use this as your subject . . .

. . . or write your own subject, perhaps modeled after Bartók's subject in the first movement of his *Music for Strings, Percussion, and Celesta* (Chapter 7.4) or after Shostakovich's subject in the fifth movement of his Eighth String Quartet (Exercise 7F). Find a way to give your fugue shape and coherence using transpositional relations, countersubjects, devices such as stretto, and so forth.

3. Compose a movement in sonata form modeled after the first movement of Stravinsky's Piano Sonata (Chapter 7.3) and/or the second movement of Hindemith's Fourth String Quartet (Exercise 7E). A good way to begin is to compose the two main themes first, in contrasting characters. Then plan how you will change the presentation of the second theme in the recapitulation in order to produce some sort of formal closure. After that, you're ready to compose the movement, working out introductory and connective material, and deciding which aspects of the theme(s) you'll feature in the development section.

FOR FURTHER STUDY

TERNARY FORM:

Béla Bartók: *Concerto for Orchestra* (1945), mvt. 2; String Quartet no. 4 (1928), mvt. 2; String Quartet no. 5 (1934), mvt. 3
Alban Berg: Four Pieces for Clarinet and Piano, op. 5, no. 2 (1913)
Irving Fine: Music for Piano (1947), mvt. 2 (Waltz-Gavotte)
Paul Hindemith: Piano Sonata no. 3 (1936), mvt. 2
György Ligeti: Trio for Violin, Horn, and Piano ("Hommage à Brahms") (1982), mvt. 1
George Perle: Sinfonietta II (1987): Scherzo I, Scherzo II
Arnold Schoenberg: Three Pieces for Piano, op. 11, no. 2 (1909)
Anton Webern: Five Movements for String Quartet, op. 5, no. 3 (1909)

RONDO FORM:

Béla Bartók: Three Rondos on Slovak Folk Tunes (1916, 1927); *Concerto for Orchestra* (1945), mvt. 4; Piano Sonata (1926), mvt. 3
Alban Berg: *Wozzeck*, act 2, scene 5 (1917–22)
Alberto Ginastera: *Rondo sobre temas infantiles argentinos*, op.19 (1947)

Paul Hindemith: Piano Sonata no. 2 (1936), mvt. 3

Igor Stravinsky: Concerto in D for String Orchestra (1946), mvt. 3

SONATA FORM (ALL FIRST MOVEMENTS):

Béla Bartók: Piano Sonata (1926); Sonata for Two Pianos and Percussion (1937); *Concerto for Orchestra* (1945); String Quartets no. 4 (1928), no. 5 (1934), no. 6 (1939)

Paul Hindemith: Piano Sonata no. 3 (1936)

Sergey Prokofiev: Symphony no. 5 (1944); Piano Sonata no. 7 (1939–42)

Arnold Schoenberg: String Quartet no. 2 (1907–8)

Dmitri Shostakovich: String Quartet no. 2 (1944)

Igor Stravinsky: Symphony in Three Movements (1942–45); Octet for Winds (1923); Septet (1953)

FUGUE:

Samuel Barber: Sonata for Piano, op. 26 (1949), mvt. 5

Béla Bartók: String Quartet No. 5 (1934), mvt. 5 (fugato); Piano Concerto no. 3 (1945), mvt. 3 (fugato); *Concerto for Orchestra* (1945), mvt. 5 (fugato in development section of sonata form)

Amy Beach: Prelude and Fugue, op. 81 (1917)

Ernst Bloch: Symphony in C♯ Minor (1901–2), mvt. 4

Elliott Carter: Piano Sonata (1945–46), mvt. 2

Paul Hindemith: *Ludus Tonalis* (1942); Piano Sonata no. 3 (1936), mvt. 4; String Quartet no. 5 (1923), first movement; Violin Sonata in C Major (1939), mvt. 3

Alan Hovhaness: Symphony no. 2 "Mysterious Mountain" (1955), mvt. 2

Charles Ives: "Fugue in Four Keys on *The Shining Shore*" (1903)

Ernst Krenek: String Quartet (1948), mvt. 7

György Ligeti: *Musica Ricercata*, no. 11 (1951–53); Requiem ("Kyrie" movement) (1963–65)

Witold Lutoslawski: Preludes and Fugue for Thirteen Solo Strings (1972)

Olivier Messiaen: *Vingt regards sur l'Enfant-Jésus* (1944), no. 6 ("Par Lui tout a été fait")

Darius Milhaud: *The Creation of the World* (first section) (1923)

George Rochberg: String Quartet no. 4 (1977), mvt. 2

Alfred Schnittke: Violin Sonata no. 2 (third section of single-movement work) (1968)

Dmitri Shostakovich: String Quartet no. 8 (1960), mvt. 5; 24 Preludes and Fugues for Piano, op. 87 (1950–51)

Igor Stravinsky: *Symphony of Psalms* (1930), mvt. 2; Concerto for Two Pianos (1935), mvt. 4; Septet (1953), mvt. 3; Symphony in Three Movements (1942–45), mvt. 3

Ernst Toch: *Geographical Fugue* (1930)

Heitor Villa-Lobos: *Bachianas Brasileiras* no. 1 (1930), mvt. 3

PASSACAGLIA:

Alban Berg: *Wozzeck*, act 1, scene 4 (1917–22)

Paul Hindemith: String Quartet no. 5 (1923), mvt. 4

György Ligeti: *Passacaglia ungherese* (1978)

Maurice Ravel: Piano Trio (1914), mvt. 3

Dmitri Shostakovich: Symphony no. 8 (1943), mvt. 4; Symphony no. 15 (1971), mvt. 4; Piano Trio no. 2 (1944), mvt. 3 (chaconne?); String Quartet no. 10 (1964), mvt. 3; Violin Sonata (1968), mvt. 3

Igor Stravinsky: Septet (1953), mvt. 2

Anton Webern: Passacaglia for Orchestra, op. 1 (1908)

THEME AND VARIATIONS:

Béla Bartók: "Variations on a Folk Tune" (*Mikrokosmos* 112, vol. 4 [1932–39]); "Free Variations" (*Mikrokosmos* 140, vol. 6 [1932–39]); Violin Concerto no. 2 (1938), mvt. 2

Luciano Berio: *Cinque variationi* for piano (1952–53; 1966)

Elliott Carter: Variations for Orchestra (1953–55)

Aaron Copland: *Piano Variations* (1930)

George Crumb: *Gnomic Variations* (1981)

Charles Ives: *Varied Air and Variations* (1920–22)

Sergey Prokofiev: Piano Concerto no. 3 (1917–21), mvt. 2

George Rochberg: *Partita-Variations* (1976)

Arnold Schoenberg: Variations for Orchestra, op. 31 (1926, 1928); Variations on a Recitative for Organ, op. 40 (1941); Theme and Variations for Band, op. 43a (1943)

Dmitri Shostakovich: Symphony No. 7 (1941), mvt. 1(march section)

Igor Stravinsky: Octet for Winds (1923), mvt. 2; Sonata for Two Pianos (1944), mvt. 2

COLLAGE:

Luciano Berio: *Sinfonia* (1968–69)

William Bolcom: Violin Sonata no. 2 (1978); *Black Host* (1967)

Peter Maxwell Davies: *Eight Songs for a Mad King* (1969)

Sofia Gubaidulina: Piano Sonata (1965)

Charles Ives: *The Fourth of July* (1914–18; 1930–31); *Three Places in New England* (1912–17; 1919–21), mvt. 2 ("Putnam's Camp")

Gustav Mahler: Symphony no. 1 (1884–1906), mvt. 3

George Rochberg: *Music for the Magic Theater* (1965); *Partita-Variations* (1976)

Arvo Pärt: *Collage on the theme BACH* (1964); *Pro et contra* (1966); Symphony no. 2 (1966); *Credo* (1968)

Alfred Schnittke: Concerto Grosso no. 1 (1977); Symphony no. 1 (1972); Violin Sonata no. 2 (1968)

Bernd Alois Zimmermann: *Musique pour les soupers du roi Ubu* (1962–66); *Requiem* (1967–69); *Die Soldaten* (1958–60)

MOMENT FORM:

Olivier Messiaen: *Chronochromie* (1960)

Karlheinz Stockhausen: *Kontakte* (1960); *Mixtur* (1964); *Momente* (1972)

Igor Stravinsky: *Symphonies of Wind Instruments* (1920/1947)

OPEN FORM (ALEATORY MUSIC/INDETERMINACY):

Earle Brown: *Available Forms I* and *II* (1961–62)

John Cage: *Music of Changes* (1951); *Atlas Eclipticalis* (1962); *Europera* (1988)

Morton Feldman: *Intersections* (1953)

Lukas Foss: *Echoi* (1961–63)

Christian Wolff: *Duo II for Pianists* (1958)

CHAPTER 8

MODERN APPROACHES TO METER AND RHYTHM

8.1 RETHINKING METERS AND METRIC STRUCTURE

For composers eager to break with tradition, an unusual metric scheme can be as appealing as a dissonant harmony or irregularly structured melody. Meter signatures such as $\frac{5}{4}$ or $\frac{7}{8}$, sometimes called **asymmetrical meters**, occasionally appear in music of the tonal era, but since 1900 they have become much more common. Modern composers are also likely to create asymmetrical groupings within common meters.

In Bartók's second "Dance in Bulgarian Rhythm" at the end of his *Mikrokosmos* collection, for example, the grouping within a seven-beat measure is specified within the meter signature itself, using "2 + 2 + 3" as the upper value (Ex. 8.1a). A similar signature in the sixth Dance gives "3 + 3 + 2" as the upper value, thus regrouping a number of beats that in other contexts would typically be notated in $\frac{4}{4}$ or $\frac{2}{2}$ (Ex. 8.1b). A "2 + 2 + 2 + 3" grouping in the fifth dance offers an unusual configuration of a $\frac{9}{8}$ measure (Ex. 8.1c).

EXAMPLE 8.1 Some unusual meter signatures in Bartók's *Mikrokosmos*

a. Bartók, Dance in Bulgarian Rhythm No. 2
(*Mikrokosmos* vol. 6, no. 149)

b. Bartók, Dance in Bulgarian Rhythm No. 6
(*Mikrokosmos* vol. 6, no. 153)

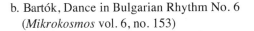

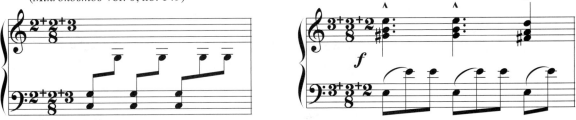

c. Bartók, Dance in Bulgarian Rhythm No. 5
(*Mikrokosmos* vol. 6, no. 152)

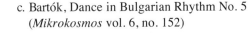

Bartók's Bulgarian Dances adhere to the conventional principle of metric consistency from one measure to the next. Composers of his era and beyond, especially Stravinsky but also many others, equally favored gestures built from meters that are constantly changing. Bartók draws attention to the novel approach in the second movement of his *Music for Strings, Percussion, and Celesta*, when his main theme from the Exposition of a sonata form, an energized proclamation in regular duple meter, returns with metric variation in the Recapitulation (Ex. 8.2a). The meter changes in Hindemith's Fourth String Quartet, which we studied in Exercise 7E, aren't even indicated on the score; performers are left to work out the metric values for themselves (Ex. 8.2b). Boulez's meter changes in the third movement of *Le marteau sans maître* include a measure with an upper value of "⁴⁄₃" in the meter signature, indicating four thirds of a beat to the bar (Ex. 8.2c). As if this weren't challenging enough for performers, each measure is also marked at a different tempo.

EXAMPLE 8.2   Examples of changing meters

a. Bartók, *Music for Strings, Percussion, and Celesta*, mvt. 2

b. Hindemith, String Quartet op. 22, no. 4, mvt. 2, mm. 1–3

c. Pierre Boulez, *Le marteau sans maître*, mvt. 3, mm. 1–6, G flute

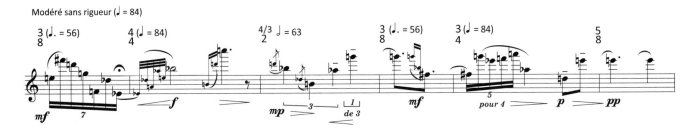

Perhaps the logical culmination of the reconception of metric structure is music notated with extremes of rhythmic and metric variability, sometimes described as the **New Complexity**. Composers associated with this trend (who reject the characterization) include Brian Ferneyhough, James Dillon, and Michael Finnissy. Their scores are ostentatiously—some might say outrageously—complicated, utilizing notations of extraordinary rhythmic durations and proportions (Ex. 8.3). More than one skeptical performer has certainly wondered why such radical conceptions aren't simply created for performance by computerized electronics, thereby assuring a level of precision that's surely unattainable by humans. But by rejecting this possibility, these composers raise provocative questions about the nature of musical notation and about the relationship between composer and performer. How precise, they might ask, is the notation of a Mozart aria or a Chopin etude? Is there such a thing as a "definitive" performance of music from any historical era?

EXAMPLE 8.3   Brian Ferneyhough, *Études transcendentales* no. 3

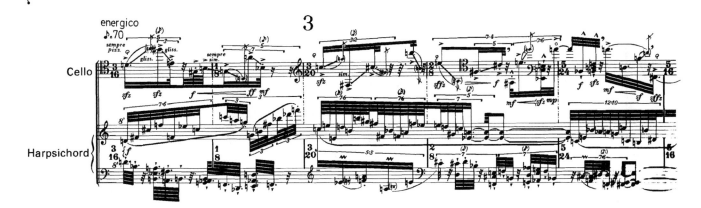

STUDY QUESTIONS 8.1

1. **What is "asymmetrical" about "asymmetrical meters?"**

2. **Why would an astute listener (without access to a score) be able to make a reasonable guess about the metric notation of Example 8.2b?**

8.2 METRIC LAYERING

Listen to the first of Stravinsky's Three Pieces for String Quartet. Example 8.4 shows the score of a twelve-bar excerpt, about a quarter of the entire movement. Metrically, the music is notated in a three-bar pattern, $\frac{3}{4}\frac{2}{4}\frac{2}{4}$—which is another way of notating a single bar of $\frac{7}{4}$ broken up into $3 + 2 + 2$. The three-bar pattern is articulated by the viola and cello, continually playing the same figures on each downbeat.

At the same time, the first violin's line generally avoids alignment with the meter changes. It recycles a limited repertory of notes and rhythms without ever establishing an obvious pattern. It seems to have a metric structure all its own, even if the precise metric organization of that structure is never completely clear.

Likewise, the second violin creates its own independent strand. Any individual statement of its four-note motive could be heard as a single bar of $\frac{2}{4}$, but these bars wouldn't line up in any predictable way with either of the other layers; the motive seems to enter and exit randomly. Indeed, by comparison with the regularity of the lower instruments, both violin lines give the impression of independence and randomness, in this excerpt and for the remainder of the movement.

Stravinsky here demonstrates a characteristic layering of distinct musical ideas. Sometimes this type of layering is described as **polyrhythm** or **polymeter**, indicating a concurrence of separate rhythmic continuities (whether or not the exact notation of each of those strands is clear and/or precise). We'll use the general term **metric layering** for any such juxtaposition of distinct musical ideas, regardless of how their independence is established and maintained.

EXAMPLE 8.4 Stravinsky, Piece no. 1 for String Quartet, mm. 4–15

It's a concept that was well established before the modern era, in opposing rhythmic groupings known as **cross-rhythms**. In the Tempo di Minuetto of his G-Major Keyboard Partita, for example, J. S. Bach establishes a cross-rhythm of two groups of three eighth notes against the notated triple meter, which groups the eighths as three groups of two (Ex. 8.5a). Contrasting beat divisions, as in a passage from Mozart's F-Major piano sonata (Ex. 8.5b), can also be considered a type of cross-rhythm. In both cases, separate rhythmic continuities coexist, working together and yet asserting their metric independence.

EXAMPLE 8.5   Examples of cross-rhythms in tonal music

a. J. S. Bach, Partita no. 5 in G Major, Tempo di Menuetto, mm. 37–44

b. Mozart, Piano Sonata in F Major, K. 332, mvt. 1, mm. 49–50

Composers in more recent times have explored this conception to a much fuller extent. Much of Schoenberg's second opus 11 piano piece establishes rhythmic oppositions, such as a quarter-note beat in one hand against a dotted quarter beat in another (Ex. 8.6). The oscillating left-hand figure alone is rhythmically ambiguous: its beaming indicates four groups of three, but a back-and-forth between two notes can easily be reinterpreted (and perceived) as a series of two-note groupings.

EXAMPLE 8.6 Schoenberg, Three Piano Pieces op. 11, no. 2, m. 8

Henry Cowell leaves no doubt about the identity of metric layers in his piano piece *Exultation* (Ex. 8.7). While the left hand repeats a three-chord pattern of black-key clusters establishing a triple meter, the right hand plays an exuberant melody notated in alternating measures of $\frac{4}{4}$ and $\frac{5}{4}$. The layers share a quarter-note pulse and seem curiously compatible in spite of their very different metric identities, in part because the beginning of each two-bar pattern in the right hand coincides with the downbeat of a $\frac{3}{4}$ bar in the left hand—the two-bar right-hand pattern is the same duration (nine beats) as three bars of the left hand's triple meter.

EXAMPLE 8.7 Henry Cowell, *Exultation* for piano, beginning

György Ligeti's Piano Étude no. 1 is consumed with metric interplay and layering (Ex. 8.8). It begins with coincidental groupings of 3 + 5, 3 + 5, and 5 + 3 in both hands in the first three measures. In measure 4, however, a larger flourish of eighth notes is one note shorter in the right hand than in the left, leaving the hands out of sync when they again present 3 + 5, 3 + 5, and 5 + 3 groupings. Next, a longer grouping of eighths is again shorter in the right hand, leaving the strands further out of sync, now by two eighths. This process continues throughout the first part of the piece, laying the groundwork for even more intricate metric oppositions to come.

EXAMPLE 8.8   Ligeti, Piano Étude no. 1 ("Désordre"), opening

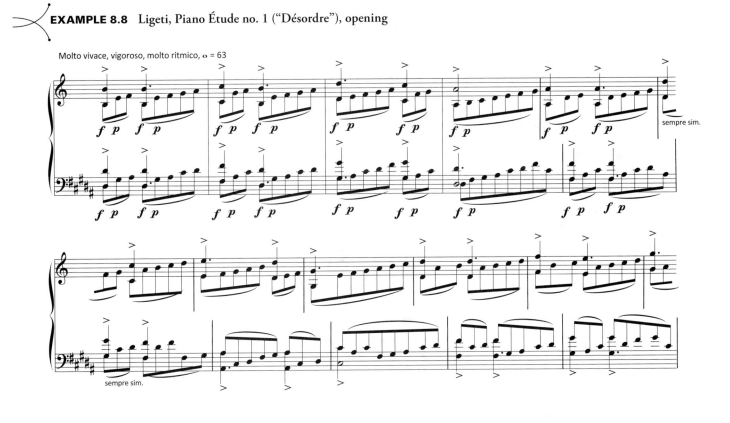

STUDY QUESTIONS 8.2

1. **Which layer in the Stravinsky example (Ex. 8.4) articulates the notated meter?**

2. **Besides the grouping differences, how else are the layers in the Ligeti example (Ex. 8.8) differentiated from each other?**

3. **What are the implied metric layers in Example 8.9 below?**

8.3   METRIC MODULATION

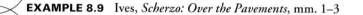

In 1906, while living on a busy street in New York City, Charles Ives took an interest in the rhythmic interplay he heard outside his window, from the footsteps of pedestrians of different sizes walking at different speeds, the clip-clops of horses on the street, and the occasional clacking of the wheels of a trolley car on its tracks. He wrote, "I was struck with how many different and changing kinds of beats, time, rhythms, etc. went on together—but quite naturally, or at least not unnaturally when you got used to it."[1] Eventually he incorporated these observations into a work for chamber ensemble entitled *Scherzo: Over the Pavements*. It begins with a layering of a clarinet in triple meter over a bassoon playing duple patterns (Ex. 8.9).

EXAMPLE 8.9   Ives, *Scherzo: Over the Pavements*, mm. 1–3

Later in the score, capturing the sounds of a sidewalk that has evidently become thick with activity, the music is a mass of cross-rhythms and tuplet figures (Ex. 8.10). The trumpet line most closely adheres to the notated $\frac{5}{8}$ meter, although with syncopations that avoid strong confirmation of an eighth-note pulse. The other layers express two different tuplet patterns: (1) three pulses per bar (quarter-note triplets) in the piccolo, clarinet, bassoon, and piano left hand; and (2) nine pulses per two bars (but also notated as quarter-note triplets) in the trombones, percussion, and piano right hand. The durations Ives used in the notation of the latter layer are inexact, but we can infer their rhythmic placement from their visual alignment in the score.

[1]Charles E. Ives, *Memos*, edited by John Kirkpatrick (New York: Norton, 1972), 62.

EXAMPLE 8.10 Ives, *Scherzo: Over the Pavements*, mm. 59–60

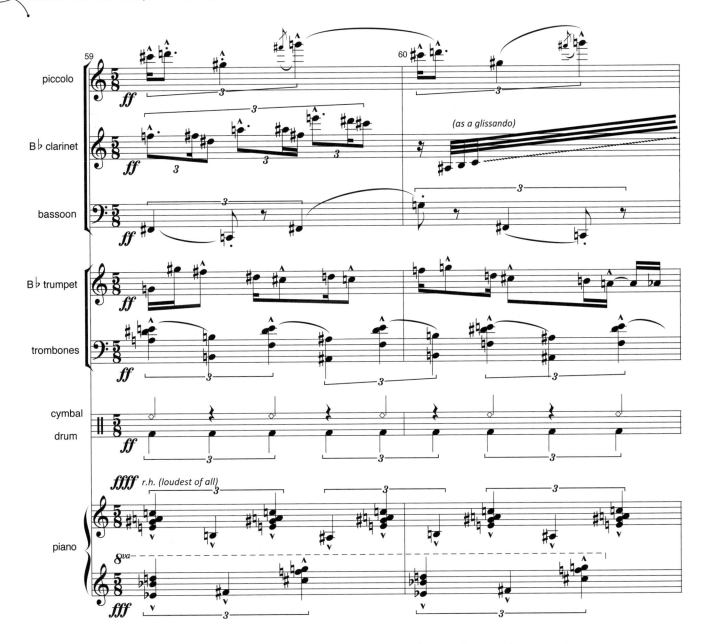

Notice what happens in the next measure (Ex. 8.11). Ives changes the meter signature to $\frac{9}{8}$ and adds a verbal instruction specifying that three notes of the preceding (piano) right hand are equal to a dotted quarter in the new meter. In a footnote, he clarifies that two of the previous $\frac{9}{8}$ measures (Ex. 8.10) are equivalent to one measure in the new $\frac{9}{8}$ meter. So the unusual quarter-note triplets in the previous nine-pulses-per-two-bars layer (trombones, percussion, piano right hand) are reinterpreted as eighth notes in the new meter.

EXAMPLE 8.11   Ives, *Scherzo: Over the Pavements*, m. 61

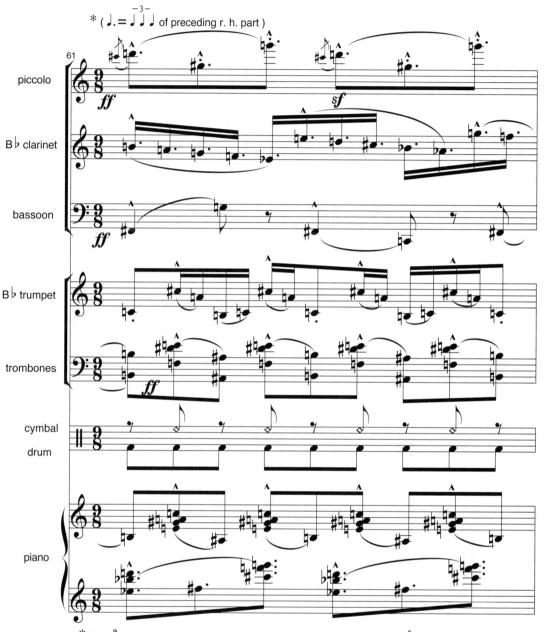

* This $\frac{9}{8}$ measure is of the same time duration as two of the preceding $\frac{5}{8}$ measures.

This sort of metric reinterpretation was later popularized by a composer who was once a young protégé of Ives, Elliott Carter. Carter sometimes described the technique as a "tempo modulation," but the more common term is **metric modulation**. In a metric modulation, a repeating rhythm that falls outside the notated meter, such as a triplet or other tuplet, or a duration different from the beat, is reinterpreted as a new basic pulse. The result can be a smooth transition from one tempo to another, like that provided by a pivot chord in a modulation from one tonality to another.

In Example 8.12a, from Carter's Fantasy for Woodwind Quartet, quarter-note triplets (mm. 15–16) are reinterpreted as regular quarter notes (starting in m. 17). As a result, the tempo speeds up from 84 bpm to 126. To calculate the change in metronome marking, determine the number of notes occupying the same amount of time in the old and new tempos. In this case, two quarter notes in the old tempo take up the same amount of time as three triplet quarter notes representing the new tempo:

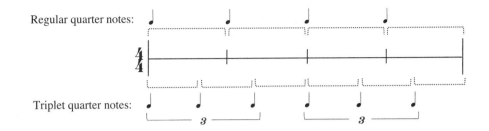

This 2:3 relationship is reflected in the change of metronome marking: 2:3 = 84:126 (84 is ⅔ of 126). Or to put it another way, increasing the tempo from 84 to 126 decreases the duration of the beat by ⅓.

Later in the Fantasy, the tempo returns from 126 to 84 by reinterpreting dotted quarter notes as the new pulse (Ex. 8.12b). Three regular quarter notes in the old tempo take up the same amount of time as two dotted quarters representing the new tempo:

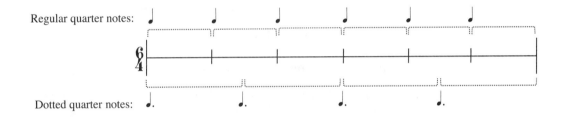

3:2 = 126:84 (126 is ³⁄₂ of 84). Or: decreasing the tempo from 126 to 84 increases the duration of the beat by half.

EXAMPLE 8.12 Carter, Fantasy from *Eight Etudes and a Fantasy* for Woodwind Quartet, excerpts

b.

STUDY QUESTIONS 8.3

1. In a metric modulation starting in $\frac{2}{2}$ meter at $\circ$ = 60 bpm, a triplet half note is reinterpreted as the regular half note. How many notes occupy the same amount of time in the old and new tempos? What is the metronome marking of the new tempo?

2. In a metric modulation starting in $\frac{4}{8}$ meter at $\eighth$ = 120 bpm, a dotted eighth note is reinterpreted as the regular quarter note. How many notes occupy the same amount of time in the old and new tempos? What is the metronome marking of the new tempo?

3. In a metric modulation starting in $\frac{4}{4}$ meter at $\circ$ = 80 bpm, a quintuplet quarter note is reinterpreted as the regular quarter note. How many notes occupy the same amount of time in the old and new tempos? What is the metronome marking of the new tempo?

8.4   RHYTHMIC PATTERNS

As we explored in Chapter 6, the search for novel principles of pitch organization led some post-tonal composers to draw inspiration from **structural models** such as wedge shapes or systems of interval relations. A similar motivation can explain the interest of some of these same composers in rhythmic patterns or other principles of rhythmic organization. In either case, freedom from an established orthodoxy triggered a search for alternative systems of logic and order—for new constraints to replace old ones.

Olivier Messiaen was especially interested in rhythmic patterns and structure. In his book *The Technique of My Musical Language* (1944), he explains his employment of principles of rhythmic transformation such as augmentation and diminution.[2] His methods include the "added value" technique, which transforms a rhythm by inserting an additional note or rest or dot. Messiaen also avoided meter signatures in his works, preferring instead to notate precise durations with or without a regular pulse or consistency from one measure to the next. In the beginning of the full-textured portion of his organ work "L'ange aux parfums,"

---

[2] Olivier Messiaen, *Technique de mon langage musical* (Paris: Leduc, 1944).

for example, Messiaen provides no meter signature, but we can make sense of the rhythmic notation by counting sixteenth notes within each grouping (Ex. 8.13). In the upper staff there is first a quarter note (four sixteenths), then a beam connecting three sixteenths, followed by a beam grouping together an eighth note, dotted eighth, eighth (seven sixteenths), and finally a half note (eight sixteenths). If the measure had an actual meter signature, the lower value would be 16, and the upper value would be the total duration in terms of sixteenth notes:

$$4 \, (\text{\musQuarter}) + 3 \, (\text{\musThreeSixteenth}) + 7 \, (\text{\musEighthDottedEighth}) + 8 \, (\text{\musHalf}) = 22/16$$

Messiaen points out in his book that the upper line of the excerpt, played by the organist's right hand, repeats the same rhythm in both measures (rhythm "a" in Ex. 8.13, notated separately in Ex. 8.14a). Just below that, the left-hand line presents the "a" rhythm in reverse and beginning one eighth note later ("b" in Exx. 8.13 and 8.14b). Each time this rhythm returns in the left-hand line, its beginning is delayed by an additional eighth note, causing it to lag farther and farther behind the right hand as the piece progresses (see m. 2 in the excerpt). Meanwhile, in the lower register, the organist's feet play a third line demonstrating what Messiaen describes as a "nonretrogradable rhythm," meaning that its durations read the same from left to right as from right to left ("c" in Exx. 8.13 and 8.14c).

EXAMPLE 8.13   Messiaen, "L'ange aux parfums" from *Les corps glorieux*, mm. 74–75

EXAMPLE 8.14 Messiaen, "L'ange aux parfums" rhythms

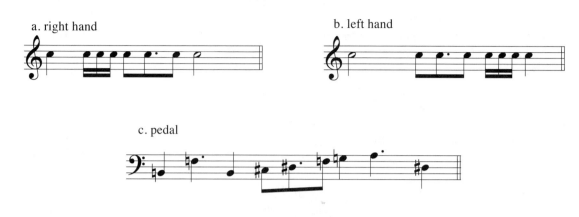

a. right hand

b. left hand

c. pedal

In act 3, scene 3 of *Wozzeck*, described by Berg as "invention on a rhythm," a repeating rhythmic pattern symbolizes the title character's jealous obsession with his lover, Marie, whom he has just murdered. We hear the motive first in the immediate aftermath of the crime, played by a large drum (Ex. 8.15a). Then when the scene changes to a tavern, a pianino on stage repeats the rhythm in its main melody over an oom-pah accompaniment (Ex. 8.15b). Within Wozzeck's first utterance in the scene, as he exhorts the dancing bar patrons to "schwitzt" (sweat) and "stinkt" (stink), the motive appears in augmentation, with each value doubled (Ex. 8.15c). We hear the rhythm more and more as the scene progresses and as Wozzeck becomes increasingly haunted by his despicable act, including a stretto (overlapping) of the original motive and its augmentation when Marie's friend Margret confronts Wozzeck about the blood on his hands and arms (Ex. 8.15d). The scene culminates at a fever pitch, with the winds blasting the motive in six-part stretto (Ex. 8.15e).

EXAMPLE 8.15 Berg, *Wozzeck*, rhythmic motives in act 3, scene 3 (all parts sound as notated)

a. large drum, mm. 114–115

fff *sehr rhythmisch*

b. pianino, mm. 122–125

Fast Polka (♩ = 160)

ff

c. Wozzeck, mm. 130–136

springt,   schwitzt _____   und   stinkt,   es _____   holt Euch doch

d. Margret and Wozzeck, mm. 197–200

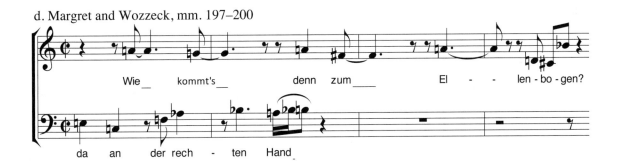

e. stretto of rhythmic pattern in measures 216–218

The music of this scene is closely focused just on the rhythm; the pitch-class contents of the various statements of the rhythmic motive are not comparably patterned. But of course, intertwining patterns of pitch and rhythm have been around for centuries, notably in the **isorhythmic motet** of the pretonal era, which is constructed of variously aligned patterns of melody ("color") and rhythm ("talea"). Charles Ives achieves a similar result in a raucous passage from the second movement of his Second String Quartet, with a six-beat pattern of successively decreasing metric subdivisions ("talea" in Ex. 8.16) in combination with a repeated ordering of eleven pitch classes ("color" in Ex. 8.16). As Ives explains, the second movement of his quartet is a series of "Arguments" among four men personified by the instrumental lines.[3] The viola seems to be arguing here with special vigor in favor of rigid organizing principles for music without tonality.

[3]Ives, *Memos*, 74.

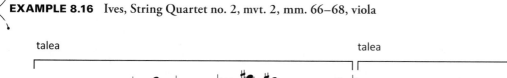

EXAMPLE 8.16 Ives, String Quartet no. 2, mvt. 2, mm. 66–68, viola

STUDY QUESTIONS 8.4

1. In what sense are Messiaen's rhythmic patterns in Example 8.13 more "radical" than Berg's rhythmic patterns in Example 8.15 and Ives's rhythmic patterns in Example 8.16?

2. What are the two different source sets for the right hand chords, and for the pedal melody, in Example 8.13? (Be specific.)

3. In Example 8.15, which versions of the rhythmic motive are presented in augmentation? What is the proportion between the durations of the original motive and the durations of the augmentations?

VOCABULARY

asymmetrical meter	metric layering	polymeter
cross-rhythm	metric modulation	polyrhythm
isorhythmic motet	New Complexity	

EXERCISES

A. METER SIGNATURES

Add an appropriate meter signature to the first measure of each exercise. If any subsequent measures have different metric structures, insert a new meter signature to indicate the change. Assume that any meter signature continues to be valid unless indicated otherwise (don't add a meter signature to any measure that has the same signature as the previous measure).

B. ANALYSIS OF METRIC LAYERING

Identify and describe the metric layers in each excerpt.

Demo. Igor Stravinsky (1882–1971), "Marche chinoise," *Chant du Rossignol,* **rehearsal 23**

The excerpt has two metric layers:

1. The celesta (which is entirely pentatonic) follows the notated meter. It returns to the same sonority on the downbeats of the first, third, and fifth measures (D$\sharp_4$–G$\sharp_4$–C$\sharp_5$–F$\sharp_5$). Upward leaps emphasize the downbeats of the last two measures.
2. The harp and low strings create groupings of three eighth notes suggesting a $\frac{3}{8}$ meter, irrespective of the notated meter. The low strings play only on the third note of each group. Further, the last notes of the three-groupings (in harp and in cello and bass) move downward by step in the first three groups and then repeat that same descent for the groups thereafter. Thus each three-eighth-note group is actually part of a larger grouping with two other three-eighth-note groups: the pattern is three groups of three, essentially $\frac{9}{8}$ meter, unfolded three times over the course of the excerpt.

1. Olivier Messiaen (1908–1992), "Le Verbe," *La nativité du Seigneur*, mm. 208–12

2. Igor Stravinsky (1882–1971), "Petit concert," *L'histoire du soldat*, rehearsal 20

3. Béla Bartók (1881–1945), String Quartet no. 3, mvt. 2, after rehearsal 37

C. ANALYSIS OF RHYTHMIC PATTERNS

1. Olivier Messiaen (1908–1992), "Amen des anges, des saints, du chant des oiseux,"
Visions de l'Amen for two pianos, mm. 24–30

What is the role of "nonretrogradable rhythm" in this excerpt?

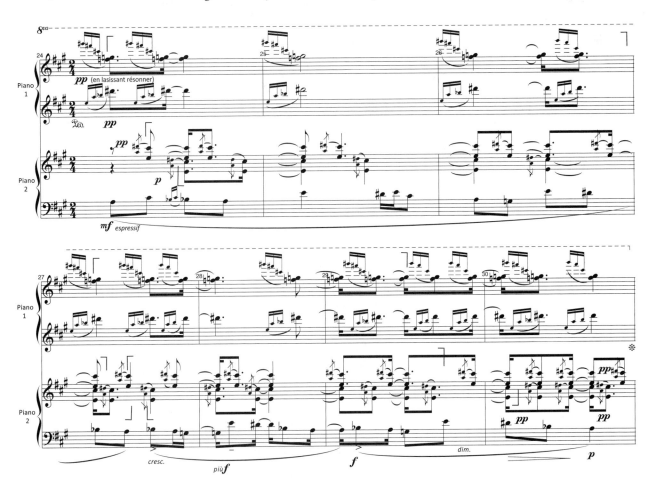

2. Charles Ives (1874–1954), Scherzo ("Holding Your Own") for String Quartet, middle section (mm. 22–28)

How is the music in each instrument related to the other instruments with respect to rhythmic patterns and pitch materials?

D. COMPOSITION EXERCISES

Demo. Compose a melody that gradually changes tempo through a process of "metric modulation." Give the metronome markings for both tempos and explain their mathematical relationship with respect to the musical change.

As the initial metronome marking implies, the first tempo is too fast for an eighth-note pulse. The beat in the first five measures would be felt either as a quarter note or a dotted quarter note. (♩ ♩ ♩. in measure 1, ♩. ♩. ♩ in measure 2, and so forth.) So to determine the precise relationship between the two tempos, take the quarter note as the regular beat of the first tempo.

The modulation reinterprets the dotted quarter as the new beat. So, three beats in the old tempo (quarter notes) take up the same amount of time as two notes (dotted quarter notes) representing the new tempo, and 3:2 = 180:120.

1. **Compose a melody that gradually changes tempo through a process of "metric modulation." Give the metronome markings for both tempos and explain their mathematical relationship with respect to the musical change.**

2. **Compose a melody that features non-coincidental patterns of pitch and rhythm, modeled after the melody by Charles Ives discussed earlier in this chapter (Ex. 8.16).**

3. Compose a melody within the metrically irregular framework provided below. Think of your melody as the main theme for a movement of a sonata for an instrument you know well, and take advantage of the expressive and technical potential of that instrument. For the pitch material, use a familiar resource such as the whole-tone or octatonic collection, or try pitch materials of some other kind.

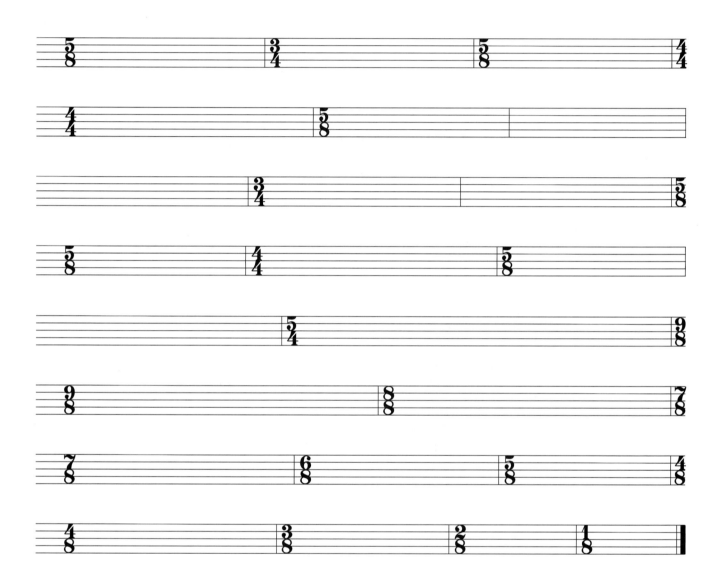

4. **Study the given metrically irregular melody. Imagine it being played by a treble instrument such as violin, flute, trumpet, or marimba. On the staffs below the melody, create ostinatos that are metrically regular, each establishing its own metric layer (without altering the notated meter signatures). Decide for yourself which instrument(s) will play each layer. For inspiration and guidance, consult Stravinsky's metric layerings shown in section 8.2 of this chapter (Ex. 8.4) and in the section B exercises. What is the regular meter implied by each of your layers?**

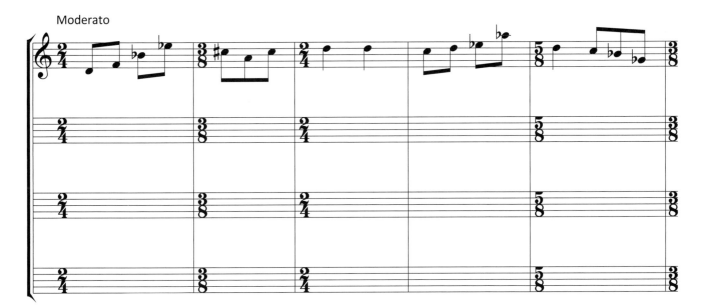

FOR FURTHER STUDY

UNUSUAL METERS:

Béla Bartók: *Contrasts* (1942), mvt. 3; String Quartet no. 5 (1934), mvt. 3; Sonata for Two Pianos and Percussion (1937), mvt. 1

Pierre Boulez: *Improvisations sur Mallarmé*, no. 1(1957)

György Ligeti: Étude no. 4 for Piano, "Fanfares" (1985)

Karlheinz Stockhausen: *Zeitmasse* (1955–56)

Edgard Varèse: *Intégrales* (1924–25); *Octandre* (1923); *Offrandes* (1921)

METRIC IRREGULARITY:

Béla Bartók: "Change of Time," *Mikrokosmos* 126, vol. 5 (1932–39); *Concerto for Orchestra* (1945), mvt. 4

Leonard Bernstein: Serenade for Violin, Strings, Harp, and Percussion (1954), mvt. 1; Symphony no. 1 ("Jeremiah"), mvt. 2(1942)

Aaron Copland: *El Salón México* (1932–36), last part

Carl Orff: *Carmina Burana* (1936), mvt. 6 ("Tanz")

Arnold Schoenberg: Five Pieces for Piano, op. 23, no. 4 (1920, 1923)

Igor Stravinsky: "Danse sacrale," *Le sacre du printemps* (1911–13)

METRIC LAYERING (INCLUDING CROSS-RHYTHMS):

Béla Bartók: *Music for Strings Percussion, and Celesta* (1936), mvt. 2

Henry Cowell: *Exultations* for piano (1919)

Paul Hindemith: Symphony: "Mathis der Maler" (1933–34), mvt. 1

Charles Ives: "In the Night," *Set for Theater Orchestra* (1915–16; 1929–30)

György Ligeti: Études for Piano I, no.1, "Désordre" (1985)

Olivier Messiaen: *Quartet for the End of Time* (1940–41), mvt. 4 ("Intermède"); "Le Verbe," *La nativité du Seigneur* (1935)

Arnold Schoenberg: Three Pieces for Piano, op. 11, no. 2 (1909); Five Pieces for Orchestra, op. 16, no. 1 (1920)

Igor Stravinsky: Dumbarton Oaks Concerto (1938), mvt. 3; Symphony in C (1940), mvt. 1; "Jeu du rapt," *Le sacre du printemps* (1911–13)

METRIC MODULATION:

Elliott Carter: Cello Sonata (1948); String Quartet no. 1 (1950–51); String Quartet no. 2 (1959)

RHYTHMIC PATTERNS:

Alban Berg: *Chamber Concerto* (1923–25), mvt. 3

Charles Ives: *From the Steeples and the Mountains* (1905–6); *Hallowe'en* (1914); *In Re Con Moto et al.* (1915–16; 1923–24)

Olivier Messiaen: *Quartet for the End of Time* (1940–41), mvt. 1 ("Liturgie de cristal"); "Le vent de l'Esprit," *Messe de la Pentacôte* (1949–50)

CHAPTER 9

THE TWELVE-TONE METHOD

9.1 ANTON WEBERN'S SONG FOR VOICE AND PIANO, OP. 23, NO. 2

In 1933 and 1934, Anton Webern composed six songs for high voice and piano, all settings of poetry by his friend Hildegard Jone. He organized the songs into two groups, designated opus 23, *Three Songs from "Viae Inviae" by Hildegard Jone*, and opus 25, *Three Songs on Poems by Hildegard Jone*. These sets were Webern's last contributions to the song genre (he died in 1945).

The second setting from opus 23 is filled with images of motion and light:

1	*Es stürtzt aus Höhen Frische,*	*Plunging from above is freshness*
2	*die uns leben macht:*	*which causes us to live:*
3	*das Herzblut*	*the heart's blood*
4	*ist die Feuchte uns geliehen,*	*is the moistness lent to us,*
5	*die Träne ist die Kühle uns gegeben:*	*the tear is the coolness given to us;*
6	*sie fliesst zum Strom der Gnade*	*wondrously it flows back*
7	*wunderbar zurück.*	*to the stream of grace.*
8	*Ach, ich darf sein,*	*Oh, I am privileged to be*
9	*wo auch die Sonne ist!*	*Where the sun also is!*
10	*Sie liebt mich ohne Grund,*	*It loves me without reason;*
11	*ich lieb' sie ohne Ende.*	*I love it endlessly.*
12	*Wenn wir einander Abend, Abschied scheinen,*	*When in the evening we bid goodbye,*
13	*den Himmel und die Seele überglüht*	*the sky and my soul*
14	*noch lange Glut.*	*remain aglow long after.*

In its first sentence (lines 1–7), a flow of energy and life connects heaven and earth, perhaps as an expression of awe and elation over an actual affair of the heart. The second and third sentences (lines 8–11) fill the imagery with sunlight, extolling the gratification of mutual love—between sky and soil just as between blissful earthly souls. After the sun goes down in the final sentence (lines 12–14), the mutual warmth and wonder remain.

Let's look at Webern's setting of the poem's second and third sentences (Ex. 9.1). First, sentence 2 (lines 8–9) unfolds five bars of $\frac{1}{2}$ meter, with frequent triplet rhythms and single notes alternating with multi-note chords. In the piano of measure 15, for example, a single note B$_2$ in the left hand is answered by a grace-note-plus-trichord in the right, and then in measure 16 a solitary B♭$_5$ is answered by another right-hand trichord; later we hear pentachords (m. 18) and a tetrachord (m. 19) expressed as vertical harmonies. For the setting of sentence 3 (lines 10–11), however, the meter changes to $\frac{5}{4}$ and the piano notes are stated mostly in succession, abandoning the previous triplets and multi-note chords. A quick glance at the score to the entire song will reveal that Webern organizes texture in this same way throughout, moving back and forth between mostly chords and triplets in $\frac{1}{2}$ meter (mm. 1–7, 25–27, 29–30), and regular (non-triplet) notes in succession in $\frac{5}{4}$ meter (mm. 8–14, 23–24, 28).

EXAMPLE 9.1   Webern, op. 23, no. 2, mm. 15–22 with annotations highlighting members of (014)

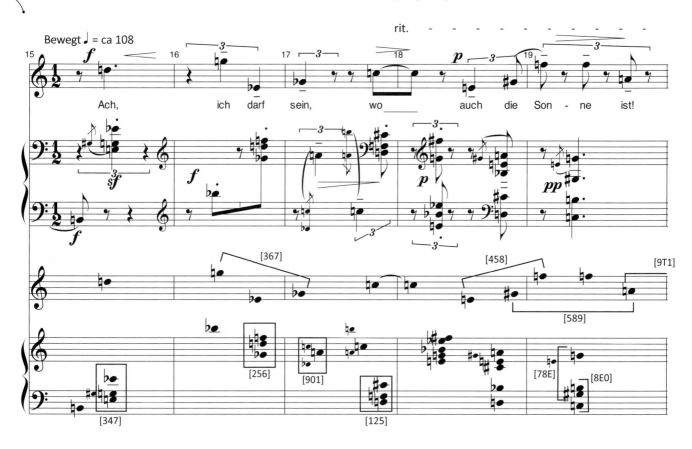

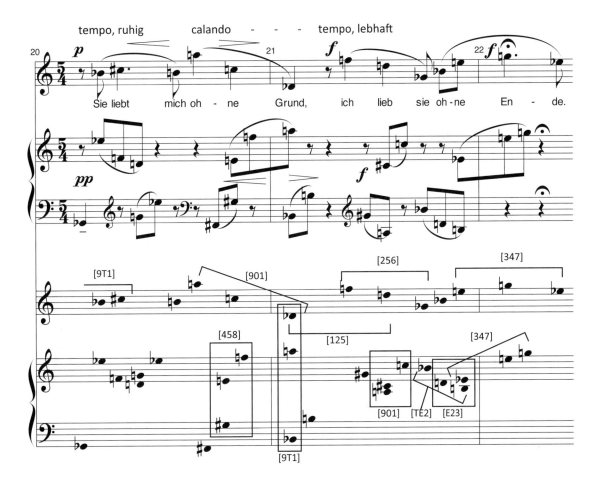

Amid the contrasts in rhythm, meter, and note groupings is a wealth of harmonic consistency, not just in the settings of sentences 2 and 3 but throughout the song. One aspect of this is highlighted in the analytic shorthand beneath the score in Example 9.1: each boxed or bracketed trichord is a member of set class (014). In the vocal line, for example, sentence 2 neatly expresses (014)s at "ich darf sein" and overlapping in "auch die Sonne ist!," followed by an additional (014) that connects the last note of sentence 2 with the first note of sentence 3 [9T1], and then we hear members of this set class four more times, with overlappings, in sentence 3 (mm. 20–22). Meanwhile, the first three trichordal simultaneities in the piano are (014) members (mm. 15–17); (014)s are also prominent among adjacencies in the larger chords (e.g., overlapping in the tetrachord in m. 19). In the piano part for sentence 3 (mm. 20–22), members of (014) are frequently formed by combining notes of the two hands.

But these are just the (014)s. It's also easy to find recurrences of other trichords (e.g., (013), (015)) and larger sets. Members of (0145) are prominent, for example, in the vocal line in measures 15–17 [2367] and 18–19 [4589], and in the piano in measures 15 [3478], 19 [78E0], and 21 [8901]/[TE23]. The pentachordal simultaneity in measure 18 [3467T], a member of (01347), echoes that same pentachord type in the nearby vocal line on "ich darf sein, wo auch" [03467], heard again in the last five notes of the excerpt's vocal line [3467T].

STUDY QUESTIONS 9.1

Identify the following pc sets from Example 9.1 in normal form and prime form:

1. **The first three notes in the vocal line.**

2. **All the piano notes in measure 16.**

3. **The first three notes in the piano right hand in measure 20.**

4. **In the piano right hand, the last two notes of measure 20 plus the first note of measure 21.**

5. **The first three notes of the vocal line in measure 20.**

9.2   THE TWELVE-TONE ROW

As we've seen in earlier chapters, Webern's work often features a saturation of set types in a musical environment (especially these specific set types). Set recurrence in this song, however, is controlled with special intensity and precision because the song was composed using a system of composition developed in the 1920s by Webern's teacher, Arnold Schoenberg, and known as the **twelve-tone method** (or **serial method**). In **twelve-tone music** (**serial music**), all pitch relations, including melodies and harmonies, originate from a single unique ordering (serialization) of the twelve pitch classes known as a **twelve-tone row**. The composer determines the ordering of pitch classes in the row as the first stage in the compositional process and then features structural elements of the row in the pitch organization of the complete work.

Later in this chapter, we'll take a close look at Webern's techniques for using the row to determine melodies and harmonies in his opus 23, no. 2 song. First, however, let's examine the underlying row itself. One of the clearest presentations of the row for opus 23 appears in song 2, in the vocal setting of sentence 2 of the poem and the beginning of sentence 3. Example 9.2 displays this row, both as a melody (9.2a) and as a series of pitches (9.2b). We'll use the label "P_2" for this particular ordering of notes: P for "prime," and the subscript indicating the row's first pitch class. Think of the row in pc-space, not in p-space. In other words, P_2 is the ordered pc segment $\langle 2-7-3-6-0-4-8-5-9-T-1-E \rangle$, not specifically the pitch series $\langle D_5-G_5-E\flat_4-G\flat_4-C_5-E_4-G\sharp_4-F_5-A_4-B\flat_4-C\sharp_5-B_4 \rangle$.

EXAMPLE 9.2   Webern, op. 23, no. 2, vocal line, mm. 15–20 (row "P_2")

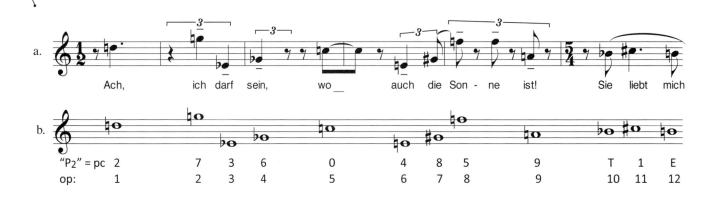

The integers 1–12 designate the **order positions** ("op") within a row, as notated at the bottom of Example 9.2b. Notice that in this melodic realization of row P$_2$ (Ex. 9.2a), the pitch class in op 8 (pc 5) occurs twice in measure 19, for both syllables of the word "Sonne." An immediate repetition of this sort is fairly common in twelve-tone music, although pitch-class repetitions that are farther apart are usually avoided, especially in Webern's twelve-tone practice.

As you might have guessed in light of our earlier set class analysis, members of (014) are formed four times between adjacent notes within P$_2$. Instances of this trichord type are formed at order positions <2–3–4> [367], <6–7–8> [458], <7–8–9> [589], and <9–10–11> [9T1]. From this we can infer that Webern initially constructed the row to highlight this trichord type, and that he then made efforts to draw attention to this feature when he composed his song setting.

Let's also consider what other trichords are formable between consecutive notes in P$_2$, whether or not they're musically highlighted. All possible three–note segments of a row are known as its **internal trichords**. To list them all, identify the trichord formed by order positions <1–2–3>, then <2–3–4>, <3–4–5>, and so forth, concluding with <10–11–12> (Ex. 9.3). In this row, (014) is the most frequently occurring internal trichord. Only one other trichord type, (015), appears twice (op <1–2–3> and <8–9–10>), and the remaining internal trichords include one each of members of set classes (036) (op <3–4–5>), (026) (op <4–5–6>), (048) (op <5–6–7>), and (013) (op <10–11–12>). We might also make note of the **wraparound trichords** at order positions <11–12–1>, which is [E12] (013), and <12–1–2>, which is [7E2] (037). The wraparounds aren't necessarily relevant in any given implementation of the twelve-tone method, however.

EXAMPLE 9.3 Webern, op. 23, no. 2, row P$_2$ and internal trichords

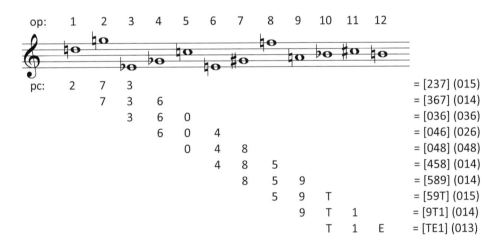

A twelve-tone composer makes decisions about which internal trichords to highlight and which to underplay. In the melody we've been looking at (Ex. 9.2a), Webern uses rhythm and phrasing to draw attention to the (014)s at order positions <2–3–4> and <6–7–8>, and to the final (013) (op's <10–11–12>). Notice, however, that P$_2$'s internal trichords also include a diminished triad at op <3–4–5> and an augmented triad at <5–6–7> that are hardly noticeable in this melodic setting, which breaks them apart with an isolated pc 0 (op 5) surrounding the measure 18 barline. An alternative setting of this row that highlights these triads could potentially sound quite different from Webern's version. These factors help explain how a single twelve-tone row can provide ample source material for compositional variety within multi-movement works, or, in the case of opus 23, separate songs within a set.

Example 9.4 lists the **internal tetrachords** for row P$_2$. Two tetrachord types appear twice: members of (0145) at op <1–2–3–4> and <6–7–8–9>, and members of (0148) at <5–6–7–8> and <8–9–10–11>. Webern's melody (Ex. 9.2a) especially brings out the (0145)s in the initial setting of "Ach, ich darf sein," and then at the end of that sentence, "auch die Sonne ist!," where the pc 0 surrounding the measure 18 barline again acts as a separator.

EXAMPLE 9.4   Webern, op. 23, no. 2, row P$_2$ and internal tetrachords

op:	1	2	3	4	5	6	7	8	9	10	11	12		
pc:	2	7	3	6									= [2367]	(0145)
		7	3	6	0								= [0367]	(0147)
			3	6	0	4							= [0346]	(0236)
				6	0	4	8						= [0468]	(0248)
					0	4	8	5					= [4580]	(0148)
						4	8	5	9				= [4589]	(0145)
							8	5	9	T			= [589T]	(0125)
								5	9	T	1		= [9T15]	(0148)
									9	T	1	E	= [9TE1]	(0124)

Ultimately, when studying a twelve-tone work, we'll want to be aware of a row's **internal sets** of all sizes. Example 9.5 lists all of them of sizes 2–9 for row P$_2$. (Wraparounds, whose relevance varies, aren't included.) Each column of the chart gives the set formed starting with the order position at the top of that column. So the first line of labels, labeled "ic" and starting with "5 4 3 6 . . . ," lists the two-note sets, or interval classes, formed between adjacent notes in the row: ic 5 from pc 2 in op 1 to pc 7 in op 2, ic 4 from pc 7 (op 2) to pc 3 (op 3), and so forth. The next line gives the prime forms of the internal trichords, starting with (015) at op <1–2–3> and moving on to (014) at op <2–3–4>, (036) at op <3–4–5>, and so forth. Trichords and tetrachords are listed in prime form, while larger sets are listed by Forte name.

EXAMPLE 9.5   Webern, op. 23, no. 2 row P$_2$, internal sets of sizes 2–9

Pc:	2	7	3	6	0	4	8	5	9	T	1	E
Starting op:	1	2	3	4	5	6	7	8	9	10	11	12
Ic:	5	4	3	6	4	4	3	4	1	3	2	
Trichords:	**(015)**	(014)	(036)	**(026)**	(048)	(014)	**(014)**	(015)	(014)	**(013)**		
Tetrachords:	**(0145)**	(0147)	(0236)	(0248)	**(0148)**	(0145)	(0125)	(0148)	**(0124)**			
Pentachords:	5-Z18	5-16	5-26	5-13	5-21	5-6	5-Z37	5-13				
Hexachords:	**6-Z10**	6-15	6-39	6-15	6-16	6-Z44	**6-Z39**					
Septachords:	7-13	7-3	7-16	7-13	7-21	7-Z18						
Octachords:	8-2	8-3	8-Z29	8-19	8-7							
Nonachords:	9-2	9-2	9-11	9-4								

STUDY QUESTIONS 9.2

In the internal sets of Webern's op. 23 row (Ex. 9.5),

1. **What is the trichord type formed at op <6–7–8>?**

2. **Which trichord types, in which order positions, include op 4?**

3. **What order positions combine to form members of (0148)?**

4. **Which tetrachord types, in which order positions, include op 7?**

5. **What are the wraparound tetrachords (<op> [normal form] (prime form))?**

6. **What is the pentachord type formed at op <5–6–7–8–9>?**

7. **What order positions combine to form instances of the same pentachord type (and name it)?**

8. **What is the hexachord type formed at op <6–7–8–9–10–11>?**

9. **What are the order positions of the two hexachord types that can each be formed twice within the row?**

10. **After seeing the Forte name of the first internal pentachord, how can you predict the Forte name of the last internal septachord?**

11. **What is the significance of the set names shown in bold lettering in Example 9.5?**

How did you answer the last study question? To locate the entries in bold type in Example 9.5 within P$_2$, organize the notes of the row into separate, non-overlapping segments. For the trichords, these would be op <1–2–3>, <4–5–6>, <7–8–9>, and <10–11–12>. In other words, organize the twelve notes of the row into four non-overlapping groups of three. To locate the bold-type tetrachords, then, make three non-overlapping groups of four: op <1–2–3–4>, <5–6–7–8>, and <9–10–11–12>. The other bold-type sets in Example 9.5 are the two hexachordal halves, op <1–2–3–4–5–6> and <7–8–9–10–11–12>. As a group, these non-overlapping trichords, tetrachords, and hexachords are known as the **regular partitions** of the row (Ex. 9.6). It's useful to be aware of the regular partitions of a row because composers often accentuate these segments in their musical realizations. As we've seen, however, other internal sets can be just as relevant; in the melody we've studied from Webern's op. 23 no. 2 (Ex. 9.2a), four members of set class (014) are prominent, only one of which (op <7–8–9>) is a regular partition.

EXAMPLE 9.6 Webern, op. 23, no. 2 row P$_2$, regular partitions

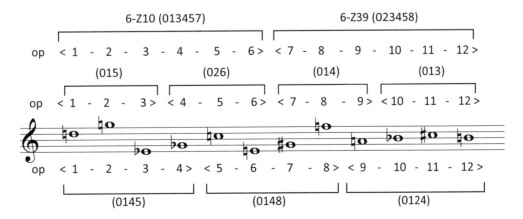

The regular trichordal partitions are a primary compositional focus in music Webern wrote just before the opus 23 songs, although given a later opus number. The row of his Concerto, op. 24, is constructed with members of (014) in order positions <1–2–$3>$, <4–5–$6>$, <7–8–$9>$, and <10–11–$12>$ (Ex. 9.7). Milton Babbitt originated the term **derived row** to describe a row with equivalent regularly partitioned trichords, a concept that can extend to equivalent regularly partitioned tetrachords.[1] This terminology recognizes that a row of this type is essentially derived, or generated, from the initial trichord and its multiple transformations into non-overlapping pc sets. When Webern first presents the row at the beginning of the Concerto, he isolates each of the trichords in a different instrument, and gives it a distinctive rhythm (Ex. 9.8).

EXAMPLE 9.7   Webern, Concerto for Nine Instruments, op. 24, row P_E, regular partitions

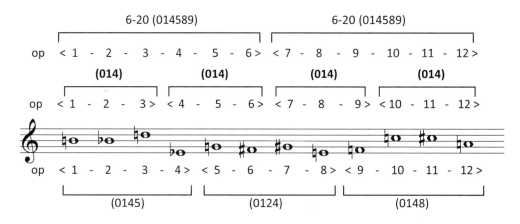

EXAMPLE 9.8   Webern, Concerto for Nine Instruments, op. 24, mvt. 1, mm. 1–3 (sounds as notated)

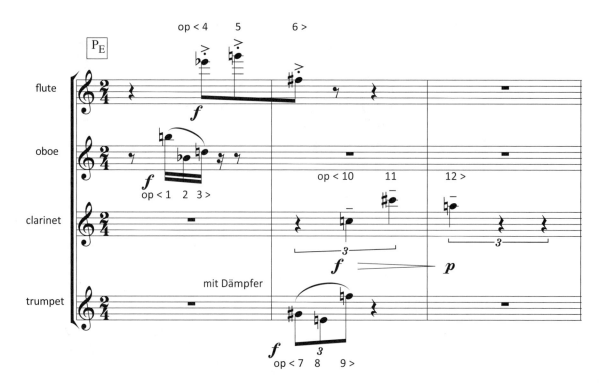

[1]Milton Babbitt, "Some Aspects of Twelve-Tone Composition," *The Score and I. M. A. Magazine* 12 (June 1955): 59.

9.3   TWO BASIC ROW TRANSFORMATIONS

In the typical implementation of the twelve-tone method, rows are transformed by **ordered transposition** or **ordered inversion**. As we learned in Chapters 2 and 3, ordered operations keep the original ordering of a musical object intact. The object is defined by its ordering. Indeed, ordering is the only way to distinguish one twelve-tone row from another; in terms of pitch-class *contents* (ordering aside), all twelve-tone rows are the same.

So when we speak of transposing or inverting a row, we're always talking about ordered transposition or ordered inversion. To transpose a row, for example, keep the ordering intact while shifting all the pitch classes by the same amount. To transpose P_2 by T_6, add 6 (mod 12) to each pitch-class integer in P_2:

$$
\begin{array}{lcccccccccccc}
P_2 = & 2 & 7 & 3 & 6 & 0 & 4 & 8 & 5 & 9 & T & 1 & E \\
+ & \underline{6} & \underline{6} & \underline{6} & \underline{6} & \underline{6} & \underline{6} & \underline{6} & \underline{6} & \underline{6} & \underline{6} & \underline{6} & \underline{6} \\
T_6(P_2) = & 8 & 1 & 9 & 0 & 6 & T & 2 & E & 3 & 4 & 7 & 5
\end{array}
$$

You might find it useful to conceptualize row transposition as a literal move upward of each note in pitch space (Ex. 9.9). Keep in mind, however, that a row is an ordering of pitch *classes*, not pitches, and so its musical realization could place the notes in any octave. A literal, uniform shift upward is just one of many possibilities.

EXAMPLE 9.9   Webern, op. 23, no. 2 row P_2, T_{+6} transposition

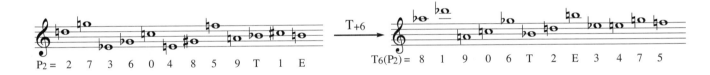

$$P_2 = \quad 2 \quad 7 \quad 3 \quad 6 \quad 0 \quad 4 \quad 8 \quad 5 \quad 9 \quad T \quad 1 \quad E \qquad\qquad T_6(P_2) = \quad 8 \quad 1 \quad 9 \quad 0 \quad 6 \quad T \quad 2 \quad E \quad 3 \quad 4 \quad 7 \quad 5$$

We'll continue to use the P label for the result of this operation, or for any other transposition of P_2, plus a subscript indicating the initial pitch class. Therefore, $T_6(P_2) = P_8$. ("T_6 of P_2 equals P_8.") The transpositional distance is clearly displayed in the relationship of the subscripts: because $2 + 6 = 8$, row P_2 transposed by T_6 yields row P_8. In general, to determine the subscript for row P_y of a particular transposition T_n of P_x, add $x + n$ (mod 12):

$$P_x \xrightarrow{\;T_n\;} P_y \qquad x + n = y \text{ (mod 12)}$$

So T_7 of P_2 would yield P_9 (because $2 + 7 = 9$); T_E of P_2 would generate P_1 (because $2 + 11 = 1$); and so forth.

If you want to determine the transpositional operator between a given P_x and P_y, subtract the first subscript from the second (mod 12):

$$P_x \xrightarrow{\;T_n\;} P_y \qquad n = y - x \text{ (mod 12)}$$

For example, the operation that maps P_2 to P_4 is T_2 (because $4 - 2 = 2$); the operation that generates P_7 from P_E is T_8 (because $7 - 11 = 8$); and so forth.

The twelve different transpositions of the row, displaying subscripts 0–11, are the **P-forms** of this row. These transpositional partners are twelve members of an equivalence class known as the **row class**, analogous to a set class of equivalent pitch-class sets.

And like a set class, a row class also includes inversional equivalences. Let's first think of row inversion in pitch space, keeping in mind that the row actually consists of pitch classes that may be expressed in any octave. We'll start by specifying the pitch intervals (Chapter 2.3) in the realization of P_2 in Webern's song (see Ex. 9.2): it begins with pitch interval $+5$ from D_5 to G_5, then jumps down -16 from G_5 to Eb_4, followed by $+3$ from Eb_4 to Gb_4, and so forth (Ex. 9.10a).

EXAMPLE 9.10   Webern, op. 23, no. 2 row P_2, p-space I_T inversion

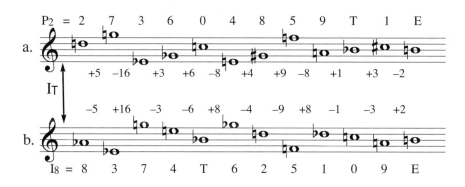

To create a pitch-space inversion, start on any note and move these same distances in opposite directions; replace all pluses with minuses and minuses with pluses. Since this version of P_2 begins with pitch intervals $+5$, -16, and $+3$, start the inversion with pitch intervals -5, $+16$, and -3. Example 9.10b demonstrates a pitch-space inversion of this row statement starting on Ab_4, $(-5 =)$ Eb_4, $(+16 =)$ G_5, $(-3 =)$ E_5. The result is labeled I_8, which indicates an inversional form of the row beginning on pitch-class 8.

The index number of this inversion (Chapter 2.4) is the sum of corresponding pitch classes, 10:

$P_2 =$	2	7	3	6	0	4	8	5	9	T	1	E
$I_8 =$	8	3	7	4	T	6	2	5	1	0	9	E
Index $=$	10	10	10	10	10	10	10	10	10	10	10	10

This is easy to see just in the subscript labels: we know that the index number between P_2 and I_8 is 10 because the sum of their subscripts, 2 and 8, is 10. Thus row form I_8 is the I_T-transform of row form P_2, and row form P_2 is the I_T-transform of row form I_8. In general, to find the index of inversion between rows P_x and I_y, add $x + y$ (mod 12):

$$P_x \xleftrightarrow{\;\;I_n\;\;} I_y \qquad x + y = n \;(\text{mod } 12)$$

Row forms P_8 and I_8 are equivalent by operation I_4 (because $8 + 8 = 4$); row forms I_5 and P_2 are I_7-transforms of each other (because $5 + 2 = 7$); and so forth.

If you want to find the subscript of an inversional partner I_y of P_x for a given index I_n, subtract $n - x$ (mod 12):

$$P_x \xleftrightarrow{\;\;I_n\;\;} I_y \qquad y = n - x \;(\text{mod } 12)$$

Likewise, to find the subscript of an inversional partner P_x of I_y for a given index I_n, subtract $n - y$ (mod 12):

$$P_x \xleftarrow{\quad I_n \quad} I_y \qquad x = n - y \ (\text{mod } 12)$$

For example, the I_8 partner of row form P_3 is row form I_5 (because $8 - 3 = 5$); the I_1 partner of row form I_7 is row form P_6 (because $1 - 7 = 6$); and so forth.

The row class includes twelve different inversional forms, or **I-forms**, with subscripts 0–E. Each of the twelve P-forms can be partnered with some I-form at a given index number. Row forms P_2 and I_8 are I_T-partners, as we've seen, but so are other P- and I-forms with subscripts that sum to 10: P_3/I_7, P_4/I_6, P_5/I_5, P_6/I_4, P_7/I_3, P_8/I_2, P_9/I_1, P_T/I_0, P_E/I_E, P_0/I_T, and P_1/I_9.

The twelve I-forms themselves are equivalent via ordered transposition, at distances revealed in their subscripts:

$$I_x \xrightarrow{\quad T_n \quad} I_y \qquad x + n = y, \ n = y - x \ (\text{mod } 12)$$

So, T_5 maps row form I_9 to row form I_2 (because $9 + 5 = 2$); the transpositional mapping from row form I_1 to row form I_T is T_9 (because $10 - 1 = 9$); and so forth.

STUDY QUESTIONS 9.3

1. **What are the labels for the following row forms?**

   1.1. T_6 of P_8 1.2. T_1 of P_8 1.3. T_E of P_3

   1.4. T_5 of I_9 1.5. T_6 of I_1

2. **What is the (ordered) transformation between the row forms with these labels?**

   2.1. P_2 and P_5 2.2. P_5 and P_2 2.3. P_T and P_4

   2.4. I_4 and I_5 2.5. I_8 and I_4

3. **What is the index number between these row forms?**

   3.1. P_2 and I_7 3.2. I_7 and P_2 3.3. P_5 and I_T 3.4. I_9 and P_9

4. **What are the labels for the following row forms?**

   4.1. I_9 of P_2 4.2. I_9 of I_7 4.3. I_3 of I_T

   4.4. I_4 of P_7 4.5. I_4 of I_9 4.6. I_T of P_0

9.4 THE INT, AND TWO MORE BASIC ROW TRANSFORMATIONS

One important means of defining and understanding a row is contained in the series of pitch-class intervals (Chapter 2.3) between consecutive notes, also known as the **INT**.[2] The INT of Webern's P_2 row is:

P_2	=	2		7		3		6		0		4		8		5		9		T		1		E
INT	=		5		8		3		6		4		4		9		4		1		3		T	

[2] Robert D. Morris, *Class Notes for Atonal Music Theory* (Hanover, NH: Frog Peak Music, 1991), 43.

The INT isn't the same as the list of two-note sets, or interval classes, on the first line of the list of internal sets for this row in Example 9.5. Interval classes combine interval inverses into the same category (Chapter 2.3). Pitch-class intervals distinguish between an interval and its inverse. The second element in this INT, for example, is 8, while in the internal set list (Ex. 9.5)—which lists interval classes, not pitch-class intervals—this distance is represented by its inverse, 4.

The operation of transposition has no effect on the INT; the INTs of P_2, P_8, and of any other P-form are the same (Ex. 9.11ab). When a row is inverted, each pc interval in the INT is replaced with its inverse, resulting in the **INT′** ("INT inverse"). The INT of the P-form of the op. 23 row, for example, begins with pc intervals 5, and 8, and 3, while the INT′ begins with pc intervals 7, 4, and 9 (Ex. 9.11c). Transposing an I-form of a row has no effect on the INT′; all I-forms of a row have the same INT′.

EXAMPLE 9.11   Webern, op. 23, no. 2 P- and I-forms with INT/INT′ labels

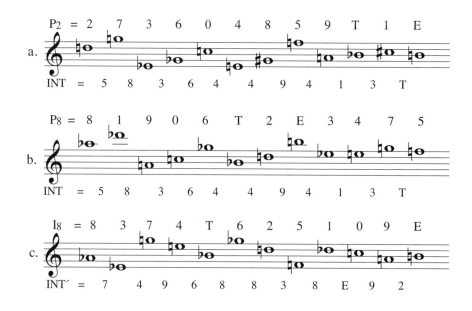

So far we've accounted for the twelve P-forms of a row, and the twelve I-forms, but these constitute only half of the complete row class (assuming the row isn't symmetrical). In the classic twelve-tone method, any of the P- and I-forms can also be reversed, creating **retrograde** forms of the row. Retrogrades of P-forms are known as **R-forms**, and retrogrades of I-forms are designated **RI-forms**. With the R- and RI-forms we have now doubled the size of the row class to forty-eight members: twelve P-forms and their twelve reversals as R-forms, plus twelve I-forms and their twelve reversals as RI-forms.

Labels for the R- and RI-forms retain the subscripts of the row forms they reverse. The retrograde of P_2, for example, is R_2, short for "retrograde of P_2." Thus the subscript for an R-form is actually its last note, not its first:

$$P_2 \quad = \quad 2 \; 7 \; 3 \; 6 \; 0 \; 4 \; 8 \; 5 \; 9 \; T \; 1 \; E$$
$$R_2 \quad = \quad E \; 1 \; T \; 9 \; 5 \; 8 \; 4 \; 0 \; 6 \; 3 \; 7 \; 2$$

To label the order positions of an R-form, start with 12 and progress down to 1. In other words, use the same pairings of order positions and pitch classes found in the P-form that's being reversed:

R_2	=	E	1	T	9	5	8	4	0	6	3	7	2
op	=	12	11	10	9	8	7	6	5	4	3	2	1

P_2	=	2	7	3	6	0	4	8	5	9	T	1	E
op	=	1	2	3	4	5	6	7	8	9	10	11	12

So, pc 2 is op 1 in both P_2 and R_2; pc 5 is op 8 in both P_2 and R_2; and so forth. Similarly, the first trichord in P_2, pc <2–7–3> at order positions <1–2–3>, reappears in reverse order as the last trichord in R_2, pc <3–7–2> op <3–2–1>. Another example: the second internal tetrachord of P_2 (not a regular partition) is pc <7–3–6–0> op <2–3–4–5>, which reappears as the penultimate internal tetrachord in R_2, pc <0–6–3–7> op <5–4–3–2>.

Subscripts and labels for I- and RI-forms work the same way:

I_8	=	8	3	7	4	T	6	2	5	1	0	9	E
RI_8	=	E	9	0	1	5	2	6	T	4	7	3	8

RI_8	=	E	9	0	1	5	2	6	T	4	7	3	8
op	=	12	11	10	9	8	7	6	5	4	3	2	1

I_8	=	8	3	7	4	T	6	2	5	1	0	9	E
op	=	1	2	3	4	5	6	7	8	9	10	11	12

Retain the same pairings of order position numbers and pitch classes found in the I-form being reversed. Pitch–class 2 is op 7 in both I_8 and RI_8. The second regularly partitioned trichord in I_8, pc <4–T–6> op <4–5–6>, reappears as the third regularly partitioned trichord of RI_8, pc <6–T–4> op <6–5–4>. Another example: the third internal pentachord of I_8, pc <7–4–T–6–2> op <3–4–5–6–7>, reappears as the antepenultimate internal pentachord in RI_8, pc <2–6–T–4–7> op <7–6–5–4–3>.

Notice what happens to the INT or INT′ when you retrograde a row or its inversion. An R-form of a row reverses the numbers in the INT but also inverts them (compare Exx. 9.12a and 9.12b). In other words, the succession of pitch-class intervals for R-forms is R(INT′). An RI-form of a row reverses the INT (compare Exx. 9.12a and 9.12d). The succession of pitch-class intervals for RI-forms is R(INT).

EXAMPLE 9.12   Webern, op. 23, no. 2 P-, R-, I-, and RI-forms with INT/INT′ labels

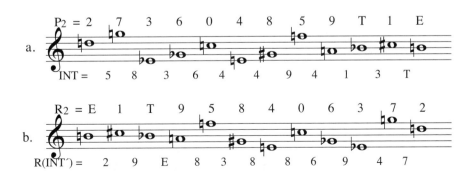

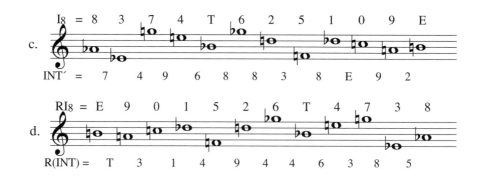

c.   I$_8$ = 8   3   7   4   T   6   2   5   1   0   9   E

INT′ =   7   4   9   6   8   8   3   8   E   9   2

d.   RI$_8$ = E   9   0   1   5   2   6   T   4   7   3   8

R(INT) =   T   3   1   4   9   4   4   6   3   8   5

These INT/INT′ relationships vividly capture the solidarity and power of the row class and, ultimately, of the twelve-tone method itself. For most listeners, intervallic relationships are the primary means of distinguishing one row form from another. A twelve-tone work is typically an interplay and exploration of a carefully selected group of these forms. The music invites us to absorb their close relationships and follow the composer's pathway through their sounds and combinations.

As we do so, basic structural features pop to the surface again and again, as we noticed in our study of the middle section of Webern's opus 23 song at the beginning of this chapter. This naturally occurs because every member of the row class has the same internal set structure. The table of internal sets for row P$_2$ (Ex. 9.5) also applies to row form P$_8$, or to row form I$_8$, or to any other P-form or I-form and their retrogrades.

Recall, for example, that members of (014) occur four times within row P$_2$, at order positions <2–3–4>, <6–7–8>, <7–8–9>, and <9–10–11> (Ex. 9.5). Example 9.13a highlights the contents of the first of these, <2–3–4>, when this row is variously transposed and inverted. In P$_2$, the trichord in these order positions is pc-set [367]. If P$_2$ is then transposed by T$_6$ to yield P$_8$, of course this pc-set is also transposed at T$_6$, to [901]. Likewise, when P$_2$ is inverted by I$_{10}$ resulting in row form I$_8$, [367] is inverted at I$_{10}$, to [347]. Example 9.13b shows the similar journey of the (014) trichord in order positions <6–7–8>, from pc-set [458] in P$_2$ to [TE2] in P$_8$ and [256] in I$_8$. Follow similar transformational progressions for the trichords at order positions <7–8–9> in Example 9.13c and <9–10–11> in Example 9.13d.

EXAMPLE 9.13   Members of (014) within P- and I-forms

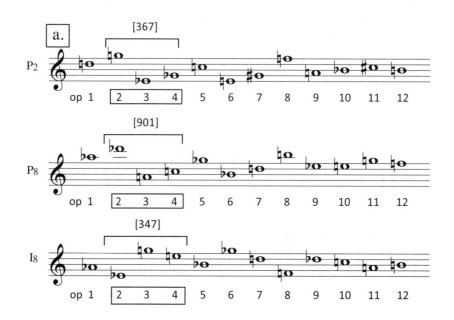

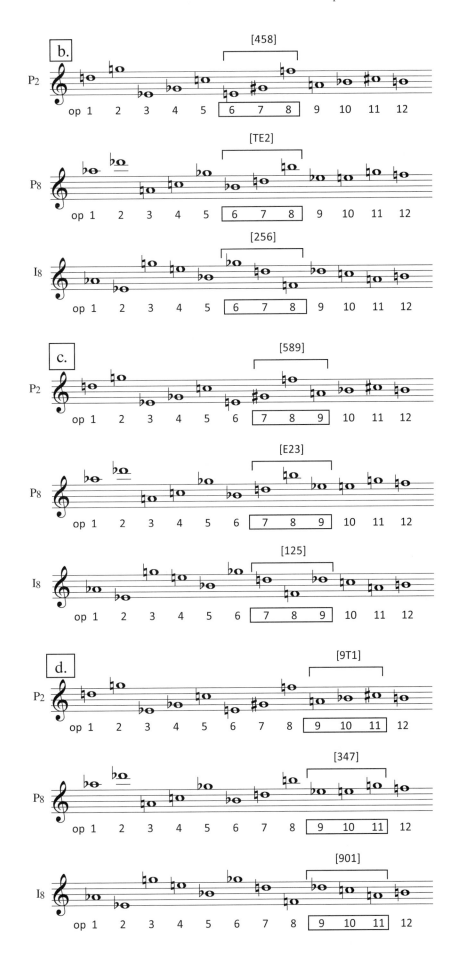

Choose any set of any size within the row and you'll find a member of the same set class at the same order positions in any transpositional or inversional form of the row. Any R- or RI-form contains those same recurrences in reverse order, numbered with the same order-position labels. The chart of internal sets in Example 9.5 applies equally to every member of this row class.

STUDY QUESTIONS 9.4

1. **Assuming that pc string <273604859T1E> is labeled P_2, give the labels for these forms of the same row:**

    1.1. <81906T2E3475>   1.2. <E1T958406372>   1.3. <5743E2T60918>
    1.4. <8374T625109E>   1.5. <E901526T4738>

2. **Give the <pc string> and <order positions> of these row segments (P_2 = <273604859T1E>):**

    2.1. The first trichord of P_8.
    2.2. The first trichord of R_2.
    2.3. The last tetrachord of R_8.
    2.4. The third regularly partitioned trichord of I_8.
    2.5. The first hexachord of RI_8.

3. **Define and explain the relationships between the series of pitch-class intervals in:**

    3.1. All P-forms.   3.2. All I-forms.
    3.3. All R-forms.   3.4. All RI-forms.

4. **Look again at Webern's "derived row" and its initial musical realization in Examples 9.7 and 9.8:**

    4.1. What are the pc intervals formed between consecutive notes in each of the regularly partitioned trichords?
    4.2. Think of the pc intervals of the first trichord (op <1–2–3>) as a mini-INT; which of the other regularly partitioned trichords expresses the mini-INT'?
    4.3. How do the pc intervals of the other two trichords relate to the mini-INT and mini-INT'?
    4.4. If the first trichord (op <1–2–3>) is a "P-form" of a three-tone mini-row, how would you identify the other three regularly partitioned trichords as forms of that mini-row, based on your awareness of the consecutive pc intervals in each?

9.5 THE ROW CHART

A **row chart** organizes all forty-eight members of the row class into one graphic summary (Ex. 9.14). (This type of chart is also known as a "twelve-tone matrix," "Babbitt square," or "magic square.") Each line of the chart is a P-form, starting with P_0 across the top, and each column is an I-form, starting with I_0 down the left side. The lines reading right to left are R-forms, and the columns reading bottom to top are RI-forms. Notice the diagonal of zeroes from upper left to lower right.

The notes of row form I$_0$ in the leftmost column determine the first notes of the P-form in each line: because the second note (op 2) of I$_0$ is pc 7, the P-form on the second line of the chart is P$_7$; because the third note (op 3) of I$_0$ is pc E, the P-form on the third line is P$_E$; and so forth. Likewise, the notes of the P$_0$ across the top determine the first notes of the I-form in each column: because the second note (op 2) of P$_0$ is pc 5, the I-form in the second column of the chart is I$_5$; because the third note (op 3) of P$_0$ is pc 1, the I-form in the third column is I$_1$; and so forth.

Placement on the top line or leftmost column of the chart doesn't imply prominence in a particular musical setting. The top line simply contains the P$_0$ form of the row, the left column the I$_0$ form. P$_0$ and I$_0$ may have no roles in the music at all. The row forms we've been studying in Webern's song appear on the fourth and fifth lines (P$_8$ and P$_2$) and in the third column from the right (I$_8$).

EXAMPLE 9.14   Row chart for Webern, op. 23, no. 2

0	5	1	4	T	2	6	3	7	8	E	9
7	0	8	E	5	9	1	T	2	3	6	4
E	4	0	3	9	1	5	2	6	7	T	8
8	1	9	0	6	T	2	E	3	4	7	5
2	7	3	6	0	4	8	5	9	T	1	E
T	3	E	2	8	0	4	1	5	6	9	7
6	E	7	T	4	8	0	9	1	2	5	3
9	2	T	1	7	E	3	0	4	5	8	6
5	T	6	9	3	7	E	8	0	1	4	2
4	9	5	8	2	6	T	7	E	0	3	1
1	6	2	5	E	3	7	4	8	9	0	T
3	8	4	7	1	5	9	6	T	E	2	0

To construct a row chart, start by writing P$_0$ from left to right and then I$_0$ sharing the first note of P$_0$ and extending downward. To generate I$_0$, you can work from the INT′, or you can simply calculate the mod-12 inverses of each note in P$_0$: in the row chart for any row, op 2 of I$_0$ (pc 7) is the mod-12 inverse of op 2 of P$_0$ (pc 5); op 3 of I$_0$ (pc E) is the mod-12 inverse of op 3 of P$_0$ (pc 1); and so forth (Ex. 9.15).

EXAMPLE 9.15   Mod-12 inverses between P_0 and I_0

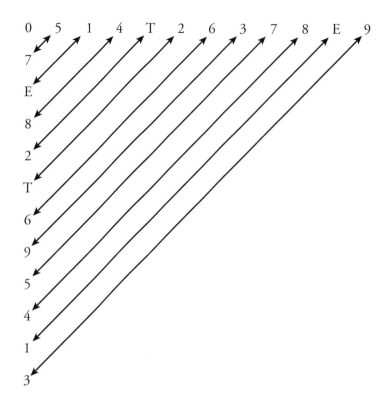

After you've established I_0 in the leftmost column, you could then calculate all the remaining lines as transpositions of the lines immediately above: because line 2 begins with pc 7, which is T_7 of the pc 0 above, all other notes in line 2 will also be T_7 of the pc above; because line 3 begins with pc E, which is T_4 of the pc 7 immediately above, all other notes in line 3 will also be T_4 of the pc immediately above; and so forth.

You can also use the INT to create each line of the chart (because all P-forms have equivalent INTs). After you've determined the starting pc of each line (i.e., after you've written I_0 down the left side), simply use each note of I_0 as the beginning of a pc series projecting the series of pitch-class intervals of the INT, <5–8–3–6–4–4–9–4–1–3–T>, on each line.

You could also apply your knowledge of index numbers to complete a row chart. Since every pc in each P-form in each line is also a note in each I-form in each column, you can calculate P-forms as sums between a member of P_0 and a member of I_0. Line 2 consists of the sums of the pc in op 2 of I_0 (pc 7) with every pc in P_0 (Ex. 9.16); line 3 consists of the sums of the pc in op 3 of I_0 (pc E) with every pc in P_0 (Ex. 9.17); and so forth.

EXAMPLE 9.16   Using sums to calculate P₇ on line 2 of the op. 23 row chart

The pc in this op of P_7 . . .	. . . is the sum of this op in I_0 . . .	. . . and this op in P_0 . . .	. . . with this result . . .
2	2 (pc 7)	2 (pc 5)	pc 0
3	2 (pc 7)	3 (pc 1)	pc 8
4	2 (pc 7)	4 (pc 4)	pc E
5	2 (pc 7)	5 (pc T)	pc 5
6	2 (pc 7)	6 (pc 2)	pc 9
7	2 (pc 7)	7 (pc 6)	pc 1
8	2 (pc 7)	8 (pc 3)	pc T
9	2 (pc 7)	9 (pc 7)	pc 2
10	2 (pc 7)	10 (pc 8)	pc 3
11	2 (pc 7)	11 (pc E)	pc 6
12	2 (pc 7)	12 (pc 9)	pc 4

I_0

op	1	2	3	4	5	6	7	8	9	10	11	12
P_0 → 1	0	5	1	4	T	2	6	3	7	8	E	9
P_7 → 2	7	0	8	E	5	9	1	T	2	3	6	4

EXAMPLE 9.17   Using sums to calculate P_E on line 3 of the op. 23 row chart

The pc in this op of P_E . . .	. . . is the sum of this op in I_0 . . .	. . . and this op in P_0 . . .	. . . with this result . . .
2	3 (pc E)	2 (pc 5)	pc 4
3	3 (pc E)	3 (pc 1)	pc 0
4	3 (pc E)	4 (pc 4)	pc 3
5	3 (pc E)	5 (pc T)	pc 9
6	3 (pc E)	6 (pc 2)	pc 1
7	3 (pc E)	7 (pc 6)	pc 5
8	3 (pc E)	8 (pc 3)	pc 2
9	3 (pc E)	9 (pc 7)	pc 6
10	3 (pc E)	10 (pc 8)	pc 7
11	3 (pc E)	11 (pc E)	pc T
12	3 (pc E)	12 (pc 9)	pc 8

I_0

op	1	2	3	4	5	6	7	8	9	10	11	12
P_0 → 1	0	5	1	4	T	2	6	3	7	8	E	9
2	7	0	8	E	5	9	1	T	2	3	6	4
P_E → 3	E	4	0	3	9	1	5	2	6	7	T	8

STUDY QUESTIONS 9.5

1. **What are the labels for the following row forms in the row chart for Webern's op. 23 (Ex. 9.14)?**

    1.1. The P-form on the bottom line.

    1.2. The R-form on the bottom line.

    1.3. The I-form in column 5.

    1.4. The RI-form in column 2.

2. **Locate the diagonal of zeroes from upper left to lower right on the row chart (Ex. 9.14).**

    2.1. What is the relevance of the diagonal number sequence to the immediate right of the diagonal of zeroes?

    2.2. What is the relevance of the diagonal number sequence to the immediate left of the diagonal of zeroes?

9.6   EXPLORING THE ROW CLASS

Let's investigate more possibilities for relations between row forms. As we've seen, all P-forms are transpositional partners with each other, as are all I-forms with each other. Of course, the same is true of their retrogrades: all R-forms are transpositional partners with each other, as are all RI-forms transpositions of each other. And since the subscript doesn't change between P-forms and their reversals as R-forms, and between I-forms and their reversals as RI-forms, the subscript relations we've already observed continue to apply:

$$R_x \xrightarrow{\;T_n\;} R_y \qquad x + n = y,\; n = y - x \;(\text{mod } 12)$$

$$RI_x \xrightarrow{\;T_n\;} RI_y \qquad x + n = y,\; n = y - x \;(\text{mod } 12)$$

If, for example, row form P_5 is T_3 of row form P_2 (because $2 + 3 = 5$), then row form R_5 is likewise T_3 of row form R_2. And if row form I_7 is T_8 of row form I_E (because $11 + 8 = 7$), then row form RI_7 is T_8 of row form RI_E.

I-partners and their retrogrades are similarly predictable. What's true of the relationship between row forms T_x and I_y is also true between their retrogrades, row forms R_x and RI_y:

$$R_x \xleftarrow{\;I_n\;} RI_y \qquad x + y = n,\; y = n - x,\; x = n - y \;(\text{mod } 12)$$

For example, if row forms P_4 and I_7 map to each other at operation I_E (because $4 + 7 = 11$), then row forms R_4 and RI_7 map to each other by that same operator. Likewise, since the I_2 mapping of row form P_8 is row form I_6 (because $2 - 8 = 6$), it follows that the I_2 mapping of row form R_8 is row form RI_6. And so forth.

When an operation involves retrograde in addition to transposition or inversion, the "R" indicator is placed before the T or I ("RT_n" or "RI_n"), but the retrograde is performed last, after the transposition or inversion. The addition of the retrograde operation doesn't alter the subscript. Transposition followed by retrograde relates a P-form and an R-form, or an I-form and an RI-form:

$$P_x \xrightarrow{\text{RT}_n} R_y \qquad x + n = y, n = y - x \ (\text{mod } 12)$$

$$R_x \xrightarrow{\text{RT}_n} P_y \qquad x + n = y, n = y - x \ (\text{mod } 12)$$

$$I_x \xrightarrow{\text{RT}_n} RI_y \qquad x + n = y, n = y - x \ (\text{mod } 12)$$

$$RI_x \xrightarrow{\text{RT}_n} I_y \qquad x + n = y, n = y - x \ (\text{mod } 12)$$

So, RT_2 of row form P_1 produces P_3 (because $1 + 2 = 3$) followed by retrograde, or row form R_3. The operation that transforms row form RI_7 into row form I_3 is T_8 (because $3 - 7 = 8$) followed by retrograde, or RT_8.

Inversion followed by retrograde relates a P-form and an RI-form, or an I-form and an R-form:

$$P_x \xleftarrow{\text{RI}_n} RI_y \qquad x + y = n, y = n - x, x = n - y \ (\text{mod } 12)$$

$$I_x \xleftarrow{\text{RI}_n} R_y \qquad x + y = n, y = n - x, x = n - y \ (\text{mod } 12)$$

For example, if row forms P_6 and I_9 map to each other at operation I_3 (because $6 + 9 = 3$), then row forms P_6 and RI_9 map to each other at operation RI_3. Likewise, since the I_0 mapping of row form I_2 yields row form P_T (because $0 - 2 = 10$), it follows that the RI_0 mapping of row form I_2 is row form R_T. And so forth.

STUDY QUESTIONS 9.6

1. **What are the labels for the following row forms?**

    1.1. T_6 of R_8 1.2. T_1 of RI_8 1.3. I_3 of R_3

    1.4. I_3 of RI_0 1.5. I_E of RI_1

2. **What is the (ordered) transformation between the row forms with the following labels?**

    2.1. R_T to R_1 2.2. RI_5 to RI_2 2.3. R_0 to RI_1

    2.4. RI_1 to R_0 2.5. RI_8 to R_2

3. **What are the labels for the following row forms?**

    3.1. RT_5 of P_3 3.2. RT_9 of R_8 3.3. RT_1 of I_4 3.4. RT_7 of RI_T

    3.5. RI_7 of P_3 3.6. RI_7 of RI_4 3.7. RI_2 of RI_8

    3.8. RI_E of R_8 3.9. RI_E of I_3 3.10. RI_1 of I_6

4. **What is the (ordered) transformation between the row forms with the following labels?**

    4.1. P_0 to R_5 4.2. R_5 to P_0 4.3. R_T to P_8 4.4. I_2 to RI_6

    4.5. RI_5 to I_4 4.6. P_7 to RI_6 4.7. RI_6 to P_7

    4.8. RI_2 to P_8 4.9. I_6 to R_3 4.10. R_7 to I_7

5. **Return one more time to Webern's "derived row" and its initial musical realization in Examples 9.7 and 9.8:**

    5.1. Specifically which ordered transformations map the first trichord to each of the others?

    5.2. Specifically how does the musical presentation of these trichords help portray their relationships?

9.7   ROW USAGE IN WEBERN'S SONG, OP. 23, NO. 2

All the set relations in Webern's op. 23 no. 2 song that we noticed at the beginning of this chapter, and many others that we didn't, are indicators of the structure of the row and its impact on pitch relations. Let's explore exactly how this works. Example 9.18 republishes the score of the middle section as it appears in Example 9.1 but with annotations showing the order position numbers of the row forms used in this passage: P_2, I_8, RI_8, I_2, and P_8. Remember that order positions for R-forms begin with 12 and progress down to 1. The first trichord of RI_8, for example, comprises order positions <12–11–10>, not <1–2–3>.

The distribution of notes from row forms here is typical of Webern's implementation of the twelve-tone method. One of his favorite techniques, for example, is the overlap, evident in the vocal line in measure 20, where the B_4 serves as both the final note (op 12) of P_2 and the first note (op 12) of RI_8. Just after that, two notes in the vocal line overlap with row forms in the piano: C_5 at the end of measure 20 serves as both op 10 of RI_8 and op 5 of the P_2 below; and the next vocal note, Db_4, is both op 9 of RI_8 and op 11 of P_2.

Otherwise, Webern follows basic principles in his implementation of the row forms. Notes within a row form typically occur in succession and may occasionally repeat immediately (as does the op 8 of P_2 in m. 19) but may not recur out of order. When the notes in a segment of a row form occur together, as a vertical sonority, they may appear in any vertical ordering as long as all the notes being simultaneously expressed are contiguous within the row. Webern's methods make no assumptions about rhythm or emphasis or instrumentation of the row presentation; these are expressive details determined during the compositional process.

EXAMPLE 9.18   Webern, op. 23, no. 2, mm. 15–22, row usage

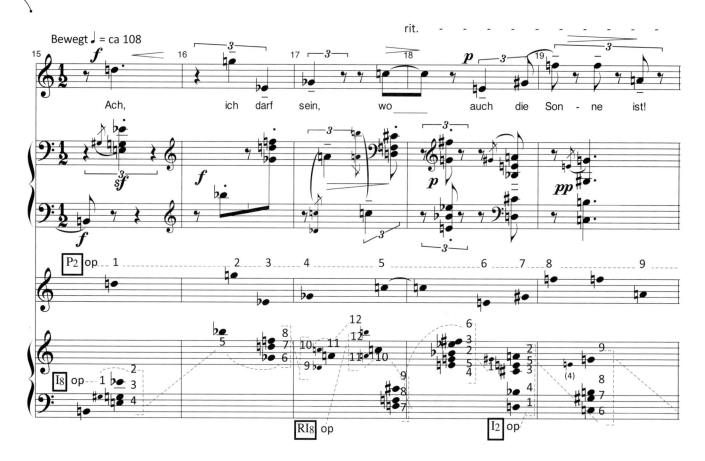

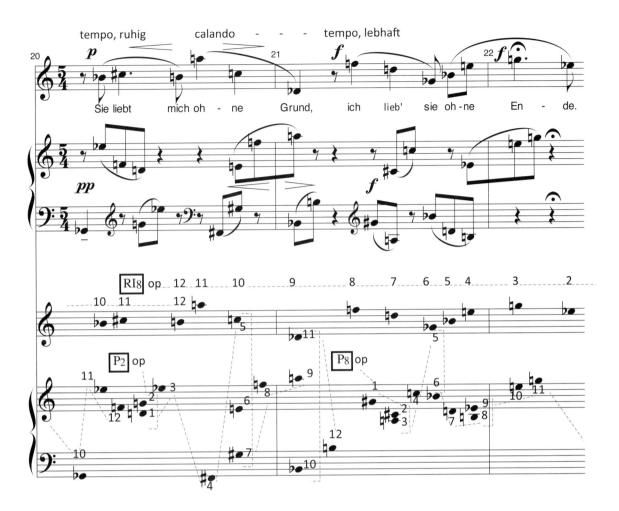

The recurrences of members of (014) that we noticed earlier (Ex. 9.1) are evident in any grouping of order positions <2–3–4>, <6–7–8>, <7–8–9>, or <9–10–11>, regardless of row form. These groupings are especially prounounced in the vocal line, often echoed by chordal presentations in the accompaniment. In the first five measures of the piano, for example, we highlighted (014)-members [347] (I_8 op <2–3–4>) in measure 15; [256] (I_8 op <6–7–8>) in measure 16; [901] (I_8 op <9–10–11>) and [125] (RI_8 op <9–8–7>) in measure 17; and the overlapping [78E] (I_2 op <9–8–7>) and [8E0] (I_2 op <8–7–6>) in measure 19.

Earlier in this chapter, we also noticed recurrences of members of set class (0145), which we can now recognize as groupings of order positions <1–2–3–4> or <6–7–8–9> of any row form (see the chart of internal sets in Example 9.5). The piano presents this tetrachordal grouping first, in measure 15 (I_8 op <1–2–3–4>), and the singer then echoes the same tetrachord type unfolded by four sustained tones (P_2 op <1–2–3–4>). In measures 18 and 19, the voice announces this tetrachord (P_2 op <6–7–8–9>) and the piano answers (I_2 op <6–7–8–9>). Later, when the piano switches from chords to mostly single-line gestures, we hear this tetrachord type again at the end of measure 20 (P_2 op <6–7–8–9>) and twice in measure 21 (P_8 op <1–2–3–4>, <6–7–8–9>).

The row analysis also helps heighten our awareness that the two vertical pentachords in the piano in measure 18 (RI_8 op <6–5–4–3–2> and I_2 op <1–2–3–4–5>) are rather unique occurrences within this part of the song. Of course, they echo five–note segments of the vocal line above (P_2 <1–2–3–4–5> and <2–3–4–5–6>), but they don't anticipate pentachordal groupings of these same order positions later in the excerpt. Their interrelations within the song stretch wider, to earlier and later passages.

Think about Webern's choice of row forms for this passage. In the vocal line alone, as we've already observed, the B_4 in measure 20 becomes a "pivot" between two row forms, serving as both op 12 of the initial P_2 and op 12 of the RI_8 that continues thereafter. More specifically, the vocal line's two row forms are related by RI_T:

$$P_2 \xrightarrow{\text{RI}_T} RI_8$$

Further, the voice's RI_8 also recalls that same row form in reverse, I_8, earlier in the piano, accompanying the voice's P_2 starting in measure 15, and RI_8 itself in measures 17 and 18. Look closely at the transition between the end of the I_8 and the beginning of the RI_8 in measure 17: at first, the RI_8 draws attention to the RT_0 relationship by reversing the previous I_8 in pitch space (compare the exact pitches, in register, of I_8 op $<9–10–11–12>$ with RI_8 op $<12–11–10–9>$). After that is another I-form in the piano, I_2 (mm. 18–20), which is RT_6 of the previous RI_8, or just T_6 of the earlier I_8.

All the row forms accompanying the initial P-form in the voice are I- or RI-forms. After that, all the row forms accompanying the voice's RI-form are P-forms: P_2 in measures 20–21, and P_8 in measures 21–22. In this short passage, Webern has managed to summarize the basic row relationships within the twelve-tone method itself:

- **Transposition**: T_6 from P_2 to P_8 in the piano (mm. 20–22);
- **Inversion**: I_T between P_2 (voice) and I_8 (piano); I_4 between P_2 (voice) and I_2 (piano);
- **Retrograde**: RT_0 from I_8 to RI_8 (piano); RT_6 from RI_8 to I_2 (piano);
- **Retrograde Inversion**: RI_T from P_2 to RI_8 within the complete vocal line and between voice and piano in the second half; RI_4 between the voice's final RI_8 and the P_8 down below.

STUDY QUESTIONS 9.7

1. **What are the order positions of these set classes in the row, and where in the vocal line of measures 15–22 (Ex. 9.18) does Webern draw attention to them?**

   1.1. (013)   1.2. (015)   1.3. (0147)   1.4. 6-Z44 (012569)

2. **What are the normal forms and prime forms of the following note groupings that *aren't* formed by adjacent notes in the same row form, and how do they relate to the row structure?**

   2.1. Measure 20, piano right hand, first three notes.
   2.2. Measure 20, piano right hand, last two notes, plus the completion of this gesture with the A_5 in measure 21.
   2.3. Measure 17, the initial trichord in the piano plus the concurrent $G\flat_4$ in the voice.
   2.4. All the notes in measure 15 (voice and piano).

9.8   LOCATING ROW FORMS

An analysis of a twelve-tone work begins, of course, by finding and studying the row. In some twelve-tone music, you'll be able to find a definitive statement of the row near the beginning, while in others, the initial statements of the row may be broken up into chords or be otherwise unpredictable (or unorthodox), and you'll need to look for a clear ordering later. Schoenberg makes it easy at the beginning of his Fourth String Quartet, op. 37, establishing the prime ordering of the row melodically in the first six measures of the first violin part (Ex. 9.19). In Webern's Variations for Piano, op. 27, on the other hand, the definitive row ordering isn't clear until the beginning of the final movement (which was composed first). Generally speaking, the process of finding the definitive ordering of the row in a twelve-tone work may involve varying amounts of score study, research, and trial-and-error. Above all, as with musical analysis of any kind, it must involve getting to know the music really well.

EXAMPLE 9.19 Schoenberg, String Quartet op. 37, no. 4, mm. 1–6, first violin

When you're sure you've identified the row correctly, study it thoroughly. Play it on the piano or on some other instrument, both in its original pitches and rhythms, and in a neutral register and rhythm. Calculate its INT, and use the INT and the INT transforms to play other row forms in p- and pc-space on various starting notes: (1) The same INT for different P-forms; (2) The INT' for different I-forms; (3) The R(INT') for different R-forms; and (4) The R(INT) for different RI-forms. Break the row down into its internal sets and identify the regular partitions and any recurring set-class types. Use the P_0 and I_0 forms to create a row chart for the row.

After you and the row are BFFs, you're ready to figure out which row forms appear in the music. Let's do this for the beginning of Webern's opus 23, no. 2 song, excerpted in Example 9.20.

EXAMPLE 9.20 Webern, op. 23, no. 2, mm. 1–8

To start, let's review what we know about the row. We can see in the INT (Ex. 9.21) and in the top line of the chart of internal sets (Ex. 9.22) that the row has a fair amount of intervallic variety: every interval class is represented at least once, as are eight of the eleven pitch-class intervals (only pc intervals 2, 7, and E aren't represented). The most common interval class is 4, represented in the INT by the pc interval 8 between op's 2 and 3, and by pc interval 4's at op's <5–6>, <6–7>, and <8–9>. The consecutive pc interval 4's indicate an augmented triad at op <5–6–7>, but we've also observed the more prevalent (014) trichords at op's <2–3–4>, <6–7–8>, <7–8–9>, and <9–10–11>; and (015) at op's <1–2–3> and <8–9–10>. Recall also that the first regularly partitioned tetrachord, (0145), reappears at op <6–7–8–9>, and that the row likewise contains dual appearances of members of set classes (0148) (<5–6–7–8>, <8–9–10–11>), 5–13 (<4–5–6–7–8>, <8–9–10–11–12>), and 6–15 (<2–3–4–5–6–7>, <4–5–6–7–8–9>).

We're thinking about these features as we're starting to look at the opening phrase (Ex. 9.20). Since the ordering of notes within a row form isn't immediately obvious in the piano's chords, let's start with the much clearer ordering in the vocal line. Is there a row form that begins with the first three vocal notes, pc's <5–3–6>?

EXAMPLE 9.21 Webern, op. 23, row P_2 and INT

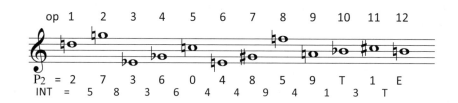

op	1	2	3	4	5	6	7	8	9	10	11	12
P2 =	2	7	3	6	0	4	8	5	9	T	1	E
INT =	5	8	3	6	4	4	9	4	1	3	T	

EXAMPLE 9.22 Webern, op. 23, row P_2, internal sets of sizes 2–9, with regular partitions in **bold**

Pc:	2	7	3	6	0	4	8	5	9	T	1	E
Starting op:	1	2	3	4	5	6	7	8	9	10	11	12
Ic:	5	4	3	6	4	4	3	4	1	3	2	
Trichords:	**(015)**	(014)	(036)	**(026)**	(048)	(014)	**(014)**	(015)	(014)	**(013)**		
Tetrachords:	**(0145)**	(0147)	(0236)	(0248)	**(0148)**	(0145)	(0125)	(0148)	**(0124)**			
Pentachords:	5-Z18	5-16	5-26	5-13	5-21	5-6	5-Z37	5-13				
Hexachords:	**6-Z10**	6-15	6-Z39	6-15	6-16	6-Z44	**6-Z39**					
Septachords:	7-13	7-3	7-16	7-13	7-21	7-Z18						
Octachords:	8-2	8-3	8-Z29	8-19	8-7							
Nonachords:	9-2	9-2	9-11	9-4								

One way to answer this question would be to search randomly in the outer edges of the row chart in Example 9.14. For two reasons, however, you'll be better off using your knowledge of the structure of the row to search for row forms. First of all, thinking more organically about what happens at any given spot in a row will help you to get deeper "inside" the row and the score, and this will benefit you when you're searching for row forms in passages with obscure or unusual row presentations. But also, you can't assume that those first three vocal notes are actually the beginning of a row form. It makes sense to start your search by assuming that they are, but you shouldn't be surprised if it turns out that they're a continuation of a row form that begins in measure 1 in the piano, or that the row statement actually jumps back and forth from voice to piano, note by note.

So a better way to start is to focus on the row structure, as revealed by the internal sets and INT transforms. The first three notes in the voice form trichord [356], a member of set class (013). Since this trichord appears only once in the internal sets, as the last regularly partitioned trichord of P- and I-forms, we can reasonably assume that we're dealing here with a row form that starts at the end of a P- or I-form and works backwards: in other words, an R- or RI-form.

At this point, you could just browse through the R- and RI-forms on the chart until you find one that matches the pitch-class ordering in the melody. But let's stay focused on the row structure, and use the INT transforms as our guide:

INT	=	5	8	3	6	4	4	9	4	1	3	T	(P-forms)
INT′	=	7	4	9	6	8	8	3	8	E	9	2	(I-forms)
R(INT′)	=	2	9	E	8	3	8	8	6	9	4	7	(R-forms)
R(INT)	=	T	3	1	4	9	4	4	6	3	8	5	(RI-forms)

The melody begins with pc intervals <T–3–1>. These are the same pc intervals found at the beginning of R(INT). Since only RI-forms express the R(INT), it looks like we're dealing with an RI-form. So find the RI-form on the row chart that begins with pc 5, and confirm that the pc ordering of the melody is the same. Annotate the score with the order-position numbers, starting with 12 (Ex. 9.23). Remember that the label for an RI-form uses the last note as the subscript, so this row form is RI₂, not RI₅.

EXAMPLE 9.23   Webern, op. 23, no. 2, vocal line, mm. 2–6

Well, we have a couple of curiosities. One is that op's 7 and 6 are immediately repeated in measure 5. This type of repetition is not unusual in twelve-tone composition.

Another is that the melodic phrase ends before the row form is completed, on op 3 in measure 6. So, where are the remaining two notes of RI₂, pc's 9 and 2? This section of the song ends in measure 6, and the next notes in the vocal line, segment <B♭₄–D₅–B₄> in measures 6–7, are clearly part of some different row presentation. Is the RI₂ left incomplete? This is always a possibility, but we should assume that a row form is somehow complete until convinced otherwise. (Webern, for one, would never leave a row form incomplete.) To find the remaining two notes of RI₂, look elsewhere: this row form is completed by the A₄ and D₅ within the piano chord in measure 7 (Ex. 9.20). After we've located all the row forms within the piano, we'll know whether these two notes overlap with other row forms or are derived solely from the RI₂.

Back to the beginning: What is the row source for the opening piano pentachord? Start by assuming that it's a five-note segment at the beginning of a row form, but make no assumptions about the ordering. In other words, assume that the order positions for the notes of this pentachord will be either <1–2–3–4–5> or <12–11–10–9–8>, without knowing which number goes with which note. To assign the order positions, recall the first four or last four pc intervals in the INT transforms, which profile the row's first and last pentachord, respectively. Find a way to arrange the notes of the pentachord so that they unfold one of these pc interval series.

The INT begins with pc intervals <5836> and ends with <413T>. Rearranging the notes of the measure 1 chord as <E–9–0–1–5> produces the pc interval series <T–3–1–4> (Ex. 9.24). Since this is the reverse of the end of the INT, we know that we are again dealing with R(INT), indicating an RI-form. Find the RI-form on the chart that begins with pc E: RI$_8$. Label the order positions within the score starting with 12 and progressing into the first chord in measure 2 (Ex. 9.25).

EXAMPLE 9.24 Webern, op. 23, no. 2, derivation of first chord

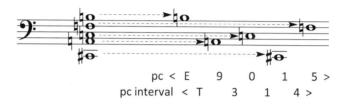

```
pc  < E    9    0    1    5 >
pc interval  < T    3    1    4 >
```

EXAMPLE 9.25 Webern, op. 23, no. 2, RI$_8$ in mm. 1–2

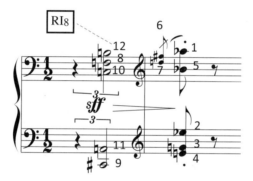

After that, the voice enters, leaving open the possibility that notes can be shared between voice and piano, as we saw happen twice in measure 21 (Ex. 9.18). Sharing is also possible from one row form to the next in the piano, as we saw in the shared pc E in the vocal line in measure 20 (Ex. 9.18). It makes sense to continue our row searching, however, as if notes aren't shared, and hypothesize that the trichord in the piano at the end of measure 2 is the first trichord of a row statement. Investigate the most obvious, most regular possible row distributions first.

Could the piano trichord at the end of measure 2 be the beginning of a row statement? Yes: the trichord is [TE1] (013), which is the row's last regularly partitioned trichord. So it's reasonable to assume that the grace note B$_3$ is the beginning of an R- or RI-form. And we can arrange the second and third notes to match the beginning of the R(INT'): <B$_3$–C♯$_4$> = pc interval 2, followed by <C♯$_4$–B♭$_4$> = pc interval 9. These pc intervals are the beginning of R(INT'), so we're now dealing with an R-form.

Consult the row chart to find the R-form that begins on pc E, labeled R$_2$, and follow its progress through measure 3 and the beginning of measure 4 (Ex. 9.26). Its last two notes account for two of the three notes in the trichord at the beginning of measure 4.

EXAMPLE 9.26   Webern, op. 23, no. 2, R_2 in mm. 2–4

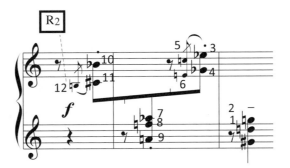

STUDY QUESTION 9.8

Start on the piano's $G\sharp_4$ in measure 4 and identify the row forms in the remainder of Example 9.20. The last chord in the piano (m. 7) contains the beginning of a row form that isn't completed in this excerpt, but you can still identify the row form based on how it begins.

Ultimately, just finding the row forms isn't enough; it's not the "analysis." A study of a twelve-tone work should determine not only *what* row forms appear but also *why*. It should address questions such as:

- What aspects of the row are musically highlighted?
- How are the row forms related to each other as pitch-class strings?
- How are the row forms compositionally related to each other in this particular context?
- How do the row forms contribute to the articulation of form (or to the text setting, if any)?

We've seen in this chapter, for example, that Webern often isolates (014) trichords in the middle section of his opus 23. no. 2 song (Ex. 9.1), and we see this in the opening bars as well (e.g., m. 3, piano left hand). You probably noticed several more instances of this trichord type when you were answering Study Question 9.8. (Remember, any combination of op's <2–3–4>, <6–7–8>, <7–8–9>, or <9–10–11> in any row form produces a member of this set class.) You also probably noticed that the opening bars of the song use some of the same row relationships we found in the song's middle section: a T_6 transformation from the piano's initial RI_8 to the voice's RI_2, an I_T transformation between the piano's first two row forms (RI_8, R_2), and so forth. We're on the way toward a fuller understanding of the pitch structure of Webern's song, one that weaves all these factors together into a coherent narrative.

VOCABULARY

derived row	ordered transposition	row class
I-form	P-form	serial method
INT	R-form	serial music
INT′	regular partitions	twelve-tone method
internal sets	retrograde	twelve-tone music
internal tetrachord	retrograde inversion	twelve-tone row
internal trichord	RI-form	wraparound tetrachord
order position	row chart	wraparound trichord
ordered inversion		

EXERCISES

A. P-SPACE TRANSPOSITIONS AND INVERSIONS

1. Underneath the original row form, indicate its pitch intervals;

2. Using whole notes on the staff, notate the indicated transpositional form of the row by starting on the note specified by the subscript and projecting the identical series of pitch intervals;

3. Using whole notes on the staff, notate the indicated inversional form of the row by starting on the note specified by the subscript and projecting the same pitch intervals but in opposite directions;

4. For both the transposition and the inversion, fill in the boxes with the label for the pc operation (T_n or I_n) that relates the original row form with the row forms you wrote.

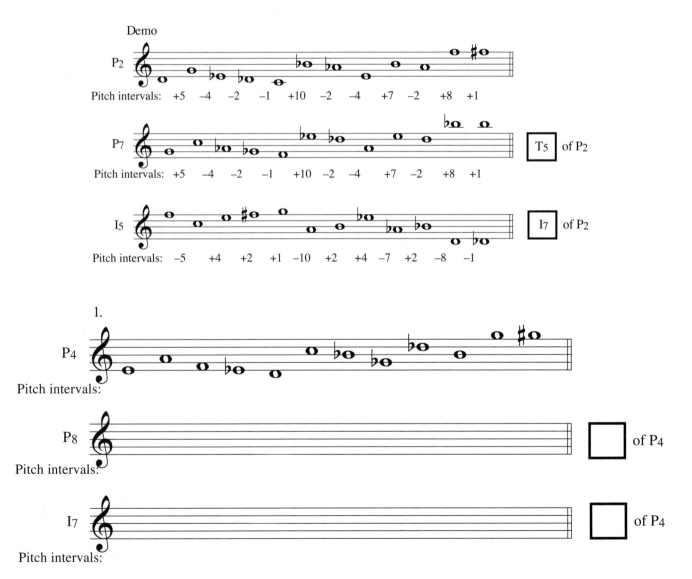

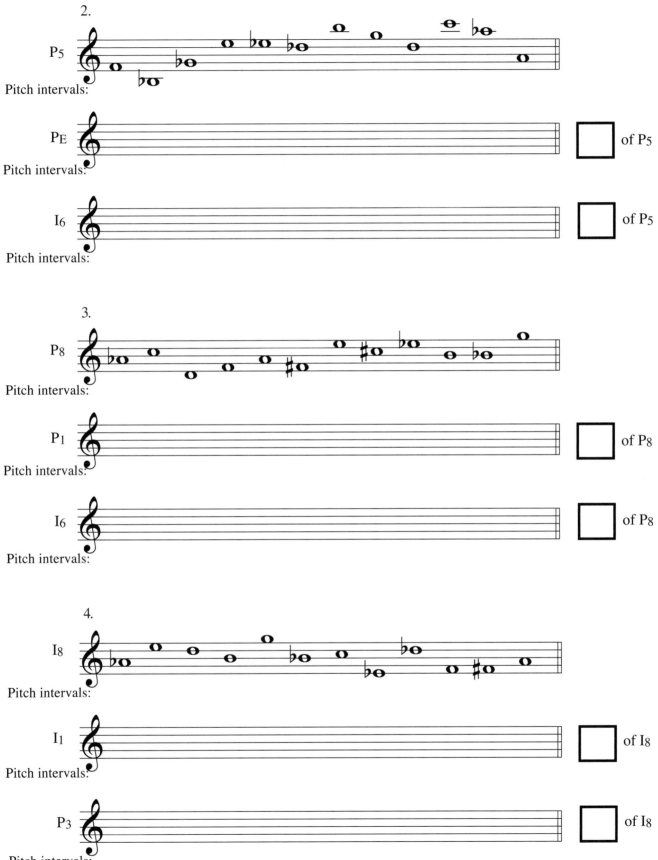

2.

P5

Pitch intervals:

PE   of P5

Pitch intervals:

I6   of P5

Pitch intervals:

3.

P8

Pitch intervals:

P1   of P8

Pitch intervals:

I6   of P8

Pitch intervals:

4.

I8

Pitch intervals:

I1   of I8

Pitch intervals:

P3   of I8

Pitch intervals:

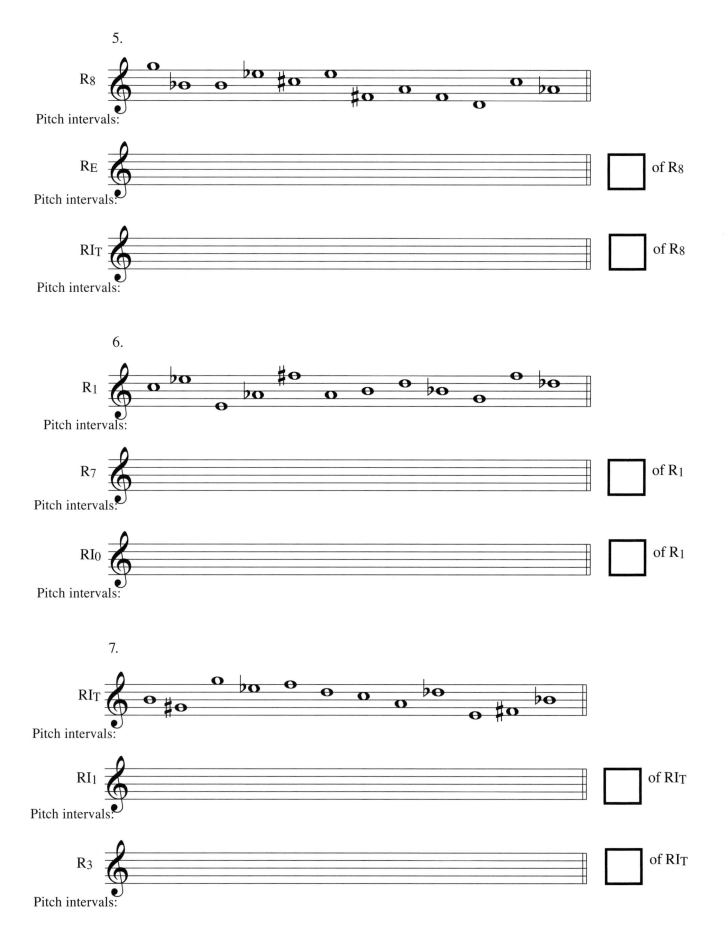

5.

R8

Pitch intervals:

RE   of R8

Pitch intervals:

RIT   of R8

Pitch intervals:

6.

R1

Pitch intervals:

R7   of R1

Pitch intervals:

RI0   of R1

Pitch intervals:

7.

RIT

Pitch intervals:

RI1   of RIT

Pitch intervals:

R3   of RIT

Pitch intervals:

B. ROW STRUCTURING

Convert the notes of each melody to the twelve-tone row on which it's based, expressed as an ordered series of twelve different pitch-class integers (ignoring any repetitions). Underneath that, write the INT. Then answer the questions.

Demo. Arnold Schoenberg (1874–1951), String Quartet no. 4, op. 37, mvt. 1, mm. 1–6, first violin

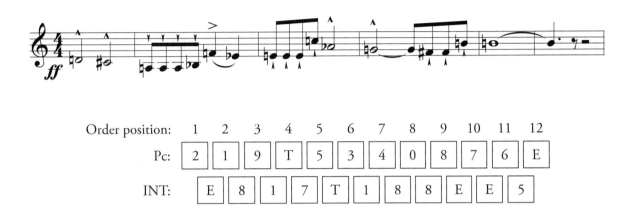

Order position:	1	2	3	4	5	6	7	8	9	10	11	12
Pc:	2	1	9	T	5	3	4	0	8	7	6	E
INT:		E	8	1	7	T	1	8	8	E	E	5

1. **Give the normal form and prime form of the regularly partitioned trichords and tetrachords.**

   trichords: [912] (015) / [35T] (027) / [048] (048) / [67E] (015)

   tetrachords: [9T12] (0145) / [0345] (0125) / [678E] (0125)

2. **Give the order positions of other members of any of these same set classes formed within the row.**

   a. op <3–4–5> = [59T] (015)

   b. op <8–9–10> = [780] (015)

3. **Assuming that the given row form is P_2, write the following forms as <pc series>. For transformations, also give the label of the resulting row form.**

   a. P_5 =   <54018673ET92>

   b. R_5 =   <29TE37681045>

   c. R_2 =   <E6780435T912>

   d. I_2 =   <2376E10489T5>

   e. RI_2 =   <5T98401E6732>

   f. $T_9(P_2)$ =   <ET6720195438> (P_E)

   g. $I_8(P_5)$ =   <348702159TE6> (I_3)

   h. $RI_1(I_2)$ =   <8345910276TE> (R_E)

   i. $RT_2(I_3)$ =   <810E73429T65> (RI_5)

1. Arnold Schoenberg (1874–1951), Violin Concerto, op. 36, mvt. 1, mm. 8–11.1, solo violin

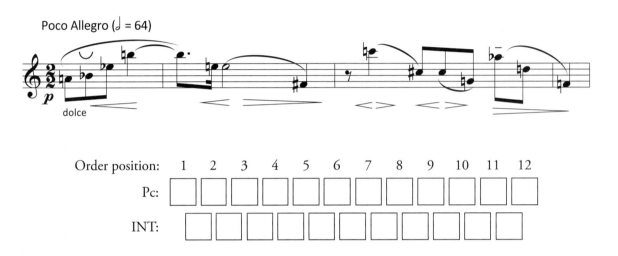

1. **Give the normal form and prime form of the regularly partitioned trichords. What are the order positions of other internal trichords that are equivalent to any of the regularly partitioned trichords?**

2. **Give the normal form and prime form of the internal tetrachords at op <2–3–4–5> and <6–7–8–9>. What are the order positions of other internal tetrachords that are equivalent to these?**

3. **Identify the normal form and prime form of the first internal pentachord (i.e., op <1–2–3–4–5>) and give the order positions for two other instances of this same pentachord type within the row's internal sets.**

4. **Assuming that the given row form is P_9, write the following forms as <pc series>. For transformations, also give the label of the resulting row form.**

   a. P_0 =

   b. R_0 =

   c. R_T =

   d. I_5 =

   e. RI_5 =

   f. RI_9 =

   g. $T_5(P_9)$ =

   h. $I_8(P_2)$ =

   i. $RT_1(I_5)$ =

   j. $RI_7(I_3)$ =

2. Alban Berg (1885–1935), Violin Concerto, mvt. 1, mm. 15–20, solo violin

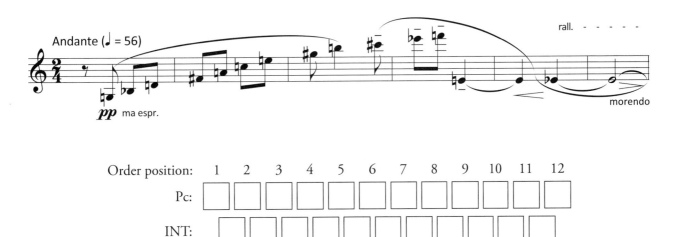

Order position: 1   2   3   4   5   6   7   8   9   10   11   12

Pc:

INT:

1. With respect to its intervallic structure, how is the end of this row very different from its beginning? At what order position does the difference begin?

2. What is the pattern in the INT, and how does Berg bring this out in his melody?

3. Use the regularly partitioned tetrachords to demonstrate further the contrast within the structure of the row.

4. What are the order positions of other internal tetrachords that are equivalent to any of the regularly partitioned tetrachords?

5. Assuming that the given row form is P_7, write the following forms as <pc series>. For transformations, also give the label of the resulting row form.

  a. I_7 =
  b. R_1 =
  c. RI_T =
  d. P_5 =
  e. $RT_6(I_2)$ =
  f. $RI_1(R_1)$ =
  g. $T_T(P_4)$ =
  h. $I_5(RI_7)$ =

3. Anton Webern (1883–1945), String Quartet, op. 28, mvt. 3, mm. 1–7, first violin

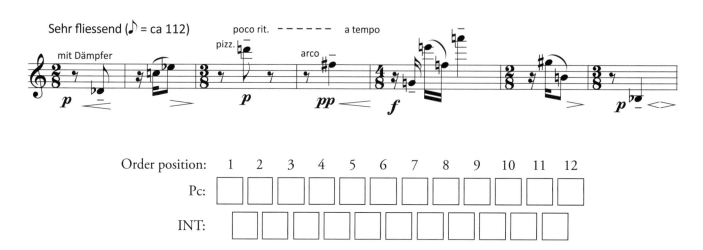

1. Notice the symmetry in the INT: INT = R(INT). What form of the INT is equivalent to INT′?

2. Recognizing that INT = R(INT), what conclusion can you draw about the relationship between P-forms and RI-forms within this row class?

3. Demonstrate the row's symmetry by relating all the row's internal trichords, notated in normal form and prime form.

4. Explain the role of the B–A–C–H motive in the structure of this row. (In p-space, the motive is $<B\flat_4–A_4–C_5–B_4>$.)

5. Assuming that the given row form is P_1, write the following forms as <pc series>. For transformations, also give the two possible labels for the resulting row form.

   a. P_T =
   b. I_7 =
   c. RI_7 =
   d. $I_E(P_1)$ =
   e. $RI_E(P_1)$ =
   f. $T_8(I_7)$ =
   g. $RI_9(I_3)$ =

4. Luigi Dallapiccola (1904–1975), *Il prigioniero*, act 1, scene 1, mm. 241–44

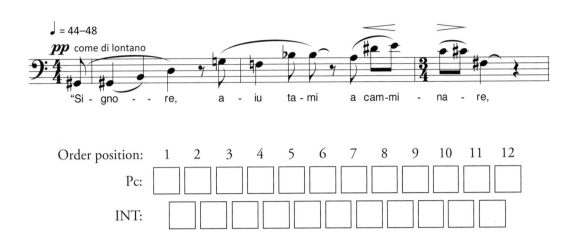

1. **Give the normal form and prime form for all of the internal trichords. Which trichord type is most prevalent?**

2. **Which type of source set (Chapter 5) is prominent in the structure of this row? Explain.**

3. **Assuming that the given row form is P_8, write the following forms as \<pc series\>. For transformations, also give the label of the resulting row form.**

   a. I_2 =

   b. $T_6(P_8)$ =

   c. $RI_1(P_8)$ =

   d. $RT_E(RI_1)$ =

   e. $T_8(P_E)$ =

5. Ulysses Kay (1917–1995), First Nocturne for Piano, mm. 1–5.1

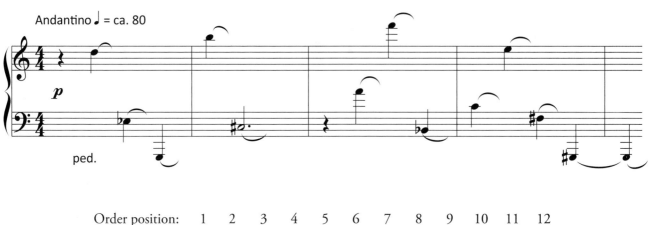

1. **In the INT for this row, how many of the pc intervals are odd, and how many are even? What does this tell you about the nature of the row and the melodies and harmonies that might be derived from it?**

2. **Give at least four examples of internal sets (of various sizes) that further support your answer to question 1.**

3. **Write the series of pc intervals for the following:**

   a. all P-forms of this row

   b. all I-forms of this row

   c. all R-forms of this row

   d. all RI-forms of this row

6. Elisabeth Lutyens (1906–1983), *Maybe* **[for piano], first row statement**

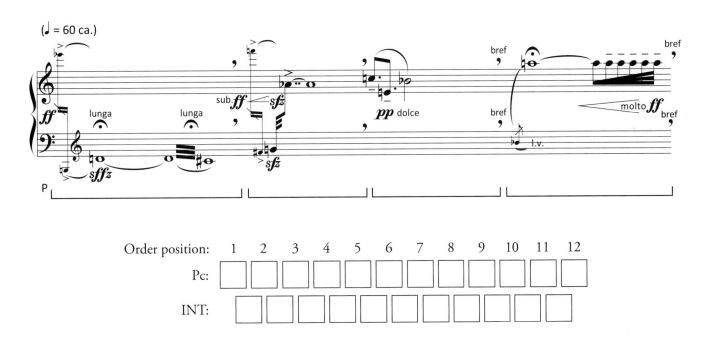

Order position: 1   2   3   4   5   6   7   8   9   10   11   12

Pc:

INT:

1. **Members of ic 1 are prominent in this row: which internal trichords *don't* include ic1's? Give order positions, normal forms, and prime forms.**

2. **What aspects of this row (such as specific internal sets and/or regular partitions) are featured in the musical realization of the row shown above? Provide plentiful musical details in your answer.**

C. LOCATING ROW FORMS

Draw from your knowledge of the rows explored in the section B exercises above to identify the row forms used in the excerpts from those same works below. Give the label for the row form(s) and place order-position numbers next to the appropriate notes in the scores.

Demo. Arnold Schoenberg (1874–1951), String Quartet no. 4, op. 37, mvt. 2, mm 541–42 (consult B.demo)

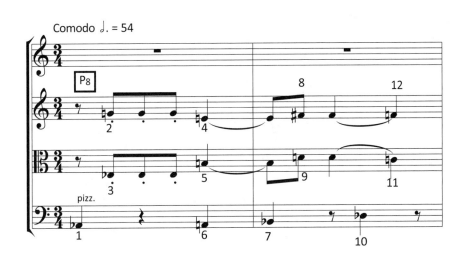

1. Arnold Schoenberg (1874–1951), Violin Concerto, op. 36, mvt. 1, mm. 1–8.1 (consult B.1)

2. Alban Berg (1885–1935), Violin Concerto, mvt. 1, mm. 11–15 (accompanying parts, sounds as notated) (consult B.2)

3. Anton Webern (1883–1945), String Quartet, op. 28, mvt. 1, mm. 0–6 (consult B.3)

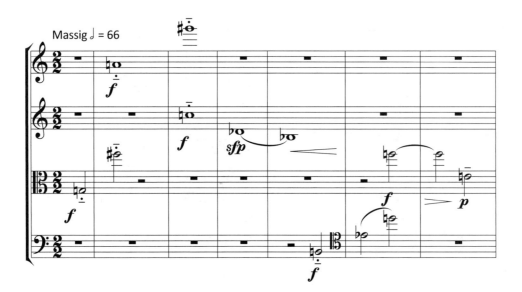

4. Luigi Dallapiccola (1904–1975), *Il prigioniero,* **Prolog, mm. 77.3–79.4 (consult B.4)**

5. Ulysses Kay (1917–1995), First Nocturne for Piano, mm. 5–9 (consult B.5)

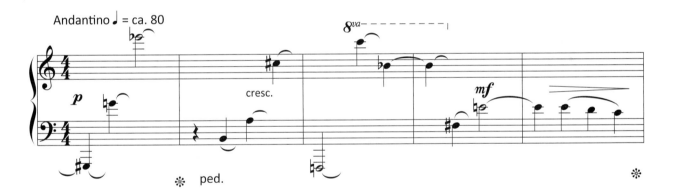

6. Elisabeth Lutyens (1906–1983), *Maybe,* **end of page 3 (consult B.6)**

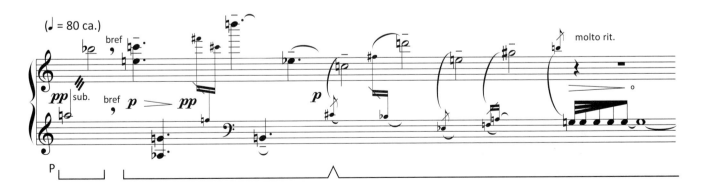

D. CONSTRUCTING ROW CHARTS

Using one of the methods described in section 9.5 of this chapter, construct a row chart for the given rows.

Demo. Arnold Schoenberg (1874–1951), String Quartet no. 4, op. 37, mvt. 1, mm. 1–6

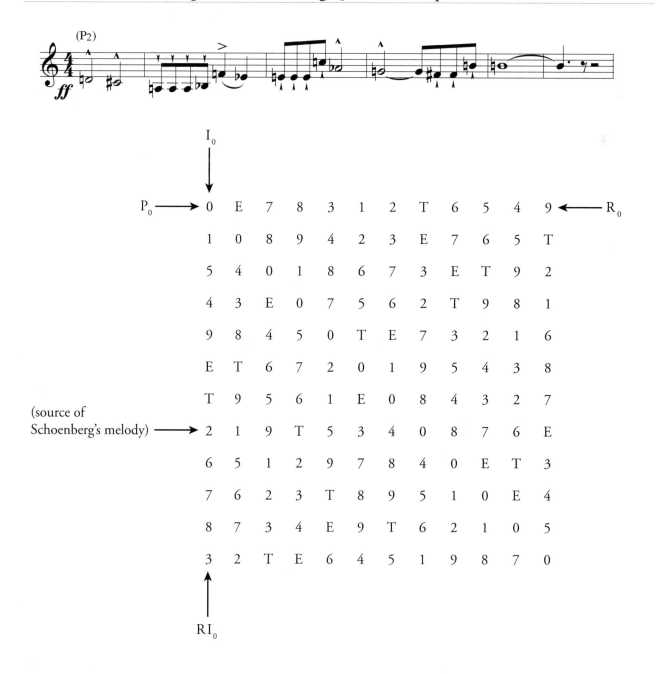

1. Arnold Schoenberg (1874–1951), Suite for Piano, op. 25, no. 1, Präludium, mm. 1–3, right hand

2. Wallingford Riegger (1885–1961), Sonatina for Violin and Piano, mvt. 2

3. Hale Smith (1925–2009), *Three Brevities* for flute solo, mvt. 3, mm. 1–4

4. Sofia Gubaidulina (b. 1931), "The Elk Clearing," *Musical Toys*, mm. 1–9

5. Charles Wuorinen (b. 1938), *Flute Variations*, mvt. 2, mm. 1–4

E. TWELVE-TONE ANALYSIS

1. Anton Webern (1883–1945), Three Songs for Voice and Piano, op. 23, no. 2, mm. 8–14

This excerpt falls between the beginning of the song studied in section 9.8 and the middle section studied in sections 9.1 and 9.7. The row is thoroughly explored in sections 9.2 through 9.5, including a row chart as Example 9.14.

Identify the row forms used in the excerpt and place order position numbers next to all notes within the score. (The voice begins by completing the P_8 started in measure 7; see Example 9.20 and Study Question 9.8.) Then answer the questions.

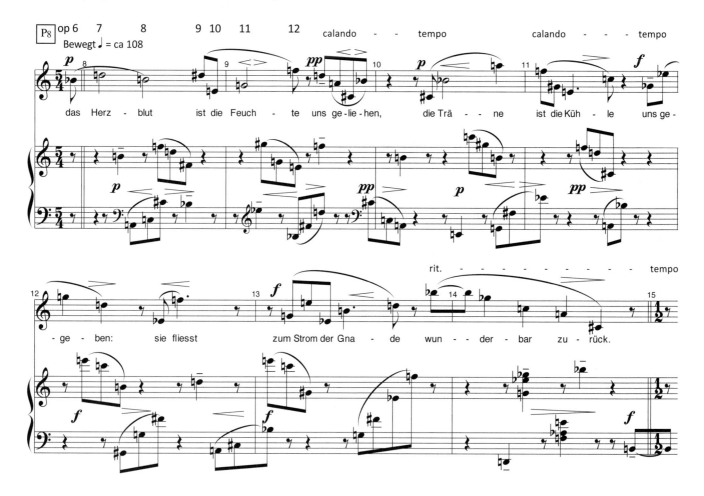

1. **Where in the passage do you find a row form followed immediately by its RT_0 transformation? How does Webern draw attention to the close relationship between these two row forms?**

2. **Where in the passage do you find a row form followed immediately by the same row form again? How does Webern draw attention to the repetition of this row form?**

3. **Identify a trichord type that's highlighted in this excerpt. Explain how many different ways the trichord can be formed within the row, and cite specific examples of moments in the excerpt when members of this set class are highlighted.**

4. Identify a tetrachord type that's highlighted in this excerpt. Explain how many different ways the tetrachord can be formed within the row, and cite specific examples of moments in the excerpt when members of this set class are highlighted.

5. Compare the presentation and rhythmic grouping of row elements in this passage with the next section of the song (Ex. 9.18).

6. Here again is the text for the song, with the text of the current excerpt in bold:

1	*Es stürtzt aus Höhen Frische,*	*Plunging from above is freshness*
2	*die uns leben macht:*	*which causes us to live:*
3	**das Herzblut**	**the heart's blood**
4	**ist die Feuchte uns geliehen,**	**is the moistness lent to us,**
5	**die Träne ist die Kühle uns gegeben:**	**the tear is the coolness given to us;**
6	**sie fliesst zum Strom der Gnade**	**wondrously it flows back**
7	**wunderbar zurück.**	**to the stream of grace.**
8	*Ach, ich darf sein,*	*Oh, I am privileged to be*
9	*wo auch die Sonne ist!*	*Where the sun also is!*
10	*Sie liebt mich ohne Grund,*	*It loves me without reason;*
11	*ich lieb' sie ohne Ende.*	*I love it endlessly.*
12	*Wenn wir einander Abend, Abschied, scheinen*	*When in the evening we bid goodbye,*
13	*den Himmel und die Seele überglüht*	*the sky and my soul*
14	*noch lange Glut.*	*remain aglow long after.*

How do Webern's choices of row forms and their musical presentations in measures 8–14 help express the song text?

2. Arnold Schoenberg (1874–1951), Suite for Piano, op. 25, no. 5, Menuet, Trio

The opus 25 Suite was Schoenberg's first complete work composed with the twelve-tone method. Its six movements draw inspiration from instrumental suites of the Baroque period: Prelude, Gavotte, Musette, Intermezzo, Menuet, Gigue.

You're already acquainted with the opening melody from the first movement of the Suite, and the P$_4$ form of the row, from exercise D.1 above. What you learned from that exercise, and from creating a row chart for this row, will also apply to the Trio section of the Menuet movement on the next page. Identify all the row forms in the Trio and place order-position numbers next to notes in the score. Then answer the questions.

You'll notice one aspect of Schoenberg's row usage in this music that's different from the methods of Webern that we studied in this chapter. Look, for example, at this passage from the first movement, which accompanies the right-hand melody shown in exercise D.1:

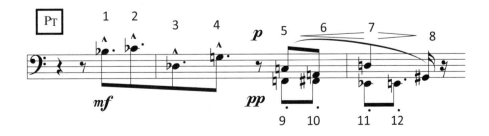

The P_T row form is divided here into its three regularly partitioned tetrachords, op <1–2–3–4>, <5–6–7–8>, and <9–10–11–12>. The first one is presented alone, but the other two are stacked and presented together. So the F_2–C_3 dyad that follows op 4 is not op's 5 and 6 (as you might at first expect), but actually a pairing of op's 5 and 9. The next dyad ($F\sharp_2$–A_2) is op's 6 and 10, and so forth. You'll find this same sort of row distribution in some parts of the Trio.

TRIO

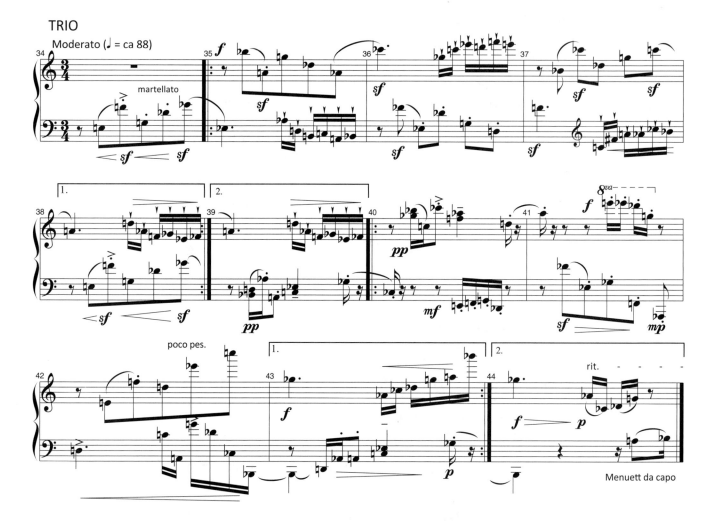

1. **Discuss the canon between the pianist's hands. How, exactly, are the two canonic voices related? How is this relationship revealed in the row subscripts and played out in pitch space? How do these relationships change in the second half of the Trio?**

2. **Now inspect each canonic voice by itself: just the left hand, and just the right hand. How does the music in each hand individually reflect and interact with the canonic relationships?**

3. **Discuss the internal sets brought out by Schoenberg's row treatment, making note of any places in the form where the groupings are different.**

4. **For a short portion of the Trio, it's possible to make groupings of notes that aren't actually adjacent in the same row form. What are the resulting set types, and how do these relate to the row's internal sets?**

3. Luigi Dallapiccola (1904–1975), "Quartina" from *Quaderno musicale di Annalibera*

"Quartina" is the eleventh and final movement of Dallapiccola's pianistic tribute to his daughter, Annalibera. The entire work is based on a single twelve-tone row, deployed and developed in a variety of ways. Before you start investigating the row and its usage, listen to the "Quartina" movement several times. Think about the significance of its title, which means "quatrain."

1. The P_0 form of the row is presented in "Quartina" in the top staff of measures 14–17, not including the A_4 in measure 16 (which is part of a different row statement). Write out P_0 as a series of pitch classes. Calculate its INT, internal trichords, and internal tetrachords, taking special notice of the regular partitions.

2. What are the order positions of the trichord types and tetrachord types that appear more than once in the internal sets?

3. Which internal trichords and tetrachords (at which order positions) are familiar chord types in tonal theory? Give the specific chord names for these chords in P_0 (even if they aren't particularly showcased in measures 14–17 of "Quartina").

4. Make a row chart for this row class.

5. Identify all the row statements in the movement and place order-position numbers next to notes in the score. Where does Dallapiccola apply note stems in an unusual way to draw attention to the row derivations?

6. In your row identifications, you've found two streams, or layers, of row presentation. Each row form in one stream is paired with a different row form in the other stream. Describe musical differences between the two streams and their methods of organizing the row.

7. Make a diagram showing the labels of all row forms in the movement and their separation into the two streams. Discuss Dallapiccola's choices of row forms within each stream separately.

8. What are the operations that relate the row forms from different streams being presented at the same time? Discuss Dallapiccola's choices of row forms to pair with each other.

9. In one of the streams, there are two (nonconsecutive) row statements that are retrogrades of each other (RT_0). When you hear the second one, what aspects of the musical presentation might remind you of the first one?

10. Any simultaneous presentation of row forms holds the possibility of making close connections between equivalent pc sets in both rows. For example, since the regularly partitioned trichord at op $<1–2–3>$ is a member of the same set class in every row form (P-, I-, R-, and RI-forms), a composer might do something musically to draw attention to occurrences of op $<1–2–3>$ in simultaneous row unfoldings. Further, a composer might also make connections between internal sets that appear in multiple positions in the row, such as those you listed in your answer to question 2 above. Where in the movement does Dallapiccola musically draw attention to these types of correspondences? Give the order positions and normal/prime forms of the internal sets being highlighted.

Molto lento; fantastico (♩ = 40)

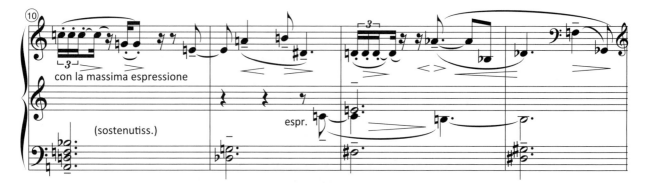

F. ROW CONSTRUCTION AND MELODY COMPOSITION

1. Create a "derived row" (Chapter 9.2) in which all the regularly partitioned trichords are members of set class (014). Use a variety of intervals, so that redundancy of the row isn't clearly displayed in the INT. Compose a melody that highlights the (014)s. Then compose a different melody that obscures them.

Demo.

2. Create a twelve-tone row in which some internal trichords are equivalent, but each of the regularly partitioned trichords is a member of a different set class. Compose a melody that highlights the trichordal equivalences. Then compose a different melody that obscures those, but highlights the regular trichordal partitions.

3. Create a twelve-tone row in which two of the three regularly partitioned tetrachords are members of set class (0236), and at least one other internal tetrachord is also a member of (0236). Compose a melody that highlights all the (0236)s within the row.

G. COMPOSITION PROJECTS

1. Create a twelve-tone row that includes internal trichords and/or tetrachords that you feel should be featured in a short composition. Make a row chart for the row. Use this row as the source for a duet for two single-line instruments with compatible sound qualities (such as two violins, or trumpet and trombone) in which a following part answers a leading part in pitch-space inversional canon. Compose the canonic line to bring out the row's most interesting features and to produce effective interplay between the two instruments. Select row forms according to some sort of pattern such as:

Answering voice:		I	P		R	RI
Leading voice:	P		I	RI	R	

2. Create a twelve-tone row that includes internal sets you'd like to express simultaneously, as harmonies supporting a melody. Make a row chart for the row. Compose a short piano piece, inspired by Dallapiccola's "Quartina," in which a row form expressed melodically is supported by a different row form expressed as a series of chords. Create a coherent formal structure from the row pairings.

3. Compose a set of variations on one of your melodies from section F above. In each variation, highlight different aspects of the row. Demonstrate principles of theme and variation form discussed in Chapter 7.

FOR FURTHER STUDY

ALBAN BERG:

Der Wein (1929)

LUIGI DALLAPICCOLA:

Goethe Lieder (1953)
Quaderno musicale di Annalibera (1952)

ARNOLD SCHOENBERG:

Suite for Piano, op. 25 (1923)
Wind Quintet, op. 26 (1924)

ANTON WEBERN:

Cantata 1, op. 29 (1939)
Concerto, op. 24 (1948)
Drei Lieder, op. 25 (1934)
String Quartet, op. 28 (1938)
Symphony, op. 21 (1928)
Variations for Orchestra, op. 30 (1940)
Variations for Piano, op. 27 (1936)

CHAPTER 10

TWELVE-TONE TECHNIQUES

10.1 INVARIANCE

During our studies of Webern's op. 23, no. 2 song in Chapter 9, you may have noticed a conspicuous correspondence between note groupings in the voice and piano at the end of the middle section (Ex. 10.1). The last three notes in the vocal phrase, pc's <4–7–3>, form the same pc set as the last three notes in the right hand of the piano, pc's <3–4–7>. Of course, it's no surprise to find recurrences of members of (014) in this song, but these two trichords are exactly the same members of that set class, pc set [347]. And this happens between two different parts of two different row forms: the pc <4–7–3> in the voice is op <4–3–2> of row form RI$_8$, and the pc <3–4–7> in the piano is op <9–10–11> of row form P$_8$.

EXAMPLE 10.1 Webern, op. 23, no. 2, mm. 20–22

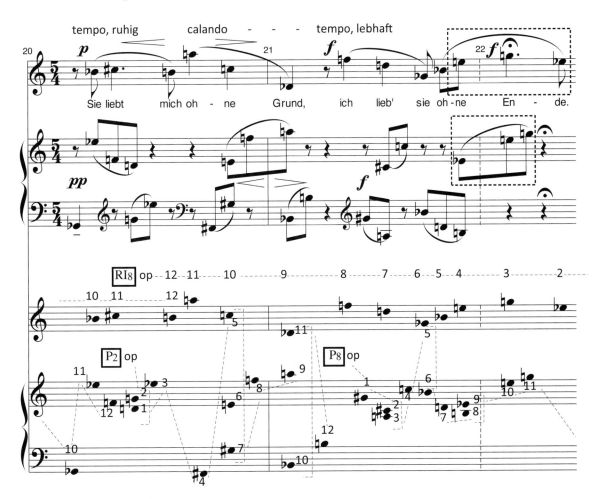

A correspondence in pitch-class contents between segments of two different forms of the same row is known as an **invariance**. Set [347] is an **invariant trichord** between RI_8 op <4–3–2> and P_8 <9–10–11> of the opus 23 row. Invariances may also occur between dyads or between sets of larger sizes. Webern and other twelve-tone composers typically construct rows to hold invariant possibilities and then find interesting, artful ways to highlight these correspondences in their musical realizations.

Let's imagine how Webern might have thought about this invariant trichord when he was creating the opus 23 row and composing the songs based on it. He knew, as we noticed by inspecting the row's internal trichords (Ex. 9.3), that members of (014) appear in order positions <2–3–4> and <9–10–11> (among other locations). This indicates that it's possible to transform any form of the row so that the actual pitch-class set in op <2–3–4> of one row form will also appear at op <9–10–11> of another. To find out exactly which transformation does this, find the operation that transforms one trichord to another within the same row form. Then use that same operation to transform the entire row form.

In row form P_8, for example, the trichords in order positions <2–3–4> and <9–10–11> are [901] and [347], respectively. These two pc sets are equivalent via transformation I_4:

$$\begin{array}{ccccccccccccc}
 & & & [901] & \xleftarrow{\quad} & & I_4 & & \xrightarrow{\quad} & [347] & & & \\
P_8 & = & 8 & \boxed{1 \quad 9 \quad 0} & 6 & T & 2 & E & \boxed{3 \quad 4 \quad 7} & 5 & & & \\
\text{op} & & 1 & \boxed{2 \quad 3 \quad 4} & 5 & 6 & 7 & 8 & \boxed{9 \quad 10 \quad 11} & 12 & & &
\end{array}$$

This tells us that when we transform the entire P_8 row form by I_4, we'll move pc set [901] from op <2–3–4> into op <9–10–11>, and pc set [347] from op <9–10–11> into op <2–3–4>. The two pc sets "switch places." So calculate the I_4 transformation of the entire row form: transformation I_4 of row form P_8 is row form I_8. (Add the two row subscripts together to equal the index number: $8 + 8 = 4$.) The I_8 form of the row displays those same two trichords in reversed positions:

$$\begin{array}{ccccccccccccc}
 & & & [347] & \xleftarrow{\quad} & & I_4 & & \xrightarrow{\quad} & [901] & & & \\
I_8 & = & 8 & \boxed{3 \quad 7 \quad 4} & T & 6 & 2 & 5 & \boxed{1 \quad 0 \quad 9} & E & & & \\
\text{op} & & 1 & \boxed{2 \quad 3 \quad 4} & 5 & 6 & 7 & 8 & \boxed{9 \quad 10 \quad 11} & 12 & & &
\end{array}$$

When Webern was composing op. 23 no. 2, then, he used the P_8 form of the row in the accompaniment at the end of the middle section so that he could highlight the pitch-class invariance between its op <9–10–11> and the op <4–3–2> of RI_8 occurring nearly simultaneously in the voice (Ex. 10.1).

Yes, you're wondering, but what about the companion invariance that links P_8 <2–3–4> with RI_8 <11–10–9>? Does Webern also draw attention to the invariant pc set [901] within this row pairing? Find these row segments in Example 10.1. What do you think? Are the invariant [901]s in measures 20 and 21 likely to be as noticeable as the invariant [347]s at the end of the phrase?

There's one additional invariance to explore between P_8 and I_8. The trichord at op <5–6–7> is pc set [26T], a member of (048), the augmented triad. This highly symmetrical set maps to itself in multiple ways, and in the P_8 form of the row, one of those self-mappings is I_4. To detect this, find a way to add the pc numbers within the set to equal index 4:

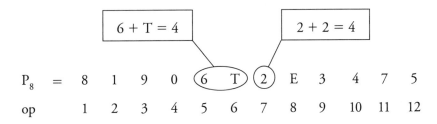

This tells us that the I_4-transform of this row, row form I_8, will hold the [26T] invariant: pc's 6 and T at op <5-6> map to each other, and pc 2 at op 7 maps to itself. So this is one additional invariance that could be emphasized when RI_8 is paired with P_8 at the end of the middle section of Webern's song (Ex. 10.1). Does this correspondence jump to the ear's attention in measure 21? Perhaps: pc 6 is shared by voice and piano as $G\flat_4$, while pc's 2 and T are stated in very close proximity in both voice and piano. The pc T, in fact, is directly repeated as $B\flat_4$ in the piano, then voice.

A close look at Webern's complete song will uncover several other moments when invariant sets emerge from the texture. Some of these occur between P_8 and I_8 (and/or their retrogrades), but others appear between different row pairings. We can predict what other row pairings will exhibit the same pattern of invariances, at the same order positions, because the relationship remains intact if both row forms are transposed by the same amount. In other words, an invariance occurs at the same order positions if you add a constant number to both subscripts. For example, the correspondences we've noticed between op's <2–3–4> and <9–10–11>, and the self-mapping at <5–6–7>, of row forms P_8 and I_8, will also occur if we add 1 to each subscript, pairing row forms P_9 and I_9 (or their retrogrades). Here's what that looks like for a pairing of P_9 with RI_9:

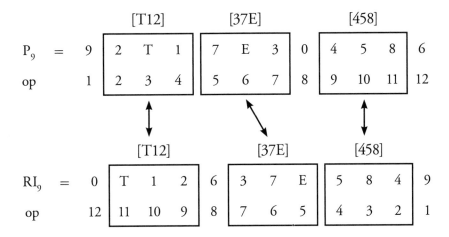

But Webern doesn't actually use these row forms in any of the opus 23 songs. The other pairing that he does use can be obtained by adding 6 to both subscripts in the P_8/I_8 pairing, yielding P_2/I_2. Here's what that looks like for a pairing of P_2 with RI_2:

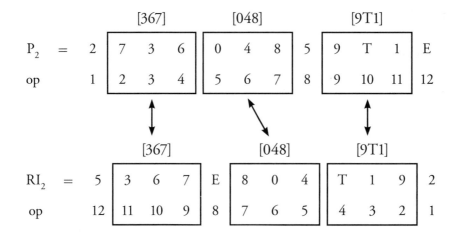

So, once we know that P_8 and I_8 share invariant segments, we automatically know that we can find invariances between equivalent pc sets in the same order positions in pairings of P_9/I_9, P_T/I_T, P_E/I_E, P_0/I_0, P_1/I_1, P_2/I_2, P_3/I_3, P_4/I_4, P_5/I_5, P_6/I_6, and P_7/I_7 (and their retrogrades).

Notice how the row forms in these pairings relate to each other as transformations. As we've seen, row forms P_8 and I_8 are equivalent via operation I_4, but row forms P_9 and I_9 relate by operation I_6, and row forms P_T and I_T by operation I_8:

ROW PAIRING	INDEX NUMBER
P_8/I_8	4
P_9/I_9	6
P_T/I_T	8
P_E/I_E	10
P_0/I_0	0
P_1/I_1	2
P_2/I_2	4
P_3/I_3	6
P_4/I_4	8
P_5/I_5	10
P_6/I_6	0
P_7/I_7	2

With each increment of one in the subscripts, the index numbers grow by two. Row pairings whose subscripts differ by six (P_8/I_8 and P_2/I_2, P_9/I_9 and P_3/I_3, and so forth) have the same index numbers. This helps explain Webern's choice of row forms in opus 23: row forms P_8/I_8 and P_2/I_2 not only share trichordal invariances, but relate to each other via the same operation, I_4.

In fact, Webern restricts himself to just these eight row forms, P_8, I_8, P_2, I_2, and their retrogrades, throughout all three of the opus 23 songs; that's just two different +6-related subscripts among all eight row forms. The trichordal invariances between row forms P_8/I_8 and P_2/I_2 (and their retrogrades) are a primary aspect of this compositional constraint. At the same time, Webern doesn't only pair row form P_8 with row form I_8, and P_2 with I_2. As we saw in Chapter 9, he uses several different combinations and configurations of the eight row forms. A complete summary of the twelve-tone structure of opus 23 would account for all possible transformational relations, including an I_T transformation between the other P/I pairings, and operation T_6 relating P-forms with P-forms or I-forms with I-forms (Ex. 10.2).

EXAMPLE 10.2   Webern, op. 23, summary of row relations

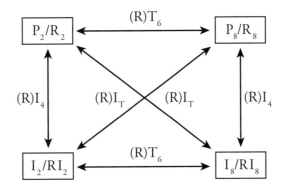

We've been focusing on invariances between row forms related by *inversion* (possibly including retrograde): P_8 (or R_8) and I_8 (or RI_8); or P_2 (or R_2) and I_2 (or RI_2). Now let's consider invariances between *transpositional* equivalences, such as two P-forms or two I-forms (again, with the possibility of retrograde). And we'll switch to a different composer, Schoenberg, and one of his first twelve-tone works, his Suite for Piano, op. 25 (1923).

The process of detecting invariances between transpositionally related row forms is essentially the same as for inversional invariances, substituting transposition for inversion, with one important difference. Let's see how this could work within the P_4 form of Schoenberg's row (Ex. 10.3).

EXAMPLE 10.3   Row from Schoenberg, Suite for Piano op. 25

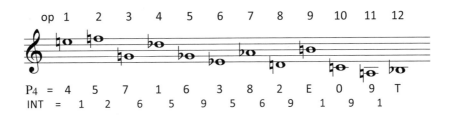

op	1	2	3	4	5	6	7	8	9	10	11	12
P4 =	4	5	7	1	6	3	8	2	E	0	9	T
INT =	1	2	6	5	9	5	6	9	1	9	1	

One distinctive feature of this row is the presence of internal (013)s in four places: as the first and last regularly partitioned trichords (op <1–2–3> and <10–11–12>), and at op <8–9–10> and <9–10–11>. Let's zoom in on the two regular partitions. The operation T_5 takes us from the [457] at op <1–2–3> to the [9T0] at op <10–11–12>:

$$[457] \xrightarrow{\quad T_5 \quad} [9T0]$$

$$P_4 = \boxed{4 \quad 5 \quad 7} \quad 1 \quad 6 \quad 3 \quad 8 \quad 2 \quad E \quad \boxed{0 \quad 9 \quad T}$$

$$op \quad \boxed{1 \quad 2 \quad 3} \quad 4 \quad 5 \quad 6 \quad 7 \quad 8 \quad 9 \quad \boxed{10 \quad 11 \quad 12}$$

This means that a transformation of the entire row form at T_5 (to P_9) will move the [9T0] into op <1–2–3>:

$$[9T0]$$

$$P_9 = \boxed{9 \quad T \quad 0} \quad 6 \quad E \quad 8 \quad 1 \quad 7 \quad 4 \quad 5 \quad 2 \quad 3$$

$$op \quad \boxed{1 \quad 2 \quad 3} \quad 4 \quad 5 \quad 6 \quad 7 \quad 8 \quad 9 \quad 10 \quad 11 \quad 12$$

So a musical pairing of row forms P_4 and P_9 could exploit an invariance between the last trichord of P_4 (or the first trichord of R_4) and the first trichord of P_9 (last trichord of R_9).

But here's the difference between row relationships by transposition and by inversion: T_5 maps pc set [457] to [9T0], but T_5 does not map [9T0] to [457]. Set [9T0] moves into op <1–2–3> when the row is transformed by T_5, but [457] doesn't likewise move to op <10–11–12>. The two trichords don't "trade places" as we saw inversional invariants do, because transpositions, unlike inversions, aren't their own inverses—with the exception of T_6, which is. The transposition within row form P_4 that sends the [9T0] at op <10–11–12> to take the place of the [457] at <1–2–3> is the inverse of $T_5 = T_7$:

$$[457] \xleftarrow{\quad T_7 \quad} [9T0]$$

P_4 =	4	5	7	1	6	3	8	2	E	0	9	T
op	1	2	3	4	5	6	7	8	9	10	11	12

Thus the row form that preserves [457] as an invariance is T_7 of $P_4 = P_E$:

$$[457]$$

P_E =	E	0	2	8	1	T	3	9	6	7	4	5
op	1	2	3	4	5	6	7	8	9	10	11	12

Pairing row forms P_4 with P_E could exploit an invariance between the first trichord of P_4 (or the last trichord of R_4) and the last trichord of P_E (first trichord of R_E).

Actually, these invariances are only inherent possiblities in Schoenberg's row. He doesn't use these specific pairings in his score. The transpositional pairing that he does use, right at the beginning of the first movement, is row form P_4 and its T_6 transposition, P_T. Let's look at the invariances between these two forms.

First, notice that the row has two tritones (ic 6's), at op <3–4> and <7–8> (Ex. 10.3). When a tritone is transposed by T_6, it self-maps; each note transforms into the other. So in the T_6 transposition of row forms, from P_4 to P_T, the pitch classes in the tritones switch places:

P_4 =	4	5	7	1	6	3	8	2	E	0	9	T
op	1	2	3	4	5	6	7	8	9	10	11	12

P_T =	T	E	1	7	0	9	2	8	5	6	3	4
op	1	2	3	4	5	6	7	8	9	10	11	12

Schoenberg draws attention to these invariant tritones in the first three measures of the first movement, between P_4 in the right hand and P_T lagging slightly behind in the left hand (Ex. 10.4).

EXAMPLE 10.4   Schoenberg, Suite for Piano, op. 25 no. 1, "Präludium," mm. 1–3

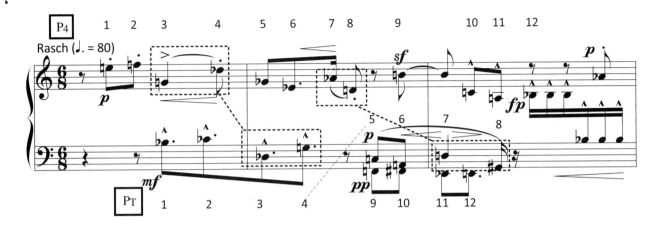

Looking further at Schoenberg's row, we can find an additional T_6 invariance between ic 3's. The [36] at op <5–6> maps by T_6 to [90] at op <10–11>, and because T_6 is its own inverse, the reverse is also true: [90] maps to [36] by the same operation:

$$[36] \xleftarrow{\qquad T_6 \qquad} [90]$$

P_4 =	4	5	7	1	6	3	8	2	E	0	9	T
op	1	2	3	4	5	6	7	8	9	10	11	12

This means that these dyads reverse positions when row form P_4 is transformed by T_6:

P_4 =	4	5	7	1	6	3	8	2	E	0	9	T
op	1	2	3	4	5	6	7	8	9	10	11	12

P_T =	T	E	1	7	0	9	2	8	5	6	3	4
op	1	2	3	4	5	6	7	8	9	10	11	12

Look again at the first three measures of Schoenberg's music in Example 10.4: are these invariant ic 3's likely to draw attention to themselves, in addition to the invariant tritones?

As Schoenberg's Suite progresses through six movements, he finds multiple ways to arrange and relate these two transpositionally equivalent rows, P_4 and P_T, and two others, I_4 and I_T. These P- and I-forms (and their retrogrades) interact with each other as well, exploring inversional invariances. In terms of row usage, the result is quite similar to Webern's approach in his opus 23 songs: eight exclusive row forms with only two different T_6-related subscripts (see Ex. 10.2). And in both works, invariant segments are primary means of building musical relationships and progressions.

For a bit more practice detecting segmental invariance, let's return to Webern's opus 23 row and look at a different built-in invariant possibility, even though he doesn't exploit this aspect in the songs. Members of tetrachord class (0145) appear as the first regularly partitioned tetrachord, op <1–2–3–4>, and later, as op <6–7–8–9>. This tells us that tetrachords in these positions will be invariant between certain forms of this row. Which ones?

It's a question with multiple answers because (0145) is symmetrical. Set class (0145) has twelve members, not twenty-four, and any pc set within the set class is equivalent to any other by both transposition and inversion. So to find the row forms with invariances at <1–2–3–4> and <6–7–8–9>, we'll need to investigate equivalences under both transposition and inversion.

First, transposition. Find the transpositional operator between the tetrachords in these positions within a single form of the row. In one of the forms we studied earlier, P_8, pc set [8901] at op <1–2–3–4> maps by T_2 to pc set [TE23] at op <6–7–8–9>:

$$
\begin{array}{ccc}
 & [8901] \xrightarrow{\;T_2\;} [TE23] & \\
P_8 = & \boxed{8\quad 1\quad 9\quad 0}\;\;6\;\;\boxed{T\quad 2\quad E\quad 3}\;\;4\;\;7\;\;5 \\
op & \boxed{1\quad 2\quad 3\quad 4}\;\;5\;\;\boxed{6\quad 7\quad 8\quad 9}\;\;10\;\;11\;\;12
\end{array}
$$

From this we can deduce that the row form that's T_2 of P_8, which is P_T, displays the contents of pc set [T2E3] in op <1–2–3–4>:

$$
\begin{array}{cc}
 & [TE23] \\
P_T = & \boxed{T\quad 3\quad E\quad 2}\;\;8\;\;0\;\;4\;\;1\;\;5\;\;6\;\;9\;\;7 \\
op & \boxed{1\quad 2\quad 3\quad 4}\;\;5\;\;6\;\;7\;\;8\;\;9\;\;10\;\;11\;\;12
\end{array}
$$

So a musical row pairing could highlight an invariance between the tetrachord at op <6–7–8–9> of row form P_8 (or R_8) and op <1–2–3–4> of row form P_T (or R_T).

Likewise, the inverse operation of T_2, which is T_T, maps the tetrachord at op <6–7–8–9> of row form P_8 to the tetrachord at op <1–2–3–4>:

$$
\begin{array}{ccc}
 & [8901] \xleftarrow{\;T_T\;} [TE23] & \\
P_8 = & \boxed{8\quad 1\quad 9\quad 0}\;\;6\;\;\boxed{T\quad 2\quad E\quad 3}\;\;4\;\;7\;\;5 \\
op & \boxed{1\quad 2\quad 3\quad 4}\;\;5\;\;\boxed{6\quad 7\quad 8\quad 9}\;\;10\;\;11\;\;12
\end{array}
$$

And this tells us that a T_T transformation of row form P_8, which is P_6, contains pc set [8901] at op <6–7–8–9>:

$$
\begin{array}{cc}
 & [8901] \\
P_6 = & 6\;\;E\;\;7\;\;T\;\;4\;\;\boxed{8\quad 0\quad 9\quad 1}\;\;2\;\;5\;\;3 \\
op & 1\;\;2\;\;3\;\;4\;\;5\;\;\boxed{6\quad 7\quad 8\quad 9}\;\;10\;\;11\;\;12
\end{array}
$$

Thus a musical row pairing might highlight an invariance between the tetrachord at op <1–2–3–4> of row form P_8 (or R_8) and the tetrachord at op <6–7–8–9> of row form P_6 (or R_6).

Now let's relate those same pc sets through inversion. The transformation I_E maps [8901] and [TE23] within row form P_8 to each other:

$$[8901] \xleftarrow{\quad I_E \quad} [TE23]$$

P_8 =	8	1	9	0	6	T	2	E	3	4	7	5
op	1	2	3	4	5	6	7	8	9	10	11	12

Therefore the I_E transformation of row form P_8, which is row form I_3, displays these two pc sets in reverse positions:

$$[TE23] \xleftarrow{\quad I_E \quad} [8901]$$

I_3 =	3	T	2	E	5	1	9	0	8	7	4	6
op	1	2	3	4	5	6	7	8	9	10	11	12

It would be possible, then, to combine these forms of this row (or their retrogrades) and musically highlight the invariances between P_8 <1–2–3–4> and I_3 <6–7–8–9>, and between P_8 <6–7–8–9> and I_3 <1–2–3–4>.

So, we've determined that row form P_8 (or R_8) could be paired with row form P_T or P_6 (or their retrogrades) to highlight invariances under transposition, and with row form I_E (or RI_E) to bring out invariances under inversion. But there are still other invariant possibilities, however, because symmetrical sets also map to themselves. Under certain operations, (0145) members will stay in their same positions in row forms. To discover how to make this happen, find the transformation that produces the self-mappings.

Members of set class (0145) map to themselves under inversion only. (Very few sets map to themselves under transposition.) So, to find the index number of the self-mapping, find a way to add pc's together within the tetrachords to total the same sums. At op <1–2–3–4> of row form P_8, we can get sum 9 from adding (8 + 1) and (9 + 0); [8901] self-maps at I_9:

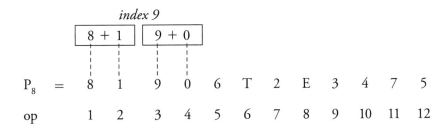

It therefore follows that when we transform row form P_8 by operation I_9, the result will be an inversional form of the row with pcset [8901] at op <1–2–3–4>. The I_9–transform of row form P_8 is row form I_1:

[8901]

I_1 =	1	8	0	9	3	E	7	T	6	5	2	4
op	1	2	3	4	5	6	7	8	9	10	11	12

In a musical association between row forms P_8 and I_1 (or their retrogrades), then, a composer could exploit an invariance between the regularly partitioned tetrachords at op <1–2–3–4>.

Follow the same procedure for the (0145) member at op <6–7–8–9>. Pc set [TE23] self-maps at I_1:

index 1

T	+	3

| | 2 + E | |

P_8	=	8	1	9	0	6	T	2	E	3	4	7	5
op		1	2	3	4	5	6	7	8	9	10	11	12

The I_1-transform of row form P_8 is row form I_5:

[TE23]

I_5	=	5	0	4	1	7	3	E	2	T	9	6	8
op		1	2	3	4	5	6	7	8	9	10	11	12

It's therefore possible to highlight the invariant tetrachord at op <6–7–8–9> in a pairing of row forms P_8 and I_5 (or their retrogrades).

STUDY QUESTIONS 10.1

1. **Find invariant trichords or tetrachords in the following pairs of row forms. Identify the invariant pc sets by order position and normal form and prime form.**
   1.1. P_3 = <3591604E287T> and I_6 = <6408395T712E>
   1.2. R_2 = <9671T3E50842> and I_4 = <42T617385E09>
   1.3. RI_5 = <T10694827E35> and I_9 = <973E6081T452>
   1.4. I_8 = <862T5E709341> and P_4 = <46T27150398E>

2. **Find two members of the same trichordal set class as internal sets in this row: P_2 = <2183604ET795>.**
   2.1. What are the order positions and normal forms of these two trichords, and what is the prime form of their set class?
   2.2. What is the operation that transforms one of these trichords into the other?
   2.3. What is the label for the row form that results from applying that same operation to the P_2 label?
   2.4. Write the new row form from question 2.3 as a <pc string>. Underline the invariant segments shared with P_2.

3. **Find two members of the same tetrachordal set class as internal sets in this row: P_1 = <10925E8T7634>.**
   3.1. What are the order positions and normal forms of these two tetrachords, and what is the prime form of their set class?
   3.2. What are the two operations that transform one of these tetrachords into the other?

3.3. What are the row labels for the two row forms that result from applying those same operations to the P_1 label?

3.4. Write the two new row forms from question 3.3, each as a different <pc string>. Underline the invariant segments shared with P_1.

3.5. What are the two inversional operations that transform each of these tetrachords into themselves?

3.6. What are the row labels for the two row forms that result from applying those same operations to the P_1 label?

3.7. Write the two new row forms from question 3.6, each as a different <pc string>. Underline the invariant segments shared with P_1.

10.2 COMBINATORIALITY

While twelve-tone composers who are interested in invariances actively seek and highlight pitch-class duplications between different forms of the same row, a whole other approach seeks actively to avoid them. The second theme area of Schoenberg's piano piece opus 33a, for example, combines two inversionally equivalent row forms whose regularly partitioned hexachords share no pitch classes (Ex. 10.5).

EXAMPLE 10.5 Schoenberg, Piano Piece, op. 33a, mm. 14–18

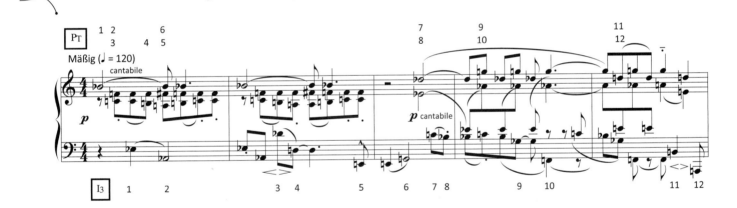

The first hexachord ("H_1") of row form P_T in the treble clef, pc set [569TE0], is completely different, with respect to pc content, from the H_1 of row form I_3 being unfolded simultaneously in the bass clef, pc set [123478]. The hexachords are members of the same set class, (012367) [6-5], but they share no pitch classes. As a result, the two hexachords combine to complete the aggregate—as a counterpart to the aggregates being unfolded by each row form individually. And of course the second hexachords ("H_2") of both row forms, likewise presented simultaneously over the next few beats, complete a second aggregate by combining these same hexachords in opposite positions, [123478] in H_2 of row form P_T over [569TE0] in H_2 of row form I_3:

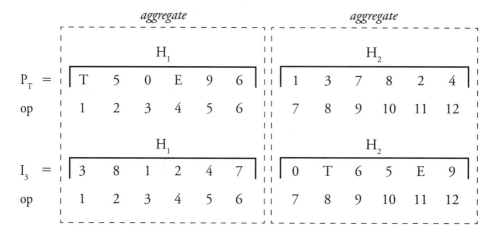

Combining row forms to complete aggregates between corresponding segments is known as **combinatoriality**. When the segments being combined are hexachords, it's **hexachordal combinatoriality**. The combinatoriality demonstrated in opus 33a is known as **I-type**, or **I-combinatoriality**, because the two row forms being combined (P_T and I_3) are equivalent by inversion. I-combinatoriality can also occur between an R-form and an RI-form of the row.

The other types of combinatoriality are **P-type**, or **P-combinatoriality**, between row forms that are equivalent by transposition; **R-type**, or **R-combinatoriality**, between row forms related by retrograde; and **RI-type**, or **RI-combinatoriality**, combining row forms related by retrograde inversion:

TYPE OF COMBINATORIALITY	ROW RELATIONS	ROW FORMS
I-type	inversion	P/I, R/RI
P-type	transposition	P/P, I/I, R/R, RI/RI
R-type	retrograde	P/R, I/RI
RI-type	retrograde inversion	P/RI, I/R

Let's ponder the circumstances for creating hexachordal combinatoriality during the compositional process. First of all, any form of any row can be combined with its retrograde to produce R-type combinatoriality. H_1 of any row form automatically completes the aggregate with H_1 of its retrograde, as does H_2 complete the aggregate with H_2 of the retrograde form. Here's how that would line up for the I_3 row form from op. 33a and its retrograde:

aggregate   *aggregate*

		H_1						H_2				
I_3 =	3	8	1	2	4	7	0	T	6	5	E	9
op	1	2	3	4	5	6	7	8	9	10	11	12
		H_1						H_2				
RI_3 =	9	E	5	6	T	0	7	4	2	1	8	3
op	12	11	10	9	8	7	6	5	4	3	2	1

Aside from this trivial R-type, however, combinatoriality is a special possibility that only works with certain rows. The composer must build this potential into the row from the beginning. Schoenberg was especially interested in rows of this type, and in writing music that explores combinatorial relationships, as in his opus 33a piano piece.

We'll explore each type of combinatoriality separately, starting with the I-type as seen in opus 33a. For a row to be capable of I-type combinatoriality, the unordered pc set of H_1 must map entirely to the pc set of H_2, and the pc set of H_2 must map entirely to the pc set of H_1, under some inversional operation. Between row forms P_T and I_3 of Schoenberg's row, that operation is I_1, easily inferrable by summing the two subscripts ($T + 3 = 1$); when either row form P_T or row form I_3 is transformed by I_1, the pc contents of the hexachords switch places. But if we didn't already know the specific operation, we could figure it out by identifying the hexachordal mapping within a single row form, just as we do when disclosing invariances:

$$H_1\ [569TE0] \xleftarrow{\quad I_1 \quad} H_2\ [123478]$$

P_T	=	T	5	0	E	9	6	1	3	7	8	2	4
op		1	2	3	4	5	6	7	8	9	10	11	12

Since the pc contents of H_1 and H_2 within row form P_T effectively switch places under the operation I_1, the I_1-transform of row form P_T, which is row form I_3, is its I-combinatorial partner, as musically realized in Example 10.5.

From this we can also conclude that any other pairing of two inversionally equivalent forms of this row that have the same +5 subscript relationship will also be I-combinatorial. If row forms P_T and I_3 are I-combinatorial, then so are row forms P_E and I_4, P_0 and I_5, P_1 and I_6, P_2 and I_7, P_3 and I_8, P_4 and I_9, P_5 and I_T, P_6 and I_E, P_7 and I_0, P_8 and I_1, and P_9 and I_2. The relationship would likewise obtain if both row forms are retrograded: row forms R_T and RI_3 are I-combinatorial, as are row forms R_E and RI_4, R_0 and RI_5, and so forth. We wouldn't expect to see all (or even many) of these pairings in a typical score, but they all have this potential.

Here's another Schoenberg row, from his Violin Concerto, op. 36:

$$H_1\ [3469TE] \xleftarrow{\quad I_E \quad} H_2\ [012578]$$

P_9	=	9	T	3	E	4	6	0	1	7	8	2	5
op		1	2	3	4	5	6	7	8	9	10	11	12

This row, whose hexachords are members of (012578) [6-18], also has I-combinatorial potential, inferable because H_1 and H_2 map to each other under operation I_E. So the I-combinatorial partner of row form P_9 is its I_E-transform, row form I_2:

$$H_1\ [012578] \xleftarrow{\quad I_E \quad} H_2\ [3469TE]$$

I_2	=	2	1	8	0	7	5	E	T	4	3	9	6
op		1	2	3	4	5	6	7	8	9	10	11	12

Schoenberg lines up the hexachords of row forms P_9 and I_2 near the beginning of his concerto, in the first linear presentation of the row in the solo violin and the accompanying bassoons, violas, and cellos (Ex. 10.6).

EXAMPLE 10.6   Schoenberg, Violin Concerto, mm. 8.2–11.1

The rows in Schoenberg's piano piece and concerto are capable of I-combinatoriality because they're built from hexachords that enable the H_1/H_2 mappings. But how special is this feature? What other hexachords enable I-type combinatoriality, and what hexachords enable other types? The answers are in Example 10.7, which summarizes the combinatorial possibilities for all fifty hexachordal set classes. Part A of the example lists hexachords having no potential for combinatoriality at all, other than the trivial R-type. Part B shows the twelve hexachords that foster I-type combinatoriality exclusively, including the source hexachords for Schoenberg's opus 33a and opus 36 rows, (012367) [6-5] and (012578) [6-18]. Hexachords that enable I-type along with at least one other type are listed in parts E, F, and G.

Notice that none of the hexachords that are capable of I-type combinatoriality are Z-related. That's because I-type combinatoriality requires hexachordal mapping, and Z-related hexachords can't map to each other; they're not equivalent. The hexachords that aren't members of Z-pairs, the self-complementary hexachords, are the ones used most often by Schoenberg to build his rows. Only one of the twenty self-complementary hexachords, (013458) [6-14], doesn't have I-combinatorial potential (Ex. 10.7C).

EXAMPLE 10.7 Hexachords Categorized by Combinatorial Potential

A. None (trivial R-type only)

(012347) 6-Z36	(012356) 6-Z3
(012358) 6-Z40	(012457) 6-Z11
(012368) 6-Z41	(012467) 6-Z12
(012469) 6-Z46	(013468) 6-Z24
(012478) 6-Z17	(012568) 6-Z43
(012479) 6-Z47	(013568) 6-Z25
(012569) 6-Z44	(013478) 6-Z19
(013457) 6-Z10	(023458) 6-Z39

B. I-type only

(012346) 6-2
(012357) 6-9
(012367) 6-5
(012458) 6-15
(012468) 6-22
(012578) 6-18
(013469) 6-27
(013579) 6-34
(014568) 6-16
(014579) 6-31
(023468) 6-21
(023579) 6-33

C. P-type only

(013458) 6-14

D. RI-type only

(012348) 6-Z37	(012456) 6-Z4
(012369) 6-Z42	(013467) 6-Z13
(012378) 6-Z38	(012567) 6-Z6
(012579) 6-Z48	(013578) 6-Z26
(013479) 6-Z49	(013569) 6-Z28
(014679) 6-Z50	(023679) 6-Z29
(023469) 6-Z45	(023568) 6-Z23

E. R/I-type

(013679) 6-30

F. P/I/RI-type

*(012345) 6-1
*(023457) 6-8
*(024579) 6-32

G. P/I/R/RI-type

*(012678) 6-7
*(014589) 6-20
*(02468T) 6-35

*"all-combinatorial" (Babbitt)

P-type = complement-mapping under transposition
I-type = complement-mapping under inversion
R-type (nontrivial) = self-mapping under transposition
RI-type = self-mapping under inversion

P-type combinatoriality requires a transpositional mapping from H_1 to H_2 and therefore cannot occur between Z-partners. The possibilities for P-type are much more limited than for I-type; only the hexachord listed in part C of Example 10.7, (013458) [6-14], can provide P-type combinatoriality; no other type can. Here's a row built from that hexachord:

$$H_1 \text{ [124569]} \xleftarrow{\quad T_6 \quad} H_2 \text{ [78TE03]}$$

P_2 =	2	4	6	9	1	5	T	E	8	3	7	0
op	1	2	3	4	5	6	7	8	9	10	11	12

Because H_1 and H_2 map to each other via T_6, the T_6-transform of the row, P_8, will display the hexachordal pc contents in opposite positions:

$$
\begin{array}{llllllllllllll}
& & & & H_1 \ [\text{78TE03}] & & \xleftarrow{\quad T_6 \quad} & & H_2 \ [\text{124569}] & & & & & \\
P_8 & = & 8 & T & 0 & 3 & 7 & E & 4 & 5 & 2 & 9 & 1 & 6 \\
\text{op} & & 1 & 2 & 3 & 4 & 5 & 6 & 7 & 8 & 9 & 10 & 11 & 12
\end{array}
$$

It's therefore possible to pair forms P_2 and P_8 of this row and line up the hexachords to produce aggregates. More generally, P-combinatoriality is possible within this row class between any P_n and P_{n+6}; or any I_n and I_{n+6}; or any R_n and R_{n+6}; or any RI_n and RI_{n+6}. For example, RI_7 and RI_1:

$$
\begin{array}{lllllllllllllll}
& & \overset{\textit{aggregate}}{} & & & & & & & & \overset{\textit{aggregate}}{} & & & & \\
& & & & H_1 & & & & & & & & H_2 & & \\
RI_7 & = & 9 & 2 & 6 & 1 & T & E & & & 4 & 8 & 0 & 3 & 5 & 7 \\
\text{op} & & 12 & 11 & 10 & 9 & 8 & 7 & & & 6 & 5 & 4 & 3 & 2 & 1 \\
& & & & H_1 & & & & & & & & H_2 & & \\
RI_1 & = & 3 & 8 & 0 & 7 & 4 & 5 & & & T & 2 & 6 & 9 & E & 1 \\
\text{op} & & 12 & 11 & 10 & 9 & 8 & 7 & & & 6 & 5 & 4 & 3 & 2 & 1
\end{array}
$$

Let's move on to R-type and RI-type combinatoriality, excluding the trivial case of every row form having combinatorial potential with its own retrograde. If I- and P-types require a row's hexachords to map to each other, then R- and RI-types require their respective hexachords to map to themselves. This means, among other things, that R- and/or RI-type combinatoriality can occur only if the hexachords are symmetrical. For nontrivial R-type combinatoriality, the hexachord must map to itself under transposition, and for RI-type, the hexachord must map to itself under inversion.

Example 10.7 shows which hexachords have this potential. No hexachords are capable of only nontrivial R-type—that is, no hexachords only map to themselves under transposition—but four enable nontrivial R-type plus other types (listed in groups E and G). RI-types are more plentiful: group D lists seven pairs of Z-related hexachords that are capable of RI-type only (map to themselves under inversion). Here's a row built from one of them:

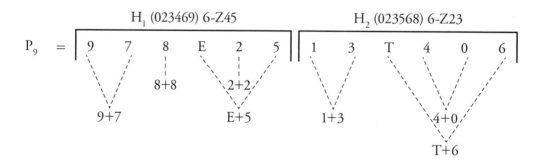

To recognize the inversional self-mappings, find ways to sum notes within each hexachord to the same index number. The index number in this case is 4, achieved by adding together 9+7, 8+8, E+5, and 2+2 in H_1, and 1+3, T+6, and 4+0 in H_2. This tells us that the I_4-transform of this row form will preserve the pc contents of the two hexachords. The I_4-transform of row form P_9 is row form I_7:

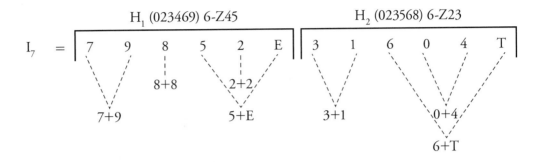

The combinatorial pairing with row form P_9, then, would be the retrograde of row form I_7:

		aggregate								*aggregate*				
				H_1							H_2				
$P_9 =$		9	7	8	E	2	5		1	3	T	4	0	6
op		1	2	3	4	5	6		7	8	9	10	11	12
				H_1							H_2				
$RI_7 =$		T	4	0	6	1	3		E	2	5	8	9	7
op		12	11	10	9	8	7		6	5	4	3	2	1

And from this we can conclude that pairings of other RI-related forms of this row that have the same +10 relationship of subscripts will also display RI-type combinatoriality: not only row forms P_9/RI_7 but also row forms P_T/RI_8, P_E/RI_9, P_0/RI_T, P_1/RI_E, P_2/RI_0, P_3/RI_1, P_4/RI_2, P_5/RI_3, P_6/RI_4, P_7/RI_5, and P_8/RI_6. The relationship would likewise exist between pairings of retrogrades of P-forms with unretrograded I-forms: row forms R_9/I_7, R_T/I_8, R_E/I_9, R_0/I_T, R_1/I_E, R_2/I_0, R_3/I_1, R_4/I_2, R_5/I_3, R_6/I_4, R_7/I_5, and R_8/I_6.

The latter categories of Example 10.7 include a list of three hexachords capable of P-, I-, and RI-type combinatoriality (group F), and another list of three that are capable of all four types (group G). In recognition of their combinatorial versatility, Milton Babbitt referred to these six as the "all-combinatorial" hexachords.[1] (He didn't distinguish between trivial and nontrivial R-type combinatoriality.) Babbitt not only drew attention to this aspect of Schoenberg's music but also wrote many works of his own that explore combinatoriality of all types in vastly interesting ways.

---

[1]Milton Babbitt, "Some Aspects of Twelve-Tone Composition," *The Score and I. M. A. Magazine* 12 (June 1955): 57.

STUDY QUESTIONS 10.2

1. **Answer the following questions by studying Example 10.7.**

   1.1. Why do the hexachords in group A exemplify a "trivial" type of combinatoriality?

   1.2. How many hexachords are capable of only I-type combinatoriality?

   1.3. How many hexachords in total are capable of I-type combinatoriality?

   1.4. Why does group B NOT include Z-pairs?

   1.5. Which group includes hexachords that only map to themselves under inversion?

2. **Which type of combinatoriality is exemplified by the following row pairings, assuming that their corresponding hexachords combine to form aggregates?**

   2.1. P_3 and I_7 2.2. RI_2 and R_1 2.3. R_1 and R_7 2.4. I_T and P_6

   2.5. I_3 and I_9 2.6. RI_0 and P_2 2.7. I_8 and R_7

3. **Within a row involved in each of the combinatorial row pairings listed in question 2, precisely how (by what transformation) are the hexachords related?**

10.3   SECONDARY SETS

Imagine doing an analysis of the opening bars from the Schoenberg op. 25 piano piece that we studied earlier in this chapter (Ex. 10.4) without thinking about the row. You would make logical, musical note groupings and consider how they might be related and integrated within the overall structure of the piece, just as we did in earlier chapters. When the left hand first enters, you'd likely group together its initial $<B\flat_3–C\flat_3>$ dyad with the right hand's $<G_4–D\flat_5>$ to form a tetrachord, [7TE1] (0236) (Ex. 10.8). At the beginning of measure 2, it would make sense to combine dyads in each hand to form [1367] (0146). After that, you'd probably make tetrachordal groupings in the left hand of [5690] (0147) at the end of measure 2 and [2348] (0126) at the beginning of measure 3.

EXAMPLE 10.8   Schoenberg, op. 25, no. 1, mm. 1–3

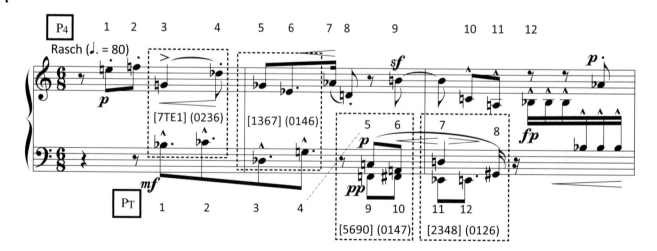

These tetrachordal formations have a significant impact on our perception of the opening bars, and yet they aren't formed by adjacent notes within row forms. The [7TE1] and [1367] are each created by combining two notes from P_4 with two from P_T, while the other two bring together dyads from different places in P_T, first op <5–6> with <9–T> to form [5690], then <7–8> with <11–12> to form [2348]. Important note groupings that aren't contiguous within a single row form, such as dyads from two different forms, or different segments of the same row form, are called **secondary sets**.

Secondary sets are especially worthy of our attention when studying music such as Schoenberg's piano piece, in which the unfoldings of different row forms are so closely intertwined. They do raise important questions, however, because they seem to draw attention away from the row itself. If the row is the source and guiding principle of a twelve-tone work, then of what significance are note combinations that clearly aren't expressed within a single row statement?

The answer lies in the relationship between the secondary sets and the row. Each of these four tetrachords in Schoenberg's piece is a member of a set class that's represented at least once in the internal sets of the row itself (Ex. 10.9). The first one, [7TE1], is a member of (0236), just like the tetrachords at op <1–2–3–4> and <7–8–9–10>. In other words, when op <3–4> of P_4 and <1–2> of P_T combine to form [7TE1] in measure 1, this tetrachord interacts with formations of this same tetrachord type by the first four notes (op <1–2–3–4>) of each hand by itself. Similarly, the [1367] formed in measure 2 by P_4 <5–6> and P_T <3–4> echoes, and interlocks with, the same tetrachord type (0146) just stated by P_4 <3–4–5–6> in the right hand.

EXAMPLE 10.9 Schoenberg, op. 25, row P_4, internal sets of sizes 2–9

Pc:	4	5	7	1	6	3	8	2	E	0	9	T
Starting op:	1	2	3	4	5	6	7	8	9	10	11	12

Ic:	1	2	6	5	3	5	6	3	1	3	1	
Trichords:	**(013)**	(026)	(016)	**(025)**	(025)	(016)	**(036)**	(013)	(013)	**(013)**		
Tetrachords:	**(0236)**	(0126)	(0146)	(0257)	**(0146)**	(0147)	(0236)	(0235)	**(0123)**			
Pentachords:	5-4	5-9	5-14	5-14	5-32	5-16	5-10	5-2				
Hexachords:	**6-2**	6-9	6-Z6	6-Z47	6-Z49	6-Z13	**6-2**					
Septachords:	7-2	7-5	7-20	7-Z12	7-31	7-4						
Octachords:	8-1	8-Z29	8-8	8-13	8-12							
Nonachords:	9-2	9-5	9-5	9-2								

STUDY QUESTIONS 10.3

1. **Look at the [5690] boxed in measure 2 of Example 10.8. Of which set class is this a member, and where is another member of this set class formed within the row? How is this relationship brought out in measures 2 and 3?**

2. **Look at the [2348] boxed in measure 3 of Example 10.8. Of which set class is this a member, and where is another member of this set class formed within the row? Does Schoenberg make an effort to connect the [2348] with the equivalent row segment?**

10.4 EXTENSIONS OF THE TWELVE-TONE METHOD

Each composer who adopted, or at least dabbled in, the twelve-tone method found different aspects to absorb and develop. Arnold Schoenberg, the originator, favored hexachordal orientations and I-combinatorial row pairings. His student Anton Webern was drawn to set-class saturation, symmetry, and invariance. Another great serialist, Luigi Dallapiccola, blended elements of Webern's style with nods to Schoenberg within a distinctively lyrical, often passionately dramatic compositional voice. Considering their shared technical roots, other adaptations of the method—by Milton Babbitt, Pierre Boulez, Ernst Krenek, Luigi Nono, Wallingford Riegger, Roger Sessions, Karlheinz Stockhausen, Charles Wuorinen, and many others—have yielded musical results that are strikingly diverse.

What distinguish the twelve-tone compositions of Schoenberg's other great student, Alban Berg, are his idiosyncratic methods of transforming and relating row forms. We get a taste of this in the first movement of his *Lyric Suite* for string quartet (Ex. 10.10). After a one-bar introduction, the first violin plays the P_5 form of the row in measures 2–4. Look carefully at the INT of this row:

$$P_5 \quad = \quad 5 \quad 4 \quad 0 \quad 9 \quad 7 \quad 2 \quad 8 \quad 1 \quad 3 \quad 6 \quad T \quad E$$
$$INT \quad = \quad E \quad 8 \quad 9 \quad T \quad 7 \quad 6 \quad 5 \quad 2 \quad 3 \quad 4 \quad 1$$

EXAMPLE 10.10 Berg, *Lyric Suite*, mvt. 1, mm. 1–4.1

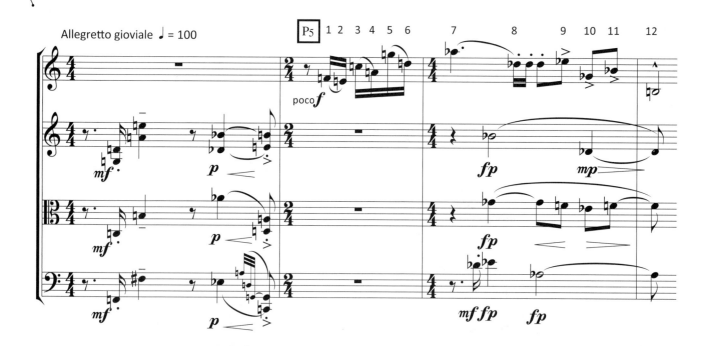

It's an **all-interval row**: every pc interval is represented once. The INT also reveals the row's symmetry: with the 6 in the center as the axis, pc intervals at equal distances before and after the axis are mod-12 complements:

$$P_5 = \quad 5 \quad\; 4 \quad\; 0 \quad\; 9 \quad\; 7 \quad\; 2 \quad\; 8 \quad\; 1 \quad\; 3 \quad\; 6 \quad\; T \quad\; E$$
$$INT = \qquad E \quad 8 \quad\; 9 \quad\; T \quad\; 7 \quad\; 6 \quad\; 5 \quad\; 2 \quad\; 3 \quad\; 4 \quad\; 1$$

$$7 \cdots\cdots + \cdots\cdots 5$$
$$T \cdots\cdots\cdots + \cdots\cdots\cdots 2$$
$$9 \cdots\cdots\cdots\cdots\cdots + \cdots\cdots\cdots\cdots\cdots 3$$
$$8 \cdots\cdots\cdots\cdots\cdots\cdots\cdots + \cdots\cdots\cdots\cdots\cdots\cdots\cdots 4$$
$$E \cdots\cdots\cdots\cdots\cdots\cdots\cdots\cdots\cdots + \cdots\cdots\cdots\cdots\cdots\cdots\cdots\cdots\cdots 1$$

This means that any retrograde form of the row will have the same INT as some P-form. To see this, just reverse row form P_5 and look at the resulting INT:

$$R_5 = \quad E \quad\; T \quad\; 6 \quad\; 3 \quad\; 1 \quad\; 8 \quad\; 2 \quad\; 7 \quad\; 9 \quad\; 0 \quad\; 4 \quad\; 5$$
$$INT = \qquad E \quad 8 \quad\; 9 \quad\; T \quad\; 7 \quad\; 6 \quad\; 5 \quad\; 2 \quad\; 3 \quad\; 4 \quad\; 1$$

The INT of row form R_5 is the same as it is for row form P_5. Further, the pc ordering of R_5 itself is the same as row form P_E. (See for yourself: add 6, mod 12, to each pc in row form P_5; the result is the same as R_5.) In other words, $R_5 = T_6(P_5) = P_E$. Or just look within the row itself: the last pc is T_6 of the first one (and vice versa, since T_6 is its own inverse), the pc's in op 2 and 11 are T_6 of each other, and so forth:

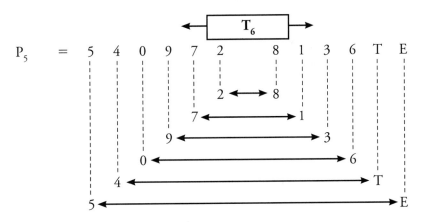

More generally, any P-form of this row is the same as the retrograde of its T_6 transposition ($P_x = R_{x+6}$). ($P_5 = R_E$, $P_6 = R_0$, $P_7 = R_1$, and so forth.) Likewise, any I-form of this row is the same as the retrograde of its T_6 tranposition ($I_x = RI_{x+6}$). ($I_E = RI_5$, $I_6 = RI_0$, $I_7 = RI_1$, and so forth.) Every form of the row has two possible labels. The row class comprises not forty-eight but twenty-four unique members.

Back to the score: What's the connection between the introduction (measure 1) and the main theme (first violin, measures 2–4)? The opening sounds in the lower three instruments are mostly stacked perfect fifths, what we called in Chapter 5 **quintal harmonies**. What do these chords have to do with the row?

Berg musically illustrates the connection later in the movement, when the first theme returns to begin the recapitulation section of the sonata form (Ex. 10.11). Row form P_5 is loudly announced here, alternating between the viola playing the notes in the odd-numbered order positions, and the cello playing the notes in the even-numbered positions. The notes played by each instrument individually are progressions of perfect fourths or perfect fifths. So the quintal harmonies of measure 1 essentially take these alternate notes from the row and express them as chords.

EXAMPLE 10.11   Berg, *Lyric Suite*, mvt. 1, mm. 42–44

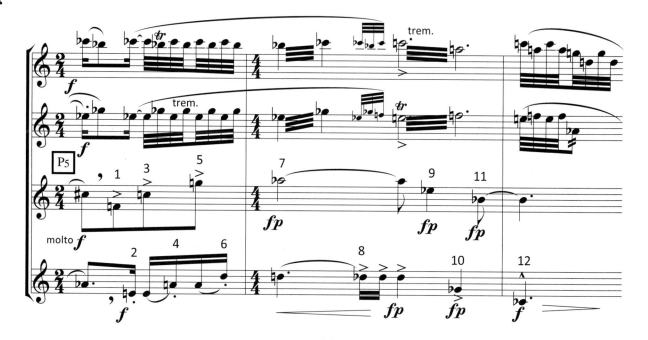

We can make the derivation more specific to measure 1 by reordering one hexachord at a time, starting with H_1 of P_5. Step through the odd-numbered order positions, then bounce back through the even-numbered positions in reverse:

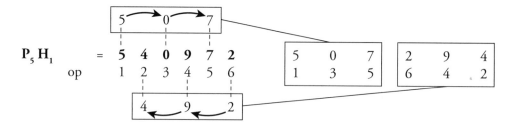

Next, do the same for H_2 of P_5 but with reverse directions. Start at the end, with op 12, and extract the even-numbered order positions right to left, then the odd-numbered positions left to right:

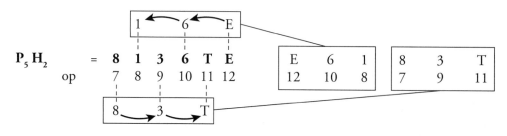

Combine the new hexachords as a newly ordered row, named S_5, for **S**econdary row beginning on pc 5:

		H_1						H_2					
P_5 op	=	1	3	5	6	4	2	12	10	8	7	9	11
S_5	=	5	0	7	2	9	4	E	6	1	8	3	T
S_5 op	=	1	2	3	4	5	6	7	8	9	10	11	12

The chords in measure 1 begin by jumping from S_5's first regularly parititioned tetrachord <1–2–3–4> to its second <5–6–7–8>, placing the <A_4–E_5> in op <5–6> at the top to suggest a p–space continuation of the perfect fifths just heard (Ex. 10.12). The chordal expression of the final tetrachord <9–10–11–12>, however, is configured to de-emphasize the pure open fifths. Then purity quickly returns with a six-note quintal stacking at the end of the measure, best understood as the first hexachord in a transposition of row form S_5 to S_0. After a pause, the second hexachord of row form S_0 appears in measure 3, again organized to downplay its intervallic echoes of the chords in measure 1.

EXAMPLE 10.12   Berg, *Lyric Suite*, mvt. 1, mm. 1–4.1 (S-forms marked)

Berg's twelve-tone works in general are looser, less strict, with the typical principles of twelve-tone composition. He is more likely than many of his contemporaries to expand standard boundaries or abandon systematic writing altogether to suit particular expressive or dramatic needs. It's fairly easy to follow his methods in *Lyric Suite*, especially when he literally demonstrates derivational procedures within the fabric of the music. In other works, however, the logic behind his variations and derivations is less clearly defined or displayed and may make complete sense only after consulting verbal explanations and compositional notes or sketches.

STUDY QUESTIONS 10.4

1. **Give two possible labels for these forms of the *Lyric Suite* row:**

   1.1. 5409728136TE   1.2. 21964E5T0378

   1.3. E04792831T65   1.4. ET6318279045

2. **In one passage in the middle of the first movement of *Lyric Suite*, each instrument plays alternating six-note segments of C major and F♯-major scales: <C–D–E–F–G–A> and <F♯–G♯–A♯–B–C♯–D♯>. How do these segments relate to the main row and its derivatives?**

10.5 ROTATION

Just after the opening bars of Berg's *Lyric Suite*, a melody appears in the first violin, echoed in other instruments, that sounds immediately familiar (Ex. 10.13). Its rhythms and overall shape directly recall the main theme (Ex. 10.12). Its melodic intervals, however, are different: the original theme begins with pc intervals <E–8–9–T–7–6>, while this new melody begins with pc intervals <3–4–1–6–E–8>. Upon closer inspection, you realize that the melody employs the P_5 form of the row, but starting with op 9.

EXAMPLE 10.13 Berg, *Lyric Suite*, mvt. 1, mm. 7–8, first violin

Moving segments of a row into different positions, while retaining the ordering within the segments themselves, is called **rotation**. Berg has rotated P_5 here by moving the first eight notes to the end:

op	1	2	3	4	5	6	7	8	9	10	11	12
P_5 =	5	4	0	9	7	2	8	1	3	6	T	E
INT =	E	8	9	T	7	6	5	2	3	4	1	

P_5 op	9	10	11	12	1	2	3	4	5	6	7	8
pc	3	6	T	E	5	4	0	9	7	2	8	1
INT =	3	4	1	6	E	8	9	T	7	6	5	

The INT, of course, is also rotated, and has lost its symmetry and its all-interval quality: pc interval 6 appears twice in the rotated INT, and pc interval 2 is absent.

For Berg, rotation was simply one of many techniques of order variation in his adaptation of the twelve-tone method. For other composers, however, rotation was a primary technical tool. The twelve-tone works of the Austrian-born Ernst Krenek, starting around 1940, employ rotation extensively. And when Igor Stravinsky began to move beyond neo-classicism toward the end of his career, he wrote twelve-tone works in which rotation was a central organizing feature.

Stravinsky, like Krenek, used rotation to create stacks of rotated rows or row segments that could be used as sources for melodies and harmonies. The stacking is known as a **rotational array**. The rotational array resembles the row chart in appearance, and in that it collects and organizes primary compositional materials, but its basic structure is significantly different.

Let's reconstruct one of the rotational arrays Stravinsky used in his orchestral work *Variations: Aldous Huxley in memoriam*. We'll use an R_2 form of the row as our starting point:

R_2	=	5	6	7	3	1	8	T	4	E	9	0	2
op		12	11	10	9	8	7	6	5	4	3	2	1

It's a two-step process. First, establish R_2 as the top line of the array ("rot1"). Then below that, place R_2 with the first note rotated to the end ("rot2"). On the third line ("rot3"), place R_2 with its first two notes rotated to the end. On the fourth line ("rot4"), place R_2 with its first three notes rotated to the end. And so forth. This process could continue up until the array has twelve lines, but to keep it relevant to the beginning of the *Variations*, we'll stop after line six ("rot6"):

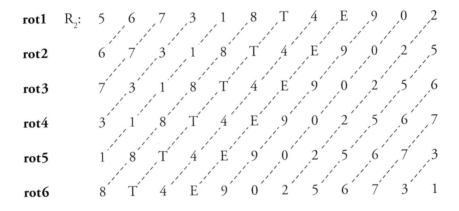

rot1	R_2:	5	6	7	3	1	8	T	4	E	9	0	2
rot2		6	7	3	1	8	T	4	E	9	0	2	5
rot3		7	3	1	8	T	4	E	9	0	2	5	6
rot4		3	1	8	T	4	E	9	0	2	5	6	7
rot5		1	8	T	4	E	9	0	2	5	6	7	3
rot6		8	T	4	E	9	0	2	5	6	7	3	1

After you've completed the rotations, the other step is to take the rotated array and transpose lines two through six so that they all begin on the same note as line 1, in this case pc 5. Since rot2 begins on pc 6, it must be transposed by T_E ("down a half step") to begin on pc 5 (6 + E = 5). Since rot3 begins on pc 7, it must be transposed by T_T (T + 7 = 5). And so forth:

Column:		**1**	**2**	**3**	**4**	**5**	**6**	**7**	**8**	**9**	**10**	**11**	**12**
rot1	R_2:	5	6	7	3	1	8	T	4	E	9	0	2
T_E(**rot2**)		5	6	2	0	7	9	3	T	8	E	1	4
T_T(**rot3**)		5	1	E	6	8	2	9	7	T	0	3	4
T_2(**rot4**)		5	3	T	0	6	1	E	2	4	7	8	9
T_4(**rot5**)		5	0	2	8	3	1	4	6	9	T	E	7
T_9(**rot6**)		5	7	1	8	6	9	E	2	3	4	0	T

Stravinsky used this rotational array, and others similarly constructed, as basic source material in the *Variations*. Think about this array's structure. The all-important intervallic content of the row is essentially intact within each line. Whether transposed or not, the lines of the array project some rotation of the INT. So a melodic realization of a line from the array would be a close cousin of the row itself, in the same way that Berg's rotation of the *Lyric Suite* melody makes a strong connection to its original presentation (Exx. 10.12, 10.13). And Stravinsky uses the lines of his arrays in exactly that way in some parts of the *Variations*.

The columns, however, are another story. The columns aren't at all like the vertical displays of I- and RI-forms in a Schoenbergian row chart, but are connected to the row at some conceptual distance. The first column consists only of multiple instances of a single pitch class, and the other columns often include at least one pc duplication, forming a variety of tetrachords, pentachords, and hexachords:

COLUMN	NORMAL FORM	PRIME FORM
2	[01367]	(01367) 5-19
3	[7TE12]	(01347) 5-16
4	[0368]	*(0258) 4-27
5	[13678]	*(01257) 5-14
6	[8912]	(0156) 4-8
7	[9TE34]	(01267) 5-7
8	[2467T]	(02458) 5-26
9	[89TE34]	(012378) 6-Z38
10	[479TE0]	*(012358) 6-Z40
11	[8E013]	(02347) 5-11
12	[2479T]	*(01368) 5-29

*also an internal set

Look at the variety of set types in this listing. None of the set types appears more than once among the columns, and only four of them are also internal sets within the original row: a member of (0258) [4-27] appears in the original row at op <5–6–7–8>, (01257) [5–14] at <7–8–9–10–11>, (012358) [6–Z40] at <3–4–5–6–7–8>, and (01368) [5–29] at both <5–6–7–8–9> and <6–7–8–9–10>. In short, the columns of a rotational array don't generally provide the sort of systematic interconnections typically found between vertical and horizontal dimensions in twelve-tone music.

As a result, when Stravinsky begins the *Variations* with a presentation of the columns as a series of chords, he's not only announcing primary source material, but also celebrating its diversity. These opening chords have a detached, defiant essence, as if daring us to hear them with conventional organic expectations. Each of the chords is isolated in the score of the opening, shown in Example 10.14, and labeled with the corresponding column numbers from the array.[2] Columns 1 and 2 of the array are combined within one chord, as are 5 and 6, presumably because Stravinsky wanted fuller, richer chords than those columns can individually provide. In general, the diversity of the pitch structure is matched by variety within the instrumentation: forceful brass (realizing columns 1, 2, and 3 of the array) are answered by *forte* strings and woodwinds (columns 4, 5, and 6), giving way to soft muted brass in a different meter (columns 7–11).

---

[2]Example 10.14 includes two corrections of apparent errors in the published score: E_4 in trumpet 3 in measure 2 (originally F_4), and C_3 in trombone 2 in measure 5 (originally E_3). Joseph N. Straus gives justifications for such corrections in "Stravinsky's Serial 'Mistakes,'" *Journal of Musicology* 17 no. 2 (1999): 231–71.

EXAMPLE 10.14 Stravinsky, *Variations: Aldous Huxley in memoriam*, mm. 1–5 (all parts sound as notated)

Stravinsky composed with rotational arrays for his last major works, including the cantata *A Sermon, a Narrative, and a Prayer*; the "sacred ballad" *Abraham and Isaac*; and a setting of portions of the requiem mass text, *Requiem Canticles*. Rather than rotating the entire twelve notes of the row, as we saw in the *Variations*, he more often followed Krenek's practice and rotated the row's regularly partitioned hexachords separately, creating two different 6 × 6 arrays from one row form. Although Stravinsky pursued a dramatically different artistic course after he abandoned neoclassicism, these late works are unmistakably endowed with hallmarks of his style.

STUDY QUESTIONS 10.5

1. **Write the <pc string> of the following rotations of Stravinsky's R_2 row from the *Huxley Variations*.**

   1.1. rot7   1.2. rot10

2. **Specifically how would you transpose your answers to question 1 so that they begin on the same pitch class as the other transposed rotations in the array?**

3. **Imagine a rotational array with the P_2 form of Stravinsky's row in the first line. What would be the contents of the first column?**

4. **Inspect this ordered listing of the subscripts of the transpositions that cause each line of Stravinsky's array to begin on pc 5: <E–T–2–4–9>. How can you derive this series from the row itself? Hint: The first subscript (E) is the inverse of the first pc interval in R_2 (pc 5–6 = pc interval 1).**

10.6   INTEGRAL SERIALISM

Some composers in the mid-twentieth century began to feel that Schoenberg's method held enormous potential as an organizer of pitch structure but that it didn't go far enough. They also knew music by Webern, such as the Symphony op. 21 (1928), and the Concerto op. 24 (1934), and by Messiaen, such as his piano piece "Mode de valeurs et d'intensités" (1949), that took a systematic approach to the organization of other musical parameters, including rhythm and articulation. They began to experiment with different methods of assembling multiple musical dimensions into complex organizational schemes. Their works exemplify what is known as **integral serialism** (also sometimes called **total organization** or **multi-serialism**).

The meetings and classes attended by composers in Darmstadt, Germany, in the 1950s became an important source of inspiration for the integral serialists, a group that included Pierre Boulez, Bruno Maderna, Luigi Nono, and Karlheinz Stockhausen. Let's look at one of Stockhausen's earliest efforts in this genre, a work for oboe, bass clarinet, piano, and percussion called *Kreuzspiel*, which translates as "Cross-Play." We'll start with the main tone row, which appears in the piano after a thirteen-bar introduction (Ex. 10.15).

The notes of the row are unfolded between the pianist's hands in extreme registers of the instrument. The row begins with pc 3 (op 1) in the right hand, continues with pc's 1 and 0 (op's 2 and 3) in the left hand, returns to the right hand for pc 2 (op 4), completes the first hexachord with pc's T and 5 (op's 5 and 6) in the left hand, and so forth. Within the hands, the notes stay in fairly close p-space proximity. But Stockhausen isn't just announcing the primary tone row here; he's also establishing an affiliation between each note of the row and a particular dynamic marking and rhythmic placement (summarized below the score in Ex. 10.15). The first note of the row, pc 3, establishes a pairing with *sfz*; the second note, pc 1, becomes a partner with *mf*; the third note, pc 0, is also marked *mf*; and the pairings continue for op's 4 (pc 2, *p*), 5 (pc T, *ff*), 6 (pc 5, *pp*), and so forth. (All dynamic markings except *pp* and *sfz* are used twice each.) In subsequent row statements in the piano, oboe, and bass clarinet parts, these same pairings of pitch class with dynamic marking are maintained, with occasional variations. All occurrences of pc 1 in this section, for example, are marked *mf*. All occurrences of pc 9 are marked *mp*. And so forth.

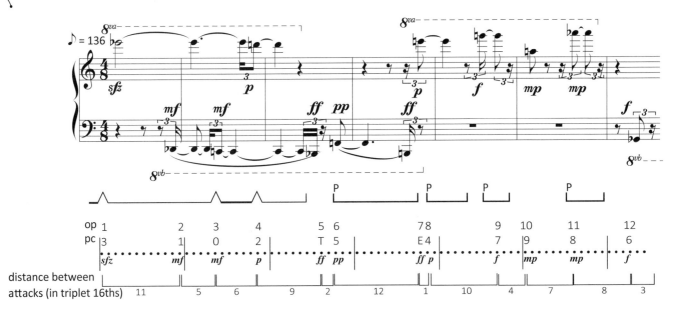

EXAMPLE 10.15 Stockhausen, *Kreuzspiel*, mm. 14–20.1, piano

The organization of the rhythmic dimension relies on a division of the measure into triplet sixteenth-note durations in $\frac{4}{8}$ meter. We'll refer to these divisions as **rhythmic units**, or **RUs**. There are three RUs per beat, twelve per measure. Look at the distances between the attack points of the twelve notes in the row in Example 10.15: each of these distances is a different number of RUs, 1–12. For example, the second note of the row, pc 1, begins eleven RUs after the beginning of the first note (pc 3). The row's third note, pc 0, begins five RUs after the beginning of the second note. The next note, pc 2, starts six RUs after the previous one. And so forth. Throughout the row presentation, no two of these distances between attack points are the same.

In the remainder of the first section, each of the numerical measurements of distances between attack points, or **RU distances**, continues to be paired with these same pitch classes and dynamic markings. You might say that the RU distances constitute a row of their own, which unfolds in tandem with the series of dynamic markings and pitch classes:

P_3	=	3	1	0	2	T	5	E	4	7	9	8	6
Dynamic marking	=	*sfz*	*mf*	*mf*	*p*	*ff*	*pp*	*ff*	*p*	*f*	*mp*	*mp*	*f*
RU distance	=	11	5	6	9	2	12	1	10	4	7	8	3

Let's see how this works in the next row statement, occurring in roughly the next seven measures of the piece (Ex. 10.16). The row here isn't transposed or inverted but reordered by shifting the first and last notes into the center:

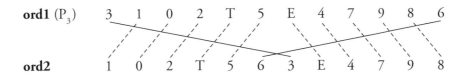

It's not exactly a rotation in the style of Berg, Krenek, and Stravinsky, although it certainly applies rotational principles. Let's just call each version an *ordering*. The initial version (P_3) is ordering 1, or "ord1," and the first reordering is "ord2." Notice, however, that despite the

reordering, the affiliations between pitch classes, dynamic markings, and RU distances in ord1 and ord2 are the same. Pitch-class 3, for example, has moved from the beginning of ord1 to the center of ord2, but it's still *sfz* and RU distance 11. In the wake of pc 3's relocation, pc 1 has moved to the beginning of ord2, but it's still *mf* and RU distance 5. The last note of ord1, pc 6, has moved to the center of ord2, earlier than the pc 3 moved from the beginning of ord1, but it's still *f* and RU distance 3. And so forth. Each of the twelve pitch classes in ord2 has the same dynamic marking and RU distance that it has in ord1.

EXAMPLE 10.16   Stockhausen, *Kreuzspiel*, mm. 20.1–26, piano (ord2)

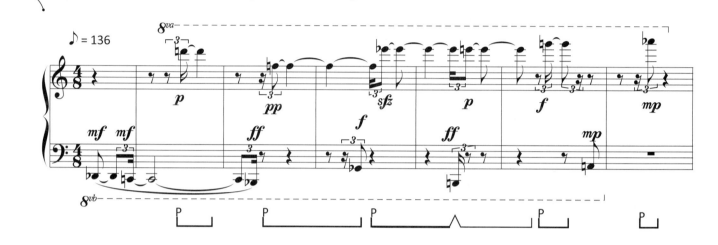

In the long first section of *Kreuzspiel* (through m. 90), similar procedures derive ten more aggregate orderings in the piano, oboe, and bass clarinet, each preserving these same affiliations between pitch class, dynamic marking, and RU distance (with occasional irregularities). The array in Example 10.17 summarizes the musical progression. In ord3, ord4, ord5, and ord6, notes from the ends continue to crisscross to the center as we saw from ord1 to ord2, moving other notes farther back and ahead. The lower half of the array is best understood from the bottom up, applying the same relocation pattern from ord12 to ord11 that we saw from ord1 to ord2, likewise matching the difference between ord11 and ord10 with the reordering of ord2 as ord3, and so forth.

While all this is happening, the percussion parts unfold a different, though similarly conceived, organizational scheme (Ex. 10.18). Tumba (conga) drums establish two different patterns in the introduction, the first (mm. 1–7.2) consisting of an ordering of all RU distances 1–12 as <2–8–7–4–11–1–12–3–9–6–5–10> (not directly related to the durational row in the piano), the second (mm. 7.3–13) a simple numerical sequence, 1 through 12. Each of these orderings then becomes the generator of its own separate array. The array for the first pattern (Ex. 10.19) is organized exactly like the pc array (Ex. 10.17), with outer notes crossing to the center, and the last six orderings mirroring the first six. The array for the second pattern (Ex. 10.20) applies the reordering from ord1 to ord2 as found in the other arrays (outer notes crossing to the center) to generate each subsequent reordering.

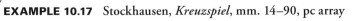

EXAMPLE 10.17 Stockhausen, *Kreuzspiel*, mm. 14–90, pc array

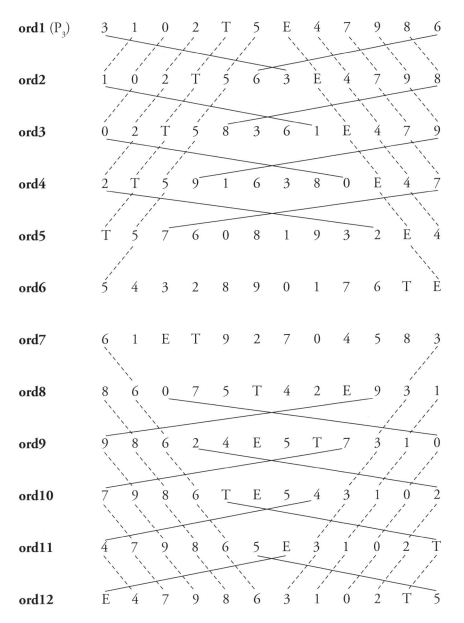

EXAMPLE 10.18 Stockhausen, *Kreuzspiel*, mm. 1–13, Tumbas

EXAMPLE 10.19   Stockhausen, *Kreuzspiel*, array starting with pattern 1 of Example 10.18

ord1 (RU distance)	2	8	7	4	11	1	12	3	9	6	5	10
ord2	8	7	4	11	1	10	2	12	3	9	6	5
ord3	7	4	11	1	5	2	10	8	12	3	9	6
ord4	4	11	1	6	8	10	2	5	7	12	3	9
ord5	11	1	9	10	7	5	8	6	2	4	12	3
ord6	1	2	3	4	5	6	7	8	9	10	11	12
ord7	10	8	12	11	6	4	9	7	3	1	5	2
ord8	5	10	7	9	1	11	3	4	12	6	2	8
ord9	6	5	10	4	3	12	1	11	9	2	8	7
ord10	9	6	5	10	11	12	1	3	2	8	7	4
ord11	3	9	6	5	10	1	12	2	8	7	4	11
ord12	12	3	9	6	5	10	2	8	7	4	11	1

EXAMPLE 10.20   Stockhausen, *Kreuzspiel*, array starting with pattern 2 of Example 10.18

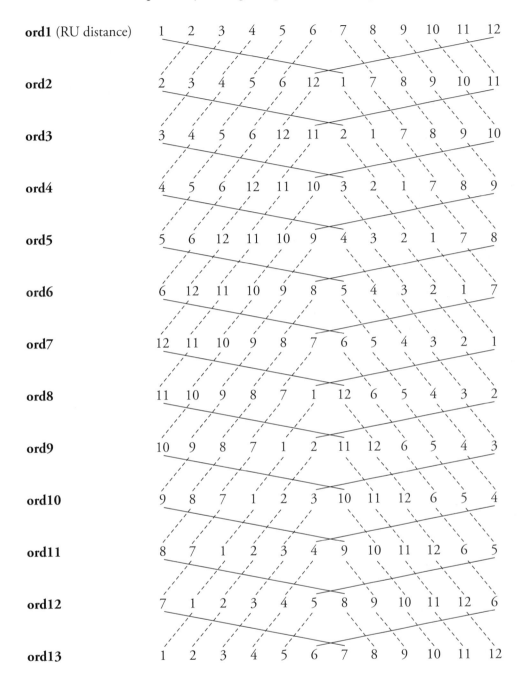

Let's now observe how these arrays are realized at the beginning of the section, when the piano is presenting its ord1 (Ex. 10.21). The unfolding of ord1 of the percussion array <2–8–7–4–11–1–12–3–9–6–5–10> moves back and forth between the two tom-tom players, setting up pairings of RU distances with dynamic markings just as in the piano (but not in the same pattern as the piano). Meanwhile, the tumba (conga) part moves on to ord2 of the array generated by the earlier pattern 2 (Ex. 10.20), although without affiliated dynamic markings. Thus begins the series of patterns and reorderings that constitute the first section of the piece. The piano, oboe, and bass clarinet move through their array in full synchronicity, with the progress from line to line through the arrays presented by tom-toms and tumbas. The "cross-play" of Stockhausen's title is the continual sequential reordering, plus the interplay and cross-references between the simultaneously unfolding patterns.

EXAMPLE 10.21   Stockhausen, *Kreuzspiel*, mm. 14–20.2

STUDY QUESTIONS 10.6

1. Assuming the array in Example 10.17 is strictly realized, what would be the series of RU distances during the presentation of ord3 in the piano, bass clarinet, and oboe?

2. In the percussion parts of Example 10.21, indicate the patterns of RU distances (calculated in triplet sixteenths) as found in the arrays in Examples 10.19 and 10.20.

3. What are the pairings of dynamic markings with RU distances (calculated in triplet sixteenths) in the tom-tom parts in Example 10.21? (Ignore the markings in smaller fonts.)

4. Assuming the pairings of dynamic markings and RU distances you wrote in your answer to question 3 continue in the next portion of the piece, what would be the series of dynamic markings during the presentation of ord2 of the Example 10.19 array in the tom-tom parts?

VOCABULARY

all-interval row
combinatoriality
hexachordal combinatoriality
I-type combinatoriality
integral serialism

invariance
invariant trichord
multi-serialism
P-type combinatoriality
R-type combinatoriality

RI-type combinatoriality
rotation
rotational array
secondary set
total organization

EXERCISES

A. ROW INVARIANCE

For each given row:

1. Find the specified internal sets (give order positions, normal forms, and prime form).
2. Determine whether any of the sets identified for question are symmetrical.
3. Indicate the transformation that relates the pc sets identified for question 1. If the sets are symmetrical, they will map to each other by both transposition and inversion, and they will also map to themselves.
4. Give the label(s) for the row form(s) related by the mapping(s) named for question 3.
5. Write the <pc string> of the row form(s) identified in question 4, and draw a ring around the invariant segment(s).

Demo.

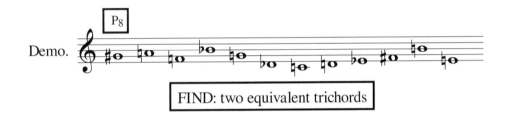

FIND: two equivalent trichords

1. Members of (014) appear at op <1–2–3> [589] and op <8–9–10> [236].
2. (014) is not symmetrical.
3. [589] and [236] map to each other by I_E.
4. Row form P_8 maps by I_E to row form I_3.
5. I_3 = <3 2 6 1 4 T E 9 8 5 0 7 >

1.

FIND: two equivalent trichords

2.

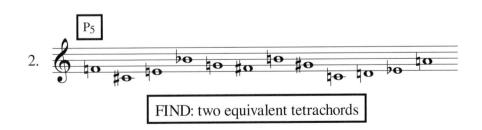

FIND: two equivalent tetrachords

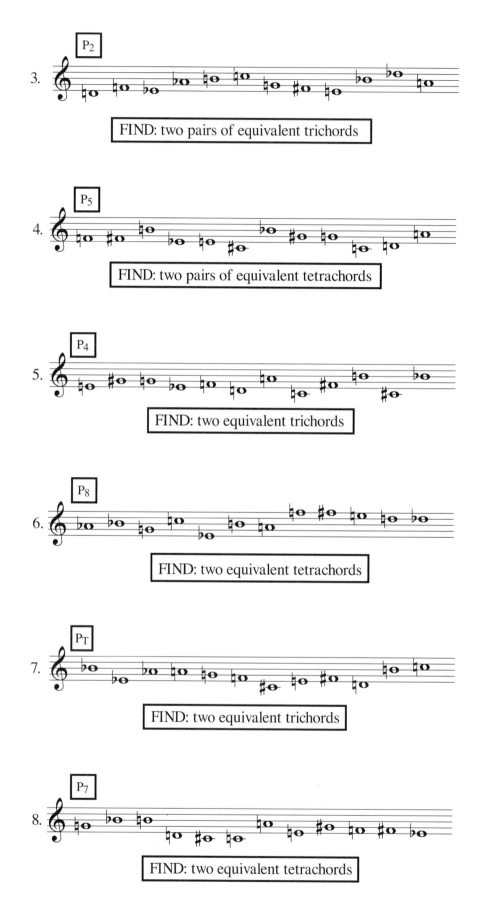

B. HEXACHORDAL COMBINATORIALITY

For each given row:

1. Give the normal form and prime form of the two regularly partitioned hexachords within the given row.
2. Consult Example 10.7. Determine whether the hexachords you identified for question 1 are capable of nontrivial combinatoriality. If not, you're finished with this row; go on to the next one. If the hexachords do have combinatorial potential, indicate which type(s) and then go on to the remaining three questions about this row.
3. Find the transformation(s) demonstrating the relationship(s) you discovered for question 2.
4. Use the transformation(s) given in your answer for question 3 to derive the label(s) for the row form(s) that combine with the given row to create hexachordal combinatoriality.
5. Write the <pc string> of the row form(s) identified in question 4, lined up with the <pc string> of the given row form. Draw a ring around the aggregates formed by corresponding hexachords.

Demo.

1. H_1 = [E13456] (012357); H_2 = [789T02] (012357).
2. Yes, I-type only.
3. [E13456] and [789T02] map to each other at I_1.
4. The I_1-transform of row form P_5 is row form I_8.
5. P_5 = <5 6 E 3 4 1 | T 8 7 0 2 9>
   I_8 = <8 7 2 T 9 0 | 3 5 6 1 E 4>

1.

2.

3.

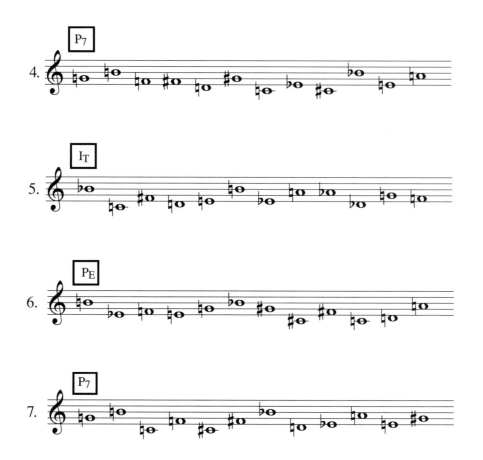

C. ARNOLD SCHOENBERG (1874–1951), PHANTASY FOR VIOLIN WITH PIANO ACCOMPANIMENT, OP. 47, MM. 32–39

1. Using the first row form in the violin part (P_T) indicated in the score as a guide, insert labels and order positions for the other row forms in the excerpt. Don't include the first two notes in the piano (A_2–$F\sharp_3$), which are part of a previous row form.

2. Schoenberg draws attention to an invariant trichord that P_T shares with which other row form in the excerpt? Write out both row forms as <pc strings>, with the invariant trichord highlighted in both. Identify the row transformation that moves the trichord from its location in one row form to a different location in the other.

3. Explain the role of combinatoriality in the excerpt. Identify the type of combinatoriality being demonstrated, and explain the relationship of the row pairs. Write out both row forms in combinatorial pairs as <pc strings> and draw a ring around the aggregates formed by corresponding hexachords. Identify the hexachord type(s) and locate it/them in Example 10.7. Explain the row transformation(s) that result in the combinatorial relationships between the pitch-class contents of the hexachords.

D. ARNOLD SCHOENBERG (1874–1951), VARIATIONS FOR ORCHESTRA, OP. 31, THEME (MM. 34–57)

1. The cellos present the main theme of this theme and variations form starting in measure 34. Where does the main theme shift to another instrumental section? When that change happens, how do the cellos contribute to a texture change?

2. On the score, indicate the order positions of the row forms in the main theme only, assuming that the cellos begin with P_T. In what sense do the row forms in the theme form a cohesive group?

3. Identify the row forms and mark the order positions in the other instruments throughout the excerpt. How are these row forms consistently paired with the row forms in the main theme? What is the logic governing these particular row pairings? Explain your answer using technical terminology and methods studied in this chapter.

4. By now you've noticed that the last row form in the cellos (mm. 52–57) is a bit of a deviation from orderliness of the row pairings in the preceding measures. In choosing to use this row form at this point, what relationship does Schoenberg wish to

emphasize between this cello row form and the row form being presented in the main theme (first violins)? Explain your answer using technical terminology and methods studied in this chapter.

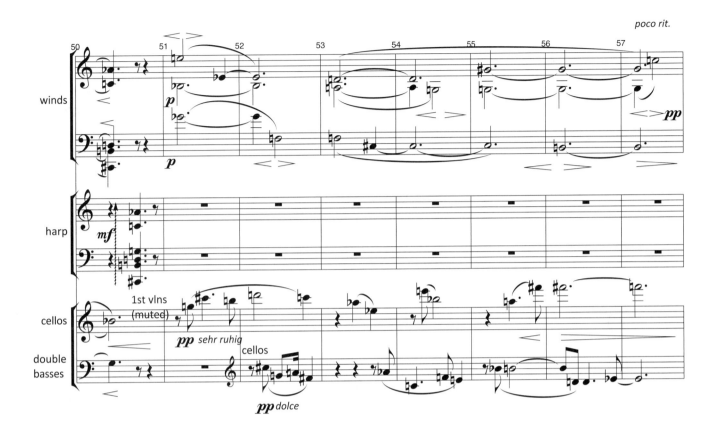

E. ANTON WEBERN (1883–1945), VARIATIONS FOR PIANO, OP. 27, MVT. 2

1. **Annotate the score with row labels and order positions.** The prime ordering of the row (and the "theme" of the variations) is clearly defined at the beginning of a different movement (the third, which was composed first). Use the row form of that theme as your point of reference: $P_3 = $ <3ET210647598>.

2. **What internal trichord (at what order positions) is especially highlighted in the row presentations and how?**

3. **What are the pairings of simultaneously presented row forms?** How many different row pairings occur in the movement, and in what sense are they consistently related?

4. **How are the row pairings articulated in pitch-space, and how might this affect the peformer's approach to the music?**

5. **Where in the movement does Webern draw attention to an invariant trichord between concurrent row forms?** Give technical details of this invariance.

6. **The two grace-note gestures in measures 2–3,** <B_2–D_3> answered by <G_6–E_6>, can be grouped together to form a tetrachord, defined as a "secondary set" because it includes notes from different row forms. What is this secondary tetrachord in normal form and prime form? Look at all the other secondary sets in the movement formed by combining two grace-note figures. (There are six of them in total.) What are the set class types formed by each of these secondary sets? Which of these set types can also be found as internal sets within the row?

Sehr schnell ♩ = ca 160

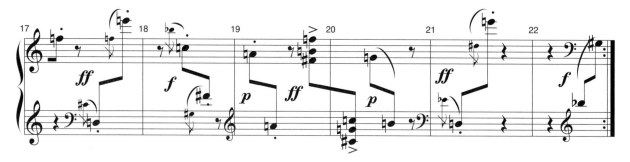

F. LUIGI DALLAPICCOLA (1904–1975), *GOETHE-LIEDER*, NO. 1

1. The prime ordering of the row is clearest in the vocal part starting in measure 14. Using that row form as P_E, make a row chart.

2. Annotate the score from measure 13 (last three eighth notes) to the end with row form labels and order positions.

3. What is the relationship between the B♭ clarinet part and the vocal line in this last section, with respect to row forms, rhythm, and p-space transformations?

4. How does the bass clarinet part interact with the relationships explained in your answer to question 3?

5. An invariant trichord occurs between voice and bass clarinet in measure 16. Write out the row forms involved in the invariance as <pc strings> and highlight the invariant trichords. Explain the invariance with respect to the transformational relationship between the row forms.

6. What other invariances are highlighted between voice and bass clarinet?

7. Now annotate the score of measures 1–9 to show the row forms and order positions. How do the methods of row presentation differ here from the last section? What aspects of the row are emphasized?

8. At the beginning of measure 6, all four parts come together in unified rhythm to present two vertical tetrachords. What are these tetrachords, and how do they relate to the row and the row presentation?

9. Where in this first section do you find a row form combined with its own retrograde? In what sense is this combination not really an example of the trivial R-type combinatoriality, but actually an example of invariance?

10. From measure 10 through the beginning of the canonic lines in measure 13, Dallapiccola abandons normal row presentations. Instead we hear repeated statements and transformations of a three-note motive. What is the motive, and how is it transformed? How does it relate to the row? How do the motivic statements in different instruments relate to each other as pitch-class sets?

11. Study the text of the song:

In tausend Formen magst du dich verstekken,	*In a thousand forms you may conceal yourself.*
Doch, Allerliebste, gleich erkenn ich dich;	*Yet, most beloved, I recognize you immediately.*
Du magst mit Zauberschleiern dich bedecken,	*You may cover yourself with veils of magic,*
Allgegenwärt'ge, gleich erkenn ich dich.	*But, all-present being, I still recognize you immediately.*

How do Dallapiccola's compositional choices support the images and meanings in the poem?

*sounds as notated

G. IGOR STRAVINSKY (1882–1971), *A SERMON, A NARRATIVE, AND A PRAYER*, MVT. 2, MM. 77–85

Pitch structure in this passage is based on an R-form of the row:

R_3	=	5	8	9	7	6	E	T	1	2	0	4	3
op		12	11	10	9	8	7	6	5	4	3	2	1

The rotational array is derived by dividing the row into hexachords H_1 and H_2: $H_1(R_3)$ = <58976E>, and $H_2(R_3)$ = <T12043>.

Demo. Make a rotational array with H_2 as the top line. Create the other lines in the array by moving the previous starting note to the end. Then transpose each line to make it begin on the same pitch class as line 1. Label the array "H_2A" (i.e., "H_2 array").

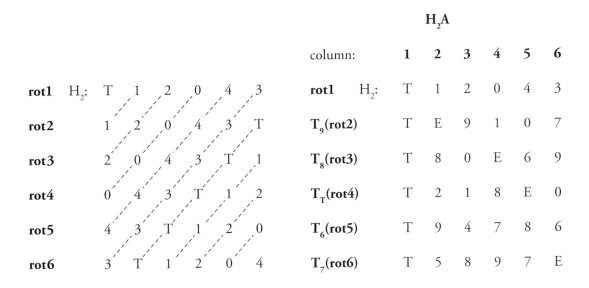

			H_2A					
			column:	**1**	**2**	**3**	**4**	**5**	**6**
rot1	H_2:	T 1 2 0 4 3	**rot1**	H_2:	T	1	2	0	4	3
rot2		1 2 0 4 3 T	**T_9(rot2)**		T	E	9	1	0	7
rot3		2 0 4 3 T 1	**T_8(rot3)**		T	8	0	E	6	9
rot4		0 4 3 T 1 2	**T_T(rot4)**		T	2	1	8	E	0
rot5		4 3 T 1 2 0	**T_6(rot5)**		T	9	4	7	8	6
rot6		3 T 1 2 0 4	**T_7(rot6)**		T	5	8	9	7	E

1. Make a rotational array with H_1 as the top line. Create the other lines in the array by moving the previous starting note to the end. Then transpose each line to make it begin on the same pitch class as line 1. Label the array "H_1A."

2. Find the normal form and prime form of columns 2–6 in H_1A and H_2A. What's the pattern of set-class recurrence within each array? Are any of these set classes also represented as internal sets in the row itself?

3. Annotate the score to show how Stravinsky uses the row and H_1A and H_2A in this passage. To reference the columns, add an additional subscript to the label: H_1A_1 signifies the first column of H_1A, H_2A_4 symbolizes the fourth column of H_2A, and so forth. Use order positions only for lines (rows), not for columns (chords). Some of the columns are clearly presented as individual musical units, while others are more dispersed and involve overlappings between separate note groupings.

H. MILTON BABBITT (1916–2011), THREE COMPOSITIONS FOR PIANO, NO. 1, MM. 1–8

1. The P_T form of the row is presented by the left hand in the first two measures. Write it out as a <pc string>, and find the normal form and prime form of the regularly partitioned hexachords. Of what type of combinatoriality are they capable?

2. Find the row form presented by the right hand in the first two measures. Write it out as a <pc string>. What musical result did Babbitt achieve by pairing this row form with the P_T in the left hand? Explain the relationship between the two row forms using technical terminology and methods from this chapter.

3. In the remaining measures of the excerpt, the pianist's hands continue to present different row forms at roughly the same time. Make a diagram showing the row forms being paired in measures 1–8. What are the rationales and musical consequences of these row pairings? In what sense has Babbitt presented a complete group of possibilities?

4. The P_T in measures 1–2 also presents a rhythmic pattern: <5142>. How is this pattern articulated?

5. Look at the rhythms of the other row forms in the excerpt. Which other row forms also use the <5142> pattern, and which ones use its retrograde, <2415>?

6. Now look at the rhythmic patterns in measures 1–8 that you haven't identified in your answers to the previous two questions. How do these fit into Babbitt's organizational plan? Hint: Subtract from a constant.

7. How do the dynamic markings participate in the overall organizational plan?

8. How do the articulation markings participate in the overall organizational plan?

I. ROW CONSTRUCTION AND REALIZATION

1. **Create a twelve-tone row that includes two inversionally equivalent members of set class (014) among its internal sets. Determine the mapping between the two (014) members, then calculate the row form that can combine with your original row to highlight these trichords as invariances. Compose a short phrase for piano in which the invariances are highlighted.**

   Demo:

   P_8 = < 8 9 5 T 7 1 0 2 3 6 E 4 >. [589] maps by I_E to [236]. The trichords are invariant with the I_E-transform of P_8, which is I_3 = < 3 2 6 1 4 T E 9 8 5 0 7 >.

2. **Compose additional phrases as described above but with different invariant segments. Try different trichord types or larger sets. Try segments that are transpositionally equivalent. Try invariant segments that are symmetrical, and compose phrases that feature the same pc set among a variety of row pairings.**

3. **Create musical realizations of some of the row pairings derived for questions 1 and 2, but instead of presenting the two rows simultaneously, present them one after the other within a melody for a solo instrument or voice. Find different ways to draw attention to the invariant segments, even though they may not occur in close proximity.**

4. **Choose one of the hexachords capable of I-type combinatoriality from Example 10.7. Create a row based on that hexachord. Find the I-combinatorial partner of your row, and compose a short phrase for piano that pairs the two row forms to form aggregates between corresponding hexachords.**

Demo:
Hexachord = (014568) 6-16. H_1 pc set = [34789E]; H_2 pc set = [T01256]. P_3 = <397E8460152T>. Because [34789E] maps to [T01256] by I_9, the I-combinatorial partner of P_3 is the I_9-transform of P_3 = I_6 = <602T1539847E>.

5. **Create rows with other types (or multiple types) of combinatorial potential, find the combinatorial row pairing(s), and compose phrases for piano or instruments that form aggregates between corresponding hexachords.**

J. COMPOSITION PROJECTS

1. **Develop one or more of the phrases from the previous exercises into a complete composition. Restrict yourself to a small number of row forms, using Webern's op. 23, no. 2 song as a model. Work on finding different ways to present the same or similar row pairings, by changing the rhythm, texture, dynamics, and so forth.**

2. **Compose a movement for instrumental duet featuring combinatorial row pairings, either borrowed from the previous exercises or created anew. Change the row pairings while retaining the combinatorial relationship, by altering subscripts in equal amounts. (For example, if row form P_1 is combinatorial with row form I_7, then any P_n is combinatorial with any I_{n+6} form, etc.) Use changes in, and recollections of, row pairings as a means of formal articulation.**

3. **Compose a movement for string quartet inspired by the first movement of Berg's *Lyric Suite*. Create an all-interval row (or a row that's distinctive in some other way) and use a systematic procedure to convert your row into a different one. Find ways to musically associate the different rows, as Berg does when he demonstrates one of his derivations in Example 10.11.**

4. **Create a row and then imagine techniques for presenting your row in a permutational sequence and alongside organizational patterns for other musical dimensions, such as rhythm, dynamics, and articulation. Compose a movement for small instrumental ensemble that realizes your scheme.**

FOR FURTHER STUDY

MILTON BABBITT:

Three Compositions for Piano (1947)
Composition for Four Instruments (1948)

ALBAN BERG:

Lyric Suite (1926)
Der Wein (1929)

PIERRE BOULEZ:

Structures Ia (1952)

OLIVIER MESSIAEN:

"Mode de valeurs et d'intensités," *Quatre études de rythme* (1949)

ARNOLD SCHOENBERG:

Suite for Piano, op. 25 (1923)
Variations for Orchestra, op. 31 (1926)

IGOR STRAVINSKY:

A Sermon, a Narrative, and a Prayer (1961)
Abraham and Isaac (1963)
Requiem Canticles (1966)

ANTON WEBERN:

Symphony, op. 21 (1928)
Concerto, op. 24 (1934)
Variations for Piano, op. 27 (1936)

CHARLES WUORINEN:

Twelve Short Pieces for Piano (1973)

APPENDIX 1
SET-CLASS LIST

bold = symmetrical set

prime form	sets in set class	TIC						Forte name	Z-partner
		1	2	3	4	5	6		
TRICHORDS									
(012)	12	2	1	0	0	0	0	3-1	
(013)	24	1	1	1	0	0	0	3-2	
(014)	24	1	0	1	1	0	0	3-3	
(015)	24	1	0	0	1	1	0	3-4	
(016)	24	1	0	0	0	1	1	3-5	
(024)	12	0	2	0	1	0	0	3-6	
(025)	24	0	1	1	0	1	0	3-7	
(026)	24	0	1	0	1	0	1	3-8	
(027)	12	0	1	0	0	2	0	3-9	
(036)	12	0	0	2	0	0	1	3-10	
(037)	24	0	0	1	1	1	0	3-11	
(048)	4	0	0	0	3	0	0	3-12	
TETRACHORDS									
(0123)	12	3	2	1	0	0	0	4-1	
(0124)	24	2	2	1	1	0	0	4-2	
(0125)	24	2	1	1	1	1	0	4-4	
(0126)	24	2	1	0	1	1	1	4-5	
(0127)	12	2	1	0	0	2	1	4-6	
(0134)	12	2	1	2	1	0	0	4-3	
(0135)	24	1	2	1	1	1	0	4-11	
(0136)	24	1	1	2	0	1	1	4-13	
(0137)	24	1	1	1	1	1	1	4-Z29	(0146) 4-Z15
(0145)	12	2	0	1	2	1	0	4-7	
(0146)	24	1	1	1	1	1	1	4-Z15	(0137) 4-Z29
(0147)	24	1	0	2	1	1	1	4-18	
(0148)	24	1	0	1	3	1	0	4-19	
(0156)	12	2	0	0	1	2	1	4-8	
(0157)	24	1	1	0	1	2	1	4-16	
(0158)	12	1	0	1	2	2	0	4-20	

prime form	sets in set class	TIC						Forte name	Z-partner
		1	2	3	4	5	6		
(0167)	6	2	0	0	0	2	2	4-9	
(0235)	12	1	2	2	0	1	0	4-10	
(0236)	24	1	1	2	1	0	1	4-12	
(0237)	24	1	1	1	1	2	0	4-14	
(0246)	12	0	3	0	2	0	1	4-21	
(0247)	24	0	2	1	1	2	0	4-22	
(0248)	12	0	2	0	3	0	1	4-24	
(0257)	12	0	2	1	0	3	0	4-23	
(0258)	24	0	1	2	1	1	1	4-27	
(0268)	6	0	2	0	2	0	2	4-25	
(0347)	12	1	0	2	2	1	0	4-17	
(0358)	12	0	1	2	1	2	0	4-26	
(0369)	3	0	0	4	0	0	2	4-28	
PENTACHORDS									
(01234)	12	4	3	2	1	0	0	5-1	
(01235)	24	3	3	2	1	1	0	5-2	
(01236)	24	3	2	2	1	1	1	5-4	
(01237)	24	3	2	1	1	2	1	5-5	
(01245)	24	3	2	2	2	1	0	5-3	
(01246)	24	2	3	1	2	1	1	5-9	
(01247)	24	2	2	2	1	2	1	5-Z36	**(01356)** 5-Z12
(01248)	24	2	2	1	3	1	1	5-13	
(01256)	24	3	1	1	2	2	1	5-6	
(01257)	24	2	2	1	1	3	1	5-14	
(01258)	24	2	1	2	2	2	1	5-Z38	(01457) 5-Z18
(01267)	24	3	1	0	1	3	2	5-7	
(01268)	12	2	2	0	2	2	2	5-15	
(01346)	24	2	2	3	1	1	1	5-10	
(01347)	24	2	1	3	2	1	1	5-16	
(01348)	12	2	1	2	3	2	0	5-Z17	**(03458)** 5-Z37
(01356)	12	2	2	2	1	2	1	5-Z12	(01247) 5-Z36
(01357)	24	1	3	1	2	2	1	5-24	
(01358)	24	1	2	2	2	3	0	5-27	
(01367)	24	2	1	2	1	2	2	5-19	
(01368)	24	1	2	2	1	3	1	5-29	
(01369)	24	1	1	4	1	1	2	5-31	
(01457)	24	2	1	2	2	2	1	5-Z18	(01258) 5-Z38
(01458)	24	2	0	2	4	2	0	5-21	
(01468)	24	1	2	1	3	2	1	5-30	
(01469)	24	1	1	3	2	2	1	5-32	
(01478)	12	2	0	2	3	2	1	5-22	
(01568)	24	2	1	1	2	3	1	5-20	
(02346)	12	2	3	2	2	0	1	5-8	

prime form	sets in set class	TIC						Forte name	Z-partner
		1	**2**	**3**	**4**	**5**	**6**		
(02347)	24	2	2	2	2	2	0	5-11	
(02357)	24	1	3	2	1	3	0	5-23	
(02358)	24	1	2	3	1	2	1	5-25	
(02368)	24	1	2	2	2	1	2	5-28	
(02458)	24	1	2	2	3	1	1	5-26	
(02468)	12	0	4	0	4	0	2	5-33	
(02469)	12	0	3	2	2	2	1	5-34	
(02479)	12	0	3	2	1	4	0	5-35	
(03458)	12	2	1	2	3	2	0	5-Z37	**(01348)** 5-Z17
HEXACHORDS									
(012345)	12	5	4	3	2	1	0	6-1	
(012346)	24	4	4	3	2	1	1	6-2	
(012347)	24	4	3	3	2	2	1	6-Z36	(012356) 6-Z3
(012348)	12	4	3	2	3	2	1	6-Z37	**(012456)** 6-Z4
(012356)	24	4	3	3	2	2	1	6-Z3	(012347) 6-Z36
(012357)	24	3	4	2	2	3	1	6-9	
(012358)	24	3	3	3	2	3	1	6-Z40	(012457) 6-Z11
(012367)	24	4	2	2	2	3	2	6-5	
(012368)	24	3	3	2	2	3	2	6-Z41	(012467) 6-Z12
(012369)	12	3	2	4	2	2	2	6-Z42	**(013467)** 6-Z13
(012378)	12	4	2	1	2	4	2	6-Z38	**(012567)** 6-Z6
(012456)	12	4	3	2	3	2	1	6-Z4	**(012348)** 6-Z37
(012457)	24	3	3	3	2	3	1	6-Z11	(012358) 6-Z40
(012458)	24	3	2	3	4	2	1	6-15	
(012467)	24	3	3	2	2	3	2	6-Z12	(012368) 6-Z41
(012468)	24	2	4	1	4	2	2	6-22	
(012469)	24	2	3	3	3	3	1	6-Z46	(013468) 6-Z24
(012478)	24	3	2	2	3	3	2	6-Z17	(012568) 6-Z43
(012479)	24	2	3	3	2	4	1	6-Z47	(013568) 6-Z25
(012567)	12	4	2	1	2	4	2	6-Z6	**(012378)** 6-Z38
(012568)	24	3	2	2	3	3	2	6-Z43	(012478) 6-Z17
(012569)	24	3	1	3	4	3	1	6-Z44	(013478) 6-Z19
(012578)	24	3	2	2	2	4	2	6-18	
(012579)	12	2	3	2	3	4	1	6-Z48	**(013578)** 6-Z26
(012678)	6	4	2	0	2	4	3	6-7	
(013457)	24	3	3	3	3	2	1	6-Z10	(023458) 6-Z39
(013458)	24	3	2	3	4	3	0	6-14	
(013467)	12	3	2	4	2	2	2	6-Z13	**(012369)** 6-Z42
(013468)	24	2	3	3	3	3	1	6-Z24	(012469) 6-Z46
(013469)	24	2	2	5	2	2	2	6-27	
(013478)	24	3	1	3	4	3	1	6-Z19	(012569) 6-Z44
(013479)	12	2	2	4	3	2	2	6-Z49	**(013569)** 6-Z28
(013568)	24	2	3	3	2	4	1	6-Z25	(012479) 6-Z47

prime form	sets in set class	TIC						Forte name	Z-partner
		1	2	3	4	5	6		
(013569)	12	2	2	4	3	2	2	6-Z28	**(013479)** 6-Z49
(013578)	12	2	3	2	3	4	1	6-Z26	**(012579)** 6-Z48
(013579)	24	1	4	2	4	2	2	6-34	
(013679)	12	2	2	4	2	2	3	6-30	
(014568)	24	3	2	2	4	3	1	6-16	
(014579)	24	2	2	3	4	3	1	6-31	
(014589)	4	3	0	3	6	3	0	6-20	
(014679)	12	2	2	4	2	3	2	6-Z50	**(023679)** 6-Z29
(023457)	12	3	4	3	2	3	0	6-8	
(023458)	24	3	3	3	3	2	1	6-Z39	(013457) 6-Z10
(023468)	24	2	4	2	4	1	2	6-21	
(023469)	12	2	3	4	2	2	2	6-Z45	**(023568)** 6-Z23
(023568)	12	2	3	4	2	2	2	6-Z23	**(023469)** 6-Z45
(023579)	24	1	4	3	2	4	1	6-33	
(023679)	12	2	2	4	2	3	2	6-Z29	**(014679)** 6-Z50
(024579)	12	1	4	3	2	5	0	6-32	
(02468T)	2	0	6	0	6	0	3	6-35	
SEPTACHORDS									
(0123456)	12	6	5	4	3	2	1	7-1	
(0123457)	24	5	5	4	3	3	1	7-2	
(0123458)	24	5	4	4	4	3	1	7-3	
(0123467)	24	5	4	4	3	3	2	7-4	
(0123468)	24	4	5	3	4	3	2	7-9	
(0123469)	24	4	4	5	3	3	2	7-10	
(0123478)	24	5	3	3	4	4	2	7-6	
(0123479)	12	4	4	4	3	4	2	7-Z12	(0123568) 7-Z36
(0123567)	24	5	4	3	3	4	2	7-5	
(0123568)	24	4	4	4	3	4	2	7-Z36	**(0123479)** 7-Z12
(0123569)	24	4	3	5	4	3	2	7-16	
(0123578)	24	4	4	3	3	5	2	7-14	
(0123579)	24	3	5	3	4	4	2	7-24	
(0123678)	24	5	3	2	3	5	3	7-7	
(0123679)	24	4	3	4	3	4	3	7-19	
(0124568)	24	4	4	3	5	3	2	7-13	
(0124569)	12	4	3	4	5	4	1	7-Z17	**(0134578)** 7-Z37
(0124578)	24	4	3	4	4	4	2	7-Z38	(0145679) 7-Z18
(0124579)	24	3	4	4	4	5	1	7-27	
(0124589)	24	4	2	4	6	4	1	7-21	
(0124678)	12	4	4	2	4	4	3	7-15	
(0124679)	24	3	4	4	3	5	2	7-29	
(0124689)	24	3	4	3	5	4	2	7-30	
(012468T)	12	2	6	2	6	2	3	7-33	
(0125679)	24	4	3	3	4	5	2	7-20	

prime form	sets in set class	TIC						Forte name	Z-partner
		1	2	3	4	5	6		
(0125689)	12	4	2	4	5	4	2	7-22	
(0134568)	24	4	4	4	4	4	1	7-11	
(0134578)	12	4	3	4	5	4	1	7-Z37	**(0124569)** 7-Z12
(0134579)	24	3	4	4	5	3	2	7-26	
(0134679)	24	3	3	6	3	3	3	7-31	
(0134689)	24	3	3	5	4	4	2	7-32	
(013468T)	12	2	5	4	4	4	2	7-34	
(0135679)	24	3	4	4	4	3	3	7-28	
(013568T)	12	2	5	4	3	6	1	7-35	
(0145679)	24	4	3	4	4	4	2	7-Z18	(0124578) 7-Z38
(0234568)	12	4	5	4	4	2	2	7-8	
(0234579)	24	3	5	4	3	5	1	7-23	
(0234679)	24	3	4	5	3	4	2	7-25	
OCTACHORDS									
(01234567)	12	7	6	5	4	4	2	8-1	
(01234568)	24	6	6	5	5	4	2	8-2	
(01234569)	12	6	5	6	5	4	2	8-3	
(01234578)	24	6	5	5	5	5	2	8-4	
(01234579)	24	5	6	5	5	5	2	8-11	
(01234589)	12	6	4	5	6	5	2	8-7	
(01234678)	24	6	5	4	5	5	3	8-5	
(01234679)	24	5	5	6	4	5	3	8-13	
(01234689)	24	5	5	5	5	5	3	8-Z15	(01235679) 8-Z29
(0123468T)	12	4	7	4	6	4	3	8-21	
(01234789)	12	6	4	4	5	6	3	8-8	
(01235678)	24	6	5	4	4	6	3	8-6	
(01235679)	24	5	5	5	5	5	3	8-Z29	(01234689) 8-Z15
(01235689)	24	5	4	6	5	5	3	8-18	
(0123568T)	24	4	6	5	5	6	2	8-22	
(01235789)	24	5	5	4	5	6	3	8-16	
(0123578T)	12	4	6	5	4	7	2	8-23	
(01236789)	6	6	4	4	4	6	4	8-9	
(01245679)	24	5	5	5	5	6	2	8-14	
(01245689)	24	5	4	5	7	5	2	8-19	
(0124568T)	12	4	6	4	7	4	3	8-24	
(01245789)	12	5	4	5	6	6	2	8-20	
(0124578T)	24	4	5	6	5	5	3	8-27	
(0124678T)	6	4	6	4	6	4	4	8-25	
(01345679)	24	5	5	6	5	4	3	8-12	
(01345689)	12	5	4	6	6	5	2	8-17	
(0134578T)	12	4	5	6	5	6	2	8-26	
(0134679T)	3	4	4	8	4	4	4	8-28	
(02345679)	12	5	6	6	4	5	2	8-10	

prime form	sets in set class	TIC						Forte name	Z-partner
		1	2	3	4	5	6		
NONACHORDS									
(012345678)	12	8	7	6	6	6	3	9-1	
(012345679)	24	7	7	7	6	6	3	9-2	
(012345689)	24	7	6	7	7	6	3	9-3	
(01234568T)	12	6	8	6	7	6	3	9-6	
(012345789)	24	7	6	6	7	7	3	9-4	
(01234578T)	24	6	7	7	6	7	3	9-7	
(012346789)	24	7	6	6	6	7	4	9-5	
(01234678T)	24	6	7	6	7	6	4	9-8	
(01234679T)	12	6	6	8	6	6	4	9-10	
(01235678T)	12	6	7	6	6	8	3	9-9	
(01235679T)	24	6	6	7	7	7	3	9-11	
(01245689T)	4	6	6	6	9	6	3	9-12	

APPENDIX 2
GLOSSARY

abstract complementation   The combining of members of complementary *set classes* without achieving *aggregate completion*.

Aeolian   The sixth *rotation* of the major scale, also known as the minor scale.

aggregate completion   A note formation consisting of all twelve pitch classes.

aleatory music   Music created by chance operations.

all-interval row   A *twelve-tone row* with an *INT* that includes every *pitch-class interval*.

all-interval tetrachords   *Tetrachords* whose *total interval-class contents* consist of one instance of each *interval class*.

asymmetrical meter   Meter signatures with an unusual number of beats per bar, usually five or seven.

augmentation   A presentation of a *fugue subject* in longer note values.

axis of inversion   The focal point of a symmetrical display in *pitch space*.

axis of symmetry   See *axis of inversion*.

binary form   Two-part form.

centricity   A note within a *source set* that is more musically emphasized than the other notes.

chaconne   A term sometimes used to describe a *passacaglia* that includes a repeating chord progression.

chromatic cluster   A collection of consecutive notes from a chromatic scale.

chromatic trichord   Set class (012), or any member thereof.

closing   A concluding passage with a *connective formal function*.

collage (in music)   A musical combination of disparate, seemingly unrelated, elements.

combination cycle   A *source set* defined by the alternation of two *pitch-class intervals*.

combinatoriality   A combination of forms of a *twelve-tone row* to complete *aggregates* between corresponding *segments*.

connective formal function   The role of a section within a form that is transitory and often unstable, serving to link, lead to, or lead away from, sections with other functions.

constructive technique   A means of fulfilling a *formal function*. See *repetition*, *variation*, and *contrast*.

contrast   A *constructive technique* involving a new musical idea, in a contrasting style and/or character

countersubject   A secondary contrapuntal line in a *fugue* paired with the *subject* in the *exposition* and usually accompanying the *subject* as it recurs throughout the remainder of the work.

cross-rhythm   Opposing rhythmic groupings presented simultaneously.

derived row   A *twelve-tone row* constructed of equivalent *regularly partitioned trichords* or *tetrachords*.

development (sonata form)   The middle area of a *sonata form*, featuring harmonic instability and some sort of fragmentation and variation of previous themes or motives.

developmental formal function   The role of a section within a form featuring previous musical ideas that are fragmented and combined in ways that distort and transform their original structure and character.

diatonic mode   Any *rotation* of the scale represented by the white keys within one octave on the piano, or any transposition thereof.

diatonic source set   A *source set* consisting of the notes of the *diatonic modes* (*Forte class* 7-35)

diminution   A presentation of a *fugue subject* in shorter note values.

Dorian   The second *rotation* of the major scale (i.e., minor with $\sharp\hat{6}$).

double fugue   A *fugue* with two separate *subjects* and (usually) two separate *expositions*, possibly concluding with the *subjects* in some sort of combination.

dyad   A two-element *pitch-class set*.

embedded complement   A type of *abstract complementation* in which a member of the smaller set class is featured within a member of the larger one.

episode   A passage in a *fugue* featuring motivic fragmentation and development of ideas from the *subject* and/or *countersubject*.

equivalence class   A collection of elements whose nature and relations are specifically defined.

exposition (fugue)   The presentation of the *subject* in all voices at the beginning of a *fugue*.

exposition (sonata form)   The first main section of a *sonata form*, featuring a move away from tonic, often involving two contrasting themes.

form   The organization of musical components into comprehensible units.

formal function   A chracterization of the role of a section of music within the *form*. See *thematic*, *connective*, and *developmental*.

Forte name   A *set-class* designator devised by Allen Forte consisting of the set size, a hyphen, and an ordinal number.

fugato   A fugal passage within a larger form.

fugue   A contrapuntal technique typically starting with an *exposition* and continuing to alternating passages of *subject* entries and *episodes*.

ground bass   The repeating bass melody in a *passacaglia*.

hexachord   A six-element *pitch-class set*.

hexachordal combinatoriality   *Combinatoriality* in which the corresponding *segments* are *hexachords*.

hexatonic source set   A six-tone scale built from alternating *pitch-class intervals* 1 and 3 (*Forte name* 6-20).

I-form   The inversion of a prime ordering of a *twelve-tone row* and its transpositions.

I-type combinatoriality   *Combinatoriality* between a *P-form* and an *I-form*, or between an *R-form* and an *RI-form*, of a *twelve-tone row*.

indeterminacy   Music giving performers freedom to improvise within broad guidelines.

index number   The mod 12 sum of correponding notes that are related by inversion.

INT   The series of *pitch-class intervals* between adjacent notes in the *P-form* of a *twelve-tone row*.

INT′   The series of *pitch-class intervals* between adjacent notes in the *I-form* of a *twelve-tone row*.

integral serialism   The serial organizational of multiple musical parameters.

intcrnal sets   Segments of all sizes within a *twelve-tone row*.

internal tetrachords   All possible four-note *segments* of a *twelve-tone row*.

internal trichords   All possible three-note *segments* of a *twelve-tone row*.

interval class (ic)   An equivalence class consisting of *pitch-class intervals*, with intervals larger than 6 reduced to their *mod-12 inverses*.

interval cycle   A *source set* defined by the repetition of a *pitch-class interval*.

interval space   A *musical space* recognizing distances between musical objects.

introduction   A prefatory passage with a *connective formal function*.

invariance   A correspondence in pitch-class contents between *segments* of two different forms of the same *twelve-tone row*.

invariant trichord   An *invariance* involving three-note *segments* of a *twelve-tone row*.

inversional axis   See *axis of inversion*.

Ionian   The major scale.

isorhythmic motet   An early writing style featuring non-coordinated patterns of melody and rhythm.

literal complementation   The combining of different *pitch-class sets* to achieve *aggregate completion*.

Locrian   The seventh *rotation* of the major scale (i.e., minor with $\flat\hat{2}$ and $\flat\hat{5}$).

Lydian   The fourth *rotation* of the major scale (i.e., major with $\sharp\hat{4}$).

mapping   A process that sends one object to another in a specifically defined way.

maximal subset   A subset that is one element smaller than the larger set.

metric layering   The juxtaposition of rhythmically and/or metrically distinct musical continuities.

metric modulation   The reinterpretation of a non-beat duration, such as a tuplet, as the beat in a new tempo.

minor pentatonic   A *source set* consisting of a five-note segment of a 5- or 7-cycle, ordered to display *pitch-class intervals* <3–2–2–3>.

Mixolydian mode   The fifth *rotation* of the major scale (i.e., major with $\flat\hat{7}$).

mod-12 arithmetic   A mathematical calculation in which results are converted to a number between 0 and 11.

mod-12 inverses (complements)   Numbers that add together to equal 0, mod 12 (e.g., 3 and 9).

moment form   Music designed to deny a sense of forward progression and narrative.

monad   A one-element *pitch-class set*.

multi-serialism   See *integral serialism*.

musical space   A specifically defined perspective on a musical idea.

musical unit (grouping)   Collections of notes according to musical factors such as rhythm, phrasing, articulation, and instrumentation.

New Complexity   Music notated using complex rhythmic notation, posing extreme difficulties for performers.

nonachord   A nine-element *pitch-class set*.

normal form   A neutral ordering of a *pitch-class set*, derived through a specific procedure.

note space   A *musical space* in which notes and note groupings appear in a neutralized state, without regard for their original rhythmic settings, durations, dynamic markings, modes of articulation, and spellings.

octachord   An eight-element *pitch-class set*.

octatonic source set   An eight-tone scale built from alternating half- and whole-steps (*Forte class* 8-28).

open form   A conception of musical form based on randomness and improvisation.

order position   A sequential number applied to each of the notes in a *twelve-tone row*.

ordered inversion   *Inversion* that preserves the order of the object being inverted.

ordered transposition   *Transposition* that preserves the order of the object being transposed.

P-form   The prime ordering of a *twelve-tone row* and its transpositions.

P-type combinatoriality   *Combinatoriality* between two *P-forms*, or two *I-forms*, or two *R-forms*, or two *RI-forms*, of a *twelve-tone row*.

passacaglia   A type of variation form featuring a repeating bass melody.

pedal point   A held note, often somehow set apart from its musical surroundings.

pentachord   A five-element *pitch-class set*.

pentatonic   A *source set* consisting of a five-note segment of a 5- or 7-cycle, ordered to display *pitch-class intervals* <2–2–3–2>.

Phrygian   The third *rotation* of the major scale (i.e., minor with ♭2̂).

pitch   A note in its specific register, notated using the ACA standard (middle C = C₄).

pitch class (pc)   An collective of notes that are octave-equivalent and enharmonically equivalent.

pitch interval   The distance between objects in *pitch space*, counted in number of half steps up or down.

pitch space   A type of *note space* in which notes are recognized in their specific octaves.

pitch-class interval (pc interval)   The distance between objects in *pitch-class space*, calculated by subtracting the first pc from the second, *mod 12*.

pitch-class set (pc set)   *Pitch classes* in a meaningful musical grouping.

pitch-class space (pc space)   A type of *note space* in which notes are identified without regard to register.

polymeter   See *metric layering*.

polyrhythm   See *metric layering*.

primary grouping   Groupings that arise from the strongest grouping criteria.

prime form   The identifier and representative of a *set class*, derived through a specific procedure.

quartal harmony   Chords formed from literal (i.e., order-preserved) segments of a 5-cycle expressed in *pitch space*.

quintal harmony   Chords formed from literal (i.e., order-preserved) segments of a 7-cycle expressed in *pitch space*.

R-form   The reversals of *P-forms* of a *twelve-tone row*.

R-type combinatoriality   *Combinatoriality* between a *P-form* and an *R-form*, or between an *I-form* and an *RI-form*, of a *twelve-tone row*.

recapitulation (sonata form)   The final primary section of a *sonata form*, featuring a restatement of the earlier thematic material and some sort of harmonic resolution.

regular partitions   The non-overlapping *trichords*, *tetrachords*, and *hexachords* that are *segments* of a *twelve-tone row*.

repetition   A *constructive technique* in which music heard previously occurs again, either exactly as first presented, or with very minor alterations.

retrograde   The reversed ordering of a *twelve-tone row*, usually specifically referring to the reversal of a *P-form* to create an *R-form*.

retrograde inversion   The reversed ordering of an *I-form* of a *twelve-tone row*.

RI-form   The reversals of *I-forms* of a *twelve-tone row*.

RI-type combinatoriality   *Combinatoriality* between a *P-form* and an *RI-form*, or between an *I-form* and an *R-form*, of a *twelve-tone row*.

rondo form   A musical form featuring a recurring refrain.

rotation   Reordering of a *segment* (possibly a *twelve-tone row*) by moving elements from the beginning to the end, otherwise preserving original orderings.

rotational array   A stacking of systematic *rotations* of a *twelve-tone row*, usually including additional adjustments such as transposing so that each line begins on the same *pitch class*.

row chart   An organized listing of all forty-eight members of a *row class* for a *twelve-tone row*.

row class   The *equivalence class* consisting of all *P-forms*, *I-forms*, *R-forms*, and *RI-forms* of a *twelve-tone row*.

secondary grouping   The grouping of notes, according to reasonable musical criteria, from different *primary groupings*.

secondary set   Important note groupings in *twelve-tone music* that aren't contiguous within a single form of a *twelve-tone row*.

segment   A meaningful musical grouping (in *pitch-* or *pitch-class space*) with a specific ordering.

self-complementation   A hexachord that can combine with a transformation of itself to complete the aggregate.

septachord   A seven-element *pitch-class set*.

serial method   See *twelve-tone method*.

serial music   See *twelve-tone music*.

set   A musically meaningful collection of notes (*pitches* or *pitch classes*) that may appear in any possible ordering in a musical realization.

set class   An *equivalence class* in which the elements are *pitch-class sets*.

set complementation   A pairing of *set classes* whose members have the capability of combining to achieve *aggregate completion*.

singleton   A note in a *wedge model* that pairs with itself.

sonata form   A form type consisting of an *exposition*, *development*, and *recapitulation*.

source set   A collection of notes constituting the primary *pitch-class* content of a *musical unit* of any size.

stretto   Overlapping *subject* entries in a *fugue*.

structural model   An organizing principle of a musical passage, possibly involving a musical analogy to a geometric shape or some sort of patterned repetition of intervals or harmonies or durations.

subject (fugue)   The primary theme of a *fugue*.

symmetrical set   A *pitch-class set* with self-mappings, in a *set class* that has fewer than twenty-four members.

ternary form   Three-part form.

tetrachord   A four-element *pitch-class set*.

thematic formal function   The role of a section within a form that presents an important melody and sounds stable and settled, with fully formed phrases and well-defined cadential gestures.

total interval-class content (TIC)   A listing of all possible *interval classes* among notes in a *pitch-class set* or *set class*.

total organization   See *integral serialism*.

transition   A linking passage with a *connective formal function*.

trichord   A three-element *pitch-class set*.

trichord class   The *set class* of a *trichord*.

twelve-tone method   A compositional method developed by Arnold Schoenberg in which all pitch relations, including melodies and harmonies, originate from a single unique ordering of the twelve *pitch classes*.

twelve-tone music   Music composed using the *twelve-tone method* or some variant thereof.

twelve-tone row   The unique ordering of the twelve *pitch classes* in *twelve-tone music*.

variation   A *constructive technique* in which music heard previously is presented with significant alterations, while keeping important elements intact.

voice (contrapuntal)   A distinct line of music within a contrapuntal setting.

wedge model   A *structural model* consisting of identical or similar lines moving simultaneously in opposite directions to unfold an incremental progression of harmonic intervals.

wedge voice-leading   Identical or similar lines moving simultaneously in opposite directions to unfold an incremental progression of harmonic intervals.

whole-tone source set   A six-tone scale built from repeating whole steps (*Forte class* 6-35).

wraparound tetrachord   *Tetrachords* formed by combining notes at the beginning and end of a *twelve-tone row*.

wraparound trichord   *Trichords* formed by combining notes at the beginning and end of a *twelve-tone row*.

Z-relations   A condition in which *pitch-class sets* that are not equivalent have identical *total interval-class contents*.

APPENDIX 3
ANSWERS TO STUDY QUESTIONS

CHAPTER 1

1.1 1. The motivic melody in the first violin, and the supporting chords in the other three instruments.
2. A three-note stepwise figure (ascending or descending) filling in a third.

1.2 1. By rhythm, articulation, and/or registral proximity.
2. The Mozart excerpt is more motivically saturated. Webern's Bagatelle doesn't have as much motivic density and is distinguished more by its variety than by its uniformity.
3. Because many post-tonal materials and relationships are contextually defined, the analyst brings fewer assumptions and expectations to the analytical process.

1.3 1. "Harmony" in post-tonal music can apply to any element of consistency or structural salience within a work's pitch structure.
2. In measure 1, the notes of the cluster occur in a non-scale order (D–E♭–C♯), and the third note is in a different register from the others. In measure 10, similarly, the ordering is B–C♯–C, and all three notes are in different octaves.
3. In measure 1, the root is doubled between cello and second violin, surrounding the fifth in the viola, and the third appears briefly in the first violin, at first displaced by an accented passing tone (A♭$_4$) and then followed by a motivic continuation to the repeated B♭$_4$'s. In measure 8, the root is doubled between the violins, again surrounding the fifth in the viola, and the third is in the cello.

1.4 1. Rhythm, articulation, instrumentation, and temporal proximity.
2. By associating a two-note grouping with a third note from another grouping in close proximity.

3. The first four notes: D$_4$ (cello) + E♭$_4$ (viola) + C♯$_5$ (1st violin) + C$_4$ (2nd violin).
4. The last four notes in the viola and cello: B♭$_4$ (viola) + B$_2$ (cello) + C♯$_4$ (cello) + C$_5$ (viola).

CHAPTER 2

2.1 1. Rhythm, dynamic marking, mode of articulation, and spelling.
2. Chromatic cluster.

2.2 1.1. pitch-class space   1.2. pitch-space
1.3. note space, pitch-space, pitch-class space
2.1. yes   2.2. F♯$_3$–E$_4$–F$_4$ 2.3. C$_3$–B$_4$–A$_5$
2.4. B$_2$–C♯$_3$–G♭$_4$–G$_4$–F$_5$–G$_6$
3.1. 4–6–5   3.2. 8–T–0   3.3. 7–1–7–6–5–E
3.4. 1–2–3–4–5–6–7

2.3 1.1. +5   1.2. –5   1.3. +7   1.4. +19
1.5. –19   1.6. +11   1.7. –1
1.8. +18   1.9. –16   1.10. +28
2.1. pc 1/6; pc interval 5
2.2. pc 6/1; pc interval 7
2.3. pc 6/1; pc interval 7
2.4. pc 6/1; pc interval 7
2.5. pc 1/6; pc interval 5
2.6. pc 5/4; pc interval E
2.7. pc 5/4; pc interval E
2.8. pc 2/8; pc interval 6
2.9. pc 7/3; pc interval 8
2.10. pc 3/7; pc interval 4
3.1. ic 5   3.2. ic 5   3.3. ic 5   3.4. ic 5
3.5. ic 5   3.6. ic 1   3.7. ic 1   3.8. ic 6
3.9. ic 4   3.10. ic 4

2.4 1. T$_{-1}$
2.1. F♯$_3$ A$_3$ F$_3$ 2.2. D$_3$ F$_3$ D♭$_3$ 2.3. F♯$_4$ A$_4$ F$_4$
2.4. D$_4$ C$_4$ A♭$_3$ B♭$_4$ 2.5. E♭$_2$ F$_3$ E$_4$ D$_5$

3.1. +3 −4   −3 +4 G_3 E_3 $G\sharp_3$ 2
3.2. −3 +4   +3 −4 $D\flat_4$ E_4 C_4 2
3.3. +5 −6 −2   −5 +6 +2 F_5 C_5 $F\sharp_5$ $G\sharp_5$ 10
3.4. +7 +1 −16   −7 −1 +16 G_3 C_3 B_2 $D\sharp_4$ 2
3.5. +1 −2 +3 −4 +5   −1 +2 −3 +4 −5
     $B\flat_4$ A_4 B_4 $G\sharp_4$ C_5 G_4 8

CHAPTER 3

3.1 1.1. set   1.2. segment   1.3. set   1.4. segment
1.5. segment   1.6. set   1.7. segment
1.8. segment   1.9. set   1.10. segment
1.11. segment
2. $<F_4–A_4–E_4>$ = +4 −5; $<F_4–E_4–A_4>$ = −1 +5;
$<A_4–F_4–E_4>$ = −4 −1; $<A_4–E_4–F_4>$ = −5 +1;
$<E_4–F_4–A_4>$ = +1 +4; $<E_4–A_4–F_4>$ = +5 −4

3.2 1. The Nacht motive is an ordered segment in pitch space. The Nacht trichord is a pitch-class set.
2.1. Transposition or inversion.   2.2. 24
3. A segment is defined by its order, while a set is a collection of notes that may appear in any order. A set class is a grouping of sets that are equivalent in some specifically defined way (such as by transposition or inversion).
4.1. {594} {6T5} {7E6} {807} {918} {T29} {E3T} {04E} {150} {261} {372} {483}
4.2. {516} {627} {738} {849} {95T} {T6E} {E70} {081} {192} {2T3} {3E4} {405}

3.3 1.1. T_{+10}, T_T 1.2. T_{+20}, T_8 1.3. T_{+10}, T_T
1.4. T_{-1}, T_E 1.5. T_{-11}, T_1
2.1. I_1 2.2. I_5 2.3. I_0 2.4. I_E

3.4 1. [347], [125], [E03], [9T1]   2. [347], [E23]
3. [125], [236], [E23], [T12]   4. [156]
5. [123]   6. [45T]   7. [147]   8. [E26]
9. [E16]   10. [37E]

3.5 1. [034] (014)   2. [7TE] (014)   3. [459] (015)
4. [912] (015)   5. [45T] (016)   6. [E12] (013)
7. [025] (025)   8. [E26] (037)
9. [7E2] (037)   10. [379] (026)

3.6 1. (012), (024), (036), (027), (048)
2. (048)
3.1. 8   3.2. 10   3.3. 0   3.4. 2

3.7 1.1. [01] [14] [04]   1.2. [02] [24] [04]
1.3. [02] [26] [06]   1.4. [03] [37] [70]
1.5. [04] [48] [80]
2.1. (013), (014), (015), (016), (025), (026), (037)
2.2. (016), (026), (036)

2.3. (016), (036)
2.4. (036) = diminished triad; (037) = major or minor triad; (048) = augmented triad

CHAPTER 4

4.1 1. [0123]   2. [E046]   3. [3457T]   4. [0167]
5. [2569]   6. [57E1]   7. [9035]
8. [68T13]   9. [147T]   10. [236789]

4.2 1. (0123)   2. (0157)   3. (01247)
4. (0167)   5. (0347)   6. (0268)
7. (0258)   8. (02479)   9. (0369)
10. (012367)

4.3 1. Z-partners, like members of the same set class, have identical TICs.
2. They aren't transpositionally or inversionally equivalent.
3. Each interval class is represented exactly once in their TICs.

4.4 1. [9TE0145].
2. Abstract complementation.
3. The entries for interval-classes 1–5 differ by 4. The entry for interval-class 6 differs by 2.
4. The entries for interval-classes 1–5 differ by 2. The entry for interval-class 6 differs by 1.
5. A hexachord in a Z-pair.

4.5 1. (0137) 4-Z29; (0146) 4-Z15
2. (01245) 5-3
3. Find the set of complementary size that has the same number after the hyphen in its Forte name.
4. tetrachords

4.6 1. [013] (013); [015] (015); [035] (025); [135] (024)
2. [023] (013); [025] (025); [035] (025); [235] (013)
3. All the maximal subsets of (0235) are also maximal subsets of (0135). (0135) also has two other maximal subsets, (015) and (024), that aren't maximal subsets of (0235).

CHAPTER 5

5.1 1. F-major triads are formed in measure 3 of the Mozart phrase and in measures 2 and 4 of the Debussy phrase.
2. In the Mozart phrase, the F-major triad acts as a neighboring chord to the tonic that precedes it and follows it. In the Debussy phrase, the F-major triad doesn't have any such functional role and is used for its coloristic value within the parallel movement of triads.

3. C_1 is held as a pedal point through the entire phrase, and the phrase begins and ends on C-major triads.

5.2   1. 98

2. 35

3. 6 (three major triads and three minor triads, often labeled in a major key as I, ii, iii, IV, V, vi)

4. 1 (one diminished triad, often labeled in a major key as vii°)

5. half-diminished and dominant 7th

6. 2 (one half-diminished, formed on $\hat{7}$ in a major key, and one dominant seventh, formed on $\hat{5}$ in a major key)

5.3   1. Ionian (major) and Aeolian (minor).

2.1. Raise $\hat{4}$.   2.2. Lower $\hat{2}$.   2.3. Raise $\hat{7}$.

2.4. Lower $\hat{6}$.

3.1. major   3.2. major   3.3. minor   3.4. minor

5.4   1. 218   2. 34   3. 8   4. 8

5. 4 (roots related by minor third)   6. 2

7. OCT_{01} = [0134679T]; OCT_{12} = [124578TE]; OCT_{23} = [235689E0].

5.5   1. 41   2. 7   3. augmented

4. WT_0 = [02468T]; WT_1 = [13579E].

5.1. [379], (026), WT_1

5.2. [246T], (0248), WT_0

5.3. [26T], (048), WT_0

5.4. [79E1], (0246), WT_1

5.6   1. Augmented triads interlock to form both source sets. In the whole-tone, the notes of the triads are separated by pc interval 2's. In the hexatonic, the notes of the triads are separated by pc intervals 1 and 3.

2. 41

3. 9

4. [2569], [69T1], [T125]

5. HEX_{01} = [014589]; HEX_{12} = [12569T]; HEX_{23} = [2367TE]; HEX_{34} = [3478E0]

6.1. [67E], (015), HEX_{23} 6.2. [9T12], (0145), HEX_{12}

6.3. [590], (037), HEX_{01}

6.4. [78E0], (0145), HEX_{34}

5.7   1.1. chromatic scale   1.2. whole-tone scale

1.3. fully diminished 7th chord

1.4. augmented triad

1.5. octatonic scale   1.6. hexatonic scale

1.7. pentatonic scale   1.8. diatonic scale/mode

1.9. tritone

2. quintal harmonies

3. quartal harmonies

4. 11-cycles

5. The mod-12 sum of the two intervals being alternated equals the size of the intervals in the interlocked single-interval cycles.

6.1. a) <8–T–E–1–2–4–5–7>   b) 3-cycles

c) 8   d) octatonic

6.2. a) <4–E–5–0–6–1–7–2–8–3–9–4–T–5–E–6–0–7–1–8–2–9–3–T>   b) 1-cycles

c) 11   d) none

6.3. a) <1–4–9–0–5–8>   b) 8-cycles

c) 6   d) hexatonic

6.4. a) <3–E–2–T–1–9–0–8–E–7–T–6–9–5–8–4–7–3–6–2–5–1–4–0>

b) 11-cycles   c) 8   d) none

6.5. a) <0–5–2–7–4–9–6–E–8–1–T–3>

b) 2-cycles   c) 12   d) none (aggregate)

6.6. a) <E–1–4–6–9–E–2–4–7–9–0–2–5–7–T–0–3–5–8–T–1–3–6–8>

b) 5-cycles   c) 5   d) none

CHAPTER 6

6.1   1. The structural model provides organizational logic and gives coherence and direction to musical progressions.

2. Both are based on gradual changes in the sizes of cyclic intervallic repetitions. Both are concerned with both vertical and horizontal dimensions.

3. The sizes of the intervals in the chords (verticals) grow incrementally in the same way that the sizes of the intervals in the lines (horizontals) gradually increase from bottom to top.

4. The chords from the model are varied and arpeggiated underneath the vocal line throughout the song, essentially projecting the structure of the model over the form of the entire work. The model is presented in its entirety at the beginning, middle, and end.

6.2   1. Even-numbered wedges always have singletons.

2. The singletons are the two possible axis notes.

3. In non-singleton wedges (those with odd-numbered indexes), the axis is often a half-step dyad.

4.1. 2-wedge   4.2. 11-wedge   4.3. 1-wedge

4.4. 1-wedge   4.5. 4-wedge

6.3   1. Combine it with a mirror of itself.

2. The other notes are <C_4–E_4–G_4>. The 6-wedge summarizes the symmetrical relations.

3. The other notes are <Bb_3–Eb_4–G_4–D_5>. The 3–wedge summarizes the symmetrical relations.

4. $G\sharp_5$/F_2 (e); E_5/A_2 (d); $D\sharp_5$/Bb_2 (c); B_4/D_3 (b); Bb_4/Eb_3 (c).

CHAPTER 7

7.1   1. Repetition, variation, contrast.
2. Thematic, developmental, connective.
3. OCT_{23}
4. When the right hand answers the left hand in inversion, they establish inversional symmetry about the $C\sharp_4$ axis. In measures 5–11, the axis shifts up to G_4.
5. Measures 12–22 continue OCT_{23}, except for the $A\flat$ upper neighbor in measure 15. Measures 23–30 aren't octatonic.
6. Despite the contrasting elements starting in measure 12, the source set is initially the same as section A (OCT_{23}). Then in the thematic passage starting in measure 23, the change to a non-octatonic environment provides an additional element of contrast just before the return of the A material.
7. The OCT_{23} collection returns in measure 31, again surrounding the G_4 axis in measures 31–33. When the right-hand motive transposes at T_{-5} in measures 34–35, it disrupts the purity of OCT_{23} and yet draws attention to the previous axis pitch (G_4). Then the right transposes again, at T_{-7} in measures 36–37, returning to OCT_{23} and to the $C\sharp_4$ axis between the hands, recalling measures 1–4. The inversional symmetry in the closing material (mm. 40–43) summarizes the OCT_{23} collection and moves the axis back to G_4.

7.2   1. The essence of ternary is statement–departure–return. Rondo extends this idea to involve multiple departures and returns.
2. ABA

7.3   1. The eighteenth century.
2. Development (often the introduction and coda also).
3. Motor rhythms and irregular phrasing.
4. The motive appears both as a surface gesture throughout and as an organizing principle on a deeper structural level.

7.4   1. The exposition is over when the subject has been presented in all of the contrapuntal voices.
2. Augmentation and diminution.
3. His transpositions up and down by fifths bring to mind the subject entries in tonic and dominant in a traditional fugal exposition.
4. The expanding-contracting wedge.

7.5.   1. The number and length of phrases.
2. Berg develops three ideas from the theme: a four-note motive (M), and two winding chromatic melodies that sometimes relate to each other as voices in a distorted chromatic wedge (P and Q).
3. Stravinsky and Bartók retain essential features of their models, while Berg substantially reworks every aspect of his. For Berg, "variation" is focused more on the technique than on the form type.

7.6   1. Form normally requires integration and interrelationships, but musical collages celebrate differences and discontinuities.
2. Both minimize the role of the composer, but this happens in aleatory during the compositional process, using chance operations to make basic compositional decisions, while in indeterminacy the creative burden is shifted from composer to performer.

CHAPTER 8

8.1   1. Their measures aren't (or can't be) divided into equal parts.
2. Each measure is musically distinct. If the listener assumes that each change of rhythm and motive is the beginning of a measure, then it shouldn't be that difficult to establish a beat value and divide the music into metric units.

8.2   1. Viola and cello.
2. The right hand plays only white keys (diatonic source set) and the left hand plays only black keys (pentatonic).
3. $\frac{3}{8}$ in the clarinet against $\frac{2}{8}$ in the bassoon.

8.3   1. Two regular half notes take up the same amount of time as three triplet half notes. The new metronome marking is $\quad = 90$ bpm (2:3 = 60:90).
2. Three regular eighth notes take up the same amount of time as two dotted eighth notes. The new metronome marking is $\quad = 80$ bpm (3:2 = 120:80).
3. Four regular quarter notes take up the same amount of time as five quintuplet quarter notes. The new metronome marking is $\quad = 100$ bpm (4:5 = 80:100).

8.4   1. Berg and Ives present rhythmic patterns within conventional metric contexts—standard meter signatures and rhythmic values. Messiaen employs unorthodox rhythmic combinations and maintains no regular beat.
2. Right hand: OCT_{01}. Pedal: WT_1.
3. Examples 8.15c and 8.15d (treble clef only) present augmentations of the motive. The proportion between the original motive and the augmentations is 1:2.

CHAPTER 9

9.1   1. [237] (015)   2. [256T] (0148)   3. [235] (013)
4. [459] (015)   5. [TE1] (013)

9.2   1. (014)
2. (014) at <2–3–4>; (036) at <3–4–5>; (026) at <4–5–6>
3. <5–6–7–8> and <8–9–10–11>
4. (0248) at <4–5–6–7>; (0148) at <5–6–7–8>; (0145) at <6–7–8–9>; (0125) at <7–8–9–10>
5. <10–11–12–1> [TE12] (0134); <11–12–1–2> [7E12] (0137); <12–1–2–3> [E237] (0148)
6. 5–21 (01458)
7. 5–13 (01248) is formed at op <4–5–6–7–8> and <8–9–10–11–12>
8. 6–Z44 (012569)
9. 6–15 (012458) is formed at op <2–3–4–5–6–7> and <4–5–6–7–8–9>. 6–Z39 (023458) is formed at op <3–4–5–6–7–8> and <7–8–9–10–11–12>.
10. The last internal septachord is the complement of the first internal pentachord. Since Forte names of complements have the same identifying number, you can look at the name of the first pentachord, 5–Z18, and know right away that the last septachord is 7–Z18.
11. [answered in section 9.2]

9.3   1.1. P_2 1.2. P_9 1.3. P_2 1.4. I_2 1.5. I_7
2.1. T_3 2.2. T_9 2.3. T_6 2.4. T_1 2.5. T_8
3.1. 9   3.2. 9   3.3. 3   3.4. 6
4.1. I_7 (see #3.1/3.2)   4.2. P_2 (see #3.1/3.2)
4.3. P_5 (see #3.3)   4.4. I_9
4.5. P_7 (see #4.4)   4.6. I_T

9.4   1.1. P_8 1.2. R_2 1.3. R_8 1.4. I_8 1.5. RI_8
2.1. <819> <1–2–3>   2.2. <E1T> <12–11–10>
2.3. <0918> <4–3–2–1>
2.4. <251> <7–8–9>
2.5. <E90152> <12–11–10–9–8–7>
3.1. INT. All P-forms display the INT.
3.2. INT′. The series of pc intervals in P- and I-forms are inverses of each other.
3.3. R(INT′). The series of pc intervals in any R-form of the row is the retrograde of the INT′.
3.4. R(INT). The series of pc intervals in any RI-form of the row is the retrograde of the INT.
4.1. <1–2–3>: <E4>   <4–5–6>: <4E>
<7–8–9>: <81>   <10–11–12>: <18>
4.2. The mini-INT of op <1–2–3> is <E4>. The mini-INT′ <18> occurs at op <10–11–12>.
4.3. The interval series at op <4–5–6> is <4E>, which is R of mini–INT. The interval series at op <7–8–9> is <81>, which is R of mini–INT′.

4.4. Because the trichord at <10–11–12> expresses the mini-INT′, it is an I-form of the trichord at <1–2–3>. The trichord at <4–5–6> is the retrograde of the INT, so it's an RI-form. The trichord at <7–8–9> is the retrograde inversion of the INT, so it's an R-form.

9.5   1.1. P_3 1.2. R_3 1.3. I_T 1.4. RI_5
2.1. It's the INT.   2.2. It's the INT′.

9.6   1.1. R_2 1.2. RI_9 1.3. RI_0 1.4. R_3 1.5. R_T
2.1. T_3 2.2. T_9 2.3. I_1 2.4. I_1 2.5. I_T
3.1. R_8 3.2. P_5 3.3. RI_5 3.4. I_5
3.5. RI_4 3.6. P_3 3.7. P_6 3.8. I_3
3.9. R_8 3.10. R_7
4.1. RT_5 4.2. RT_7 4.3. RT_T 4.4. RT_4
4.5. RT_E 4.6. RI_1 4.7. RI_1
4.8. RI_T 4.9. RI_9 4.10. RI_2
5.1. <1–2–3> maps to <4–5–6> by RI_5; to <7–8–9> by RT_6; and to <10–11–12> by I_E.
5.2. The transformations occur in pitch-space. The inversional relationships between <1–2–3> and <10–11–12>, and between <4–5–6> and <7–8–9>, surround the $F_5/F\sharp_5$ axis (which are the final pitches of the second and third trichords). The transpositional mappings are RT_{-6}, from <1–2–3> to <7–8–9> and from <4–5–6> to <10–11–12>.

9.7   1.1. A member of sc (013) appears at op <10–11–12>. The notes of this trichord are slurred together in the vocal line in measure 20 <$B\flat_4$–$C\sharp_5$–B_4>. That trichord also interlocks with another occurrence of (013) at <12–11–10> of RI_8, <B_4–A_5–C_5>.
1.2. (015) appears at op <1–2–3> and <8–9–10>. There are two occurrences of <8–9–10> in the vocal line of the excerpt (measures 19–20 and 20–21), but these don't really stand out. The <1–2–3> at the beginning of the vocal line, <D_5–G_5–$E\flat_4$> in measures 15–16, is more prominent, even though the second and third notes also connect with the $G\flat_4$ in measure 17.
1.3. (0147) appears at op <2–3–4–5>. This tetrachord is brought out as the final vocal phrase in this passage, <$B\flat_4$–E_5–G_5–$E\flat_5$>.
1.4. (012569) appears at op <6–7–8–9–10–11>. The string of these op's in measures 18–20 of the vocal line, <E_4–$G\sharp_4$–F_5–A_4–$B\flat_4$–$C\sharp_5$>, is somewhat prominent (although it crosses over the tempo change at bar 20), but the occurrence of these op's in the RI_8 is emphasized much more, in two consecutive three-note phrases in measures 20–21, <A_5–C_5–$D\flat_4$> plus <F_5–D_5–$G\flat_4$>.
2.1. [235] (013). This trichord type is an internal set at op <10–11–12>, brought out nearly

simultaneously in the vocal line, as explained above (Study Question 9.7.1.1).

2.2. [459] (015). This trichord type is an internal set at op <1–2–3> and <8–9–10>, stated prominently at the beginning of the section (see above, Study Question 9.7.1.2).

2.3. [6901] (0147). This is an internal set at op <2–3–4–5>, occurring conspicuously as the final vocal phrase (see above, Study Question 9.7.1.3).

2.4. [23478E] (012569). This is an internal set at op <6–7–8–9–10–11>, brought out in two consecutive vocal phrases, as explained above (Study Question 9.7.1.4).

CHAPTER 10

10.1 1.1. [359] (026) is held invariant between P_3 <1–2–3> and I_6 <5–6–7>. [046] (026) is held invariant between P_3 <5–6–7> and I_6 <1–2–3>.

1.2. [67T1] (0147) is held invariant between R_2 <11–10–9–8> and I_4 <3–4–5–6>. [58E0] is held invariant between R_2 <6–5–4–3> and I_4 <8–9–10–11>.

1.3. [37E] (048) is held invariant between RI_5 <4–3–2> and I_9 <2–3–4>.

1.4. [26T] (048) is held invariant between I_8 <2–3–4> and P_4 <2–3–4>. [903] (036) is held invariant between I_8 <8–9–10> and P_4 <8–9–10>.

9.8

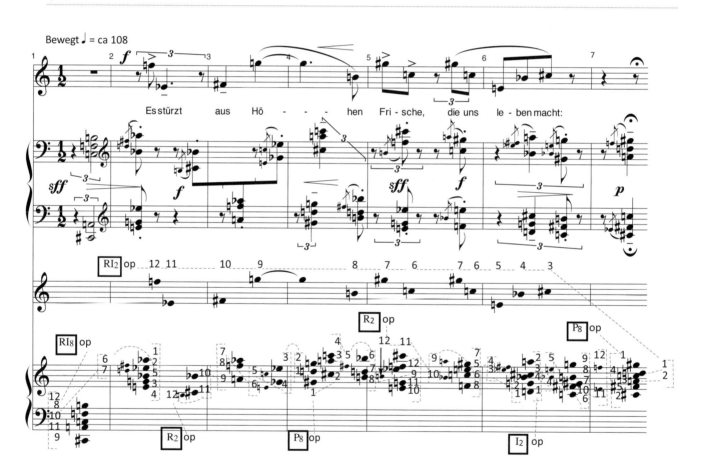

2.1. Members of (016) appear at op <1–2–3>, which forms pc set [812], and <7–8–9>, which forms pc set [TE4].

2.2. [812] maps to [TE4] at I_0.

2.3. I_0 transforms P_2 into I_T (because 2 + 10 = 0, or 0 − 2 = 10).

2.4. I_T = <$TE\overline{4960812537}$>.

3.1. Members of (01$\overline{3}$4) appear at op <6–7–8–9>, which forms pc set [78TE], and <9–T–11–12>, which forms pc set [3467].

3.2. [78TE] maps to [3467] at T_8 or I_2.

3.3. T_8 transforms P_1 into P_9 (because 1 + 8 = 9). I_2 transforms P_1 into I_1 (because 1 + 1 = 2, or 2 − 1 = 1).

3.4. P_9 = <985T1$\overline{74632}$E0>; I_1 = <1250$\overline{936478}$ET> and <1250$\overline{936478}$ET>.

3.5. [78TE] maps to itself at I_6. [3467] maps to itself at I_T.

3.6. I_6 transforms P_1 into I_5 (because 1 + 5 = 6, or 6 − 1 = 5). I_T transforms P_1 into I_9 (because 1 + 9 = 10, or T − 1 = 9).

3.7. I_5 = <5694$\overline{17T8E}$032>; I_9 = <9T185E203$\overline{476}$>.

10.2 1.1. The hexachords in group A can occur in combinatorial pairings only when a row form is paired with its own retrograde. This is a "trivial" case because it's not a special feature; any form of any row has this capability.

1.2. 12 (in group B)

1.3. 19 (12 in group B + 1 in group E + 3 in group F + 3 in group G)

1.4. Group B lists hexachords capable of I-type combinatoriality, and I–type combinatoriality requires an inversional equivalence between two halves of a row. Z–related hexachords aren't inversionally equivalent.

1.5. D (hexachords capable of RI-type combinatoriality map to themselves under inversion)

2.1. I–type   2.2. I–type   2.3. P-type
2.4. I-type   2.5. P-type
2.6. RI-type   2.7. RI-type

3. (2.1) The hexachords map to each other at I_T.
(2.2) The hexachords map to each other at I_3.
(2.3) The hexachords map to each other at T_6.
(2.4) The hexachords map to each other at I_4.
(2.5) The hexachords map to each other at T_6.
(2.6) The hexachords map to themselves at I_2.
(2.7) The hexachords map to themselves at I_3.

10.3 1. [5690] is a member of (0147). Another member of this set class is formed in the row at op <6–7–8–9>. The [5690] occurs in the left hand just as the tetrachord at P_4 <6–7–8–9> is being unfolded in the right hand.

2. [2348] is a member of (0126). Another member of this set class is formed in the row at op <2–3–4–5>. The presentations of <2–3–4–5> within P_4 (right hand) and P_T (left hand) in this passage aren't especially emphasized, and they occur in measures 1 and 2, somewhat distant from the [2348] in the left hand in measure 3. Schoenberg doesn't give this relationship particular emphasis in this passage.

10.4 1.1. P_5 or R_E 1.2. P_2 or R_8 1.3. I_E or RI_5
1.4. P_E or R_5

2. The C–major hexachord <C–D–E–F–G–A> is a rearrangement of the pitch classes of H_1 of P_5, and the F♯–major hexachord <F♯–G♯–A♯–B–C♯–D♯> is a rearrangement of the pitch classes of H_2 of P_5. They aren't systematic rearrangements of P_5, in the same way that S_5 is. They are, however, systematic rearrangements of S_5. <C–D–E–F–G–A> is an extraction of the even, then odd order positions of S_5 H_1 <2–4–6–1–3–5>; and <F♯–G♯–A♯–B–C♯–D♯> is an extraction of the even, then odd order positions of S_5 H_2 <8–10–12–7–9–11>. So you might say that the C–major and F♯–major hexachords are systematic derivations from P_5 via S_5.

10.5 1.1. <T4E902567318> (the R_2 form of the row rotated to begin on op 7)

1.2. <902567318T4E> (the R_2 form of the row rotated to begin on op 10)

2.1. T_7 transforms this rotation to begin on pc 5.
2.2 T_8 transforms this rotation to begin on pc 5.

3. Multiple instances of pc 2. After rotating each line of P_2 to begin on a different order position, you would then create the rotational array by transposing each rotation to begin on pc 2. As a result, the first column of the array would consist entirely of pc 2's.

4. Each successive subscript is the inverse of the pc interval from the first note in the row to each successive later note. The first subscript, E, is the inverse of the pc interval from the first note to the second note in R_2 (pc 6 − 5 = pc interval 1); the second subscript, T, is the inverse of the pc interval from the first to third note in R_2 (pc 7 − 5 = pc interval 2); the third subscript, 2, is the inverse of the pc interval from the first to fourth note in R_2 (pc 3 − 5 = pc interval T); the fourth subscript, 4, is the inverse of the pc interval from the first to fifth note in R_2 (pc 1 − 5 = pc interval 8); and the fifth subscript, 9, is the inverse of the pc interval from the first to sixth note in R_2 (pc 8 − 5 = pc interval 3).

10.6   1. Ord3 is $\langle 0$–2–T–5–8–3–6–1–E–4–7–$9\rangle$ (see Ex. 10.17). Each pitch class has a corresponding RU distance:

P_3 =	3	1	0	2	T	5	E	4	7	9	8	6
Dynamic marking =	*sfz*	*mf*	*mf*	*p*	*ff*	*pp*	*ff*	*p*	*f*	*mp*	*mp*	*f*
RU distance =	11	5	6	9	2	12	1	10	4	7	8	3

So the corresponding series of RU distances is $\langle 6$–9–2–12–8–11–3–5–1–10–4–$7\rangle$.

2.

3. The pattern moves back and forth between the two tom-tom parts, which are identifed with Roman numerals I and III. The first tom-tom note, marked *f* in tom-tom III, is separated from the second, marked *pp* in tom-tom I, by a distance of two RUs (triplet sixteenth-notes and/or rests). The third note, marked *p* in tom-tom I, comes along eight RUs after the second note. And so forth. The resulting pairings of dynamic markings with RU distances are as follows:

2	8	7	4	11	1	12	3	9	6	5	10
f	*pp*	*p*	*f*	*p*	*ff*	*f*	*f*	*pp*	*p*	*p*	*pp*

4. Ord2 of the Example 10.19 array is $\langle 8$–7–4–11–1–10–2–12–3–9–6–$5\rangle$. Using the correspondences from the answer to question 3, the new series of dynamic markings is:

8	7	4	11	1	10	2	12	3	9	6	5
pp	*p*	*f*	*p*	*ff*	*pp*	*f*	*f*	*f*	*pp*	*p*	*p*

CREDITS

Example 1.3 (part 1): 1924, 1952 Universal Edition

Example 1.3 (part 2): 1924, 1952 Universal Edition

Exercise 1C: Béla Bartók (1881–1945), String Quartet No. 4 (1928), first movement, mm. 1–13, 1929 Universal-Edition Renewed 1956

Exercise 3I: 1922, 1949 Universal Edition

Exercise 4C5: Copyright © 1983 by Associated Music Publishers, Inc. International Copyright Secured. All Rights Reserved. Reprinted by Permission.

Exercise 4G: 1922, 1949 Universal Edition

Example 5.7: 1921 Universal Edition. Renewed 1949

Example 5.9: 1921 Universal Edition. Renewed 1949

Example 5.20: 1939 Arrow; 1957 Associated

Example 5.23: 1939 Arrow; 1957 Associated

Example 5.24a: 1940 Hawkes & Son; corrected edition 1987 Boosey & Hawkes

Example 5.24b: 1940 Hawkes & Son; corrected edition 1987 Boosey & Hawkes

Example 5.27: 1924, 1952 Universal Edition

Exercise 5B9: 1949 Edward B. Marks

Exercise 5B11: 1988 Eschig

Exercise 5B12: 1940 Hawkes & Son; corrected edition 1987 Boosey & Hawkes

Exercise 5B13: By permission of Joan Tower

Example 5.33: 1947 Durand

Example 5.34: 1947 Durand

Example 5.45: 1947 Durand

Example 6.5: 1935 Merion

Example 6.7: 1935 Merion

Example 6.9: 1933 Merion

Example 6.19: 1953 Universal Edition

Example 6.21: 1922, 1949 Universal Edition

Example 6.24: 1924, 1952 Universal Edition

Exercise 6C5: 1936 Universal Edition Renewed 1963

Exercise 6F6: Boosey & Hawkes

Exercise 6G: 1940 Hawkes & Son; corrected edition 1987 Boosey & Hawkes

Exercise 6H: 1924, 1952 Universal Edition

Example 7.2: 1940 Hawkes & Son; corrected edition 1987 Boosey & Hawkes

Example 7.5: 1925 Édition Russe de Musique

Example 7.6a: 1925 Édition Russe de Musique

Example 7.6b: 1925 Édition Russe de Musique

Example 7.6c: 1925 Édition Russe de Musique

Example 7.7: 1925 Édition Russe de Musique

Example 7.9: 1925 Édition Russe de Musique

Example 7.10a: 1925 Édition Russe de Musique

Example 7.10b: 1925 Édition Russe de Musique

Example 7.11: 1925 Édition Russe de Musique

Example 7.12: 1925 Édition Russe de Musique

Example 7.14: 1936 Universal Edition. Renewed 1963

Example 7.15: 1937 Universal Edition. Renewed 1964

Example 7.16: 1937 Universal Edition. Renewed 1964

Example 7.18: 1937 Universal Edition. Renewed 1964

Example 7.19: 1931 Universal Edition. Renewed 1958

Exercise 7A1: The People United Will Never Be Defeated. Words and Music by Sergio Alvarado, Eduardo Carrasco and Frederic Rzewski. Copyright © 1975 Hadem Music Corporation and Co-Publishers. Copyright Renewed. This arrangement Copyright © 2017 Hadem Music Corporation and Co-Publishers. All Rights for Hadem Music Corporation in the United States and Canada Controlled and Administered by Spirit Two Music, Inc. International Copyright Secured. All Rights Reserved. Reprinted by permission of Hal Leonard LLC

Exercise 7A2: The People United Will Never Be Defeated. Words and Music by Sergio Alvarado, Eduardo Carrasco and Frederic Rzewski. Copyright © 1975 Hadem Music Corporation and Co-Publishers. Copyright Renewed. This arrangement Copyright © 2017 Hadem Music Corporation and Co-Publishers. All Rights for Hadem Music Corporation in the United States and Canada Controlled and Administered by Spirit Two Music, Inc. International Copyright Secured. All Rights Reserved. Reprinted by permission of Hal Leonard LLC

Exercise 7C1: Copyright © 1923 (Renewed) by G. Schirmer, Inc. (ASCAP) International Copyright Secured. All Rights Reserved. Reprinted by Permission.

Exercise 7C2: Copyright © 1923 (Renewed) by G. Schirmer, Inc. (ASCAP) International Copyright Secured. All Rights Reserved. Reprinted by Permission.

INDEX